Maritime security and peacekeeping

This important and original contribution to the global security debate asks how maritime forces can act as international instruments to promote peace and security in the post-Cold War era. Michael Pugh and his co-authors (Jeremy Ginifer, Frank Gregory, Eric Grove and Françoise Hampson) present an entirely innovative approach to the use of sea power, and a framework for maritime security operations authorised by the United Nations.

The book explains how maritime peacekeeping and peace support activities have expanded since the end of the Cold War, with operations ranging from naval observers in Cambodia to sanction enforcement patrols in the Adriatic Sea. It examines the distinctive roles of maritime forces in past naval peacekeeping operations, and asks, in the light of post-Cold War theories of peacekeeping, if the time has come for the international community to create a standing UN naval force. Specific topics covered include multinational constabulary roles for drug interdiction, piracy suppression, disaster relief and pollution control. The all-important political and financial factors and the prospects for a regional approach are fully addressed, as are operational issues, management and the legal framework provided by the Law of the Sea and the International Maritime Organisation.

Maritime security and peacekeeping will be invaluable to all students of international relations and anyone with an interest in the development of UN peacekeeping, naval power and maritime security.

Michael Pugh is Senior Lecturer in Politics at the University of Plymouth. Jeremy Ginifer, Frank Gregory and Eric Grove are Research Fellows in the Mountbatten Centre for International Studies, University of Southampton. Françoise Hampson is Senior Lecturer in Law, University of Essex.

Maritime security and peacekeeping

A framework for United Nations operations

Michael Pugh EDITOR

Manchester University Press

Manchester and New York

Distributed exclusively in the USA and Canada by St. Martins Press

Published by Manchester University Press
Oxford Road, Manchester M13 9NR, UK
and Room 400, 175 Fifth Avenue,
New York, NY 10010, USA

Distributed exclusively in the USA and Canada
by St. Martin's Press, Inc.,
175 Fifth Avenue, New York, NY 10010, USA

British Library Cataloguing-in-Publication Data
A catalogue record for this book is available from the British Library

Library of Congress Cataloguing-in-Publication Data
Maritime security and peacekeeping / Michael Pugh, editor.
    p. cm
  Includes bibliographical references and index.
  ISBN 0-7190-4368-9. – ISBN 0-7190-4563-0 (pbk.)
    1. Sea-power.   2. United Nations–Armed Forces.   3. Navies.
  4. International police.   I. Pugh, Michael C. (Michael Charles), 1944–   .
  V25.M37   1994
  327.1′72–dc20   94-28597

ISBN 0 7190 4368 9 *hardback*
ISBN 0 7190 4563 0 *paperback*

Typeset in Great Britain
by Servis Filmsetting Limited, Manchester, England
Printed in Great Britain
by Biddles Ltd, Guildford and King's Lynn

Contents

Figures and tables

Figures

Tables

Contributors

Jeremy Ginifer is Research Fellow at the Mountbatten Centre. In addition to his research on the UN he studies nuclear non-proliferation issues. His publications include: 'Towards a Concept of UN Maritime Operations', *Arms Control*, vol. 13, no. 3, December 1992, and chapters in D. Howlett and J. Simpson (eds), *Nuclear Non-Proliferation: a Reference Handbook*, Longmans, Harlow, 1992.

Frank Gregory is Senior Lecturer, Department of Politics, University of Southampton. He directs the Mountbatten Centre's Police Research Programme and has been an adviser to the House of Commons Home Affairs Committee on controlling drugs. His publications include: 'The Beira Patrol, *RUSI Journal*, vol. 124, no. 656, 1969 and *The Multinational Force: Aid or Obstacle to Conflict Resolution?*, *Conflict Studies*, no. 170, Institute for the Study of Conflict, London, 1984.

Eric Grove is Lecturer in International Relations, University of Hull and Research Fellow at the Mountbatten Centre. He is a Visiting Lecturer at the Royal Naval College, Greenwich and at the University of Cambridge. He helped to set up naval dialogues between the United States, Soviet Union/Russia and the UK. He is a member of the Russian Academy of Natural Sciences. His publications include: *From Vanguard to Trident: British Naval Policy Since 1945*, Bodley Head, London, 1989; *The Future of Sea Power*, Routledge, London, 1990; *Maritime Strategy and European Security*, Brassey's, London, 1990.

Françoise Hampson is Senior Lecturer, Department of Law and the Human Rights Centre, University of Essex. She is a Disseminator for the International Committee of the Red Cross, has participated in fact-finding missions and has submitted cases to the European Commission Court of Human Rights. Her publications include: 'War and Law in Conflicts in the Third World', *Third World Quarterly*, vol. 11, no. 2, 1989; 'Means and Methods of Warfare in the Conflict in the Gulf' and 'Liability for War Crimes', in P. J. Rowe (ed.), *The Gulf War in International and National Law*, Routledge, London, 1993.

Michael Pugh is Senior Lecturer in Politics, University of Plymouth. He is the author of *The ANZUS Crisis, Nuclear Visiting and Deterrence*, Cambridge University Press, Cambridge, 1989, and editor of *European Security Towards 2000*, Manchester University Press, Manchester, 1991. He has also published articles on arms control and maritime security, and is the editor of the journal, *International Peacekeeping*.

Preface

Our long-standing interest in maritime security was re-kindled by various proposals for UN operations at sea, put forward at the end of the Cold War by former Soviet officials, including Eduard Shevardnadze and Vladimir Petrovksy. Irrespective of any realpolitik considerations which may have underpinned those Soviet diplomatic initiatives, they encouraged us to formulate an academic agenda to discuss the questions raised by the concept. In addition, the end of the Cold War brought structural changes to the international system which led to new demands for multinational intervention and promoted further debate about the future of peacekeeping and its relationship to international security and peace enforcement. In this context, academic and professional interest in the concept of maritime security and peacekeeping at sea began to grow. Thus, both the international and intellectual climates justified new research for what the authors hope will become a standard text.

The research which began in October 1991 and ended in October 1992, was facilitated by a great many institutions and individuals. In particular, grateful acknowledgement is due to the Economic and Social Research Council which awarded a research grant (no. R000.232856). Colleagues at the University of Southampton who offered help and advice include: Ralph Beddard of the Department of Law, and Emily Bailey, Olivia Bosch and John Simpson of the Mountbatten Centre for International Studies. It is not possible to mention everyone further afield who helped but special thanks are due to people who participated in discussions, commented on draft chapters, supplied research material and granted interviews. They are not, of course, responsible for the views expressed in this study.

In the UK: Rear-Admiral Jeremy J. Blackham, Naval Home

Command, Portsmouth; Cdr Mike Codnor and Martin Howard, Ministry of Defence, London; Sergey Chashnikov and Vladimir Volkov, Embassy of the Russian Federation, London; Col. Richard Connaughton and Lt-Col. Richard P. Cousens, Staff College, Camberley; Sam Daws, UN Association, London; Lt Jan De Beurme, Belgian Navy; Martin Garside, NUMAST, London; Vice-Admiral Sir Roy Halliday, KBE, DSC (Royal Navy ret.), Lyndhurst, Hampshire; Professor Alan James, Department of International Relations, University of Keele; Stephen Langford, Guernsey; Dr Gerd Leipold, Greenpeace Communications, London; Capt. Olutunde A. Oladikeji (NN), Office of Deputy Nigerian CDS, Lagos; Capt. Christopher Page, Naval Defence Studies, Royal Naval College, Greenwich; Indar Jit Rikhye (Maj.-Gen. ret.), International Peace Academy, New York; Grp Capt. Anselmo M. Rojo-Arauz and Capt. Alberto Secchi, Argentine Embassy, London; Professor Geoffrey Till, Department of History and International Affairs, Royal Naval College, Greenwich; Lt-Col. D. H. Watmuff, New Zealand High Commission, London; Dr Alan Waymont, Metropolitan Police, London; David Whitehead, Racal Training Services Ltd, Heckfield, Reading; Dr James Whitman, Global Security Programme, University of Cambridge; Capt. Gordon Wilson (Royal Navy ret.), Liphook, Hampshire.

In the United States and Canada: Derek Boothby, UN Department of Political Affairs; I. Cliffe and Col. Tim Manners-Smith, UK Mission to the UN; Maxime Faille, Parliamentarians for Global Action, New York; Christian Harleman, UN Institute for Training and Research; Jeffrey Laurenti, United Nations Association of the USA; Rear-Admiral A. P. Hoddinott, and Cdr Adrian Nance, British Navy Staff, Washington DC; Capt. Joe Baggett (USN), Cdr Dick Mcraillis, Marc S. Palevitz and Rear-Admiral Schachte (USN), Department of Defense; Ron O'Rourke, Congressional Research Service, Library of Congress; Jeffrey Sands and Thomas J. Hirschfeld, Center for Naval Analyses, Alexandria; Lt-Cdr David I. Scott, Office of Marine Safety, Security and Environmental Protection, US Coast Guard; Dr William J. Durch, Henry L. Stimson Center, Washington DC; Dr Donald C. Daniel, Capt. Bradd Hayes (USN), Cdr Barry L. Coombs (USN), and Cdr Les Sim, (Royal Navy), US Naval War College, Newport; Jarat Chopra and John Mackinlay, John Watson Jr Institute, Brown University, Providence; Distinguished Professor Alfred P. Rubin, Fletcher School of Law and

Diplomacy, Tufts University, Medford; Rear-Admiral Bruce Johnston (CN), Supreme Allied Command Atlantic, Norfolk; Rear-Admiral Fred Crickard (CN, ret.) and Peter Haydon, Centre for Foreign Policy Studies, Dalhousie University, Halifax; Peter Jones, Department of External Affairs, Ottawa; Alex Morrison, Canadian Institute of Strategic Studies, Ontario.

In Oslo, Paris, Brussels, Geneva and Moscow: Marianne Heiberg, Åge Eknes and Tore Bjørgo, Norwegian Institute of International Affairs; Roy Breiviek (RNoN ret.), Én Verden; Vice-Admiral Carsten Lütken (RNoN ret.); Lt-Cdr Inge Tjøsthein, Norwegian Institute for Defence Studies; Colin Cameron, Defence Counsellor, WEU Assembly and John Roper, WEU Institute for Security Studies; Capt. Jean Dufourcq (FN), Centre d'Analyse et de Prévision, Ministère des Affaires Etrangères and Col. Alain Lamballe, Ministère de la Défense, Paris; Barry Carr, Cdre Andrew Gough (Royal Navy) and Cdre A. Roy Wood (CN) NATO HQ; Deborah F. Elizondo, Bo Schack and Naoko Obi, UNHCR, Geneva; Professor Yves Ghebali, Institut Universitaire de Hautes Etudes Internationales; Dr Sergio Piazzi and Rudolf Mueller, UN–DHA; Jiri Toman, Institut Henry-Dunant; Giles M. Whitcomb, UN Consultant; Dr Vladimir P. Kozin and Dimitri Yadin, Russian Ministry of Foreign Affairs; Capt. Alexandr G. Rudenko, Russian Ministry of Defence.

In Tokyo: Capt. Akifumi Hirata (JMSDF); Rear-Admiral Sumihiko Kawamura (JMSDF ret.); Professor Takehiko Kamo, Faculty of Law, University of Tokyo; Tetsuo Ohno, UN Information Centre; Ambassador Shizuo Saito and Professor Tomohisa Sakanaka, Aoyama Gakuin University; Professor Susumu Takai, National Institute for Defence Studies; Dr Takeo Uchida, International Relations, UN University.

Acknowledgements are also due to the staffs at: the Royal Naval College, Greenwich; the Royal Navy Maritime Tactical School, Southwick; the British Library of Political and Economic Science; the Public Record Office; the International Maritime Organisation Library; the Hartley and Institute of Maritime Law Libraries, University of Southampton.

Every effort has been made to trace and secure permission from copyright holders. For the inclusion of copyright material we are indebted to: NATO HQ for the map of the Adriatic Sea; Crown Copyright for the map of Cambodia; the Australian Government

Publishing Service for the diagram of Operation *Desert Storm* deployments; Juan Neves and the US Naval War College in respect of a quotation and the diagram of the ONUCA chain of command; the Institute for Foreign Policy Analysis, Cambridge, Massachusetts for David Miller's diagram of a UN–coalition chain of command; the International Maritime Organisation for the diagram of the goals of the IMO Global Programme for the Protection of the Marine Environment; the International Institute for Strategic Studies for the map of the South China Sea; Sage Publications Ltd., in respect of the quotation from Gwyn Prins, 'The UN and Peace-Keeping in the Post Cold War World: The Case of Naval Power', *Bulletin of Peace Proposals*, vol. 22, no. 2, June 1991; Frank Cass & Co. Ltd for permission to use material by Jeremy Ginifer and Michael Pugh, which appeared in *Arms Control*, vol. 13, no. 3, December 1992, and *Low Intensity Conflict & Law Enforcement*, vol. 2, no. 1, summer 1993.

Last but not least, we are grateful to Rosemary Morris for her administrative support, to Pat Heyland for his translation work and to Margaret Pugh and Adrian Hyde-Price who made valuable comments on the drafts.

Michael Pugh
University of Plymouth

Acronyms and abbreviations

AAW	anti-air warfare
ANZUS	Australia, New Zealand, United States [Treaty/Alliance]
ASEAN	Association of South-East Asian Nations
ASUW	anti-surface unit warfare
ASW	anti-submarine warfare
$C^{2/3/4}I$	command and control/communications/computers and intelligence
CCB	Combined Communications Board
CIS	Commonwealth of Independent States
CNO	Chief of Naval Operations
COLREG	Regulations for the Prevention of Collisions
C(S)BM	confidence- (and security-) building measure
CSCE	Conference on Security and Co-operation in Europe
DEA	Drug Enforcement Agency
DHA	see UNDHA
DoD	[US] Department of Defense
EC/U	European Community/Union
ECOMOG	Economic Community [of West African States] Monitoring Group
ECOWAS	Economic Community of West African States
ECPR	European Consortium for Political Research
EEZ	exclusive economic zone
FFA	[Pacific] Forum Fisheries Agency
FNS	French Naval Ship
FY	fiscal year (US 1 October to 30 September)
HASC	House Armed Services Committee
HF	high frequency
HMS	Her Majesty's Ship
ICJ	International Court of Justice
ICRC	International Committee of the Red Cross

IISS	International Institute for Strategic Studies
IMB	International Maritime Bureau
IMO	International Maritime Organisation
INMARSAT	International Maritime Satellite
IPC	inshore patrol craft
IPKF	Indian Peace-Keeping Force
ISA	International Studies Association
MARPOL	[Convention for the Prevention of] Marine Pollution
MFO	Multinational Force and Observers [Sinai]
MIF	Maritime Interception Force
MINURSO	United Nations Mission for the Referendum in the Western Sahara
MLF	Multilateral Force
MNF	Multinational Force [Beirut]
MoD	Ministry of Defence
MSC	Military Staff Committee
NATO	North Atlantic Treaty Organization
NBC	nuclear, biological, chemical
NGO	non-government organisation
n.m.	nautical mile
NUMAST	National Union of Marine, Aviation and Shipping Transport Officers
NUPI	Norwegian Institute of International Affairs
OAS	Organisation of American States
OAU	Organisation of African Unity
OECD	Organisation for Economic Co-operation and Development
ONUC	United Nations Operation in the Congo
ONUCA	United Nations Observer Group in Central America
PRO	Public Record Office
RAF	Royal Air Force
RAN	Royal Australian Navy
RFA	Royal Fleet Auxiliary
RIIA	Royal Institute of International Affairs
RN	Royal Navy
RNZN	Royal New Zealand Navy
ROE	rules of engagement
RUSI	Royal United Services Institute
SACEUR	Supreme Allied Commander Europe
SACLANT	Supreme Allied Commander Atlantic
SAR	search and rescue
SC	Security Council
SIPRI	Stockholm International Peace Research Institute
SLCM	sea-launched cruise missile

SNFL	Standing Naval Force Atlantic
SNFM	Standing Naval Force Mediterranean
SOLAS	[Convention on] Safety of Life at Sea
UNCTAD	United Nations Conference on Trade and Development
UNDHA	United Nations Department of Humanitarian Affairs
UNDRO	[Office of] United Nations Disaster Relief Co-ordinator
UNEF	United Nations Emergency Force [Egypt]
UNEP	United Nations Environmental Programme
UNFICYP	United Nations Peacekeeping Force in Cyprus
UNHCR	United Nations High Commission for Refugees
UNICEF	United Nations International Children's Emergency Fund
UNIDIR	United Nations Institute for Disarmament Research
UNIFIL	United Nations Interim Force in the Lebanon
UNIIMOG	United Nations Iran–Iraq Military Observer Group
UNIKOM	United Nations Iraq–Kuwait Observer Mission
UNITAR	United Nations Institute for Training and Research
UNLOSC	United Nations Law of the Sea Convention
UNMA	[proposed] United Nations Maritime Agency
UNMOGIP	United Nations Military Observer Group in India and Pakistan
UNOGIL	United Nations Observation Group in Lebanon
UNOSOM	United Nations Operation in Somalia
UNPROFOR	United Nations Protection Force
UNSNF	[proposed] United Nations Standing Naval Force
UNTAC	United Nations Transitional Authority in Cambodia
UNTEA	United Nations Temporary Executive Authority [West New Guinea]
UNTSO	United Nations Truce Supervision Organisation [Palestine]
UNYOM	United Nations Yemen Observation Mission
USCG	United States Coast Guard
USMC	United States Marine Corps
USN	United States Navy
USS	United States Ship
WEU	Western European Union

1 *Michael Pugh*

Introduction

The subject of maritime security and peacekeeping in this book is approached from an international relations perspective. Our analysis highlights the particularity of maritime–naval forces as instruments of state authority which function in an international context, and our purpose is to explore the potential for naval and maritime forces to act as international instruments at the behest of competent international authorities such as the United Nations.

The context in which maritime–naval forces operate is distinctively international in several respects. First, the maritime environment poses common risks to those who use it, irrespective of nationality. Seafarers have therefore evolved a common culture and maritime states have developed regulatory systems to cope with common dangers. Second, the environment permits flexibility of movement which global naval powers have often used to their advantage. Although states have been preoccupied by issues of maritime delimitation and the apparent creation of 'frontiers' at sea, these are not accorded the same political, legal or emotive attributes as land frontiers. This is largely because the sea is uninhabited and because international freedom of movement at sea is still jealously guarded. Indeed, nearly half of the earth's surface has the legal status of high seas and does not fall within any jurisdiction at all. Third, the marine eco-system is part of the global environment which can only be sensibly managed internationally through regulation of, and co-operation between, ocean users.

At the same time, maritime and naval assets are commonly regarded as attributes of national power, fulfilling a variety of roles which can range from defending the state from invasion, to 'showing the flag' abroad, to protecting fishing rights. In essence they have been regarded as valuable instruments for maintaining security in an international system characterised by competitive state behaviour. Even so, when states have sought common cause, through alliances or temporary coalitions, naval forces have displayed remarkably high levels of co-operation and even integration.

Usually the impulse to co-operate has either been to meet a common military threat or to remove a nuisance such as a danger to navigation. Nevertheless, there have been occasions when naval–maritime forces have co-operated on a multinational basis to deal with problems of international order: to rescue foreign nationals from civil unrest, for example, or to punish errant states through blockades and bombardment.

The existing literature on maritime security and multinational naval operations to support peace and international order is somewhat sparse, and the subject has only just begun to enter the mainstream of academic debate about international governance. A few studies of multinational maritime co-operation and use of naval units for peacekeeping have appeared in articles, papers and book chapters.[1] This book builds on that pioneering work to present a new and comprehensive study which takes account of pressure on the traditional view of maritime–naval forces as instruments acting narrowly for national or alliance purposes.

Although the study is not primarily concerned with broad philosophical and ethical questions about the purpose of international political life and the nature of security, it recognises that states in the post-Cold War world are confronted by domestic and international pressures which make maritime co-operation an attractive proposition and perhaps an essential consideration in meeting their security concerns. As discussed in the next chapter, the relevance of state-centrism in international relations has been increasingly challenged in international relations theory since the 1970s[2] and it may be false to assume that national sea power interests can be defined meaningfully any more. Yet within the system of complex interdependence and multifarious international actors, states and inter-state networks remain significant. The UN could hardly function without them.

The authors of this study have infused their individual contributions with their own views of the role of the state. But the book also reflects the general international relations perspective which detects significant evidence of the amelioration of international anarchy by the regulation of state behaviour through international institutions, international law and functional interdependence. Formal state sovereignty may remain intact but there is a perception, even in the most powerful of states, that practical autonomy in security matters, both military and non-military, is difficult if not impossible to achieve. Thus, to take only one example, economic pressures on defence budgets in Western states may persuade 'realist' decision-makers to seek cost-benefits through increased naval co-operation.

Moreover, the demand for UN activity, multinational peace-keeping and UN-authorised interventions grew dramatically with the end of the Cold War. This is not to argue that UN operations have an assured future. In 1993, euphoria gave way to a scaling down of ambitions for the UN after it encountered severe problems in Somalia and Bosnia. Nor is it certain that an East–West axis of co-operation in the Security Council can be maintained if extreme nationalism brings an anti-integration thrust to the foreign and security policies of Russia. Nevertheless, as argued in Chapter 2, the end of the Cold War system has led to a vigorous debate about improving international co-operation generally and about reforming the competence of the UN in particular. In view of the UN's widely perceived importance in conferring political legitimacy on the of force and its unrivalled experience in the realm of peace-keeping, discussion of the UN's role in the emerging international system is interwoven throughout the book.

Against this backcloth, the main focus of the book is on key concepts and practical policy issues to assess the potential for naval–maritime forces as instruments in promoting international order. Whether traditional 'peacekeeping' is an appropriate mechanism in this respect is a recurring theme. Indeed the theme can be expressed as two key questions. First, is the traditional concept of peacekeeping relevant to naval–maritime forces? Second, in the changing international situation are there multinational roles in maintaining peace and security which are applicable to naval–maritime forces and which could be legitimised by the international community for maintaining peace and security? Obviously, in seeking answers to these questions, elementary issues need to be addressed: what is peacekeeping? how have navies been used in the past? what is the nature of sea power and the maritime environment? what assumptions can be made about the international system? can any new roles be conceptually related to peacekeeping?

Broadly speaking, these theoretical and conceptual issues are considered in the first part of the study from Chapters 2 to 5, though the historical evidence of naval peacekeeping and maritime constabulary work is also considered. Chapters 6 to 10 then deal with practical issues concerning the structure, management, operational and legal requirements for naval–maritime forces. Most operations at sea are likely to be required to support and intermesh with land-based initiatives. Chapter 11 also considers the extent to which they could be functionally related to the evolving maritime regime.

However, before detailing the arrangement of the chapters and their constituent arguments, the use of terminology should be explained.

First, the terms 'naval' and 'maritime' are not synonymous in spite of considerable overlap. In this study, the term 'naval forces' encompasses warships (regular and auxiliary), units operated by marines, aviation based at sea and aviation based on land but used primarily for patrolling at sea. In wartime, however, marine police forces, such as the US Coast Guard (USCG), may also be allocated naval roles. For the most part, only naval units have been used for peacekeeping, but USCG personnel have been employed in training roles and in UN-authorised embargo enforcement operations in the Persian Gulf and Adriatic Sea. The term 'maritime forces' refers to all units in the service of governments which have a role at sea. In addition to warships, they include vessels operated by coastguards, police forces and customs officials. Thus the subject matter of Chapter 5 is deliberately couched in terms of 'maritime' constabulary roles because by engaging in such activities, naval units would be acting in support of civilian maritime agencies.

This also indicates that the primary concern of this book is with security issues which maritime–naval forces might be expected to address. To go much beyond this deliberate limitation – to consider depletion of fish stocks or satellite surveillance of the oceans, for example – would have extended the scope of the research into areas which merit detailed consideration in their own right. Obviously, 'security' can be defined much more widely than in a purely military sense. Indeed, Chapter 11 examines the development of a regime for managing and regulating maritime security as a whole. The wider security issues, including environmental security, are discussed in relation to potential constabulary and management roles for maritime forces. In these cases, however, it is also considered essential to avoid militarising non-military security.

The 'peacekeeping' concept is discussed at length in Chapter 2, but we should note at the outset that the term has often been used in both descriptive and prescriptive senses. In its traditional descriptive sense it refers to the phenomenon of military force being deployed impartially, not to win battles or to solve underlying problems, but to act as political reassurance for which the parties in a conflict have normally given their consent. Naval units have not been prominent in traditional peacekeeping roles, primarily because the origins of internationally significant disputes are predominantly land-based and because there have been few calls for autonomous maritime operations to secure the maritime domain. Nevertheless, as shown in Chapter 3, there have been several occasions when naval forces have supported land-based peacekeeping operations.

A difficulty confronting scholars in the post-Cold War period is that the narrow concept is becoming stretched – as peacekeepers themselves are being mandated to engage in activities, notably humanitarian aid protection, which have not traditionally been central to their task. This has given rise to the notion of 'second generation' operations (see Chapter 2), within which, metaphorically speaking, naval operations could find a firmer niche.

In its prescriptive sense 'peacekeeping' has come to be used as a generic term, loosely associated with any military force operating under a UN-authorised mandate to deal with a problem. However, the need for differentiation between types of operation was emphasised by the UN Secretary-General Dr Boutros Boutros-Ghali in his report 'An Agenda for Peace' of June 1992. He identified and distinguished four types of problem-solving operation which might be prescribed under UN auspices. He labelled these: preventive diplomacy; peacemaking; peacekeeping; and peacebuilding. Unfortunately even this typology does not adequately distinguish between the levels of force which, in the light of particular circumstances, may be necessary to achieve political goals. The term 'peacemaking', for example, veils various kinds of activity ranging from use of the International Court of Justice to enforcement actions which in practice are indistinguishable from warfighting. Therefore, the prescriptive framework used in 'An Agenda for Peace', valuable though it is, has not provided an organising principle for this book.

A second reason for diverging from the Secretary-General's typology relates to the attributes of naval–maritime power and the nature of the marine environment. As will become abundantly clear from the analysis which follows, concepts applicable to land-based operations are not always appropriate to sea-based activities. Indeed, naval forces can undertake multinational roles in support of peace and security for which there are no land-based equivalents.

The study begins by situating maritime security and peacekeeping in context to demonstrate the need for new conceptual thinking. Chapter 2 therefore discusses fundamental concepts – about the maritime environment, traditional sea power and traditional peacekeeping. The chapter then examines the implications of the evolving international context for the UN, for peacekeeping and for naval–maritime forces.

Chapter 3 provides a survey of past naval peacekeeping operations to reveal that these have been closely allied to land-based peacekeeping. In conformity with traditional peacekeeping principles naval peacekeepers have been deployed in unambiguously inoffensive fashion. Following from this, Chapter 3 argues that it is critically important to distinguish force thresholds, especially for naval units which in the normal course of duty are likely to be deployed with offensive capabilities. The political significance of crossing force thresholds, when navies switch from monitoring tasks to the enforcement of sanctions and interdiction of shipping, for example, is discussed.

A conceptual basis for UN maritime operations is then presented in Chapter 4, following from the proposition that traditional concepts of peacekeeping have limited relevance in the maritime environment. Distinctive roles may be undertaken which capitalise on the particular attributes of maritime forces. Two of these attributes are flexibility and ambiguity. Maritime forces are traditionally valued for their ability to roam the seas relatively freely and to operate offshore without attracting the kind of opprobrium that armies might do by manoeuvring in the vicinity of a land frontier. Because they go to sea prepared to fight, naval vessels are also capable of sending ambiguous signals of intent. Although they may come in peace, they arrive with warlike potency. It is vital, therefore, to appraise the possible effects of deploying multinational naval forces, especially in view of the historical resonances which derive from the practice of 'gunboat diplomacy'. The discriminate deployment of force may therefore be both a problem for naval units and an essential requirement if political goals are to be met by task-specific disposition.

However, operations in which the threat of force is low or non-existent are of particular relevance to navies working in conjunction with civilian agencies. These constabulary activities are normally conducted in a framework of national jurisdiction, but may be perceived to require multinational efforts, either because individual states cannot cope or because the problems are intrinsically significant for the welfare of many coastal communities and maritime users. These constabulary roles are examined in Chapter 5, with specific reference to drug interdiction, piracy suppression, disaster relief and pollution control.

Throughout history, Utopian thinkers have advocated the creation of standing international forces to maintain peace and enforce the law of nations. The idea re-surfaced after the Cold War to provide the UN with a ready means of response to crises. Standing force structures and alternative means of structuring multinational naval forces are investigated in Chapter 6. The practical implications of the main options (ad hoc, on-call and standing forces) are evaluated in the light of financial, political and operational advantages and problems.

As noted by a senior Royal Navy officer experienced in naval peacekeeping, a key to the success of any multinational naval operation is a coherent command and control architecture.[3] The extent to which the UN could develop the capacity to manage naval operations effectively is discussed in Chapter 7. A precedent for future arrangements might be seen in the Military Staff Committee (MSC) which was set up in 1945 but which had fallen into abeyance by 1948. Although it may prove impractical and politically unacceptable to resurrect the MSC, its deliberations provide insights into the problems of establishing and managing multinational forces. Whatever may be the most appropriate management structure, it is reasonable to argue that naval command and control should be an integral part of a UN system.

However, the UN may not be the most fitting organisation to control operations, and it might be more effective to subcontract tasks to politically acceptable, and militarily robust, regional security organisations. Chapter 8 discusses the prospect of developing regional naval security arrangements which might be delegated tasks by the UN. In this respect it is important to consider whether the capabilities wielded by NATO are replicated anywhere else.

The operational and technical requirements of multinational forces are examined in Chapter 9 in the light of the possible levels of integration among navies participating in a multinational operation. Particular attention is paid to rules of engagement, communications, sustainability and logistic support, common procedures, doctrine and training. There is no point, of course, in 're-inventing the wheel' and we should not ignore the lengthy experience which has already been accrued. Chapter 9 therefore considers the extent to which the elements of integration by NATO navies could provide standards for wider use.

Political legitimacy, cohesive management and technical capacity are not the only considerations which govern naval–maritime deployments. The legal regime also has to be taken into account. The extent to which there is confusion and contest in international law relevant to naval peacekeeping is discussed in Chapter 10. Legal uncertainties may be of minimal significance when peacekeepers operate by consent. But when confrontation is likely, the existence of issues appertaining to: the possible functions of international maritime forces; the impact of maritime zones on operations; the relationship between peacekeeping forces and states affected by the operations; and the rights of peacekeepers should be recognised.

Chapter 11 assesses significant regulatory developments in the maritime domain in the last quarter of the twentieth century, notably the Law of the Sea Convention and the various conventions affecting safety at sea under the purview of the International Maritime Organisation. The maritime regime governs non-military security on the basis of consensus and customary law. However, in the light of problems in maritime delimitation and a radical proposal for integrating military and non-military governance, this chapter considers the extent to which maritime forces might be functionally related to the evolving security regime.

Finally in Chapter 12 the authors draw conclusions and make proposals. The study indicates that distinctive maritime peace and security concepts, either for the purposes of supporting land-based operations or for strengthening the maritime regime, have yet to be formulated or treated seriously. This study provides a framework of analysis and discussion of practical issues which, it is hoped, will encourage the incorporation of maritime security and peacekeeping concepts into the discourse of international studies.

Notes

1 Alan James, *Peacekeeping in International Politics*, Macmillan and IISS, Basingstoke and London, 1990, pp. 175–8; Gwyn Prins, 'The UN and Peace-Keeping in the Post Cold War World: The Case of Naval Power', *Bulletin of Peace Proposals*, vol. 22, no. 2, June 1991, pp. 135–55; Robert Stephens Staley II, *The Wave of the Future: The United Nations and Naval Peacekeeping*, International Peace Academy occasional paper, Lynne Rienner, Boulder, Col., 1992; Jeffrey Sands, *Blue Hulls: Multinational Naval Cooperation and the United Nations*, paper for the Center for Naval Analyses, Alexandria, Va., 1992.

2 For discussion of the general directions in international relations theory, see Martin Hollis and Steve Smith, *Explaining and Understanding International Relations*, Clarendon Press, Oxford, 1990.

3 Rear-Admiral J. J. Blackham, 'Maritime Peacekeeping', *RUSI Journal*, August 1993, pp. 18–23.

Sea power, security and peacekeeping after the Cold War

The prospects for maritime security and peacekeeping are ultimately dependent upon developments in the structure of world politics and changing concepts of security. Developments in the international system since the end of the Cold War have clearly affected perceptions about the maintenance of international peace and security, and about the role of the UN and its military operations. The argument in this chapter is that in principle the maritime environment is an important arena for multinational approaches to security, and that traditional state-centric concepts of sea power can be re-examined in the light of the evolving international context.

Sea power and state security

The point of departure in our discussion of sea power is the relationship between the use of force to safeguard national interests on the one hand, and concepts for international peace support operations on the other. Navies have generally been regarded as symbols of national power and prestige *par excellence*, and this may make multinational naval operations more problematic than similar activities ashore.[1]

In terms of sea-power theory, concepts of competitive statism have traditionally taken precedence over international co-operation, and maritime development has been closely linked to theories of hegemony in world history. Thus, access to the sea, the control of trade routes and the development of port hinterlands have been regarded as keys to the rise and fall of states and empires.[2] The great classics of naval literature, notably those of Alfred Mahan, focused on the relationship between navies, their command of the sea and the greatness of states.[3] Not surprisingly, too, there is a large body of literature on the nuances of naval diplomacy and showing the flag.[4] Indeed the pejorative connotations of 'gunboat diplomacy', harking back to nineteenth-century imperialism, are liable to colour perceptions of naval deployments. When the former Soviet Foreign Minister, Eduard Shevardnadze, raised the possibility of establishing a UN-flagged task force to provide convoys for merchant ships during the Iran–Iraq War, the proposal was challenged as making the UN 'an instrument of gunboat diplomacy'.[5] One of the inherent problems of naval deployment, therefore, is to discriminate between gunboat diplomacy on the one hand and international peace support operations on the other.

In reality, the Mahanist tradition is far less relevant in the late twentieth century than in the heyday of mercantilism. The nexus between maritime power and state economic interests has been increasingly fractured.[6] States cannot easily command economic sovereignty because capital accumulation and economic power increasingly reside in transnational capitalism. Thus trade and commerce have to be developed and protected by means other than the unilateral deployment of national naval power. Correlations between indices of naval strength and hegemonic change can no longer conceal the fact that commercial shipping has become a supranational business.

Moreover, the special features of the maritime environment which were outlined in the previous chapter permit, even encourage, international co-operation. Maritime forces operate in an environment which is internationally regulated by well-established rules and procedures. International law recognises the common interests at sea, protecting free use of the high seas and the innocent transit of warships in territorial seas (see Chapter 10 below). Whilst the UN Law of the Sea Convention (1982) had still not been ratified by major maritime states at the start of 1994, many of its provisions reflect pre-exisiting customary law or may be in the process of passing into customary law.[7] This, and the body of conventions governing use of the seas, some of which are supervised by the UN's International Maritime Organisation, can be considered as part of the maritime regime elaborated in Chapter 11 below.

There is indeed a general level of common professional interest in safety at sea. All seafarers face a common adversary – the sea – and this gives rise to an ethos of comradeship which cuts across the divide between civilian and naval fraternities and across national barriers. Common security has been expressed, for example, in measures to prevent naval accidents, such as the Incidents at Sea Agreements, the first signed between the United States and the Soviet Union in 1972. These treaties survived the second Cold War of the 1980s when other agreements were stalled or cancelled, in part because the unity of professional purpose was able to fend off political interference.[8]

Nevertheless, such naval co-operation remained limited and was outweighed by Cold War confrontation. The Cold War sustained belief in the nexus between maritime strength, state power and global hegemony. Naval units were vital aspects of strategic competition, threatening nuclear devastation through relatively invulnerable sea-launched ballistic missiles and sea dominance through powerful surface fleets. The two blocs were engaged in an apparently open-ended naval race with little prospect of reaching arms control agreements.[9] However, as discussed in Chapters 6 and 9 below, this same confrontation also served to intensify integration between allied navies, more particularly in NATO which established multinational standing forces. The end of the Cold War in the late 1980s opened up the prospect that this kind of co-operation could be extended.

Developments in global security

The impact of the end of the Cold War on maritime strategic thinking is explored in a later section of this chapter, but in general terms the end of Cold War confrontation has presented states that were embroiled in it with opportunities to review the rationale of existing security structures and the purposes of military–naval force.[10] Regional conflicts and diffuse non-military security threats are not easily met by old modes of thinking, and if the 'humbling' of the former superpowers reduces their ability to impose stability, it may impel them to redefine their power and interests in terms which enhance maritime multilateralism. However, there is no consensus in world politics about which security goals should have priority, an irresolution that has become part of the security *problematique*. Indeed, for much of the developing world, security issues have hardly altered with the end of the Cold War and are primarily about resources, poverty and debt. Developing states are not enthusiastic about a security agenda, determined by the rich and powerful states, which pays lip-service to 'sustainable development' whilst starving international organisations of funds for economic and social purposes.[11]

At the end of 1994 we clearly cannot predict with confidence the impacts of the emergence of extreme nationalism in Russia, the prospect of disillusion in Washington with policies of global engagement may follow from US experiences in dealing with Iraq and Somalia, or the progress towards settlement of the South African and Israeli–Palestinian problems. It seems probable that the quest for global peace and security will proceed unevenly. However, a key factor in the development of maritime security and peacekeeping will be the role of the United Nations in the post-Cold War world.

In the euphoria which greeted the collapse of bipolarity, and since the last substantive use of the veto in the UN Security Council in May 1990, hopes were generated for a UN *redivivus*. It would play a more assertive role in global security as the most authoritative and internationally recognised international security organisation. By 1993 the sobering impact of continued regional conflict, though less system-threatening than superpower confrontation, led to a refocusing of the debate on the UN's difficulties in coping with the demands being placed upon it.[12] The end of the Cold War not only presented opportunities for members of the UN to strengthen its role, it also exposed the UN's limitations. The long-term outcome of this exposure is open to debate. To take a gloomy prognosis, the UN may not be able to maintain credibility into the next millennium. It may be faced with problems so intractable that they cannot be effectively treated by any agency. Paralysis may set in as a consequence of mismatch between resources and demands, the cumulative effect of 'things going wrong' in particular theatres of operation, or a renewal of the veto in the Security Council. In some accounts the UN may also wither because it represents an irrelevant elitist and state-centric power model, its military interventions being irrelevant to the economic, social and environmental mainsprings of conflict and merely becoming part of the problem of global violence.[13]

UN hegemony could also be antithetical to the needs of many communities because it would promote the security interests of the

UN's most powerful states. In this respect, a fundamental limitation is likely to arise from the UN's selectivity in dealing with crises. Member states appear unwilling to allow the UN to act except on a case-by-case basis. Despite the Charter's opening words, 'We the peoples . . .', the UN was founded as an organisation of states, and the willingness of states in the Security Council, especially of the permanent five, to recommend action under Chapters VI and VII (and in the space between), depends largely on cost–benefit calculations from national positions. A piecemeal approach therefore suits state interests and avoids the pitfalls of attempting to implement a blueprint in conflicts which are inherently unique and liable to evolve unpredictably.[14] Obviously, the UN's task is more taxing when it is doomed to react to events. Without codification of the basis for UN involvement, the path of consistent impartiality will be difficult to maintain. The UN's legitimacy is affected, for example, when its authority is used to target a Somali warlord with helicopter gunships whilst at the same time its envoys attempt to reach a peace agreement with a Bosnian-Serb leader who is suspected of war crimes.

Nor can the UN enforce co-operation. It has to rely on the development of normative behaviour or extraneous leadership. In Francis Fukuyama's view, the UN cannot lead in a crisis but is 'perfectly serviceable as an instrument of American unilateralism' and as a surrogate for US policing.[15] Such a hegemony within the UN can work if US interests generate a degree of international stability which suits other states willing to 'free ride' on the hegemon's back.[16] Naturally, however, Fukuyama's neo-realist precepts fail to address the problems of the UN's common security or 'public goods' approach.[17] A hegemon may be reluctant to accept multinational decision-making or hesitate about incurring losses in conflicts which are of little direct concern to it.[18] Indeed, the weight given to multilateralism in the United States in the early 1990s may have been designed solely to build a domestic foreign policy consensus for the post-Cold War world.[19] Yet the UN might require the leadership and the unique, sophisticated military assets of the United States, especially, as argued in Chapter 9 below, for large-scale naval missions. Such dependency would be two-edged. If the United States is perceived either to ignore or dominate the UN, the promotion of common security is likely to be self-limiting and fragile.

At the same time, the processes of globalisation, such as the diffusion of capitalism, advances in communications and awareness of environmental depredation and human rights issues, mean that the UN could mitigate the problems of state centrism in addressing world-order problems. It is reasonable to expect that unilateral action will be constrained by the institutions within which states seek legitimacy for their actions. The UN's revival can be taken as evidence of the diffusion of multilateral norms which shape state responses and which transform traditional notions of state sovereignty.[20] In this respect, the UN may constrain state behaviour and induce commitment to multilateral norms and action, including the development of military control capabilities.[21] Decisions on a multilateral basis may appeal to states which seek political influence, or protection from security threats, through an international regime with the promise of making state behaviours more predictable. State policies thereby become 'institutionalised' or embedded by the multinational context. Indeed it becomes ever more difficult to define and identify national interests as transnational and global processes undermine state autonomy.[22]

Of course, rather than either invigoration or debilitation, perhaps the most likely outcome is that the UN will muddle through. As Georges Abi-Saab notes, the struggle between multilateralism and unilateralism is a permanent factor in the work of international organisations.[23] The balance between the piecemeal approach and the process of institutionalisation may amount to states appealing to common criteria in their decision-making about intercession in crises. The criteria are likely to include: whether there is a clear evidence of the abuse of widely held values (such as evidence of genocide); whether there are clear and achievable political goals; whether there is a multilateral political will to see it through; and whether requisite resources and machinery are available on a multilateral basis.[24] At the very least, however, there should be no difficulty among states in recognising that the UN's experience gives it a distinct comparative advantage in the sphere of peacekeeping. This advantage might be strengthened and conceptually extended to include the use of maritime and naval forces. The end of the Cold War has certainly encouraged new thinking about the deployment of UN force in ways which would more readily encompass maritime–naval forces than in the past.

Peacekeeping and peace support operations

Peacekeeping became established partly as a consequence of the slight thaw in East–West relations following the death of Stalin in 1953, and partly in an attempt to prevent the spread of the Cold War.[25] It was essentially a response to the range of circumstances, often the detritus of imperial decline, for which Chapters VI and VII of the Charter were either inadequate or inapplicable.[26] Indeed, attempts to define peacekeeping have vexed scholars because it hovers between the provisions for peaceful resolution of disputes and enforcement action. One option is to avoid defining peacekeeping too precisely on the grounds that vagueness is its strength.[27] Nevertheless, definitions have been necessary for practical purposes, such as providing states with guidelines under which participation can be authorised.[28] The fundamental operational principles, originally formulated for use on land by Lester Pearson and Dag Hammarskjöld in 1956, continue to provide a paradigm of an 'ideal' type reflecting assumptions about the possibilities and limitations of international intercession in disputes.[29] The principles refer to operations which take place when there is an effective ceasefire and the parties to the dispute give their consent to the presence of impartial, militarily weak peacekeepers, not for the purpose of resolving the conflict, but to symbolise an interruption in order to facilitate political processes. 'Ideal' peacekeeping is characterised in this study as:

a peaceful intercession by impartial military–naval personnel, police or civilians as part of multinational formations, on the basis of the consent of the hosts and parties to conflict and under international organisation and direction, normally when hostilities are in abeyance.

Peacekeeping itself is politically and juridically divorced from the rights and wrongs which underlie conflicts.[30] Consent to the presence of peacekeepers, their condition of vulnerability and their efforts to engender trust are in reciprocal relationship. The military and political costs of upsetting this have usually been considered unacceptably high, though divergences from the 'ideal' have often occurred in experiments devised to suit particular circumstances including involvement in the kind of intra-state conflicts which gained prominence in the 1990s.[31]

Until the late 1980s, such improvisations were regarded as variations on the 'ideal'. But in the absence of Cold War competition, peacekeeping has been affected by several developments. Co-operation between Security Council members increased, and the UN's operations were no longer designed to avert superpower involvement. The number of UN commitments increased. Some disputes have become more amenable to UN involvement (Namibia, Central America and Afghanistan), and political pressure on the UN to intercede in conflicts grew considerably. The size, complexity and comprehensiveness of operations developed, so that several operations in the 1990s have incorporated a range of tasks from disarming factions and mineclearing to aid provision and civil administration. The creation of viable and lasting conditions for peace within states became an integral part of operations, reflecting international concern over human, civil and minority rights. The mandate for Cambodia involved seven components requiring a large civil and military management capability to protect areas under UN authority and supervise conditional self-determination (conditional on democratic processes and respect for human rights).

The UN has also authorised military deployments clearly beyond ideal peacekeeping. They have included the war against Iraq, the creation of safe havens in Iraq, the deployment of observers in a 'preventive' role in Macedonia, the enforcement of embargoes against Serbia–Montenegro and forcible disarmament and relief measures in Somalia. Indeed, in anticipation that attacks on aid provision in Somalia would have to be deterred and repelled, the Somalia mandate allowed 'all necessary means to establish as soon as possible a secure environment for humanitarian relief operations'.[32]

Proposals to strengthen and extend the UN's operations have accompanied these developments, including the UN Secretary-General's own proposals of July 1992, 'An Agenda for Peace'. These signalled no radical departure from the traditional concepts of state sovereignty upheld in the UN Charter, and in part they revived long-standing ideas.[33] But Dr Boutros-Ghali also recognised the need for a more integrated approach to operations for maintaining peace, to encompass preventive diplomacy, peacemaking (which includes enforcement action) and post-conflict peacebuilding. Improvements to the management of operations were also undertaken in 1993, as discussed in Chapter 7 below.

Other analyses of UN operations have been provided. Marianne Heiberg, for example, employed the term 'second generation peacekeeping' to distinguish the newer post-Cold War involvements.[34]

The 'second generation' concept presupposes that robust deviations from 'ideal' peacekeeping are becoming or will have to become a new operational norm, because consent may not be available from all parties; there may be no authority which can give consent; freedom of movement may be contested; and the claims of UN forces to political and military impartiality may be brushed aside. In these circumstances, rules of engagement will move beyond self-defence. Distinctions between peacekeeping and enforcement could either become blurred, to the extent that the ideal principles have to be modified, or peacekeeping will remain a distinctive form of activity within increasingly comprehensive 'packages' of UN involvement.[35] In any event, as this book proposes, the broadening of UN operations could certainly encompass maritime security and peace support missions.

However, it is important to be aware that critical issues arise from a more interventionist UN role. To the extent that the notion of second generation operations rests on the premise that peacekeeping and intervention are becoming blurred because the situations on the ground are messy, there is a risk that role differentiation will become blurred, involving an entire UN operation in self-generating violence as appeared to be the case in Mogadishu in mid-1993. Moreover, forces trained and equipped for old-style peacekeeping cannot be easily transformed into a fighting force 'simply by passing a new Security Council resolution'.[36] In effect, too, the UN is moving away from the customary peacekeeping practices of the post-war era which have served the UN well. Indeed, the implication of second generation operations is that the UN's reputation for impartiality might be undermined, risking the refusal of states to have traditional peacekeepers on their territory.[37]

In terms of the political legitimacy for such operations, the UN Charter provides guiding principles as to what justifies member states taking individual or collective action to punish errant nations. However, the weight to be accorded to state sovereignty enshrined in Article 2(7) and the conditions under which it can be legitimately breached by the UN, is a contentious issue. Indeed, the least firmly supported of all the Security Council resolutions adopted in response to the Kuwait crisis was Resolution 688 of 5 April 1991, which led to the deployment of foreign troops and UN guards to Iraq, not only to supply sustenance to the Kurds, but also to uphold law and order. Yemen and China argued that the Kurdish problem was essentially an internal difficulty and that such intervention was a dangerous precedent.[38] Subsequent events in Iraq (the US missile strike against a Baghdad intelligence centre on 26 June 1993) and in Somalia (the US helicopter gunship raids in Mogadishu, following the killing of UN soldiers on 5 June 1993) and in Bosnia (the NATO air strikes against Serb positions in April 1994), led to a further questioning of the legitimacy of intervention.[39] Although there are international provisions to protect human rights,[40] they do not have a mandatory, enforceable quality and there is no specific reference within Chapter VII of the Charter to human rights protection. Further, there are difficulties in arriving at a common definition of what constitutes human rights. For example, the rights of the individual against the state are emphasised in the West, whilst in the Third World emphasis is placed on collective rights.[41]

For reasons discussed in the next two chapters, the deployment of maritime and naval forces, where appropriate, can avoid some of these difficulties. But accusations of gunboat diplomacy have to be avoided, and in regulating international peace and security there will need to be a clear articulation of mandates and their foundation. Moreover, in reformulating peacekeeping concepts it will be logical to assume that if 'ideal' peacekeeping has never been a panacea for dealing with conflict, nor are second generation operations likely to be. With these precautions in mind, there are no overwhelming reasons why, in principle, maritime and naval forces should not contribute to multinational efforts to uphold peace and security in the new international environment.

Navies and the new security environment

To begin with, the changing security environment and developments in the world pattern of naval growth have influenced naval policies in ways which encourage multinational co-operation. In many states political and military–naval establishments have been freed from the perceived imperatives and constraints of preparing for a global, or at least a northern hemisphere, war. Decision-makers are at greater liberty to seek alternative goals, means and structures to promote security. For old allies, new uncertainties and constraints on naval growth, mainly financial, sustain the attractions of mutual support.

Most dramatically, the old Soviet Navy's development has been arrested. Russia inherited the lion's share of the Soviet fleet because it possessed the major bases in the Kola Peninsula and in the Far East. But the future of the Crimean base remains in doubt and the old Black Sea Fleet appears to be a wasting asset. Both Russia and the Ukraine are likely to retain relatively small Black Sea squadrons. The Russian Navy persists with ambitious plans, including the maintenance of a fleet of 80 nuclear and 50 conventional attack submarines and 3 aircraft carriers.[42] But whether these goals are realistic is doubtful given the parlous condition of Russia's economy.

Reductions have also occurred in those elements of the Western navies which were most heavily engaged in Cold War confrontation, most obviously in strategic nuclear forces and attack submarines. For example, by the end of the decade the United States Navy could shrink from its total strength of 450 ships in 1993 to as low as 320.[43]

But whilst the East–West naval arms race was at its peak, naval expansion also occurred elsewhere, 'sometimes transforming what was often a neglected armed service, the navy, and a neglected aspect of national development, ocean resources, into key dimensions of domestic and foreign policy'.[44] This may be perceived as a threat to the major maritime powers. In Asia, for example, regional threat perceptions, archipelagic responsibilities and, in some cases, distrust of Western intrusion have all played a part in naval expansion. The growth in coastal and minor combatants was spectacular in the 1980s: Taiwan's from 49 to 141; Thailand's from 64 to 118; Singapore's from 17 to 43; South Korea's from 57 to 112.[45] But submarines and major combatants (including helicopter-carrying frigates) were also being acquired by several states.[46]

However, such growth does not necessarily signify new challenges to the traditional naval powers, since many of the growing naval powers have had good relations with the declining ones. Moreover, grandiose ambitions to acquire ships and submarines, even second-hand or off-the-shelf, is often tempered by the requirement for large-scale investment in shore facilities, infrastructure and personnel training.[47] Western perceptions of Third World naval expansion as a threat may therefore be exaggerated, though there is clear potential for regional naval arms races, especially in the Asia–Pacific region (see Chapter 8 below). Perhaps the most likely impetus for the United States to resurrect an expansive naval policy would be a strong China with ambitions for regional hegemony. However, despite its impressive size (54 major warships and 46 submarines), the Chinese Navy probably lags behind other regional navies in technological sophistication.

In these circumstances, with major conflict at sea seemingly remote, reassessments of strategy have been undertaken. It is more difficult for the global navies to legitimise their roles in terms of traditional sea control or sea denial operations, particularly in terms of the re-emphasis during the 1970s and 1980s among navies involved in Cold War confrontation on fleet-versus-fleet encounters to obtain command of the sea.[48] In the absence of potential threats at sea, the balance of forces in the major navies will shift even further – from assets essential for battle on the high seas, to platforms primarily useful in littoral areas. Navies are likely to focus on two spheres: an ability to regulate and defend their own economic zones and an ability to participate in multinational force projection to facilitate land operations.[49]

The shift was clearly reflected in the US Navy's design for the post-Cold War security environment, 'From the Sea', released in September 1992.[50] This strategy contains elements of continuity in that the previous 'Maritime Strategy' of 1986 had proposed a prime role for the US Navy in power projection against enemy naval sanctuaries and land-based assets, but the 1986 strategy had been predicated on major naval opposition from what was clearly identified as a first-class, Soviet battlefleet. By contrast, 'From the Sea' signals the end of the Mahanist philosophy of fighting for sea dominance in favour of providing direct support for land operations, and accords new prominence to joint and integrated operations, requiring a change in naval culture to promote greater receptivity to multilateral decision-making on maritime security issues.[51] Equally significant, it implies that joint operations will need to extend beyond traditional allies to embrace other states including former adversaries.

Clearly, however, one of the greatest barriers to the formation of multinational forces is the reluctance of states to devolve operational control and capabilities to international command structures. Major naval powers are reluctant to modify their independent decision-making over the use of naval forces.[52] Yet, paradoxically, it is difficult to envisage unilateral threats to European medium powers such as Britain and France invoking unilateral responses. The sorts of threat which confront states are perceived to be diffuse in their origins, substance and targets, and correspondingly appear difficult to meet unilaterally. Nor can the medium powers command the necessary national resources to sustain a unilateral capability to meet large threats, and it is becoming increasingly difficult for the United States to do so. And although the sizeable navies of Germany and Japan are still inhibited by constitutional and political factors from independent force projection beyond their immediate security zones, it is significant that both Germany and Japan participated in multinational counter-mine operations in the Persian Gulf.

In fact, as emphasised in Chapter 9 below, parts of the international community, not only in NATO, now have experience in the operational integration of naval forces for particular purposes. Multinational co-operation can be demonstrated to have worked in the Coalition War against Iraq among the naval forces that blockaded Iraq, gave fire support to land forces and engaged in mine-countermeasures. Although the political and military conditions for the war against Iraq are unlikely to be replicated, officials, academics and naval personnel have detected pointers for future multinational maritime co-operation.[53] Indeed, further experience, though among a narrower range of navies, was subsequently gained in the naval deployments to impose sanctions against Serbia–Montenegro.[54]

Finally, naval forces may be valuable in situations where large-scale, intrusive, military action ashore is risky, and where flexible offshore operations can offer support. Multinational forces may be more acceptable and less provocative than national or alliance forces. When the aircraft carrier USS *Kennedy* was deployed off the coast of Colombia in January 1990 to combat drug smuggling, shortly after the invasion of Panama and without informing the government in Bogotá, it caused a diplomatic incident.[55] A multinational force of less formidable power acting might have proved more acceptable to Colombia.

As remarked earlier, concepts of multinationalism have been conspicuously absent from theories of sea power, even in post-Cold War studies.[56] However, the potential for international naval peacekeeping achieved some status in sea power theory in the late 1980s when naval relations across the Cold War divide showed signs of mellowing. Within three broad peacetime functions of sea power – diplomatic, constabulary and military – peacekeeping appeared to fit best on the constabulary side of a triangular model

Figure 2.1 *Uses of sea power*

(see Figure 2.1).[57] The reasoning behind this was that such roles involved the maintenance of mutually accepted norms, rather than the unilateral coercion implied by traditional naval diplomacy.

Even in the changed security environment, the military foundations upon which the triangle rested remain similar, though the primacy of power projection is enhanced still further. But in the future, exercises of naval diplomacy and indeed naval warfare, whilst being in a state's interests, would probably take place in a multinational framework. This could lead to a diminution of the importance of traditional 'gunboat diplomacy' and give coercive naval diplomacy a more acceptable international image (though it remains problematic). It might also create a new geometry of sea power (see Figure 2.2). Showing the flag and 'naval presence' could become a crucial pillar resting on foundations comprising 'the use of the sea'. Other pillars would also support national interests, but these could also be accomplished by international peacekeeping and peace support operations.

Conclusion

Action on common interests at sea has usually been subordinate to the requirements of state policy, and there is little prospect that navies will be completely de-nationalised. It may also be doubted whether national authorities and naval establishments would accept operational command and control by an international body such as a revived UN Military Staff Committee. The development of maritime co-operation is clearly conditioned by the willingness of states

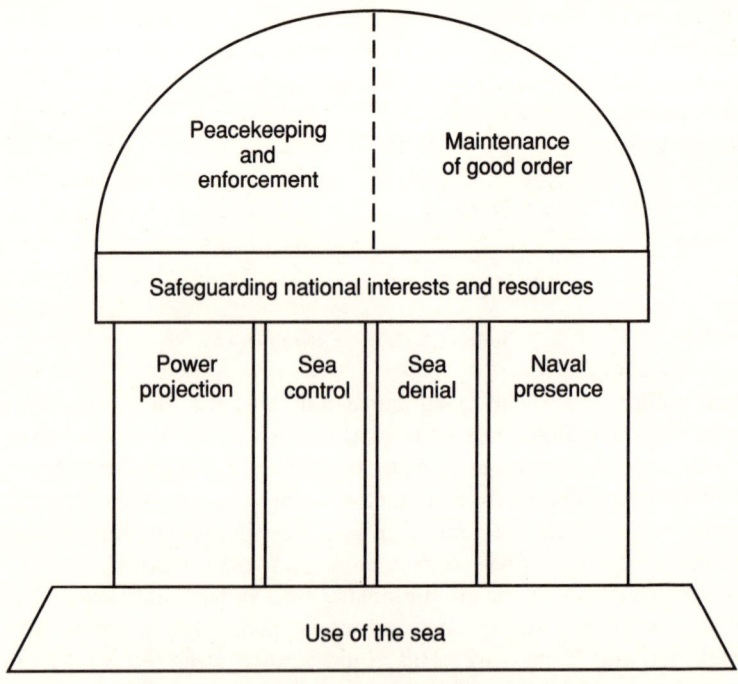

Figure 2.2 *Post-Cold War uses of sea power*

to support international co-operation in general. Nevertheless, world leaders have called for greater multilateralism in international relations and, as we have noted, there has been extensive debate about reviving and reforming the UN. Improving the UN's capability to operate on land has been frequently considered; reformers also need to be receptive to ideas which highlight the possibilities of naval–maritime operations.

This chapter has argued that in the post-Cold War international environment there is no reason in principle why naval and maritime forces should not be engaged in multinational security and peace-keeping operations. There is, of course, no justification for inventing multinational naval roles without imperatives originating in the international system. It is not reason enough to humour naval establishments searching for new functions which might help them to survive the cold blast of post-Cold War budget cuts. Nor, given that the UN is underfunded and overstretched, is it reasonable to expect the UN to extend its activities unless these increase rather than decrease its effectiveness. But if politicians perceive a need for multinational maritime operations and there is a political will to realise them, the naval establishments would be expected to find ways of implementing the policies. Mandates would have to be well defined to maintain political legitimacy, as would the rights of multinational forces under international law and their rules of engagement.

Subsequent chapters argue that, within these constraints and consonant with the changed international environment, maritime forces can present valuable deployment options for decision-makers in seeking to implement international mandates for a range of peacekeeping and peace support operations. First, however, it is important to assess the empirical evidence regarding naval units in peacekeeping operations in order to emphasise that any evolution away from ideal peacekeeping will require political support for crossing important force thresholds.

Notes

1 Harold J. Kearsley, *Maritime Power and the Twenty-first Century*, Dartmouth Publishing, Aldershot, 1992, pp. 21–3.
2 See, for example, Robert Gilpin, *War and Change in World Politics*, Cambridge University Press, Cambridge, 1983, p. 112; George Modelski and William R. Thompson, *Seapower in Global Politics, 1494–1993*, Macmillan, Basingstoke, 1988, pp. 17, 133–5.
3 Alfred Thayer Mahan, *The Influence of Sea Power upon History 1660–1783*, Little, Brown & Co., Boston, 1890. For a critique of Mahan, see Paul Kennedy, *The Rise and Fall of British Naval Mastery*, Allen Lane, London, 1976.
4 See, for example, James Cable, *Gunboat Diplomacy: Political Applications of Limited Naval Force, 1919–1979*, Chatto & Windus/IISS, London, 1971; E. N. Luttwak, *The Political Use of Sea Power*, Johns Hopkins University Press, Baltimore, 1974; Ken Booth, *Law, Force, and Diplomacy at Sea*, Allen & Unwin, London, 1985.
5 Cyrus Vance and Elliot Richardson, 'Let the UN Reflag Gulf Vessels', *New York Times*, 8 July 1987. The proposal was also challenged as legitimating a Soviet naval presence in an area of Western interests, letter from James McCoy, 'Naval Mirage in the Gulf', *The Times*, 5 July 1988.
6 Eric Grove, *The Future of Sea Power*, Routledge, London, 1990, pp. 3–4.

7 R. R. Churchill and A. V. Lowe, *The Law of the Sea*, rev. edn, Manchester University Press, Manchester, 1988, p. 19.

8 See Thomas B. Allen, 'Incidents at Sea', *Proceedings*, US Naval Institute, September 1990, pp. 41–5; Sean M. Lynn-Jones, 'A Quiet Success for Arms Control: Preventing Incidents at Sea', *International Security*, vol. 9, no. 4, spring 1985, pp. 154–84.

9 See Richard Fieldhouse and Shunji Taoka (eds), *Superpowers at Sea: An Assessment of the Naval Arms Race*, Oxford University Press/SIPRI, Oxford, 1989.

10 For example, in June 1993, the US Army's basic manual on operations for the first time recognised peacekeeping tasks in which the United States may participate unilaterally or when requested by the UN. Department of the Army, 'FM 100–5: Operations', Washington DC, June 1993, pp. 13–17.

11 See K. P. Saksena, *Reforming the United Nations: The Challenge of Relevance*, Sage Publications, New Delhi, 1993, pp. 194–205.

12 See, for example, Adam Roberts, 'The United Nations and International Security', *Survival*, vol. 35, no. 2, summer 1993, pp. 3–30.

13 John Burton, 'From Strategic Deterrence to Problem Solving', in Kevin Clements (ed.), *Peace and Security in the Asia–Pacific Region*, UN University Press, Tokyo, 1993, pp. 273–4.

14 In an effort to avoid setting precedents, the preamble of SC Res. 794, authorising enforcement of humanitarian relief in Somalia, was phrased: 'Recognizing the unique character of the present situation in Somalia and mindful of its ... extraordinary nature', S/RES/794 (1992), 3 December 1992.

15 Francis Fukuyama, 'Bush's Global Backyard', *The Guardian*, 9 September 1991, p. 17.

16 Thomas Risse-Kappen, 'American Hegemony, Minilateralism or Multilateral Norms? The Re-emergence of the United Nations in World Politics – Some Conceptual Considerations', paper at ECPR Joint Sessions, University of Leiden, 2–7 April 1993.

17 The theory of public goods, borrowed from economics, was applied to alliance burdensharing by Mancur Olson and Richard Zeckhauser in, 'An Economic Theory of Alliances', *Review of Economics and Statistics*, vol. 48, no. 3, August 1966, pp. 266–79.

18 See the application of this argument to alliances by James C. Murdoch and Todd Sandler, 'Complementarity, Free Riding, and the Military Expenditures of NATO Allies', *Journal of Public Economics*, vol. 25, no. 1/2, November 1984, pp. 83–101; Bruce Russett, *What Price Vigilance?*, Yale University Press, New Haven, Conn., 1970, p. 17.

19 See Stephen John Stedman, 'The New Interventionists', *Foreign Affairs*, vol. 72, no. 1, spring 1993, pp. 1–16. For the post-Cold War fault-lines

in US opinion, see Barry R. Posen, *Competing US Grand Strategies*, Defense and Arms Control Studies working paper, Center for International Studies, MIT, Cambridge, Mass., 3 March 1993.

20 Risse-Kappen, 'American Hegemony, Minilateralism or Multilateral Norms?'; Richard A. Falk, Samuel S. Kim and Saul H. Mendlovitz, *The United Nations and a Just World Order*, Westview Press, Boulder, Col., 1991, pp. 1–12.

21 On non-military security UN restructuring, see John G. Ruggie, 'On the Problem of "the Global Problematique": What Roles for International Organisations?', *Alternatives*, vol. 5, no. 1, January 1980, pp. 517–50. On crisis management, see Vladimir Petrovsky, 'Towards Comprehensive Security Through the Enhancement of the Role of the United Nations', UN Doc. A/43/629, annex, 22 September 1988, pp. 1–6.

22 Thomas Risse-Kappen (ed.), *Bringing Transnational Relations Back In. Non-State Actors, Domestic Structures, and International Institutions* (forthcoming).

23 Georges Abi-Saab, 'La deuxième génération des opérations de maintien de la paix: quelques réflexions préliminaires', *Le Trimestre du monde*, 4e, 1992, p. 97.

24 This was the burden of the UK Foreign Office submission to the House of Commons Foreign Affairs Committee, *The Expanding Role of the United Nations and Its Implications for United Kingdom Policy*, Session 1992–93, 3rd Report, HC Paper 235, HMSO, London, 23 June 1993, vol. II, appendices 13–15.

25 See Abi-Saab, 'La deuxième génération des opérations de maintien de la paix', pp. 89–90.

26 However, the Security Council unambiguously specified Chapter VII for humanitarian relief protection in Somalia, and for potential punitive action against Libya (implicated in the bombing of an aircraft which crashed at Lockerbie, Scotland, in 1988). In the latter instance, five Security Council members, including China, abstained from the crucial SC Res. 748 of 31 March 1992. The legal issues are fully analysed by Alfred P. Rubin, 'Libya, Lockerbie and the Law', *Diplomacy and Statecraft*, vol. 4, no. 1, March 1993, pp. 1–19.

27 Alan James, *The Politics of Peace-Keeping*, Chatto & Windus, London, 1969, p. 5. Some definitions appear to exclude monitoring and observing. See, for example, International Peace Academy, *Peacekeeper's Handbook*, Pergamon, New York, 1984, p. 22. But observation activities can be subsumed under peacekeeping because they are so often closely associated with interpositioning roles. See William J. Durch (ed.), *The Evolution of UN Peacekeeping: Case Studies and Comparative Analysis*, St Martin's Press, New York, 1993, pp. 3–4.

28 The 1992 Helsinki document of the Conference on Co-operation and Security in Europe, 'Challenges of Change', provides strict conditions

(see Chapter 8 below), but envisages that peacekeeping could involve civilian and/or military personnel 'to supervise and help maintain cease-fires, to monitor troop withdrawals, to support the maintenance of law and order, to provide humanitarian and medical aid and to assist refugees'. Article III (1) of the Japanese Law Concerning Co-operation for United Nations Peacekeeping Operations and Other Operations refers to peacekeeping: 'under the control of the United Nations . . . to ensure the observance of agreement to prevent the recurrence of armed conflicts . . . to assist in the establishment of a ruling apparatus by democratic means after the termination of armed conflicts or to maintain international peace and security in coping with disputes, provided that such operation be implemented by two or more participating countries . . . without any partiality to any of the Parties to Armed Conflicts, in cases where agreement to cease armed conflicts and maintain the cessation has been reached . . . and where consent for the undertaking of such operations have been obtained from host countries as well as the Parties to Armed Conflicts'.

29 The basic principles were subsequently adopted by the Security Council in 1973. Secretary-General's Report, 'Implementation of Security Council Res. 340 (1973)', UN Doc. S/11052/Rev.1, 27 October 1973.

30 Paul F. Diehl, 'When Peacekeeping Does Not Lead to Peace. Some Notes on Conflict Resolution', *Bulletin of Peace Proposals*, vol. 18, no. 1, 1987, p. 51. However, as Georges Abi-Saab remarks, what begins as a plaster can become an analgesic, 'La deuxième génération des opérations de maintien de la paix', p. 90.

31 It is sometimes assumed that because the post-Cold War situation is novel, so is the challenge to 'ideal' peacekeeping. But the UN had experience in intra-state conflicts in the Lebanon (UNOGIL, 1958), West New Guinea (UNTEA, 1962–63), Congo (ONUC, 1960–64), Yemen (UNYOM, 1963–64, where consensus for the UN presence was lacking) and Cyprus (UNFICYP, 1964–74). Peacekeepers have extended protection and humanitarian assistance to populations (UNIFIL and UNFICYP), protected installations (UNEF I) provided administrative support (UNTEA) and supervised disarmament (ONUCA). They have also attempted to deter aggression: at Nicosia airport in Cyprus in 1974, and in the Lebanon in 1985 when the French battalion in UNIFIL threatened to kill any Israelis who crossed its line *en route* to devastating a village. See G. R. Berridge, *International Politics: States, Power and Conflict Since 1945*, Harvester–Wheatsheaf, Hemel Hempstead, 2nd edn, 1992, p. 213; Jerzy Ciechanski, 'The Post-Cold War Security Council: remarks on the normative contents of Chapter VI½ of the UN Charter', paper at 34th ISA Convention, Acapulco, 23–27 March 1993; Major-General Indar Jit Rikhye (Ret.), *Strengthening UN Peacekeeping: New Challenges and Proposals*, US

Institute of Peace, Washington DC, 1992, pp. 14–17. For the Congo operations, the Security Council authorised 'vigorous action, including the use of the requisite measure of force, if necessary, for the immediate apprehension, detention pending legal action and/or deportation of all foreign military and paramilitary personnel and political advisers not under the United Nations Command, and mercenaries'. SC Res. S/5002, 24 November 1961, para. 4. In March 1978, Secretary-General Kurt Waldheim instructed UNIFIL that it could resist 'attempts by forceful means to prevent it from discharging its duties under the mandate'. Cited by Anthony Verrier, *International Peacekeeping: United Nations Forces in a Troubled World*, Penguin, Harmondsworth, 1981, p. 130.

32 SC Res. S/24880, para. 10, 3 December 1992.

33 The UN General Assembly Special Committee on Peacekeeping Operations (the Committee of 34) which was created in 1965 to investigate operational matters has made only desultory progress. However, a Committee on the Charter and Strengthening the Role of the Organisation presaged some of Boutros-Ghali's proposals by advocating greater scope for the Secretary-General and the Security Council to engage in fact-finding and other measures to deal with the early stages of a crisis. The General Assembly endorsed this Committee's report as a Declaration on the Prevention and Removal of Disputes and Situations Which May Threaten International Peace and Security and on the Role of the United Nations in this Field, A/43/51, 5 December 1988.

34 Marianne Heiberg, *Ethnic Conflict, Peacekeeping and Peacemaking Towards 2000: Second Generation Peacekeeping*, Notat Paper no. 442, NUPI, Oslo, April 1991.

35 See John Mackinlay and Jarat Chopra, 'Second Generation Multinational Operations', *Washington Quarterly*, vol. 15, no. 3, summer 1992, pp. 120–21; Boutros Boutros-Ghali, 'UN Peacekeeping in a New Era: A New Chance for Peace', *The World Today*, April 1993, pp. 66–9.

36 Foreign Office submission, House of Commons Foreign Affairs Committee, *The Expanding Role of the United Nations and Its Implications for United Kingdom Policy*, Session 1992–93, 3rd Report, HC Paper 235, HMSO, London, 23 June 1993.

37 Alan James has argued that: 'There is no viable half-way house between peacekeeping and peace enforcement', *Peacekeeping in International Politics*, Macmillan and IISS, Basingstoke and London, 1990, p. 368.

38 Cuba, Yemen and Zimbabwe voted against the resolution and China and India abstained. Sally Morphet, 'The Security Council and the General Assembly: Their Inter-relationship 1980–1992', paper at ECPR Joint Sessions, University of Leiden, 2–7 April 1993; Nigel S. Rodley,

To Loose the Bands of Wickedness: International Intervention in Defence of Human Rights, Brassey's/David Davies Memorial Institute, London, 1992, p. 29.

39 The missile attack on Baghdad was justified under Article 51 of the UN Charter – the right of individual or collective self-defence in the face of an armed attack. But the Article stipulates that the right to self-defence can only be invoked by an armed attack, either ongoing or imminent. There was no suggestion that Iraq was in the process of launching terrorist attacks against the United States and the US reprisal occurred, without UN authorisation, some time after the discovery of an alleged plot to kill former President George Bush. Marc Weller, 'Attack violates UN Charter', *The Times*, 28 June 1993, p. 2.

40 They include: the 1948 Universal Declaration of Human Rights; the 1966 Covenants; the UN Commission for Human Rights; and General Assembly Resolutions 43–133 and 45–100. Further, Articles 55 and 56 of the UN Charter call on states to take action to ensure the achievement of universal human rights.

41 Hedley Bull, 'Conclusion', in Bull (ed.), *Intervention in World Politics*, Clarendon Press, Oxford, 1984, p. 193. For a contrasting perspective, see Jarat Chopra and Thomas G. Weiss, 'Sovereignty Is No Longer Sacrosanct: Codifying Humanitarian Intervention', *Ethics and International Affairs*, vol. 6, 1992, pp. 95–117. At the UN World Conference on Human Rights in Vienna on 14 June 1993 on the 45th anniversary of the Universal Declaration of Human Rights, Dr Boutros-Ghali affirmed that human rights were universal and indivisible and that international organisations had the right to intervene to protect peoples from governments violating human rights. However, China, Malaysia, Mexico, Iraq and Burma denied the principle of universality. See *The Times*, 14 June 1993, p. 12; *The Guardian*, 15 June 1993, p. 8.

42 Tripartite Adderbury Talks on International Maritime Co-operation, RN College, Greenwich, 3 May 1993.

43 As envisaged by Vice-Admiral William Owens, *Navy News & Undersea Technology*, 22 March 1993, p. 3.

44 Michael A. Morris, *Expansion of Third-World Navies*, Macmillan, Basingstoke, 1987, p. 1.

45 George Kolisnek and Peter Haydon, 'Global Proliferation of Naval Weaponry', paper at Colloquium on Maritime Security and Conflict Resolution, Centre for Foreign Policy Studies, Dalhousie University, Halifax, NS, 24–27 June 1993.

46 North Korea's submarine fleet increased from 16 to 24 boats between 1979 and 1992. In the same period Indonesia's major combatants increased from 9 to 17; Thailand's from 6 to 10 and Japan's from 27 to 47. Thailand is building an aircraft carrier and Japan is building 'Aegis' destroyers. South Korea plans to acquire 7 submarines as part of a naval

expansion which would bring it into the same rank as Britain or France. Rear-Admiral Young Kang (L) (ret.), 'Korean Military Thinking and Selection of Alternatives for Naval Force Development', International Seapower Symposium, Sejong Institute, Seoul, August 1993.

47 Ian Anthony, *The Naval Arms Trade*, Oxford University Press/SIPRI, Oxford, 1990, p. 165.

48 However, from the 1960s the non-US Western navies had emphasised power projection as their major role. See, for example, the roles outlined in *Explanatory Statement on the Navy Estimates, 1962–63*, Cmnd 1629, HMSO, London, 1962, para. 2.

49 As indicated, for example, in UK Directorate of Naval Staff Duties, *A Navy for the 1990s: A Rationale for Maritime Forces in the New Strategic Environment*, MoD, London, July 1992.

50 Department of the Navy, 'From the Sea: Preparing the Naval Service for the 21st Century', Navy and Marine Corps White Paper, Washington DC, September 1992.

51 Jan S. Breemer, 'The End of Naval Strategy: Revolutionary Change and the Future of American Naval Power', paper at Colloquium on Maritime Security and Conflict Resolution, Centre for Foreign Policy Studies, Dalhousie University, Halifax, NS, 24–27 June 1993.

52 As examined in Chapter 7 below, foreign operational control can be virtually discounted. However, even the United States has allowed an air unit in UNTEA and personnel in UNTSO, UNMOGIP and UNIKOM to serve under foreign tactical control – as well as accepting non-US tactical control in NATO contexts.

53 See Michael C. Pugh, *Multinational Maritime Forces: A Breakout from Traditional Peacekeeping?*, Southampton Papers in International Policy, no. 1, Mountbatten Centre for International Studies, University of Southampton, July 1992, pp. 14–16.

54 Defence Committee of the Assembly of Western European Union, 'An Operational Organisation for WEU: Naval Co-operation – Part One: Adriatic Operations', report by Mr Marten and Sir Keith Speed, doc. 1396, 9 November 1993.

55 The *Kennedy* had to return to port. William Durch, 'The US Navy: Forces, Doctrines, Missions, and Arms Control', in Barry M. Blechman, William J. Durch, W. Philip Ellis, Cathleen S. Fisher and Mary C. Fitzgerald, *The US Stake in Naval Arms Control*, Henry L. Stimson Center, Washington DC, October 1990, p. 78.

56 For example, Kearsley, *Maritime Power in the Twenty-first Century*.

57 Grove, *The Future of Sea Power*, p. 234.

The historical record and the relevance of force thresholds

On various occasions in the past maritime forces have operated effectively to support 'ideal' peacekeeping. This chapter draws conclusions from the empirical evidence about the characteristics of such low-level operations, paying particular attention to the distinction between autonomous maritime operations and marine/riverine support to land-based peacekeeping. However, the future deployment of maritime forces may quickly outstrip the ideal peacekeeping paradigm discussed in the previous chapter. It is essential to identify force thresholds which naval units are likely to encounter, in order to complement political and diplomatic initiatives and to maintain control in situations where force could escalate. Chaos in the socio-political environments being tackled by the international community should not be compounded by chaotic interventionism.

To begin with, it might be wondered whether peacekeeping at sea has ever occurred at all. The answer depends upon whether keeping the peace at sea or offshore operations to help keep the peace on land is meant. Theoretically, there has been nothing to prevent UN authorisation of autonomous maritime operations: but in practice the Security Council has concerned itself with threats to security on land.

Autonomous maritime operations

Autonomous operations in the maritime domain, independent of land operations, have occurred rarely if at all. A protocol to the unratified Safety of Life at Sea Convention of 1920 made provision for an international iceberg patrol,[1] and precedents might be claimed for post-conflict mine and shipwreck clearances.[2] Two other cases might be thought to qualify. First, in default of any land deployments, enforcement of UN sanctions against Rhodesia was undertaken by the RN's Beira Patrol off Mozambique. But this embargo which interrupted freedom of navigation, by definition without the rebel Rhodesian government's consent, clearly deviated from peacekeeping in its idealised form. Second, the reassurance role of the Coastal Patrol Unit in the Strait of Tiran, as part of the non-UN Multinational Force and Observers (MFO) in Sinai, might be considered as having a purely maritime rationale. The three converted minesweepers, crewed by Italians, monitor freedom of navigation through the hazardous Strait of Tiran and the southern part of the sea-lane to Eilat, much used by freighters and pleasure craft. The Unit is nevertheless an integral part of the MFO. It contributes to confidence-building in the area, and its establishment is based on the 1979 Egyptian–Israeli Peace Treaty for the policing of the demilitarised zones.[3]

But the concept of interpositioning between opposing forces, whose authorities have given consent to international supervision, does not transpose neatly to the maritime environment.[4] It is difficult to see how interpositioning between forces could be regularly carried out at sea. A stand-off between opposing ships with lines patrolled by a naval peacekeeping force might have been theoretically possible for underwriting any lull in the UK–Iceland Cod War in 1958–59. A naval peacekeeping force might also be envisaged for separating navies in contested waters in the South China Sea (see Chapter 8 below). But practical problems are created by the mobility of forces and relative difficulty in establishing static positions at sea.

In any event the provenance of most disputes is on land. The maritime environment is regarded as increasingly significant in global security. But it is by no means obvious that ocean boundary issues lead to disputes which in turn deteriorate into conflicts. Differences at sea do not attract the political symbolism and popular levels of emotion which interfere with peaceful resolution processes. The unavoidable conclusion is that whilst coastal communities may develop proprietary attitudes to ocean areas and governments may seek advantages in claiming sovereignty and administrative competence over large areas of the ocean, dangerous tensions are less likely to arise in uninhabited environments.[5]

In sum, there has been no clear instance of autonomous peace-keeping in the maritime domain *per se*, though this is not to say that unarmed or lightly armed international maritime forces will not be required in the future to undertake constabulary roles of the kind discussed in Chapter 5 below, such as suppressing smuggling and piracy, securing freedom of navigation or combating pollution.

Integrated operations

By contrast, there have been several instances of maritime forces being used to assist peacekeeping on land. Navies have supplied and supported land-based peacekeepers in helping to defuse or stabilise situations and monitoring the implementation of agreements. Only the more prominent historical examples are outlined here; a full chronology is provided in the Appendix to this book.

Like international land-based peacekeeping, naval peacekeeping pre-dates the United Nations. In 1920 the League of Nations established an International Plebiscite Commission and authorised French and UK naval units to provide a presence to deter conflict, and naval personnel to police polling booths, during the Schleswig–Holstein plebiscite. A British Admiral commanded the operation from ships whose presence was regarded as necessary to maintain calm. However, the operation had been preceded by some old-fashioned gunboat diplomacy when the French cruiser, the *Marseillaise*, arrived in 1919 at the request of the Danes to deter German-sponsored unrest.[6] The sailors and marines were backed up by the big guns offshore, but they were not anticipating anything more taxing than localised rioting at the polls.

However, in the absence of political consensus, peacekeeping activities are not easily distinguished from interventionism. Significant lessons in this respect were afforded by the multinational naval activity in support of the principles of 'non-intervention' by external powers during the Spanish Civil War. To monitor the Non-Intervention Agreement of August 1936, signed by European states to prevent military exports to Spain, an International Board of Control arranged for 550 observers to embark on ships bound for Spain. The observers had a mandate to supervise the unloading of cargoes and arrival of passengers at Spanish ports, but could do no more than report suspected contraventions of the Non-Intervention Agreement to the flag states. Non-intervention was cynically flouted by Italy, Germany and the Soviet Union, and the UK used it to curb French involvement and to prevent the Spanish Republican Government exercising rights under international law. Although an International Naval Patrol was also arranged by the UK, France, Germany and Italy, the fascist powers soon withdrew, and Italian submarines attacked merchant ships trading legitimately with the Spanish Republic. In fact the monitoring of non-intervention threatened to lead to general war when, at Nyon in September 1937, the UK and France agreed to retaliate against submarines in areas where merchant ships were attacked. However, the UK and French Governments concluded that they could only effectively protect trade if they were prepared to go to war against Franco, and by implication against Italy and Germany.[7]

Humanitarian assistance in Spain was also seen as intervention. Although the rescue by sea of nationals proceeded without controversy, the evacuation of thousands of war refugees from the Bilbao enclave by the UK, France and the Soviet Union was initially resisted in the UK by the Foreign Office and Admiralty on the grounds that it would constitute intervention on behalf of the besieged Basques by reducing the mouths they had to feed. Again, the British Admiralty was initially reluctant to breach the 'blockade' of Spanish ports proclaimed by Franco in November 1936 by protecting food ships up to the 3-mile limit. The Admiralty interpreted an 'effective blockade' as the presence of a force which rendered access to the coast hazardous. In fact Nationalist activities in the Bay of Biscay created intermittent hazards and, after merchant relief ships successfully entered Bilbao, the Royal Navy resumed protection, acknowledging that Franco's blockade was unsustainable.[8] Neither the 'blockade' nor the breaching of it had much influence on the outcome of the war, but impartiality was impossible. Assisting merchant ships as far as the 3-mile limit could be represented as intervention on the Republican side. But since Franco had not declared a state of belligerency, the 'blockade' was illegal, and failure to protect the food ships would have amounted to connivance in the Nationalist cause.[9] In effect, not only was securing multinational agreement to intervene problematic, but so was maintaining non-intervention. The result in Spain was muddled unilateralism.

By contrast, the first UN naval peacekeeping operation was to render assistance to a mediation process. The blue UN ensign flew from US warships in support of Count Folke Bernadotte's mission to Palestine in 1948. Count Bernadotte, could call upon naval units which included a French minesweeper, the amphibious cargo ship USS *Marquette*, the aircraft carrier, USS *Palau* (minus its air group) and three US destroyers. The vessels patrolled the coast and transported supplies and personnel. UN officials were evacuated by sea from Haifa, were returned and re-evacuated. The American rules of engagement stipulated that US ships were not to use force to board or stop vessels and were only to be used for transport and observation.[10] Subsequently the UN Emergency Force in 1956 had a landing ship in support, though it fell into disrepair and was not replaced.

In 1962–63 the UN Temporary Executive Authority (UNTEA) monitored a ceasefire and deployed security forces for the UN administration of West New Guinea/Irian until the territory was transferred to Indonesia. Pakistan supplied crews for nine vessels which were transferred to the UN by the Netherlands.[11]

In the Americas, integrated naval operations were an important feature of the demobilisation process in Nicaragua. The Observadores de las Naciones Unidas para Centroamérica (ONUCA) had the task of monitoring the ceasefire, observing that no territory was used as a base for aggression, and monitoring cross-border interventions by irregulars, including those occurring by sea and across the river deltas which lead into the Gulf of Fonseca. Argentina agreed to deploy four 36-ton Israeli-built 'Dabur' patrol craft from the Ushuaia base crewed by thirty naval personnel. From June 1990, these vessels, together with inflatables and helicopters, undertook a complex pattern of patrols in the Gulf of Fonseca and about 350 km along the coast from Corinto in the south to the San Miguel River in the north (see Figure 3.1). However, until September 1990, patrols were not permitted within 3 n.m. of the Salvadoran coast where attacks were considered most likely.[12] The squadron commander answered to his government for the overall deployment of ships and personnel, but reported to the Fonseca Verification Centre, whose head in 1991 was also appointed from the Argentine Navy. The squadron's duties were to make contact with ships and craft, to gather and provide information to ONUCA headquarters in Tegucigalpa. Close co-operation with observers on land was essential because one of the gun-running routes between Nicaragua

Figure 3.1 *Gulf of Fonseca patrols*

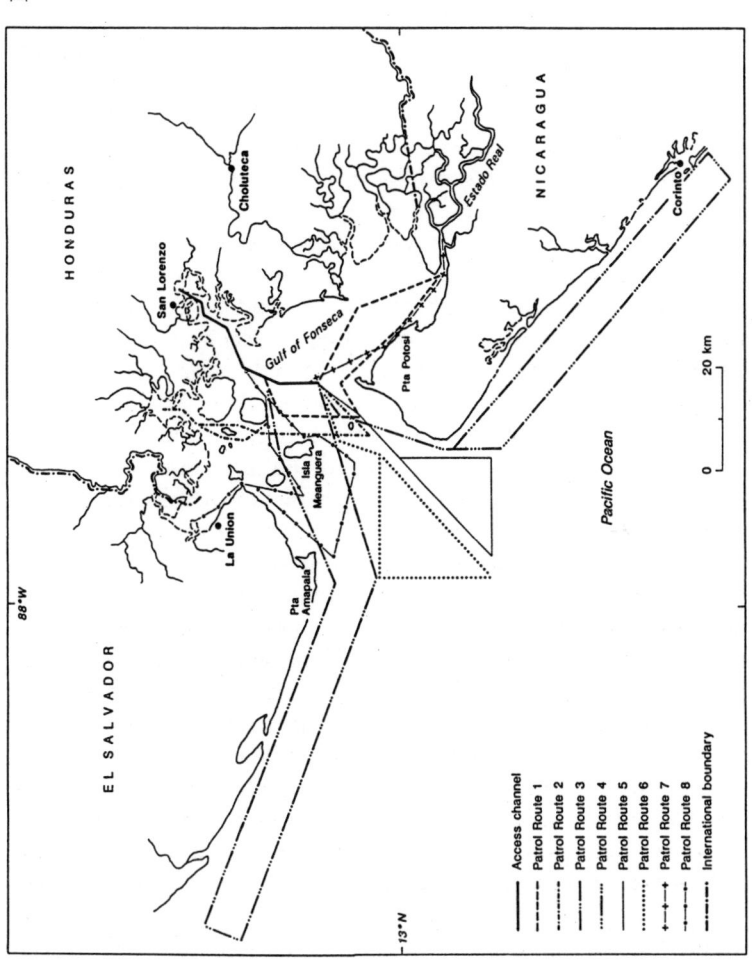

and El Salvador involved a combination of sea, river and land crossings using kayaks. In the first month some four hundred contacts
were made and this grew in succeeding months, as night patrols and
combined boat and helicopter patrols became a standard feature of
the operation. To ensure that the inoffensiveness of the ONUCA
operation would be widely recognised, the naval contingent kept in
contact with parties to the regional disputes to reduce the risk of
accidental confrontations. The boats were painted white and flew
the UN flag from the mainmast and the Argentine flag from the
stern. The UN insisted that all weapons were removed. The crews
were unarmed and the rules of engagement (ROE) permitted only
evasive action if threatened. The crews could assist the nine UN
International Military Observers, but did not have the right to stop
and inspect shipping. The squadron had a high degree of logistic and
maintenance autonomy. But the UN provided all fuel and ground
transport, chartered cargo ships to transport the boats between
Argentina and the Gulf of Fonseca, and refunded Argentina's depreciation and support costs. The operation ended on 17 January 1992,
after nearly 6,500 patrol hours in which, so the Argentine
Commander claimed, the patrols had produced 'dissuasion by
permanent presence'.[13]

Similar tasks were set for the riverine and coastal patrols of the
UN Transitional Authority in Cambodia (UNTAC) from early
1992 to the end of 1993 when UN forces began withdrawing.[14] The
220 multinational naval observers and 168 marines on some thirty
vessels on coastal, riverine and lake patrols were deployed to transport UNTAC personnel and equipment; to supervise the ceasefire
and investigate any allegations of foreign military presence; to
monitor the cantonment and demobilisation of the naval forces of
parties to the Paris Agreements of October 1991; and to deter and
intercept arms smuggling. Check-points were established at the
ports of Sihanoukville and Phnom Penh, and at river crossings into
Vietnam (see Figure 3.2). Patrol craft provided by Cambodia as
part of the 'retained units' comprising: 4 sea patrol and 27 river
patrol boats, with an additional 8 landing craft to be hired.
Canada, the Philippines and Uruguay provided navy and marine
personnel; whilst 7 countries, including Russia and the UK provided naval observers.[15] In contrast to the Gulf of Fonseca operation, the marines were armed and the ROE included a self-defence
capability.

Figure 3.2 *Naval observers in Cambodia*

Moreover, the Cambodia naval deployment stretched the bounds of peacekeeping. Additional, non-passive, roles were acquired including a deterrent function. This was necessary because the UN's mandate was not universally respected. The Khmer Rouge kidnapped UN observers and, in March 1993, massacred ethnic

Vietnamese fishing communities living on the Tonle Sap Lake. Hundreds of boats and over 13,000 people fled south to Phnom Penh and across the border into Vietnam. The exodus was monitored, and at times convoyed, by UNTAC craft and marines, whose presence offered an element of protection by deterring attacks.[16]

Similarly, operations by NATO and the Western European Union in the Adriatic Sea originally fell on the threshold between peacekeeping and enforcement. From May to November 1992, the naval vessels merely monitored merchant ships entering the Adriatic Sea. Of course the sanctions policy which the monitoring was designed to check was not agreed to by the targets of the embargo. The situation was to some extent analogous to neutral convoying and minesweeping during the 'Tanker War' in the Gulf: the parties to the dispute were thwarted by international action but could not legally oppose the international activity so long as it occurred outside territorial waters. However, from 22 November 1992, NATO and WEU units were entitled to verify adherence to UN sanctions policy by boarding or diverting merchant vessels. They were also entitled to enter the 12-mile territorial limit and to enforce the embargo by firing warning shots at suspicious vessels (without destroying them or endangering life). Although the merchant ships were not in any position to resist inspection, the fact that Serbian military units engaged in hostile behaviour towards the Adriatic task groups indicates that naval monitoring and verification had moved decisively from peacekeeping to enforcement.[17] The distinction was particularly significant to Germany which, on constitutional grounds, ordered its ship on station not to participate in enforcement operations.[18] Crossing this threshold was also reflected in the merger of the NATO and WEU task groups on 8 June 1993, under single operational control, not merely to avoid duplication of effort and resources, but to provide mutual security through a combined concept of operations drawing on NATO rules of engagement (see Figure 3.3).[19]

At the same time, although completely under national operational control, ships such as the carriers HMS *Ark Royal*, FNS *Clemenceau* and USN *Kennedy*, and their support vessels, have cooperated with peacekeeping on land, sustaining UN Protection Forces in Croatia and Bosnia with command facilities, supplies and helicopter support. They also act as sovereign base areas, standing

Figure 3.3 *NATO/WEU maritime patrol area in the Adriatic Sea*

by in case of evacuation. However, in so far as they provide air cover
to enforce no-fly zones, they are also engaged in enforcement rather
than peacekeeping actions.

In sum, the historical record indicates that there has been a
limited, though significant, requirement for naval peacekeeping in
support of territorial operations and designed to complement UN
initiatives to encourage, or allow, peaceful political processes to
occur.

Naval peacekeeping characteristics

Drawing on these experiences, it is clear that, as might be expected, naval operations have generally been low key, commensurate with land-based peacekeeping.

1 Naval operations have generally been closely tied to the peace-keeping command on land. As typified in Nicaragua and Cambodia, command links with land and air operations, have been essential.

2 The most common tasks have been as follows.
   a) Transport, sealift and sovereign base support to land-based peacekeepers, as in Bernadotte's Palestine mission, has been valuable, and inshore support was particularly useful to UN administering authorities in West Irian and Cambodia. Although sealift was superseded by airlift for the small peace-keeping operations during the Cold War, large-scale opera-tions on land are more likely to require logistic support by sea which might need to be guarded by naval units. In addition, whatever the size of the operation, offshore helicopter support, and medical and evacuation facilities may prove vital.
   b) Monitoring agreements for ceasefires, disarmament and mili-tary disengagement or supervising the cantonment of vessels have been tasks undertaken in the Gulf of Fonseca, Strait of Tiran and in Cambodia.
   c) Monitoring embargoes at sea, as in the Adriatic before November 1992, has underpinned sanctions policies which cross the threshold of coercion.

3 It has sometimes been practical and convenient to delegate naval operations to a single state. Thus the Royal Navy conducted the Beira patrol, Pakistan operated the UNTEA craft, Italy the MFO vessels, and the Argentine ONUCA's. In Cambodia the observers were multinational but the crews of local craft were Cambodian. For such distinct and usually modest operations it has made sense to give tactical control to a single national authority, thereby avoiding problems associated with the integration of multina-tional forces.

4 As in land-based peacekeeping, non-Security Council members have played important roles, for example, Pakistan, the Argentine and Italy (in the non-UN MFO). Since 1951 no ship of a major naval power has flown the UN flag.

5 Except for monitoring and verifying sanctions, the requirement has been for unglamorous, relatively cheap naval equipment with low combatant status – minesweepers, cutters, small patrol vessels and inflatables. Argentina was not permitted even to carry dismantled weapons on board its patrol vessels. Such platforms, which can engage in extensive but low-risk operations, are also most readily released from national and alliance duties. In several cases, however, locally available 'craft of opportunity' have offered practical and cheaper alternatives to bringing vessels from overseas. Corvettes, frigates and other combat ships have been deployed for sanctions monitoring when vessels have to provide extensive periods of cover and remain at sea for long periods. There may also be a higher risk of opposition or disruption by mines and therefore ships with protection and weapons systems have been required.

6 To monitor the relative ease of movement by traffic across water, naval operations are often extensive and time-consuming, placing a premium on surveillance and mobility. The volume of civilian traffic may be very high and the size and configuration of the area to be covered in relation to the number of peacekeeping vessels available may pose difficulties. The waterways of the Gulf of Fonseca and of Cambodia are very intricate and required complex patrolling patterns. The Argentine patrols averaged 12 hours a day in the period 29 June 1991 to 17 January 1992, and recorded a total of 72,000 n.m.[20] In the Adriatic, the operational area of each frigate in the WEU force was approximately 1,800 n.m. sq. However, land-based maritime patrol craft can provide more extensive surveillance cover. Alouette and Bell Jet Ranger helicopters were deployed in the Gulf of Fonseca, and a variety of fixed-wing surveillance aircraft, including P–3 Orions, are deployed on maritime patrols in the Adriatic Sea.

7 As on land, rules of engagement have usually been designed to avoid provocation and incidents which could lead to attacks on

the peacekeeping vessels, or which could lead to loss of life at sea. In this respect, the ROE in the Gulf of Fonseca were particularly strict. The UN patrols could not stop and inspect ships. The UN Secretary-General, Pérez de Cuéllar, also insisted that for the purposes of observation and patrolling no weapons were required. If they came under attack the crews were to take evasive action and withdraw from the scene, report the incident immediately to ONUCA HQ and request the assistance of the naval authorities of Nicaragua, Honduras, El Salvador, Costa Rica and Guatemala.[21] However, it is not an absolute principle that peacekeepers should be unarmed. They usually carry personal weapons and can return fire in self-defence. Where ships are deployed in multinational operations, national ROE predominate, and these may vary considerably from state to state and situation to situation.[22]

It can be concluded from the historical experience that naval operations have been valuable in association with land-based peacekeeping. But the evidence also shows that particular difficulties often confront navies. Some are practical, notably the requirement to sustain a high level of patrolling. Furthermore, as discussed in Chapter 9 below, if more than one navy is involved, technical and operational problems arise relating to the multinational integration of naval units, not least command issues and the establishment of common levels of communications and ROE. It is also the case that for naval crews which are trained for self-defence and aggressive responses, peacekeeping operations are a novelty. There is a lack of continuous experience in any state or group of states, comparable to that for land-based peacekeeping in say Fiji, Canada or Norway. As the Argentines discovered, it is important for staff to adapt to, or undertake training for, non-aggressive postures.[23]

Moreover, an extension of operations, such as embargo work in the Adriatic Sea, requires a range of techniques in seamanship, boarding and alert/force status. Searches to enforce sanctions can be particularly arduous. In maintaining the blockade against Iraq in accordance with Security Council resolutions, warships of the Coalition states issued over 13,000 challenges and conducted over 500 boardings between 26 August and 3 December 1990.[24] In the Adriatic Sea, 18,524 merchant vessels had been challenged by patrols from 22 November 1992 to 15 June 1993. Of these, 1,760 had been inspected or diverted to a port for inspection.[25]

Finally, it is axiomatic that contested humanitarian intervention, or the monitoring and verification of sanctions, and the further step of interdiction to enforce an embargo, will bring maritime units up against important thresholds which cease to have the imprimatur of uncontested peacekeeping. When, in November 1991, the Western European Union (WEU) agreed to a tripartite force comprising UK, French and Italian warships to create a 'humanitarian corridor' for the Red Cross to evacuate children and the wounded from Dubrovnik, the UK made its involvement conditional upon the agreement of the parties in the battle for Dalmatia.[26] Squeamish or prudent, the conditionality recognised that an important threshold would be crossed.

The threshold problem

Given the unique flexibility of navies in crises, are such thresholds as important at sea as on land? On the one hand, warships offshore have the advantage of being physically distanced from the intricacies of contested jurisdictions on land; an advantage which may be diminished, incidentally, when naval/marine peacekeepers are deployed to internal waterways. On the other hand, thresholds matter if escalation is to be avoided or controlled in situations where the use of naval force may sabotage the crisis management process and exacerbate the original problem.

A threshold represents a recognisable modification in effort for dealing with conflict and usually has significant legal and political, as well as military implications. Issues relating to objectives, targets, proportionality, potential collateral and environmental damage may have to be reconsidered. For peacekeepers in general, the threshold between operations by consent and contested enforcement has been regarded as a particularly useful one because it has been relatively clear; though the label 'peacekeeping' has sometimes been employed euphemistically to disguise naval enforcement tasks.[27] In the sense that it has been so easily understood and sanctified by convention, it may be regarded as analogous to the nuclear threshold beyond which additional force limitations seem less easily marked or recognised. Policies to enforce or deter assume a willingness to move through various levels of force. In addition, controlling escalation, or establishing escalation dominance beyond ideal peacekeeping, may be highly problematic in multinational contexts because of the wide variety of national views about the legitimacy of force and the permissible risks.

Participation in operations which are actually or potentially contested is a domestic issue in many states. Even under a legal dispensation granted in 1993, the German Bundestag has to endorse the deployment of troops for peacekeeping on a case-by-case basis. Turkey and Argentina are among the states whose elected assemblies have to give permission to allow involvement in armed conflict by their forces. In the embargo against Iraq, the Belgian Government specified that its three vessels could not participate in any action involving direct contact with ships trying to break the embargo.[28] Greece, Portugal and Spain also operated outside the immediate war zone. Japan was only able to participate in mine-clearing in the Persian Gulf once the war against Iraq had finished – though as a consequence of taking a leading role in the Cambodian operations, Japanese public opinion appeared to become more favourable to peacekeeping.[29] Changes from one force state to another may have domestic political implications. UN authorisation to use force to interdict merchant ships in the Adriatic caused political difficulties for Germany and Spain, and in Somalia the use of force in the Mogadishu area led to a dispute between Italy and the UN in July 1993.

Whilst such apprehensions may complicate, perhaps enfeeble, attempts to move beyond peacekeeping, a contrary problem may arise from pressures 'to do something'. Although naval and political establishments (at least in democratic states) are aware of the importance of distinguishing levels of force, public opinion and the media may demand increased involvement in a dispute without an appreciation of the inherent difficulties of controlling escalation and avoiding unnecessary risks. The dilemma was illustrated in Somalia, where many non-government organisations distributing aid joined the chorus of demands for military intervention but subsequently criticised the tactics used.[30]

The threshold problem raises issues of particular relevance for navies. First, warships are usually expected to provide a range of capabilities which facilitate transitions through a spectrum of operations. Indeed it would be unwise not to. As Peter Jones remarks: 'it would be an unfortunate commander who was ordered to sail into an unstable region without some level of access to those additional capabilities he would require if the situation worsened suddenly'.[31] Thus ships and maritime aircraft away from homeports would carry a normal complement of weapons (with the exception of nuclear weapons in the case of naval nuclear powers). The contrast with aircraft is pertinent. In mid-1993, land-based maritime patrol aircraft for the northern Adriatic were ordered to load with live anti-submarine warfare (ASW) weapons, whereas those patrolling further south were not.[32] Even if an operation were unlikely to lead to conflict, it would hardly be practical, in terms of time, cost and technical problems, to require major naval combatants to make such distinctions before sailing to their stations. Besides, it would be a tall order to expect crews to forgo any possibility of self-defence, a demand initially resisted by the Argentine Navy even for the low-key patrols by small boats in the Gulf of Fonseca.[33] Nevertheless, the selection of tactics, methods and weapons (if any) for an operation has to be guided by legal and political as well as military requirements.

Second, although warships can be valuable precisely because they have multipurpose configurations, particular circumstances will require appropriate force levels, force mixes, logistic support, training, ROE and levels of integration with other navies. In other words, task-specific elements as well as the flexibility to change tasks may be necessary, not only to ensure the effectiveness of an operation, but to send the appropriate escalation-control signals. The technical and operational requirements are discussed in Chapter 9, but the point made here is that the profile of a task force should also reflect and signal the kinds of threshold which are anticipated. There has been a world of difference between uncontested monitoring in the Gulf of Fonseca and enforcement of the embargo in the Adriatic Sea. In the former, basic technology and whitened, obviously harmless, small vessels were sufficient. For embargo operations of the Adriatic or Gulf type, combatant ships with air support and early-warning systems indicate a determination to provide escalation dominance over the target state.

Third, although lack of ambiguity may be a quintessential requirement in UN-authorised naval operations,[34] more than one objective is likely to be served by a single naval task. Thus, the declared task of a maritime surveillance operation may be to monitor compliance with an embargo; at the same time it can provide early warning of potentially hostile activity. In the Adriatic, maritime patrol aircraft operating off the Montenegrin coast have been tasked with both surface surveillance to enforce the embargo and ASW surveillance in case of a Serbia–Montenegro Federal Navy submarine threat.[35] The latter task might be perceived by the state being coerced as a more provocative military action than the former. Unless a vessel is unambiguously deployed for a single function (though even hydrographic survey vessels can engage in espionage), a target state may make a worst-case assessment. Some operational goals may be usefully served by maintaining appearances which are ambiguous, but the line between escalation and de-escalation, and the line between tempting fate and deterring effectively will be a matter of fine political judgement.

Fourth, and flowing from this, whatever blurring between peace-keeping and peace enforcement for land operations may be pro-posed, at sea, even if an operation moves smoothly from one force status to another, deliberate, highly formalised steps are essential. Naval units are furnished with distinctive levels of ROE. However, with the safety of ships and crews at stake, naval commanders no doubt acquire a fair degree of freedom of action according to the time available for consultation with political authorities. Without making invidious assessments about the relative significance of casualties at sea with those in the air and on land, there is little doubt that the loss of a major unit, whether by accident or deliberate tar-geting, could have considerable repercussions for the continued exercise of a mandate. The use of navies for UN-authorised deter-rence, opposed mineclearing, contested humanitarian intervention or embargo enforcement may involve a low probability of attack but a high risk if it occurs.

Fifth, as we have seen, sanctions monitoring is an example of a naval activity which complicates the theory of thresholds between peacekeeping and enforcement. It is conducted entirely pacifically, and perhaps without any effect on the crisis, but the element of consent and co-operation of the parties to a dispute is missing, for no such consent is needed. The next threshold, enforcement of an embargo, stretches beyond the traditional peacekeeping horizon. Diplomatic measures are necessary to secure the acquiescence of the global shipping industry and to secure access to friendly ports to which suspect ships can be diverted for inspection (such as Brindisi in the case of the Adriatic embargo). But enforcement does not necessarily entail confrontation with the target states. In this respect, entry into territorial waters of the target state to enforce an embargo may be as significant as the process of moving from monitoring to enforcement in international waters.

These factors mean that calibrating naval action to match diplomatic initiatives will be a delicate rather than cavalier process. In the very broadest terms, several linkages can be postulated: preventive diplomacy (such as fact finding) and preventive peacekeeping (such as the symbolic stationing of ships outside territorial waters); peacemaking negotiations and traditional peacekeeping; conflict management and enforcement; conflict resolution and peace observation.[36] Thus the threshold between monitoring and enforcing sanctions falls within the category of 'conflict management and peace enforcement'. Given that the financial incentive to break embargoes increases as sanctions become more effective, there is a clear need for diplomatic and operational arrangements to be made in tandem.

The point is neatly illustrated at a regional level by the move from surveillance to control of traffic on the River Danube in the autumn of 1992. Initially the Conference on Security and Co-operation in Europe (CSCE) established Sanctions Assistance Missions, comprising mainly customs officials, in the riparian and neighbouring states. Consultations were also held by the relevant authorities of Bulgaria, Romania and the Ukraine. However, Romania made an urgent request for technical assistance because ships flagrantly refused to submit to Romanian controls and one master threatened to dump his cargo in the Danube. In response, the WEU and United States provided equipment and deployed customs and police officers at centres in Hungary, Romania and Bulgaria. But Hungary then argued that WEU contingents should be unarmed and under Hungarian command, and also sought security guarantees from the WEU in the event that Serbia retaliated with force. This was refused on the grounds that the operation was limited to civilian co-operation between WEU and Central European states and that any Serbian aggression would be a matter of direct concern to the whole international community.[37]

In effect, one of the political repercussions of deploying civilians in an enforcement role, in which force was to be authorised though not necessarily with arms, was to open up wider questions about

European security. Clearly such an operation aroused territorial sensitivities. But equally critical in this respect may be Albania's agreement to allow foreign warships to use its territorial waters from 31 December 1993 for embargo enforcement in the Adriatic Sea. The gesture facilitated the embargo by sealing off the approaches to Serbian–Montenegrin ports. However, it is not clear what protection Albania could expect from foreign warships in the area if, as a consequence of the arrangement, Serbia attacked Albanian vessels.

Conclusion

It has been argued that the importance of force thresholds at sea, familiar enough to naval officers, should be fully recognised by civilian decision-makers, politicians and commentators. Simply because warships can move freely in international waters and can adapt effectively to various missions does not mean that political, legal and operational thresholds can be readily underestimated. It is one thing for UN-authorised navies to act as peacekeeping witnesses to the military effects of a political consensus, as in the Gulf of Fonseca. It is quite another to enforce sanctions under Chapter VII of the UN Charter through the interdiction of shipping. Although constabulary functions of the kind examined in Chapter 5 below, are not likely to attract great controversy, partly because they are based on minimum force or no force at all, the notion that peacekeeping and enforcement are becoming blurred should not obscure the critical implications of moving from one role and status of force to another. If not, the international community would be discarding any advantages associated with the highly disciplined and controlled deployment of military force. In this regard, assuming that the widest possible international support is sought for goals declared to be in the realm of universal 'public goods', it is not sufficient for multinational forces simply to comply with the laws of armed conflict. High standards of discipline are imperative if the UN is not to lose credibility through the errant behaviour of its forces in crises.[38]

The appropriate naval structures, their management, and the operational, technical and legal guidelines which have to be considered are the subjects of subsequent chapters in this study. The next chapter indicates that the particular character of warships presents opportunities for a departure from ideal peacekeeping, and that naval forces offer valuable deployment options for decision-makers in seeking to implement international mandates. Indeed, it is precisely beyond the classical peacekeeping paradigm that most multinational naval activities may occur in the future. It is therefore important to formulate a coherent concept of maritime operations.

Notes

1 World Peace Foundation (Denys P. Myers), *Nine Years of the League of Nations, 1920–28, (Ninth Yearbook)*, Boston, 1929, p. 80.

2 Examples of clearing mines and wrecks, unopposed by former warring parties, and analogous to restoring infrastructure on land, include: wreck clearing in the Suez Canal (1956) and Pakistan ports (1972), the hunt for mines in the Red Sea (1984) and the clearing of Kuwait's harbours and coast of mines and obstacles (1991).

3 Alan James, 'Symbol in Sinai: The Multinational Force and Observers', *Millennium: Journal of International Studies*, vol. 14, no. 3, winter 1985, pp. 261–3.

4 However, a US warship deterred opposing forces from engaging in combat during the Cyprus crisis in the early 1960s by sailing between Greek and Turkish vessels approaching each other in the Aegean Sea. Robert S. Wood, 'Intervention and the Use of Force to Achieve Limited Regional Objectives to Restore Order', paper at Colloquium on Maritime Security and Conflict Resolution, Centre for Foreign Policy Studies, Dalhousie University, Halifax, NS, 24–27 June 1993.

5 Douglas M. Johnston, 'Ocean Boundary Disputes and the Risk of Conflict', paper at Colloquium on Maritime Security and Conflict Resolution, Centre for Foreign Policy Studies, Dalhousie University, Halifax, NS, 24–27 June 1993.

6 Sarah Wambaugh, *Plebiscites Since the World War*, 2 vols, Carnegie Endowment for International Peace, Washington DC, 1933, vol. 1, pp. 65–8.

7 James Cable, *Gunboat Diplomacy: Political Applications of Limited Naval Force*, Chatto & Windus/IISS, London, 1971, pp. 196–9; Hugh Thomas, *The Spanish Civil War*, rev. edn, Penguin, London, 1965, pp. 679–80; Alan James, *Peacekeeping in International Politics*, Macmillan and IISS, Basingstoke and London, 1990, pp. 80–83.

8 James Cable, *The Royal Navy and the Siege of Bilbao*, Cambridge University Press, Cambridge, 1979, p. 92; Jeremy Ginifer, 'Naval

Operations during the Spanish Civil War: The Siege of Bilbao and the International Naval Patrol', unpublished paper, Naval Peacekeeping Research Project, University of Southampton, 14 February 1992.

9 Cable, *The Royal Navy and the Siege of Bilbao*, pp. 93–4. The concept of an effective blockade had been defined in the Declaration of Paris (1856) as the maintenance of sufficient force to prevent any actual access to the coast. It was incorporated into the 1909 Declaration of London, but there has been no consensus about what this meant: a chain of anchored warships, intermittent patrols or the establishment of an exclusion zone (as declared by a UK Order in Council for the Falklands/Malvinas). As a consequence of the increased range of weapon systems, the traditional rules of law of blockade have become increasingly tenuous. See N. Ronzitti (ed.), *The Law of Naval Warfare: A Collection of Agreements and Documents with Commentaries*, Martinus Nijhoff, Dordrecht, 1988, pp. 72–3.

10 The United States also supplied a naval medical unit, five commercial aircraft for patrols and transport, observer personnel and communications equipment. Frank Uhlig, Jr, 'The First United Nations Force', *Proceedings*, US Naval Institute, February 1951, p. 201.

11 James, *Peacekeeping in International Politics*, p. 193; William Henderson, *West New Guinea: The Dispute and Its Settlement*, Seton Hall University Press, South Orange, NJ, 1973.

12 The information for this operation is taken from: Capitán Ricardo Enrique Schroeder, '"Operacion Gaucho" en CentroAmérica', *Puestos de Maniobra*, yr. 3, no. 4, September 1991, pp. 18–21; Juan Carlos Neves, *United Nations Peace-Keeping Operations in the Gulf of Fonseca by Argentine Navy Units*, Report 01–93, Strategy & Campaign Dept, US Naval War College, Newport RI, 12 January 1993; Lt-Cmdr Graham M. Day (CD), 'Naval Peacekeeping: A Practical Account', *Peacekeeping & International Relations*, vol. 22, no. 2, March/April 1993, pp. 5–6.

13 The advantages to the Argentine were that they did not need to call on national funds and the operation gave officers multinational experience. Schroeder, '"Operacion Gaucho" en CentroAmérica', p. 21; Neves, *United Nations Peace-Keeping Operations in the Gulf of Fonseca by Argentine Navy Units*, pp. 15ff.

14 'Report of the Secretary General on Cambodia', UN doc., S/23613/Add.1, 26 February 1992.

15 *Ibid.*, UN doc., S/23613, 19 February 1992. Personnel strengths are for 1 March 1993, UNTAC 'Daily Press Briefing', UN Information Centre, New York, 4 March 1993.

16 UNTAC 'Daily Press Briefings', 11, 26, 31 March, 1, 6 April 1993.

17 Interview with naval source participating in embargo operations, 12 March 1993.

18 Michael Simmons and Ian Traynor, 'UN Enforces Its Oil Embargo on Serbia', *The Guardian*, 18 November 1992, p. 9; 'New Moves on Blockade', *Jane's Defence Weekly*, 5 December 1992, p. 9.

19 'Joint Session of the North Atlantic Council and the Council of Western European Union, Brussels, 8 June 1993', NATO press release (93)41.

20 Neves, *United Nations Peace-Keeping Operations in the Gulf of Fonseca*, p. 35.

21 Communication from Grp Capt. Anselmo M. Rojo-Arauz, Defence Attaché, Argentine Embassy, London, 20 June 1993. Also, see Neves, *United Nations Peace-Keeping Operations in the Gulf of Fonseca*, p. 21.

22 Some national ROE for ships in the Adriatic may have been so constraining as to increase the Captain's difficulties in defending his/her vessel from attack. Interview with naval source participating in embargo operations, 12 March 1993.

23 Neves, *United Nations Peace-Keeping Operations in the Gulf of Fonseca by Argentine Navy Units*, p. 40

24 Defence Committee of the Assembly of the Western European Union, *Consequences of the Invasion of Kuwait: Continuing Operations in the Gulf Region*, by De Hoop Scheffer, doc. 1248 addendum, WEU, Paris, 4 December 1990, appendix 1, p. 26.

25 Defence Committee of the Assembly of Western European Union, 'An Operational Organisation for WEU: Naval Co-operation – Part One: Adriatic Operations', report by Mr Marten and Sir Keith Speed, doc. 1396, 9 November 1993, p. 6. Of the 25–40 merchant ships monitored each day in the Straits of Otranto by three WEU ships, only about 5 were boarded for verification purposes. About 10 per cent of the containers on a ship were searched. Interview with naval source participating in embargo operations, 12 March 1993.

26 James E. Goodby, 'Peacekeeping in the New Europe', *The Washington Quarterly*, vol. 15, no. 2, spring 1992, p. 159.

27 Forceful interdiction, wrongly labelled 'peacekeeping', was carried out by the Indian and Sri Lankan navies to cut off the Tamil Tigers from external support. 'Indian Navy Blockades "Tigers"', *Navint*, 16 August 1991, p. 7; 'India Targets LTTE Arms Shipments', *Tamil Times* (London), 15 February 1993, pp. 13–14. I am grateful to Alan Bullion for drawing attention to these reports.

28 René Van Beveren, 'Belgium and the Gulf Crisis, August 1990–March 1991', in Nicole Gnesotto and John Roper (eds), *Western Europe and the Gulf*, Institute for Security Studies of Western European Union, Paris, 1992, p. 10.

29 Interviews by Jeremy Ginifer with Professor Takehiko Kamo and Dr Takeo Uchida, Tokyo, 5–6 July 1993.

30 'UN Kills Seven Repelling Attack in Mogadishu', *The Guardian*, 12 August 1993, p. 9.
31 Peter Jones, 'Preventing Conflict at Sea', paper at Colloquium on Maritime Security and Conflict Resolution, Centre for Foreign Policy Studies, Dalhousie University, Halifax, NS, 24–27 June 1993.
32 Joris Janssen Lok, 'NATO Arms against Serbian Submarines', *Jane's Defence Weekly*, 14 August 1993, p. 8.
33 Neves, *United Nations Peace-Keeping Operations in the Gulf of Fonseca*, p. 19.
34 Peter Haydon, 'Naval Peacekeeping?', *Strategic Datalink*, Canadian Institute of Strategic Studies, Toronto, December 1992.
35 Lok, 'NATO Arms against Serbian Submarines'.
36 I am grateful to Ambassador Sir John Halstead, Norman Patterson School of International Affairs, Ottawa, for his suggestions in this regard.
37 The WEU and the United States provided Romania with naval radio-telephones, patrol boats, computers and oil pollution control equipment, and sent 250–300 customs and police officers upstream and downstream of the Serbian border. Assembly of Western European Union, Defence Committee, 'WEU initiatives on the Danube and in the Adriatic – reply to the thirty-eighth annual report of the Council', report by Mr Marten and Sir Keith Speed, doc. 1367, 15 June 1993, pp. 12–20.
38 In 1993, peacekeeping contingents in Cambodia and the former Yugoslavia were accused of corruption. Unannounced attacks by UN military personnel on General Aideed's supporters in Somalia were also criticised from legal, moral and human rights perspectives in a report to the UN by a US State Department legal expert. Mark Husband, 'UN Somali Action Comes Under Fire', *The Guardian*, 5 August 1993, p. 20.

4 *Jeremy Ginifer*

A conceptual framework for UN naval operations

An adequate conceptual basis has yet to be established for United Nations maritime peace and security initiatives. There is a need for a rigorous conceptual framework appropriate to the changing context of the post-Cold War world. As shown in the previous chapter, on the occasions that the UN has undertaken action at sea in the past, the operational concepts have been derived from established territorial applications, such as peacekeeping. This approach is open to criticism on three grounds. First, territorial and maritime environments and forces are distinct and, hence, give rise to differing peace and security conceptions. Second, the emergence of new concepts of 'second generation' operations, discussed in Chapter 2 above, are particularly applicable to the maritime context. Third, new naval peace and security concepts can be identified, relating primarily to the diplomatic and deterrent functions of naval forces.

It was argued earlier that the new post-Cold War prominence accorded to the UN has created the basis for a more forceful approach to the preservation of international peace and security. In particular, norms regarding the sanctity of sovereignty, the issue of consent, and the utilisation of force have been challenged. Moves within the UN towards a more 'interventionist' approach suggest an increased role for naval forces, since they have the capacity to circumvent issues of sovereignty and consent as well as to project force. However, unless a coherent naval conceptual framework is articulated, the UN will not be in a position to effectively manage naval peace and security issues. Indeed, the effectiveness of collective security actions in part resides in the principal actors concerned comprehending the parameters that will delineate any operation.

In order to establish a coherent framework for the consideration of future UN naval or maritime operations this chapter first explains why little attention has been paid to the naval dimension within the UN. Second, it draws attention to the physical and jurisdictional differences between the territorial and maritime environments and how this impinges on international peace and security initiatives. Finally, it outlines the basis of traditional UN territorial peace and security conceptions and examines the extent to which they can be adapted for the maritime context.

Maritime and territorial contexts

Since its inception in 1945, the UN has focused almost exclusively on territorial challenges to international peace and security. The reasons for this are self-evident. Most armed conflicts, and other manifestations of international disorder, originate on land and are best addressed through territorial means. Although there are a large number of unresolved disputes centring around maritime delimitation, few attempts have been made to resolve them through the use of military force. Nor have there been many conflicts whose root cause has had a maritime dimension. More usually, maritime conflict has been an extension of territorial issues.

Furthermore, an underlying premise of the state system, within which the UN functions, is the possession of and jurisdiction over territory. A consequence of this territory-centric view of security, has been the evolution of a reasonably coherent framework for resolving territorial conflicts and disputes involving mechanisms, such as peacekeeping and mediation. In contrast, there have been few attempts to vigorously conceptualise the maritime security functions that the UN might perform. There is an empirical as well as a theoretical void in this respect. As discussed in the previous chapter, the UN has authorised only a limited number of peacekeeping operations involving the deployment of patrol boats, and a limited number of embargo and enforcement operations.

It is apparent that the physical nature of the maritime medium, the differing jurisdictional context and the nature of naval weapon systems make the formulation of parallel territorial and maritime frameworks problematic. The maritime environment has two distinctive attributes which differ from those of territory. First, parts of it are 'non-territorial' or 'neutral'. Second, the physical constitution of the sea permits the free movement of vessels.

Territorial peacekeeping operations, and to a lesser extent enforcement actions, have been traditionally constrained by the issues of sovereignty.[1] States have invariably attempted to resist incursions into their territory and the UN Charter generally supports the state's domestic jurisdiction. Chapter I, Article 2(7) states that: 'Nothing contained in the present Charter shall authorize the United Nations to intervene in matters which are essentially within the domestic jurisdiction of any state.' However, it further states that 'this principle shall not prejudice the application of enforcement measures under Chapter VII'. Only twice since 1945 (in Korea and Iraq) has the norm of sovereignty been substantively contravened in pursuance of UN-sanctioned enforcement actions. This reluctance to transgress state sovereignty has meant that peacekeeping operations, for example, have generally been conducted with the consent of the host state. Nevertheless, measures such as the establishment of the Kurdish 'safe haven' in Northern Iraq and the US and UN operations in Somalia have transgressed established notions of sovereignty.

Territorial constraints do not necessarily apply to the conduct of naval operations. Although there are apprehensions among developed, maritime states that some of the provisions of the 1982 UN Law of the Sea Convention encourage increased jurisdiction outside territorial waters and that population growth and competition for resources will lead to a new sense of territoriality, the high seas remain an area where ships, whatever their flag, can habitually operate freely in times of peace. Even within territorial waters, notions of sovereignty are less strenuously guarded than those on land. Whereas the movement of foreign troops into sovereign territory would be generally viewed as a *casus belli*, the same cannot be said of a naval deployment into territorial waters which could in any case be permitted, under *jus gentium* regarding the right of innocent passage. Thus, the basis of maritime jurisdiction – and the political perceptions it engenders – is fundamentally different from that of territory. As Martin Glassner notes, whereas virtually all the land areas of the earth are under the undifferentiated sovereignty of states, 'there are a number of zones in the sea, horizontal, vertical and functional, over which States exercise varying degrees of sovereignty or jurisdiction'.[2]

The physical nature of the maritime environment has dictated that military systems have evolved with differing characteristics to those utilised on land. Ocean-going 'blue water' vessels need to be structurally substantial to operate in adverse maritime conditions. The need to operate over considerable distances has led to the development of vessels with a high degree of self-sufficiency in logistics and communications. Even 'brown water' (i.e. coastal) vessels are substantially different in terms of size and operational characteristics from most military systems deployed on territory. The deployment of a warship, even in a potentially benign role such as peacekeeping, sends a different signal to that of a contingent of lightly armed troops by virtue of the force it can project and because of historical resonances associated with warships.[3] Thus states, particularly in the developing world, are highly sensitive to the prospect of being victims of naval diplomatic power.

As a function of the environment in which they operate, warships have developed a unique set of characteristics, described by Booth as:

> *versatility*, their ability to perform a variety of tasks; *controllability*, their escalatory and de-escalatory potential; *mobility*, their ability to move between regions with relative ease and relative independence; *projection ability*, their efficiency as bulk carriers of manpower and firepower; *access potential*, their ability to reach distant locations; *symbolism*, arising from the fact that warships are chunks of national sovereignty; and, finally, *endurance*, the staying power of warships which enables them to be adjacent to a problem but removable.[4]

These characteristics suggest that the opportunities and restraints surrounding UN naval operations will differ from their territorial counterparts. Furthermore, navies have developed distinctive strategies. The notions of 'sea control' and 'sea denial', for example, are alien to territorial strategy and the control of an area of 'neutrality' such as the high seas has no parallel in a territorial context. The diplomatic uses of naval forces – such as 'showing the flag' and 'gunboat diplomacy' – are policy instruments that have no direct parallel in a territorial context. The subtlety and flexibility of signalling that can be achieved by naval forces are not generally available to territorial forces.

The fact, then, that naval and territorial strategies differ in fundamental respects is significant. It suggests that within the framework of UN collective security operations there will be comparable conceptual divergences.

The UN and international peace and security

The framework within which UN territorial peace and security operations have been conducted can be conceptualised as follows.

First, the Charter allows for various actions under Chapter VII, including the use of force should 'peaceful means' fail to avert a dispute that might endanger international peace and security. Under Chapter VII, Article 41, the Security Council is empowered to enact economic sanctions and related measures, followed by action by 'air, sea, or land', including 'demonstrations, blockades and other operations', should the former prove inadequate.

Second, there are collective forms of peace support action not specifically mentioned in the Charter, notably the use of peacekeeping forces to create conditions conducive to international peace.

Third, as argued in Chapter 2 above, since the end of the Cold War the extension or modification of traditional peacekeeping has been proposed to include such concepts as preventive peacekeeping and deployment,[5] and second generation operations with an extended remit to use force. Peacemaking and peacebuilding – both pacific measures – although long established in a conceptual sense, have also been revitalised as viable mechanisms to promote international peace and security.

In evaluating the extent to which these territorial concepts are relevant to the maritime context, it will become apparent that second generation concepts have particular applicability to naval operations. Furthermore, the case will be made that the concept of preventive diplomacy, elucidated by the UN Secretary-General in 'An Agenda for Peace', with reference to territorial forces, can be expanded to accommodate traditional notions of naval diplomacy.

Traditional peacekeeping
As discussed in Chapter 2 above, a particular set of characteristics is associated with traditional peacekeepers. To recapitulate, they are customarily constituted from national armies or police and civilian agencies; they are lightly armed and are mandated to use force in

self-defence or in furtherance of their mission; they are expected to act impartially and are usually deployed with the consent of the parties to a dispute. Although UN peacekeeping missions have adopted roles such as election monitoring, arms collection and the provision of medical aid, the classic peacekeeping functions have been observation and interpositioning between hostile parties.

The adoption of these concepts by a naval peacekeeping force raises a set of problematic issues. The first relates to the technical characteristics of warships, particularly of the ocean-going 'blue water' variety. They tend to be heavily armed in order to survive in the high-technology threat environment posed by modern weapon systems, such as surface-to-surface missiles. Although this armament may be perceived as defensive in character, it will not necessarily be regarded as such, particularly if warships carry accurate, destructive, stand-off, weapon systems such as Sea Launched Cruise Missiles (SLCMs), which were demonstrated to be highly effective in the Persian Gulf War. The use of 'brown water' vessels (usually confined to territorial waters and exclusive economic zones) may be more reassuring in terms of threat perception, but these still have the capacity to launch potent weapon systems, such as surface-to-surface missiles.

Even the riverine and coastal peacekeeping operations undertaken by UNTAC in Cambodia cannot be said to be consistent with the interpositioning model of peacekeeping. UNTAC utilised sea and river patrol boats, landing craft and special light boats to patrol and help detect the illegal movement of arms into Cambodia in compliance with the agreement on a comprehensive political settlement signed in Paris on 23 October 1991.[6] In addition to carrying a number of observers, the craft had a complement of armed marines who had the capacity to board and search ships suspected of carrying arms. In this sense they can be said to have adopted an interdiction/deterrent posture, rather than the traditional peacekeeping remit.

Naval forces are able to operate to a considerable degree without the consent of parties to a dispute by simply not entering territorial waters, or in the case of submarines doing so illicitly without being detected. In a peacekeeping context, this presents the temptation of operating without explicit consent – perhaps conducting missions outside territorial waters when an operation becomes problematic. However, a potential difficulty resides in the realm of political signalling. Even observational patrols by sea or air can take on threatening, or at least challenging, postures in the eyes of parties suspicious of peacekeeping operations. There is a danger that a peacekeeping deployment will be seen as some form of deterrent force, or the prelude to future enforcement actions, should a party withhold its consent for peacekeeping operations. Furthermore, naval peacekeeping units are vulnerable to long-distance attacks – aircraft-delivered, surface-to-surface missiles, for example – by well-armed parties keen to derail peacekeeping efforts.

One of the few postulated naval functions which conforms to traditional norms of peacekeeping is that of interpositioning between hostile warships. This is a hypothetical function as the UN has never undertaken such a role.[7] The interpositioning of, say, lightly armed minesweepers between two hostile 'blue water' navies would be an extremely risky undertaking given the potency and range of modern weapon systems. The chances of accidental attacks on peacekeeping ships would be high given that many engagements would take place beyond visual contact. Furthermore, the nuances of traditional territorial peacekeeping, frequently involving visual and verbal contact between individual soldiers, would be difficult to achieve. Interpositioning may be more practical where disputing states deployed smaller, coastal vessels, but interstate conflicts or disputes are more likely to lead to the mobilisation of substantial naval assets. All this suggests that traditional peacekeeping will be problematic in the maritime context.

Second generation operations
Whilst naval forces, operating according to the parameters of traditional peacekeeping, are relatively constrained in their scope, naval forces have characteristics conceptually more compatible with the interventionist nature of second generation operations. It has already been argued, in Chapter 2 above, that the new vigour of the UN, following the ending of the Cold War and calls for increased interventionism and use of force on humanitarian grounds, has created a basis for new forms of peacekeeping. Second generation peace support operations are sometimes described as falling conceptually somewhere on a continuum between conventional peacekeeping ('Chapter VI and a half') and Chapter VII enforcement actions.[8] The differences between the basis of second generation operations and ideal or traditional peacekeeping can be summarised.

The consent of the parties to a dispute is not necessarily required, although obviously some form of consent is to be preferred, and the mandate to use force will be extended. Already, the commander of a peacekeeping contingent may be entitled to use force in furtherance of his prescribed mission, as well as in self-defence.[9] Second generation operations offer the prospect of increased use of remits which merge the two justifications. Furthermore, and this is psychologically important, substantial military assets are likely to be utilised in second generation operations. In order to ensure the security of forces involved in these operations and to attain military objectives, forward presence and larger zones of operations will become necessary. Last, it will not generally be possible to maintain that these types of operation are impartial. The 'enforcement of humanitarian aid', for example, is by definition a partial activity. Relief delivered by air to civilians in blockaded areas is sometimes perceived as an impartial activity in that it is non-military in character, and is designed to alleviate the suffering of non-combatants. However, warring parties tend to regard any activities that undermine the effectiveness of military measures, including those directed against or impinging upon civilians, as contrary to their interests, and, hence, partial.

If issues of impartiality, consent, and use of force are accorded less prominence in second generation operations, the utility of a naval contingent becomes apparent. Naval vessels are capable of undertaking roles in support, or independent, of territorial operations, such as: air support for humanitarian missions; the delivery of humanitarian aid; evacuations; the landing of ground troops; and the creation of 'safe havens'. In regard to the first, the potentially discriminate nature of some of the advanced weapon systems possessed by naval air forces is an important asset for the enforcement of humanitarian aid. They can fulfil observational and ultimately, if sanctioned, retaliatory capabilities should humanitarian operations come under attack, although in the case of retaliation, questions of proportionality would have to be carefully considered.

The use of naval vessels to deliver humanitarian aid by sea to blockaded ports in the Adriatic was one of the options considered by the Western European Union (WEU) in 1991 (see Chapter 3 above). Similar naval actions initiated by the UN might lessen the potential costs, both politically and militarily, of comparable missions conducted on land. As has been shown by the UN-authorised,

WEU and NATO embargo operations in the Adriatic, it is possible to conduct rigorous operations with a lower degree of resistance than would be encountered on land.[10]

The creation of a 'safe haven' for civilians and persecuted individuals – with or without the consent of warring parties – and protected by military contingents prepared to use force in order to maintain it, is a concept difficult to put into effect in the face of resistance from territorial forces.[11] Less problematic would be the establishment of 'safe havens' on the coastline of littoral states given the potential access for warships and their ability to provide defensive cover for such operations. Conditions permitting, these 'safe havens' might be gradually extended inland through joint sea–air operations.

Preventive peacekeeping and diplomacy

The deployment of territorial preventive forces to forestall the outbreak of armed conflict has been postulated over a number of years,[12] but the concept gained fresh impetus following its advocacy by Boutros Boutros-Ghali in June 1992 and the actual deployment of UN forces in Macedonia.[13] The presence of a preventive peacekeeping force along a threatened border or stretch of territory, even if lightly armed, would signal the Security Council's concern. It would carry with it the implicit 'threat' of further more drastic action, should an attack, or other forms of aggression, be mounted.

Whether a form of preventive naval deployment could fulfil a parallel function is doubtful. Such a force might bypass many of the difficulties associated with a territorial force, such as lack of consent but, unless the crisis was primarily maritime in nature, the only effective preventive function it could adopt other than a benign humanitarian role in response to a territorial crisis, would be one of deterrence. However, a distinction needs to be drawn between a preventive peacekeeping and a deterrent force. The former relies on its moral and political, rather than military, authority for effect. The effectiveness of a deterrent force resides in its military capability and perceptions regarding its use.

Other forms of preventive action, such as early warning, confidence-building and the creation of demilitarised zones have also been postulated by the UN for land forces.[14] If applied to naval forces, forward deployment to gather information through surveillance and other techniques might be regarded as a useful approach, not only in responding to traditional military threats to international peace and security, but also with respect to population migrations and environmental damage through accidents and natural disasters. It would also be possible to adopt confidence- and security-building measures (CSBMs), such as verification of constraints in regional troublespots, where some form of arms limitation or reduction was being attempted. Naval vessels, flagged or manned by an impartial agency such as the UN, might be able to provide factual information regarding compliance that would be accepted by various parties as authentic, and would have more credibility than national means of information collection. In this sense they would be fulfilling a confidence-building function. The concept of a maritime demilitarised zone established in advance of a conflict, rather than following it, as has been the norm, is another CSBM that might be advanced.[15]

Naval diplomacy

Although naval diplomacy has in the past been a unilateral instrument utilised by states to further national rather than collective interests, a case can be made for a modified form of naval diplomacy fulfilling useful functions for the UN. The political role of navies in low-intensity situations includes gunboat diplomacy and showing the flag. Navies are particularly adept at such roles. Thus to establish or cement good relations with another state, ships can be sent on goodwill port visits. However, as James Cable argues, this ceremonial and symbolic function can involve adversarial displays, whereby warships are sent merely to demonstrate concern in a location where they are not really welcome.[16] The adversarial display verges on gunboat diplomacy, a form of coercive clout associated with imperialism and usually undertaken by the strong against the weak to extract political gains. Although firepower may be used and the gunboat itself attacked, the role is at the low-intensity end of the conflict spectrum and used in situations which do not warrant the costs of full-scale war.[17]

The use by the UN of gunboat diplomacy to further international peace and security would sit uncomfortably within the traditional framework of UN operations. First, the actual use, as opposed to a threat to use, limited force in the context of gunboat diplomacy would be regarded within the UN as a military, rather than a diplomatic action. Second, the term has historical resonances that the UN would wish to avoid. However, the more benign types of gunboat diplomacy, as identified by Cable, such as 'expressive' force, where warships are employed to emphasise attitudes, to lend verisimilitude to otherwise unconvincing statements, are worthy of development, along with a 'showing of the UN flag' role.[18]

A conceptual framework for UN naval diplomacy might be postulated in the following terms with each category representing an increase in the intensity of the diplomatic signal being projected:

- a 'showing of the UN flag' to indicate concern over a potential security crisis, using few and relatively lightly armed warships;
- a more forceful (increased force disposition) 'showing of the UN flag' to express solidarity with a threatened state or states;
- the deployment of a substantial UN naval force, engaging in military manoeuvres and other forms of action that indicate a readiness to use force (a function similar to certain categories of gunboat diplomacy identified by Cable).

These deployments would be conducted in concert with active diplomacy and timed to reinforce political messages. The dispatch of a naval force following an ultimatum, for example, would send a distinct political message of intent. However, as the intensity of diplomatic deployments increases, it becomes increasingly difficult to differentiate between a deterrent and a diplomatic function.

In comparing the diplomatic uses of naval and territorial forces, the latter are constrained by the immediacy, range and strength of the political signals capable of being generated. Characteristically, troop mobilisations achieve diplomatic effects where they are physically capable of occupying territory. The diplomatic signalling that can be achieved through the mobilisation of weapon systems such as ballistic missiles or aircraft, may circumvent these difficulties because they can project force over considerable distances. However, there is a danger that these may be perceived as coercive or deterrent gestures, rather than the exercise of diplomacy. Not only is the strength and clarity of territorial diplomacy in this context questionable, but its range is also limited. By contrast, the fact that warships can approach the coastline of littoral states imbues naval diplomatic gestures with immediacy and strength. The type of warship or warships deployed also conveys a range of signals. The sending of a battle-carrier group to a crisis area is a distinct action from deploying a frigate, for example. The manner in which ships exercise also sends a signal which can be varied by alter-ing the composition of the force to achieve escalatory or de-escala-tory effects.

Peacebuilding
The concept of peacebuilding encompasses political and material measures adopted before, during or following the cessation of a con-flict, to create stable conditions that will preclude further outbreaks of violence and stimulate peace. Such measures might include: dis-arming warring parties and the restoration of order, the safe custody and destruction of weapons, repatriating refugees, the training of security forces, election monitoring, human rights promotion, and the reform and strengthening of government institutions. There has been an increasing tendency for peacekeeping missions to include peacebuilding functions.

Many of these functions are civil and territorial and, as such, do not have a direct naval input. Indirectly, however, naval forces have important support functions, such as the transportation and provi-sion of materials and personnel required to undertake basic peace-building. Where permission is difficult to obtain for the overflight or overland transportation of supplies in a crisis, due to the politi-cal animosity of adjoining states, a sea route is frequently the only feasible means of transportation. Consent may be more readily granted to naval forces because they impose less drastically than ter-ritorial forces on a host nation's culture and sovereignty.[19] The bil-leting of marines and other military personnel on vessels off shore provides greater reassurance than troops accommodated on land. The multinational provision of disaster relief to Bangladesh, fol-lowing a cyclone in April 1991 which killed more than 139,000 inhabitants, suggests the constructive aspects of this type of peace-building. The scale of the disaster was beyond the means of the indigenous government to tackle and, some have suggested, repre-sented a threat to the continuance of democratic government which had only been instituted 39 days earlier.[20] A coalition of US, Pakistani, British, French and Chinese forces delivered medical aid, food and shelter, predominantly by sea, and helped create some of the conditions for recovery.

Naval–maritime organisations could be an integral part of the international provision of 'unopposed' disaster relief and other forms of humanitarian aid, and this is analysed in Chapter 5 below in the context of the constabulary, non-military functions of maritime forces.

Deterrence

Chapter VII of the UN Charter does not make specific reference to the use of deterrence postures to maintain or restore international peace and security. However, there is little doubt that the military forces originally proposed under Article 47 of the Charter were intended to exert a deterrent effect as well as to create the capacity for actual enforcement.[21] Inherent in the concept of a global 'police force' is the notion of deterring breaches of the peace through fear of punishment.

But difficulties occur with deterrence exerted through territorial means. To appear credible, ground troops generally need to be deployed near to the state being deterred. This is rarely possible given that few states other than those fearing invasion will allow the basing of foreign troops on their territory. Nor are states generally willing to contribute troops for multinational deterrent purposes – due to concerns about lengthy deployments, cost and more compelling military requirements. Unless a sympathetic host can be identified in the vicinity of the state being deterred, the territorial basing of aircraft for deterrence purposes will also be problematic.

However, the deployment of naval vessels in a deterrence mode is a more practical, as well as a less politically sensitive, issue. Naval vessels have legitimate rights of passage and deployment in international waters. They can generally be withdrawn from or redeployed in an area without attracting extreme political opprobrium. Whether a naval force is exerting a deterrent effect or merely engaging in manoeuvres is to a great extent a matter of perception. Indeed, 'ambiguity' can be useful in bolstering the credibility of deterrence. But the size, composition and posturing of a naval force can be varied to convey political messages to states judged to be a threat to international peace and security.

The attractiveness of a credible deterrent posture may lie in the fact that it might represent a less costly and less controversial measure than enforcement actions whilst achieving a similar effect. The deployment of a UN deterrent force could be useful as an escalatory device should preventive measures be challenged and diplomatic postures proved ineffective. If a preventive land-based peacekeeping force came under attack, for example, the deployment of a naval deterrent force, with the ability to launch selective, discriminate attacks in its defence, might modify the behaviour of an aggressor. However, it should be borne in mind that doubts regarding credibility and intent have frequently hampered attempts to project conventional deterrence.[22] Furthermore, it is difficult to exert deterrent effects on actors below the state level, such as irregular forces, though many of the future challenges facing the UN are likely to have a sub-state component.

Embargoes
Article 41 of the UN Charter authorises the Security Council to call upon UN members to apply 'complete or partial interruption of economic relations' in furtherance of international peace and security, while Article 42 allows for 'demonstrations, blockade, and other operations by air, sea, or land forces'. However, a naval blockade is an attempt to completely deny access and egress of all seaborne trade to an area, and for legal reasons is unlikely to be used as an instrument by the UN. Under the non-ratified rules of the 1909 London Convention, for example, blockades could only be established by states openly engaged in hostilities. In any event, close naval blockades are increasingly difficult to apply and are demanding in resources, partly as a consequence of technological developments in mines, aircraft and coastal missile batteries which increase the danger to blockading ships. Also, because the territorial seas of neutrals cannot generally be contravened in blockades, and because some states are seeking to expand their jurisdiction, there is likely to be future constraints on this type of activity.[23]

More discriminating, are embargoes which are designed to interfere with commerce by forbidding certain categories of goods from entering and leaving ports. Sanctions may be aimed to restrict a state's capacity to act aggressively, as a deterrent and serve as a warning to others, to coerce states to accept political processes, or to punish through a form of reprisal.[24] However, debate has centred on the effectiveness of economic sanctions, particularly those applied to Iraq and Serbia–Montenegro involving naval forces.[25] Success is difficult to measure, the goals are difficult to define and the effects are likely to be variable.[26]

However, it is likely that in future UN collective security actions involving littoral states, naval embargoes will be increasingly used to attempt to ensure compliance with Security Council directives as a policy instrument short of military intervention. The 'policing' of an embargo at sea is generally a more achievable end than equivalent territorial operations. Warships can interdict on the high seas, or even in territorial waters if they possess a legitimate mandate, such as that provided in April 1993 by the Security Council to WEU and NATO ships for action in Serbian–Montenegrin territorial waters.[27] Circumvention of an embargo is also more difficult in a maritime environment where surveillance by satellite, by fixed-wing aircraft or helicopters, or by vessels conducting searches is more straightforward. Naval vessels can operate on-station for long periods and have the capacity to defend themselves should an embargo be resisted.

Furthermore, a naval embargo force fulfils a number of functions other than that of physical interdiction. First, it is symbolic of the international community's displeasure; second, it can exert a diplomatic function; third, it puts in place the structure for an enforcement action, should one be mandated. Interdiction is frequently authorised in an embargo: however its use has tended to be carefully circumscribed because, as argued in the previous chapter, it involves crossing a significant force threshold. This may make the embargo an attractive instrument for UN members concerned about the implications of full-scale enforcement actions.

Enforcement
If the measures referred to in Article 41 prove inadequate the Security Council has the option of taking under Article 42 'such action by air, sea, or land' that 'may be necessary to maintain or restore international peace and security', including enforcement actions. They differ conceptually from most other forms of UN collective action in that they are undertaken without the consent of all parties to a dispute, are not impartial, and involve fewer limitations on the use of force. Only two significant enforcement actions have been authorised by the UN since 1945 – the Korean and the Persian Gulf actions. The political and military conditions for further large-scale enforcement actions may not recur in the immediate future. More likely are situations inviting limited forms of enforcement. Discriminate air strikes had been postulated, for example, against Serbian heavy artillery and mortar positions if UN humanitarian missions were attacked in Bosnia–Herzegovina.[28] These had, in fact,

materialised by April 1994. Such instruments may also be used in future operations where conditions are different.

Within the remit of enforcement actions naval forces are capable of independent force projection, ranging from tactical shore bombardment to strategic strikes against land assets. During the Persian Gulf War, SLCMs and other forms of precision-guided munitions delivered by carrier-borne aircraft and naval vessels inflicted significant damage to the infrastructure of Iraq. Given the ability of navies to traverse the high seas and territorial waters and to launch strikes from diverse locations using the longer range of modern weapon systems, navies are no longer confined to targeting coastal states. It is conceivable that naval forces are capable of independently projecting sufficient force to compel miscreant states in certain circumstances to abide by Security Council directives, while still preserving a degree of proportionality consistent with the need to retain general support within the UN.

Conclusion

Naval forces are being employed in a changed international context. The character of the international system has altered with the collapse of bipolarity; the UN is undergoing structural change; and the conceptual basis of UN peace and security operations is being reviewed. Some of the instruments, and the political will, for enforcing the collective policy of the international community within certain, prescribed limits now appear to exist. Within this framework, naval forces will assume a new prominence. The utility of naval forces lies in a number of factors. First, their particular relationship to issues of sovereignty allows for their participation in second generation operations. Second, the discriminate manner in which they can project force opens up a number of possibilities on both land and sea. Third, they have the asset of controllability. Naval forces can play a central role in the scale of collective security actions which have been emphasised within the UN short of full-scale belligerency, such as embargoes and the selective use of low-intensity force. Fourth, naval forces have the capacity to assist in peacebuilding and the alleviation of hardship. Finally, naval forces can fulfil a set of conceptually distinct functions relating to preventive measures, diplomacy and deterrence.

Given all this, there is a strong argument for the adoption of a distinctive conceptual framework by the UN that diverges from derivative territorial notions of security. In the absence of such a framework the UN will not be in a position to act decisively when the use of naval forces is appropriate to secure international peace and security. A distinctive set of maritime parameters or guidelines, as outlined here, is essential so that participants may conduct effective maritime peace and security operations to enhance international stability. Maritime forces may also be required to engage in non-military security activities in support of civilian agencies. These special constabulary functions are the subject of the next chapter.

Notes

1 Enforcement actions, for example, are constrained to the extent that the sovereignty of states, other than those subject to enforcement actions, has to be considered. UN-sanctioned forces in the Persian Gulf War required the permission of Saudi Arabia before they could operate from Saudi territory.

2 Martin Ira Glassner, *Neptune's Domain: A Political Geography of the Sea*, Unwin Hyman, London, 1990, p. 18.

3 For 'showing the flag' and 'gunboat diplomacy' by colonial naval powers, see James Cable, *Navies in Violent Peace*, Macmillan, London, 1989, Chs 4 and 6.

4 Ken Booth, *Law, Force, and Diplomacy at Sea*, Allen & Unwin, London, 1985, p. 187. See also, Booth, *Navies and Foreign Policy*, Croom Helm, London, 1977, pp. 33–6.

5 See, Indar Jit Rikhye, 'Strengthening UN Peacekeeping: New Challenges and Proposals', United States Institute of Peace, Washington DC, May 1992, pp. 21–2; Parliamentarians For Global Action, *From National To UN-Based Security: A Report on Strengthening Collective Security – The Role of Parliamentarians, Mechanisms, and Financing*, New York, May 1992, pp. 8–10; Boutros-Ghali, 'An Agenda for Peace: Preventive Diplomacy, Peacemaking and Peace-keeping. Report of the Secretary-General pursuant to the statement adopted by the Summit Meeting of the Security Council on 31 January 1992', UN doc. A/47/277; S/24111, 17 June 1992, pp. 8–9; Brian Urquhart, 'After the Cold War: Learning from the Gulf', in Urquhart and Robert S. McNamara, *Toward Collective Security: Two Views*, Occasional Paper No. 5, Thomas J. Watson Jr. Institute for International Studies, Providence, RI, 1991, p. 18.

6 See, 'Report of the Secretary-General on Cambodia', UN doc., S/23613, 19 February 1992, pp. 15–19, 23.

7 During the 1936–39 Spanish Civil War, the Royal Navy adopted an interpositioning role off the Biscayan coast between British merchant ships and Franco's warships attempting to prevent the delivery of supplies to the Republican port of Bilbao. Although they adopted threatening postures designed to intimidate the merchant ships, the Nationalists did not directly challenge the interpositioning role of the RN. However, the operation cannot be categorised as a traditional peacekeeping operation. See Chapter 3 above.

8 Extending the analogy, these might be termed 'Chapter VI and three-quarter operations'.

9 F. R. Henn notes that: 'the guidance issued by the Secretary-General . . . governing the use of self-defence is not so constraining as may appear at first sight. Much depends on the will and discretion of the UN Commander concerned'. Referring to the initial deployment of the Second United Nations Emergency Force (UNEF II) in 1973, for example, he comments that had the peacekeeping force been 'prevented by forceful means from carrying out their task, they would have been entitled under the UN rules to have resorted to the use of force', F. R. Henn, 'Guidelines For Peacekeeping – Another View', *British Army Review*, no. 67, April 1981, pp. 33–4. See also, Michael Harbottle (letter), *The Independent*, 11 August, 1992, p. 14, and note 31, Chapter 2 above, for occasions when UN commanders have threatened a higher level of force than normally associated with peacekeeping operations.

10 Serbian forces have adopted challenging postures in response to embargo operations in the Adriatic. WEU vessels, for example, have been tracked by land-based radars; Serbian frigates have approached to within 2–3 miles and pointed weapon systems at WEU ships; and approaching Serbian fighter-bombers have opened bomb doors. However, they have not taken direct military action against vessels enforcing the embargo. Interview with naval source participating in embargo operations, 12 March 1993.

11 The two relief operations conducted in Northern Iraq, *Provide Comfort* and *Safe Haven*, following SC Resolution 688, may set a precedent for such actions.

12 See, for example, International Peace Academy, *Peacekeeper's Handbook*, Pergamon, New York, 1984.

13 Boutros-Ghali, 'An Agenda for Peace', pp. 8–9. For details of UN Macedonian preventive deployments, see Bob Furlong, 'Powder Keg of the Balkans: The UN Opts for Prevention in Macedonia', *International Defense Review*, vol. 26, May 1993, pp. 364–8.

14 Boutros-Ghali, 'An Agenda for Peace', pp. 7–10.

15 On the monitoring of military restrictions in environmental zones, see Arthur Westing, 'Environmental Dimension of Maritime Security', in Jozef Goldblat (ed.), *Maritime Security: The Building of Confidence*, UNIDIR, Geneva, 1992, pp. 91–102.

16 James Cable, *Navies in Violent Peace*, pp. 71–2.

17 See Cable, *ibid.*, for an extensive discussion of these issues.

18 Cable, *Gunboat Diplomacy: Political Applications of Limited Naval Force,* Chatto & Windus/IISS, London, 1971, p. 81.

19 H. C. Stackpole, 'Angels from the Sea', *Proceedings*, US Naval Institute, May 1992, p. 116.

20 *Ibid.*, pp. 110–16.

21 See Chapter 7 below, and Eric Grove, 'UN Armed Forces and the MSC: A Look Back', *International Security*, vol. 17, no. 4, spring 1993, pp. 172–82.

22 It is assumed that a UN deterrence policy would not encompass Nuclear, Biological and Chemical (NBC) capabilities.

23 Capt. Robert H. Thomas, 'The Use of Naval Forces in Imposing and Enforcing Sanctions, Embargoes and Blockades', paper at Colloquium on Maritime Security and Conflict Resolution, Centre for Foreign Policy Studies, Dalhousie University, Halifax, NS, 24–27 June 1993.

24 David Leyton-Brown, 'Lessons and Policy Considerations about Economic Sanctions', in Leyton-Brown (ed.), *The Utility of International Economic Sanctions*, Croom Helm, London, 1987, pp. 303–10.

25 A 1992 classified intelligence report argues that Saddam Hussein's position in Iraq had strengthened despite economic sanctions, *The New York Times International*, 16 June 1992, p. A3. The effectiveness of the UN embargo imposed on Serbia–Montenegro has been frequently questioned. See, for example, Jens Schneider, 'A River through the Sanctions', *The Guardian*, 9 February 1993, p. 11.

26 Thomas, 'The Use of Naval Forces in Imposing and Enforcing Sanctions, Embargoes and Blockades'.

27 On 17 April 1993, UN Security Council Res. 820, para. 29, authorised states enforcing the embargo to use all necessary measures including in the territorial sea of Serbia–Montenegro.

28 *The Times*, 1 July 1992, p. 1; *Daily Telegraph*, 1 July 1992, p. 1.

Maritime constabulary roles for non-military security

In the evolving international system, wide definitions of the possible scope and content of 'peace and security' have gained favour,
and attention has been directed to non-military security goals. In a
speech on peacekeeping tasks, the former Soviet official, Vladimir
Petrovsky, suggested that UN operations should be mounted 'for . . .
[tackling] qualitatively new situations, including nuclear piracy, for
suppressing illegal drug-trafficking and eradication of international
terrorism.'[1] Of the several maritime constabulary tasks which might
be undertaken multinationally, this chapter focuses on four which
illustrate the possibilities and limitations of using maritime forces:
drug interdiction, piracy suppression, disaster relief and pollution
control (or 'maritime housekeeping').

The constabulary concept

International constabulary operations require national navies to
act multinationally, outside their immediate national defence roles,
in situations which would not normally trigger action by the UN
Security Council, and in close co-operation with civilian agencies.
The levels of linkage will range from national agencies to regional
bodies, inter-governmental and non-governmental organisations
and UN bodies such as the International Maritime Organisation
(IMO) and the Department of Humanitarian Affairs (DHA). The
concept might be considered analogous to the British notions of
'military aid to the civil power' or the 'civil ministries' – supporting civilian agencies when they are unable to cope with a crisis or
maintain order. For example, the Royal Navy has a long-standing

task of providing fisheries protection to support the Ministry of Agriculture and Fisheries. Indeed, naval units are commonly engaged in resource protection, regulatory work and law enforcement.[2] The work is sufficiently specialised for separate organisations to have been created by the United States, Canada, Argentina, Japan, Taiwan, Russia and India. But in other states, including Uruguay, Iceland, Ireland, Ghana, Tanzania and New Zealand, navies in peacetime are essentially maritime constabulary forces.[3]

It is tempting to refer to the potential international roles as 'maritime policing'. However, in the 1930s the term 'policing' was applied to schemes for the international use of military forces in inter-state and internal conflicts. It is also used for inter-state co-operation between police forces, whereas the variety of agencies potentially involved in maritime security – navies, coastguards, customs services, marine police forces/gendarmerie and police forces with offshore jurisdiction – are too diverse to be linked together by the term 'policing'. A preferable term is 'constabulary work'. The term was applied by Morris Janowitz to a military establishment which 'becomes a constabulary force when it is continuously prepared to act, committed to the minimum use of force, and seeks viable international relations rather than victory because it has incorporated a protective military posture.'[4]

The need for constabulary work in the maritime environment is reflected by the existence of national and international, institutional and legal frameworks covering such issues as piracy and terrorism on the high seas, the slave trade, drug-trafficking, marine pollution, resource protection and disaster relief. In Europe, for example, fisheries protection is covered by EC regulations and national legislation, such as the UK's Police and Criminal Evidence Act (1984), setting out the procedures to be followed to enforce the Common Fisheries Policy. However, this chapter argues that the identification of issues of common concern and the evolution of regulatory frameworks does not imply a consensus, either about the process of authorising action or about the means to be used. Thus, whilst states vulnerable to drug-trafficking might support an extension of UN operations to control the problem,[5] littoral states in areas seriously affected by armed robbery at sea support international assistance for regional measures rather than an international naval presence.

Drug interdiction

At the international level the problem of controlling the illicit drugs trade is fraught with political difficulties. Production of heroin, marijuana and cocaine is economically significant for some states in the developing world, whilst developed states offer lucrative markets. This produces tension between North and South about the nature of the problem and how to address it. Further, the profits from the drugs trade are so huge that control policies can easily be thwarted by bribery and intimidation.

The US experience
Since the Nixon presidency the United States has been a leading advocate of using military force within drug-producing states and deploying military capabilities to control the supply routes. The main effort in the Caribbean began in 1974 when a joint US Coast Guard (USCG) and Drug Enforcement Agency (DEA) operation revealed the extent of marijuana smuggling, mainly from Jamaica and Mexico into Florida, though Colombia also became a major trans-shipment point and drugs would be off-loaded from larger ships to pleasure craft near the US coast.[6]

The USCG is a unique maritime law enforcement agency in terms of its size and roles. It has authority over US-registered craft and powers to search and seize without warrant, though has to operate through the Departments of State and Justice to obtain flag state permission to board foreign vessels. Further permission is required if the vessel refuses to stop, and warning shots are needed – followed if necessary by disabling firing. USCG resources have been deployed to support a choke-point strategy backed by long-range surveillance by C–130 aircraft and customs patrolling of likely landing points. But Congress considered that the USCG had inadequate resources, and cleared the way for the military to support the anti-drug effort with information, equipment, facilities, training and advisory services. The 1982 Department of Defense (DoD) Authorisation Act expanded military co-operation by allowing Coast Guards to work from naval ships (which fly the Coast Guard flag before officers board suspect vessels). This enabled more offensive patrolling to occur off the source coasts.[7] The role was expanded in the Reagan period and, partly as a consequence of increased cocaine smuggling, Congress passed the 1986 Anti-Drug Abuse Act which facilitated

DoD involvement and enabled the USCG to undertake air interdiction.

President George Bush further exploited the USCG and military resources. Although reluctant to allow the armed forces to be diverted from their primary defence roles, Richard Cheney, Secretary of Defense, conceded that reducing the flow of drugs should be a defence task. In September 1988 Congress allowed statutory missions under the FY 1989 DoD Authorisation Act and the DoD became the Federal Government's lead agency for the detection and monitoring of aerial and maritime transit of illegal drugs into the United States and for integrating command, control and intelligence used in the 'war on drugs'.[8] The Bahamas and the UK also co-operated, the latter deploying its West Indies Guard Ship on US-directed drug interdiction. In fact a jurisdictional dispute erupted with Nicaragua when US Coast Guards on board the RN frigate, HMS *Cumberland*, attempted to board a fishing vessel in August 1993.[9]

Generally, however, the militarisation policy failed. To critics, the war on drugs was a case of the Pentagon finding a new security threat which helped, for example, to justify the invasion of Panama in December 1989. The policy was also seen as inconsistent and dangerous. The United States had facilitated cocaine smuggling through Contra supply channels and, and under Bush's 'Andean strategy', the US military had enormous freedom to intervene and support the often corrupt security forces in Peru, Bolivia and Colombia which were primarily interested in striking against opposition groups. In the view of critics, the Andean strategy was inherently flawed. Production reflected the dependency of poor economies on foreign markets, and the demand which fuelled the problem was a health and social issue, rather than a military one. It was a war which could not be won. The Congressional Office of Technology Assessment found little correlation between expenditure on interdiction and the availability of imported drugs on the US market; interdiction merely raised prices.[10]

The prospect of building a consensus for an international anti-drug policy may have been improved by President Bill Clinton's retreat from reliance on costly and ineffective military responses. Maritime interdiction will continue to play a role, but by 1993 there was greater emphasis in the United States on domestic social and legal measures. Indeed, maritime constabulary operations can be only one component of a complex and loosely organised international policy of reducing demand and controlling supply.

The European approach

In contrast to the high-profile role of the military in US drug interdiction policy, West European states have emphasised regional co-operation between civilian agencies. Military units are very expensive, act only in support on an ad hoc basis and in any case cannot always be effectively exploited.[11] Nevertheless, European states have exploited the 1988 UN Convention Against Illicit Trafficking in Narcotic Drugs and Psychotropic Substances (the Vienna Convention) which contains provisions to assist co-operation against drug-trafficking in the maritime environment. Article 17 requires parties to the convention to co-operate fully to suppress the illicit trafficking by sea. It provides that where a ship suspected of being engaged in such traffic is outside territorial waters, and where the flag state has given prior permission, the ship may be boarded, searched and seized if illicit traffic is discovered.

Since the mid-1980s, informally at first, and then formally through memoranda of understanding, the UK, the Channel Islands, France, Spain, Portugal and the Netherlands have co-operated on maritime and aerial surveillance. In the UK, HM Customs and Excise reported in October 1990 that such co-operation among European Community (EC) states had 'led to significant seizures of drugs and carrier vessels'.[12] The claim has been supported statistically (see Table 5.1)

Table 5.1 *Drug seizures since maritime co-operation in the EC*

	1986	1987	1988	1989	1990	1991
Kg	3,389	4,876	18,126	24,935	9,175	3,742[a]
Craft	3	7	6	10	8	9

Source: HM Customs and Excise, [Annual] *Report*, Cm 1223 (1990) and Cm 1626 (1991), Cm 2054 (1992), HMSO, London.
Note: [a]excluding 100,000 Ecstasy tablets not quantified in kg.

In the 1990s, the targeting of Western Europe by cocaine suppliers using sea routes (though overland routes through Eastern Europe also increased in importance) led to further international co-operation to extend the geographical reach of law enforcement agencies. The UK's enabling legislation, the Criminal Justice (International Co-operation) Act 1990, anticipated that more effort would take place outside territorial waters, requiring increased aerial support and new 26- and 33-metre length customs patrol vessels.[13]

Maritime interdiction in perspective

Although the social and political significance of the illicit drug trade cannot be ignored, we should keep the scale of the problem in perspective and the feasibility of interdiction in mind when contemplating international maritime anti-drug operations. First, the USCG Pacific Area Intelligence Unit estimates that only 20 ships are regularly involved in carrying marijuana from Asia to the west coast of the United States, a small fraction of the average of 5,000 ships under way each day in the Pacific Ocean.[14] Similarly, as Table 5.1 indicates, EC maritime co-operation led to an average of only seven ships a year being seized in the 1986–92 period, out of the large total of shipping using EC waters. Obviously maritime routes are more heavily used than is revealed by the number of vessels seized. However, the second problem facing advocates of maritime interdiction is the diversity of drug-running techniques. Drugs can be carried by passengers, in containers or in small vessels and light aircraft. The maritime environment contains only a small number of craft which the operators and crew conspire to use primarily for drug-trafficking. A much larger number of vessels can be classed as 'innocent' carriers.

Thus, at present, the data relating to criminal vessels using the high seas does not suggest that a *specific* UN Maritime Force initiative could be justified or would be likely to be effective.
- European waters are already covered by established law enforcement co-operation procedures;
- Latin American–Caribbean–US routes are covered by US military forces, the USCG, US Customs and the DEA;
- Asian maritime routes might benefit from external aid but, as with Africa and Latin America, political sensitivities and corruption among officials may render external aid relatively ineffective.

Nevertheless, for maritime anti-drug operations, the UN could promote bilateral and regional co-operation and press for full international support for the 1988 Vienna Convention, given that by the end of 1991 only about a third of UN members had ratified it.[15]

Suppression of piracy, armed robbery and terrorism at sea

Piracy on the high seas may not be the oldest profession, but it was the scourge of seafarers from ancient times until regular navies came into existence to suppress it. Yet naval intervention may not be the best method of dealing with attacks at sea in the late twentieth century. So-called 'piracy' is sporadic, occurs mainly in territorial waters and does not have the potential to lead to military conflict between states.

It is, however, internationally significant, affecting relations between regional states and between coastal states where raiders are based and states which have an interest in global shipping. Also, seafarers and shipping interests have called upon flag states and the UN's International Maritime Organisation (the IMO) to act, and occasionally call for a robust response by naval forces. Russian fishermen have asked their Pacific Fleet for protection, and in 1992 the Russian Foreign Minister, Andrei Kozyrev, proposed an international naval force to safeguard shipping in the Asia–Pacific region.[16] *Lloyd's List* also reported in May 1992 that the Ministry of Defence (MoD) was considering sending the Royal Navy to participate in deterrence and escort activities in the approaches to Singapore as part of an international task force, though little more was heard of the idea.[17] In view of the cultural, legal and political constraints which surround the 'piracy problem', naval intervention by flag states, especially unilaterally, is perhaps a less appropriate response than international support for co-ordinated operations by local maritime forces.

Culture and perception

The term 'piracy' expresses a culture-bound, essentially European, concept with particular moral connotations. As Alfred Rubin shows, the Greek and Roman origins were continually misinterpreted in later periods, not least by Alberico Gentili (1552–1608) who first defined pirates as *hostes sunt communes* who took foreign life and property without the authorisation of a sovereign.[18] However, in the Malayan world, for example, marauding was endemic because it was integral to the political dynamics of inter-tribal warfare and archipelagic empire-building.[19] Yet the 'suppression of piracy', though it was more akin to privateering, became a justification for Dutch and British imperialism in South-East Asia.

Echoes of privateering continued well into the twentieth century, and even in the 1990s the professionalism of some gangs has led observers to deduce that pirates have had official backing.[20] Particularly alarming developments occurred, for example, in August 1992 around Hong Kong and in the South China Sea, where Chinese Government vessels began harassing merchants ships and seizing cargoes. It is not clear whether this represented an assertion of China's jurisdictional claims, official involvement in criminal activities or, in the case of Russian trawlers fired upon and captured by Chinese warships, a form of economic warfare.[21] Financial gain rather than political aggrandisement is the common motivation nowadays, but suppression by extra-regional states is more problematic if local official connivance is involved.

The problem is most intractable in areas where rich pickings are more easily realised at sea or in harbour than on land, where 'economic legitimacy' might be claimed for the impoverished communities for whom piracy has traditionally supplemented meagre incomes and where, as in South-East Asia, empire-building depended on control over archipelagic waters. Although organised criminal networks are also involved, an appreciation of the cultural and economic roots of the problem is essential if maritime powers are to respond effectively.

Regional perceptions of external naval intervention will, in any case, inhibit the deployment of international maritime constabulary forces. For international law not only accords rights to states in suppressing piracy but also protects states from gunboat diplomacy.

International law

In general, the obligation of states to suppress piracy is clear, but there has been a long history of confusion in law about what should be suppressed and in what circumstances.[22] Article 101 of the 1982 Law of the Sea Convention (LOSC), which inherited article 15 of the 1958 Geneva Convention on the High Seas, has been described by D. P. O'Connell as 'one of the least successful essays in the codification of the Law of the Sea', on account of its imprecision. It defines piracy as:

(a) any illegal acts of violence or detention, or any act of depredation, committed for private ends by the crew or passengers of a private ship or a private aircraft, and directed:

    (i) on the high seas, against another ship or aircraft, or against persons or property on board such ship or aircraft;

    (ii) against a ship, aircraft, persons or property in a place outside the jurisdiction of any State;

  (b) any act of voluntary participation in the operation of a ship or an aircraft with knowledge of facts making it a pirate ship or aircraft;

  (c) any act of inciting or of intentionally facilitating an act described in subparagraph (a) or (b).

In O'Connell's view, the term 'private' signifies that the essence of piracy is its repudiation of authority.[23] But confusion arises because in the absence of international courts, jurisdiction for piracy *jure gentium* has been delegated to state authorities and the definitions of piracy used in municipal law do not necessarily coincide with international law.[24] The authorities of a seizing state may arrest and deal with pirates, or hand them over to another state to be dealt with under municipal law, but whether municipal piracy law displaces international law has also been a matter of dispute.[25]

Also, to the evident disquiet of some commentators, the phrase 'for private ends' excludes mutiny or politically inspired acts by persons not recognised as belligerents.[26] Political violence at sea has been considered as a separate issue in international law. Such violence is relatively uncommon, largely because land targets are more accessible. Even so, over 100 incidents have been listed for the period 1960–90, involving passenger, cargo, fishing and military vessels and offshore installations.[27] The most prominent cases have been the seizure by a faction of the Palestine Liberation Organisation of the Italian cruise liner *Achille Lauro* in 1985, an attack by Palestinian extremists on the Greek ship, *City of Poros* in 1989, the French bombing of the Greenpeace ship, *Rainbow Warrior* in 1985, and raiding by Cuban exiles in the Caribbean Sea, by Irish nationalists off the coast of Ireland and by Polisaro guerrillas off the Western Sahara coast.[28] After the *Achille Lauro* incident, the IMO set guidelines for protecting ports and ships against terrorist attacks. Subsequently the IMO sponsored the Rome Convention for the Suppression of Unlawful Acts Against the Safety of Maritime Navigation (1988). Based on precedents in aviation it specifies offences covered by the 'prosecute or extradite' rule, such as seizing a ship and threats to interfere with a ship so as to be likely to endanger safe navigation. However, in deference to sensitivities about sovereignty, the Rome Convention excluded vessels which at the time of an incident are navigating solely within the territorial waters of a single state.[29] Nevertheless, the problem is more appropriately dealt with by civilian policing than by naval task forces.

The definitional issues may not seem critical in affecting decisions about the deployment of navies in a constabulary role. But a clear constraint on naval deployment against piracy arises from the fact that international law ties the definition of piracy to absence of jurisdiction at sea.

Maritime jurisdiction

An estimated 80 per cent of so-called 'piracy' is not piracy on the high seas as legally defined, but raiding in territorial waters. The legal prescriptions associated with maritime geographical jurisdiction also circumscribe the rights of foreign states to deter or suppress attacks. In theory a universal crime might be expected to entail universal jurisdiction and, historically, it was sometimes argued that pirates could be seized in foreign sovereign territory to be handed over to the littoral state.[30] However, the presumption is not addressed in international law because piracy was defined to meet the situation in areas where states had no jurisdiction. In South-East Asia it seems that raiders take advantage of areas of contested jurisdiction, such as the South China Sea, where it is more risky for naval vessels to operate unilaterally.[31] Coastal states are reluctant to accept the rights of maritime powers to conduct naval operations in EEZs and contiguous security zones, a matter on which, it has been argued, the Law of the Sea is ambiguous.[32]

Given the uncertainties surrounding the legal right to pursue pirates, there is considerable advantage to be gained, as Barry Dubner argues, from the establishment of local hot pursuit agreements.[33] However, states of the developed as well as developing world are wary of *posse comitatus* unless legitimised by specific arrangements. Foreign warships are powerful symbols of the exercise of alien authority, albeit when trying to enforce international law. Thus when, in May 1992, Royal Malaysian Police Marines chased a stolen trawler which was being used to prey on other vessels in disputed territory around Sabah, they had to call off the pursuit when the trawler entered Philippine waters.[34] In this instance, of course, perceptions of extra-regional 'imperialist' intervention were completely absent. Subsequently, however, Indonesia, Malaysia and Singapore signed an agreement allowing the hot pursuit of pirates into each other's territorial waters.

The Law of the Sea obliges states to co-operate to repress piracy. But the international community is disadvantaged when a state either turns a blind eye to pirates and armed robbers using its territory as sanctuary, or is unable to suppress the attacks through lack of resources.

The pattern of incidents
Before considering the prospects for dealing with piracy and armed robbery at sea, it is important to ask whether the problem is sufficiently serious to warrant international constabulary work. Gauging the frequency of attacks and their danger to shipping is problematic partly because of definitional issues, but also because perhaps less than a half of all incidents are reported. Shippers may be reluctant to report incidents which might imply negligence, and equally reluctant to disrupt a voyage to allow crews to provide evidence to local authorities. But there appears to be a cyclical pattern to incidents, which may reflect periods of varying pressure on coastal states to exert greater vigilance. The database of incidents prepared by the International Maritime Bureau (IMB) indicates an upsurge in the late 1970s and early 1980s, a decline until the late 1980s, an apparent increase from 1990 to mid-1992 (estimated to be costing shippers £200m per annum), and a downturn in the second half of 1992 after flag states and international organisations had made representations to coastal states. About 25 per cent of incidents recorded since 1990 have involved violence, and in the year ending July 1992 several officers and crew were killed.[35] Piracy and sea raiding is thus a significant threat to lives and maritime safety. In cases where vessels are out of control because the crew is detained or locked up, the risk of collision, grounding, spillage and fire is increased. In a potentially disastrous incident in April 1992, attackers used petrol bombs on an oil tanker off Singapore.

The problem is, however, largely confined to certain areas. South-East Asia and the waters around Hong Kong account for over half of the world's incidents. The problem for commercial shipping grew in the late 1980s, both with regard to frequency and level of violence. By 1991, the estimate for attacks in the Singapore approaches alone, was over two a week.[36] Although Singapore's territorial waters are well policed, there are notable haunts in the Phillip Channel and Kep Riau Islands south of Singapore, the Straits of Malacca, the South China Sea, the Gulf of Thailand and Zamboanga Peninsula on Mindanao. Latin American and Caribbean waters rank second in the number of attacks, especially around the ports of Rio de Janeiro and Santos. An estimated 50 violent robberies occurred in Santos in 1982–83, and two Greek officers were murdered off Rio in 1992.[37] In the Caribbean, the IMB recorded about 25 attacks between 1981 and 1987, but many people are thought to have disappeared in drug-related incidents.[38] West Africa has witnessed piracy by violent gangs for cargo, cash and equipment on vessels at anchor or in harbour, about half in Nigerian waters. Attacks appear to have reached a peak in the late 1970s and early 1980s, with 86 recorded, but the International Shipping Federation continues to regard West African ports as potentially dangerous, with gangs taking advantage of the break-down of civil authority in Liberia and elsewhere.[39]

Remedies

Given the complexity of the problem, navies will play only a con-tributory part in remedial measures. Shipping companies and sea-farers' unions, anxious to protect merchant vessels and their personnel have advised crews to draw up security plans, improve watchkeeping, and report attacks to the nearest shore authorities.[40] Trade Unions and shipping associations have also lobbied flag states and regional governments to act and treat the issue as seriously as attacks on aircraft.[41] In addition, seafarers would welcome a naval presence for its symbolic importance as a demonstration of resolve.[42]

However, the issue of naval protection is complicated by the fact that flags of convenience are frequently used by ship-owners to reduce labour costs, and nationals are frequently attacked when serving on foreign vessels.[43] Partly to avoid uncertainties about qualification for protection, some seafarers would opt for a UN-flagged international task force in the worst-affected areas to under-take this constabulary work. UN maritime constabulary units would extend the operational concept of traditional peacekeeping. But they would be expensive to maintain and require new command and control structures which naval powers may not yet be ready to accept. More feasible, and politically acceptable, would be ad hoc coalitions, authorised by the UN and operating with the agreement and participation of coastal states.

Alternatively, maritime powers can assist coastal states with intelligence, funds, training and equipment – as requested by the Malaysian Prime Minister, Dr Mahathir Mohamad, at the ASEAN summit in January 1992.[44] But special reporting and communication systems are also required, and observers have suggested that the UN should investigate incidents.[45] A precedent for regionally applied international assistance can be seen in the measures taken to reduce attacks on Vietnamese 'boat people'. From 1982 the attacks were gradually countered when Thailand began administering a programme devised by wealthy states and the UN High Commissioner for Refugees.[46] The scheme was slow to get under way, and for reducing renewed raiding in South-East Asia the international community might consider directing its aid specifically towards co-operative regional maritime constabulary action.

National laws, policies and control mechanisms vary considerably but, as argued at the inaugural meeting of the Asian Forum in Tokyo in April 1992, regional initiatives are essential for making the most of scarce resources and facilitating co-operation across boundaries.[47] In 1992 armed police teams from Malaysia, Indonesia and Singapore were made available to go on board ships transiting the Malacca Straits. Although armed police on ships might merely escalate the scale of violence, the scheme is important as a symbol of political will and co-operation. More effective would be high-profile patrolling by coastal states. Of course, many developing states have huge expanses of water to patrol and have usually built up capabilities with regional threats in mind. However, coastal law enforcement might be a suitable arena in which to start the process of regional confidence-building, especially through hot-pursuit agreements.

A foreign naval presence might not deter pirates so much as signal international concern and stimulate coastal states into taking action. Coercion is inappropriate in the modern context, but shippers and flag states can exert diplomatic pressure and offer financial incentives to promote regional co-operation. However, there is evidence that robbery at sea in Asia has become highly organised on a transnational basis. If local states are unable to respond effectively, extra-regional navies may have to consider providing a patrol force if requested. And if illegal activity is being sponsored to underwrite jurisdictional claims, then the UN Security Council as well as the IMO should be alerted.

Disaster relief

In addition to law enforcement functions, constabulary maritime forces can also assist civil authorities in disaster relief. Traditionally, disasters have not been interpreted as threats to peace under the terms of the UN Charter, and disaster relief can be considered as a form of 'military aid to the civil power'. Naval units contribute to national civil defence and Search and Rescue (SAR) organisations and operate outside national territory in co-operation with the International SAR Advisory Group. There is also a strong naval tradition of providing emergency aid beyond national territory, which has frequently involved international co-operation.[48] Examples include the evacuation of foreign nationals from the civil wars in Yemen (1986), Liberia (1990) and Somalia (1991), as described in the Appendix of this study. Further, it has been suggested that some of the norms developed for dealing with shipping disasters might be applied to emergency relief in general.[49]

Guidelines

Disasters produce serious disruption to the social functioning of communities, involving widespread and immediate threat to human life. The interaction of ecological, economic and political factors and the extent to which human policy or negligence contributes to disasters makes it difficult to distinguish political from natural causes. But disaster relief for victims of political conflict is obviously affected by the doctrine of non-intervention in the internal affairs of states. The UN Security Council has sometimes adopted a permissive interpretation of Article 2(7) of the Charter by linking internal problems to the international situation (as in the Congo, South Africa, Rhodesia, northern Iraq and Somalia).[50] But the draft Convention on Disaster Relief, presented by the Office of the UN Disaster Relief Co-ordinator (UNDRO) in 1984, attempts to avoid political problems by excluding disasters which arise during armed conflict.[51] Another traditional evasion has been to make external assistance dependent on the host state's agreement, itself a delicate matter if the assistance involves military personnel and equipment.

Respect for sovereignty and local political sensitivities by the providers (as well as respect for the rights of aid workers) has been affirmed in numerous international codes and resolutions, and adhered to in the practice of the International Committees of the Red Cross/Crescent (ICRC). The work of a US-dominated naval force in Bangladesh after the 1991 cyclone, was judged successful because the marines and naval personnel bowed to Bangladeshi sensitivities, respected local customs, kept a low profile and lived off shore.[52]

From a humanitarian point of view there is no objective distinction between the needs of disaster victims whose government has invited external aid and the needs of victims of deliberate government policy. Dr Bernard Kouchner, who in 1979 chartered a ship to rescue boat people in the China Sea and subsequently became French Minister of Humanitarian Action, and his legal adviser, Professor Mario Bettati, seek to revive nineteenth-century practice when states not only claimed the right to rescue nationals but also a duty to stop cruel persecutions.[53] But without a universally agreed legal right of intervention, and given that only the rich and powerful are likely to interfere, humanitarian intervention will attract accusations of gunboat diplomacy. The situation is particularly problematic when internal political conflict causes humanitarian disaster. As noted by Alan James, external assistance can be seen as taking sides in particularly vicious situations where domestic sovereignty is contested and where the authority to deal internationally may be absent.[54]

A second approach promoted by Kouchner and Bettati has been to develop 'the right of victims' to receive rapid and effective assistance. General Assembly Resolution 43/131 of 8 December 1988 takes this line in cases of natural and similar disasters. Although the Resolution upholds the primary role of the host state, where this is inadequate it is required to provide free access for those humanitarian organisations recognised by the UN and accorded impartial and neutral rights under the 1949 Geneva Convention. A second Resolution (45/100 of 14 December 1990) provides for the creation of 'humanitarian corridors', inspired by the maritime right of innocent passage in territorial waters and the maritime duty to render assistance to ships in distress (reaffirmed in Articles 17 and 18 of the LOSC).[55] Neither resolution legitimises interference in domestic jurisdiction. Ironically, when the corridor principle was put to the test *at sea* off Dalmatia, in October–November 1991, the Federal Yugoslav Navy harassed an improvised squadron (including a vessel chartered by UNICEF) assembled to evacuate children and wounded from ports such as Dubrovnik.

Although the international use of national military–civil defence forces has long been advocated, and some states have military international disaster relief units, it is only since the easing of Cold War tensions that progress has been made.[56] UN co-ordination was improved in 1991 with the creation of the Department of Humanitarian Affairs (DHA) as part of UNDRO. Its office in Geneva facilitates operational preparedness, and can dispatch civilian Disaster Assessment Teams and a Mobile Co-ordination Command Centre. In 1992–93, DHA–Geneva was also involved in planning for the use of military–naval assets in consultation with NATO and relief agencies for producing guidelines and Standard Operating Procedures.[57] The principles are similar to those issued by UNDRO, the League of Red Cross Societies, the UN Institute for Training and Research (UNITAR) and the Organisation of American States (OAS). Designed to encourage the development of norms in the practical aspects of disaster relief, they apply to navies as well as to other services. They incorporate such principles as: the requirement for a national authority to co-ordinate domestic and external assistance; non-discrimination of relief distribution; respect for territorial sovereignty; and the waiving of taxes and normal commercial documentation for relief supplies.[58] Additionally, seaborne assistance requires expeditious access to ports, harbours, beaches or offshore trans-shipment facilities, navigational aids, diplomatic clearance for warships and possibly refuelling facilities.

Maritime assistance
Obviously, air forces have a key role in providing speedy responses and access over territory, but all kinds of emergencies may require naval forces.[59] Sudden disasters which threaten coastal communities include tsunami, cyclones or tankers spilling toxic material. The national maritime services of affected states may prove inadequate in such situations. International maritime assistance may also be required for the offshore measuring of the effects of disasters which occur on land. A maritime-specific constabulary task, loosely akin to disaster relief, is peacetime mineclearing and restoring freedom of navigation, such as occurred after the Suez War of 1956, after the

laying of mines by the Islamic Jihad in the Red Sea in 1984, during the Iran–Iraq War in 1987–88 and after the Gulf War ceasefire of 28 February 1991.

Our main concern, here, is with assistance to displaced persons. When coasts and islands are affected by earthquakes, volcanic activity, cyclones or other disasters, vessels lying off shore may provide relatively safe bases. In the aftermath of the Mt Pinatubo eruption in the Philippines in 1991, the US Navy proved the value of offshore support, accommodation, medical facilities and an escape route for some 19,000 people.[60] The emergency evacuation of victims may pose considerable operational difficulties, as illustrated by the evacuation by small craft for transfer to HMY *Britannia* from open beaches at Aden in 1986. Embarkation and harbour facilities may be denied and a state of panic may interfere with orderly procedures, but political complications can also occur. In several historical cases warships were instructed to evacuate only their own nationals, but allowed moral and practical imperatives to dictate otherwise. International rules and norms are undeveloped in regard to disaster relief operations, and clear political guidelines and operating procedures for maritime evacuation need to be established.

Liaison between ships and political authorities is essential, especially when the issue of refugee status arises. Under the provisions of the maritime codes and conventions relating to safety of life at sea, ships are bound to come to the aid of persons in distress. But where refugees are not in immediate physical danger, assistance is largely discriminatory. For example, commercial vessels were not legally obliged to give temporary asylum to refugees who fled Vietnam in the 1980s, and they were often reluctant to do so without guarantees that refugees could be disembarked at the next port of call.[61] In contrast, warships are supposed to provide temporary asylum pending a process of screening.

Most displaced persons are victims of environmental land degradation and a combination of political and economic forces, and do not qualify for refugee status under criteria used by the UN High Commissioner for Refugees (UNHCR), which are based on the notion of well-founded fear of persecution in the country of nationality. However, warships may be instructed to interdict all displaced persons in order to deter illegal immigration, a task which may become ethically problematic if unsuccessful asylum seekers are forcibly repatriated. Forcible repatriation was adopted by the

Reagan Administration in November 1991 when a coup in Haiti added enormously to the existing outflow of Haitians and threatened to overwhelm the US Alien Migration Programme. President George Bush went further than his predecessor and authorised the USCG to summarily return Haitians and establish a blockade to deny them the legal right to seek asylum. The policy, which was continued by President Bill Clinton, even wrecked the UNHCR's plans for a coherent OAS asylum strategy.[62] It was not clear, however, whether the naval units in the US-led multinational group which began enforcing sanctions against Haiti in October 1993 were also expected to dissuade 'boat people' from seeking asylum, given that the UN had only authorised an economic embargo (which undoubtedly made the refugee problem worse).

Policy coherence was thus conspicuously lacking in the case of Haiti. In view of the possibility of seaborne displaced persons sailing elsewhere, for example in the Mediterranean, Baltic or China Seas, there needs to be greater international co-ordination of the kind devised for disaster relief on land, and preparation by maritime forces for operations in concert.

Maritime housekeeping

Consistent with our definition of constabulary functions as those concerned with non-military, non-state threats, there may be occasions when maritime forces are called upon to deal with marine pollution on an international basis.[63] Pollution does not respect the artificial boundaries of legal delimitation at sea, and co-operative housekeeping may be cost-effective in dealing with problems which are global in nature. The requirements of a global maritime regime are discussed in Chapter 11 below, but this section identifies the kind of marine pollution disaster which might require the specialist assistance of maritime forces.

It should be emphasised, however, that most marine pollution derives not directly from ships but from land-based industrial waste, eutrophication from agricultural run-off, urban effluent, litter from coast development and contaminated dredged material.[64] To this list we can add toxic and nuclear waste dumped in the sea. The Soviet Union, for example, discharged an estimated total of 29,000 curies in the period 1959–91. But by far the worst nuclear polluter has been the UK which discharged approximately 1 million curies from nuclear power stations into the sea in the period 1949–82.[65] The effects of low-level radiation on the marine environment are a matter of great controversy, but measuring the impact of nuclear and toxic pollution is a task which maritime agencies and naval forces might be equipped to carry out in the course of other duties.

Naval expertise would certainly be essential for coping with contamination from naval nuclear sources. Some 50 nuclear weapons have been 'lost' at sea, and several nuclear-propelled submarines have sunk since nuclear material was first carried on ships.[66] The world's most hazardous seas are around Russia – especially the Kara and Barents Seas in the vicinity of the Kola Peninsula and Novaya Zemlya. Some 16 nuclear reactors (containing a total of 2.3 million curies) were deliberately sunk by the Soviet naval authorities, and a nuclear-propelled submarine was damaged by a fire causing high levels of radioactive release at Chazhma Bay on the Sea of Japan in 1985. In the early 1990s, inspectors did not regard radionuclide leakage from these sites as unduly hazardous. However, the rate of container and sealant corrosion is uncertain, and the inevitable leakage of plutonium–239 from torpedoes on the submarine *Komsomolets* which sank in 1989, 300 miles from Norway, causes grave concern. Raising vulnerable material could be hazardous but may be necessary in order to seal it.[67]

Yet access to Russian sites by Norwegian and American scientists has been restricted or forbidden, and a Greenpeace vessel, MV *Solo*, was arrested entering territorial waters in 1992. But in dealing with nuclear emergencies, neither secrecy nor embarrassment should be permitted to obstruct international naval emergency monitoring. Assistance in raising or sealing Russian nuclear material is most likely to be available from the nuclear naval powers, the United States, the UK and France, but other states also have a direct interest in independent monitoring and safety. Co-ordination through the International Atomic Energy Agency and the IMO may assist in obtaining information and the right conditions for access.

Marine accidents in the commercial sphere may also require the intervention of coastal protection vessels. About 50 per cent of the commercial cargoes transported by sea are dangerous, hazardous or harmful from an environmental point of view.[68] The *Torrey Canyon* disaster off Land's End in 1967 focused attention on accidental oil pollution which increased in line with the increase in world tonnage and the transport of crude oil in large tankers. In 1979, serious casualties reached a rate of over 3 per cent of tankers of 6,000 gross tons minimum, and remained at about 2 per cent until the mid-1980s, reflecting in part a decline in the number of tankers in operation.[69] However, after 1988, world ship losses of all kinds rose dramatically, and further reduction in the accident rate will depend on improved crew training, wider availability of salvage tugs, the decommissioning of older vessels, the establishment of exclusion zones around dangerous and sensitive coastal areas, and traffic separation schemes in areas of high-density shipping.[70] In 1990 the IMO adopted a Convention on Oil Pollution Preparedness, Response and Co-operation to improve response to accidents, some provisions of which were enacted in the aftermath of the Gulf War in 1991 though no state had ratified the Convention.

Tanker accidents account for less than a third of total oil pollution from ships. Most pollution from ships is deliberate and, by the late 1970s, an estimated 1.5 million tons of oil was spilled annually, mainly from general shipping operations and port activities such as cleaning. Chapter 11 below examines the international framework of legislative and administrative measures for addressing pollution at sea. Given that government-owned ships, whether in the civilian or naval sectors, are often required to assist in monitoring and implementing regulations, to effect arrests for example, they may also be required for salvage and mopping-up operations. Given the transnational nature of commercial shipping, co-operation between national maritime agencies to combat pollution is increasingly necessary. Further, although such constabulary work may not command a high priority for maritime forces, a growing global consciousness of risks to the marine environment and to coastal communities means that housekeeping activities may become more important in the future.

Conclusion

Although the security contexts differ, maritime forces engaged upon international constabulary roles will normally be governed by principles similar to those that govern traditional peacekeeping. Firepower is a secondary characteristic compared to the importance of official status and ship capabilities in, for example, monitoring and boarding. When deployed outside their own areas of jurisdiction, with the consent of coastal states and as part of a complex response, maritime forces can act to support civilian organisations in international non-military security.

In drug interdiction, piracy suppression, disaster relief and pollution control, multinational maritime forces would be the instruments of national governments co-operating through or interacting with intergovernmental organisations and UN agencies such as the IMO, DHA–UNDRO and UNHCR. NGOs are less likely to be directly involved in sea-based missions than on land, though co-ordination with medical foundations and the Red Cross and Red Crescent societies may be necessary. Interaction with commercial shipping may be significant in combating piracy and in disaster relief operations. Generally speaking co-ordination between navies and shippers should present few problems, provided standard operating procedures are understood and clear lines of communication and authority established.

Disaster relief operations and criminal law enforcement activities have to compete among many claims on UN resources. Regional intergovernmental organisations, such as the Andean group in dealing with drugs, may be the most appropriate channels for co-ordinating constabulary policy and deploying resources. However, the UN agencies clearly have the potential to facilitate and legitimise the initiatives of member states. In particular the UN can play a leading role in producing guidelines and operating procedures for international constabulary functions. In this respect the DHA's disaster relief preparations are significant and might in time be extended to coping with displaced persons and humanitarian intervention in internal conflicts. It remains to be seen, however, whether the Security Council's Summit Declaration of 31 January 1992, that non-military sources of instability can be threats to peace and security, will transform the nature of constabulary roles. As argued here in regard to US drug interdiction, constabulary work is valuable to the extent that it does not militarise non-military security issues.

Notes

1 Vladimir F. Petrovsky, speech at Seminar on Problems of UN Peacekeeping Operations, Salzburg, 4 August 1989, official Austrian text.

2 Rear-Admiral J. R. Hill, 'Control of the Exclusive Economic Zone', *Naval Forces*, vol. 6, no. 2, 1985, pp. 87–8. After Waterloo and after each of the two World Wars, a large part of the Royal Navy's time and effort was spent on littoral constabulary work though, ironically, in 1839–42, wars were also fought with China to protect the opium trade. For the nineteenth century, see C. J. Bartlett, *Great Britain and Sea Power, 1815–1853*, Clarendon, Oxford, 1963. For the twentieth century, see Eric Grove, *From Vanguard to Trident: British Naval Policy Since World War II*, Bodley Head, London, 1989.

3 Eric Grove, *The Future of Sea Power*, Routledge, London, 1990, pp. 187–98, 240.

4 M. Janowitz, *The Professional Soldier: A Social and Political Portrait*, Free Press of Glencoe, Ill., 1960, p. 418. Peacekeeping operations could be viewed as an application of the constabulary concept, 'undertaken by conventional national forces which have been wielded into ad hoc organisations, and given political and administrative direction by . . . [the] United Nations'. Janowitz, 'Armed Forces and Society: A World Perspective', in J. Van Doorn (ed.), *Armed Forces and Society – Sociological Essays*, Mouton, The Hague, 1968, p. 32.

5 At the 1990 British Commonwealth Heads of Government Meeting, the Jamaican Premier called for international action to control drug-trafficking. See F. E. G. Gregory, 'Can Military Force Defeat Drugs Trafficking?', *Small Wars and Insurgencies*, vol. 2, no. 1, April 1991, p. 2.

6 In four years the USCG seized 189 vessels and 250,000 kg of marijuana. J. C. Trainor, 'United States Maritime Drug Law Enforcement', *Naval Forces*, vol. 9, no. 3, 1988, p. 78.

7 *Ibid.*, p. 79.

8 The National Guard, Naval Reserve and Naval Air Reserve were also given enhanced roles. Center for Defense, 'The Pentagon's War on Drugs: The Ultimate Bad Trip', *Defense Monitor*, vol. 21, no. 1, 1992, p. 5; Alan Waymont, 'An Analysis of the Failure of the Drugs Law Enforcement Policies of the Governments of Britain and the United States of America', unpublished PhD thesis, University of Southampton, 1993, pp. 163–4.

9 Chris Taylor, 'Britain Chastised over Attempt to Board Boat', *The Guardian*, 21 August 1993, p. 12.

10 'The Pentagon's War on Drugs', *Defense Monitor*, pp. 2–7; Alan Ned Sabrosky, 'A War Un-Won: The US Fight against Drugs', *Small Wars and Insurgencies*, vol. 2, no. 1, April 1991, pp. 8–17; US Senate Committee on the Judiciary, 'Fighting Drug Abuse: Tough Decisions for our National Strategy', USGPO, Washington DC, May 1993; Michael Reid, 'Legacy of Defeat in the Fight against a Deadly Trade', *The Guardian*, 14 August 1993, p. 8.

11 A Nimrod maritime patrol aircraft would provide target acquisition capability but, in the words of a UK police officer: 'We had nothing at sea to follow up the advantage this powerful instrument might give us.' Cited in Gregory, 'Can Military Force Defeat Drugs Trafficking?, *Small Wars and Insurgencies*, vol. 2, no. 1, April 1991, p. 3.

12 HM Customs and Excise, [Annual] *Report*, Cm 1223, HMSO, London, 1990, pp. 33–4.

13 In 1990, 227 kg of cocaine was found on a Liberian-registered ship at Liverpool, and 500 kg (with a street value of £10m) was landed in Scotland, *ibid.*, Cm 1636, 1991, p. 22.

14 Cdr William J. Lahneman (USN), 'Interdicting Drugs in the Big Pond', *Proceedings*, US Naval Institute, July 1990, pp. 56–7.

15 Bureau of Public Affairs, US Department of State, *Dispatch*, vol. 3, no. 20, 18 September 1992; *Fact Sheet: 1991 Progress in the International War Against Narcotics*, p. 393.

16 Sergei Strokan, 'Sailing under the Jolly Roger into the 21st century', *Moscow News*, 16 July 1993, pp. 1, 4.

17 Anthony Poole, 'Pirate Patrol May Boost UK Register', *Lloyd's List*, 26 May 1992, p. 1; John Harlow, 'Royal Navy Launches Task Force against Pirates', *The Sunday Times*, 24 May 1992, p. 1. The Netherlands and Sweden had urged the IMO to act in the 1980s. International Maritime Bureau, *A Report into the Incidence of Piracy and Armed Robbery From Merchant Ships* (submitted to the IMO), London, 6 June 1983, p. 3.

18 Political communities in the Eastern Mediterranean which defied Roman hegemonic ambition were treated as pirates with belligerent status whose possessions were not subject to the law of *postliminium* but could be seized by anyone. Alfred P. Rubin, *The Law of Piracy*, US Naval War College Press, Newport, RI, 1988, Ch. 1.

19 Nicholas Tarling, *Piracy and Politics in the Malayan World: A Study of British Imperialism in Nineteenth Century South-east Asia*, F. W. Cheshire, Melbourne, 1963, pp. 4–8, 133–4; Rubin, *The Law of Piracy*, pp. 220–58.

20 *NUMAST Telegraph*, vol. 25, no. 7 (piracy supplement), July 1992, p. iii; 'Do what I tell you or I will kill you', *The Guardian*, 2 October 1992, p. 5.

21 Strokan, 'Sailing under the Jolly Roger', pp. 1, 4; Jon Swain, 'Chinese terrorise Hong Kong ships', *Sunday Times*, 30 August 1992, p. 1; 'Assignment – The New Pirates', BBC2 TV October 1993.

22 See Rubin, *The Law of Piracy*, op. cit.

23 D. P. O'Connell, *The International Law of the Sea*, vol. 2, Oxford University Press, Oxford, 1984, p. 970.

24 US piracy law assimilates assault by a seaman on a captain so as to prevent him from defending his ship or cargo, and receipt of pirated goods. 18 US Code, sec: 1654, 1656, 1660.

25 The leading case is from the Scottish Courts, *Cameron v. HM Advocate* [1971], SC 50; O'Connell, *International Law of the Sea*, p. 972.

26 James Cable, *Navies in Violent Peace*, Macmillan, London, 1989, pp. 92–101; Samuel Pyeatt Menefee, 'Piracy, Terrorism and the Insurgent Passenger: A Historical and Legal Perspective', in Natalino Ronzitti (ed.), *Maritime Terrorism and International Law*, Martinus Nijhoff, Dordrecht, 1990, pp. 56–61. The term 'piracy' was used flexibly during the Spanish Civil War. The Republican Government announced that state vessels taken over by the fascists were pirate ships, and signatories to the 1937 Nyon Agreement argued that the 'unidentified' [Italian] submarines which were sinking neutral merchant vessels, were engaged in piracy. Raoul Genet, 'The Charge of Piracy in the Spanish Civil War', *American Journal of International Law*, vol. 32, no. 2, April 1938, pp. 253–63.

27 Many cases were not political but threats by the disgruntled employees of shipping companies. Tore Bjørgo, *Maritime Terrorism. A Threat to Shipping and the Oil Industry*, special report, Norwegian Institute of International Affairs, Oslo, August 1991, Appendix 3, pp. 78–95.

28 B. A. H. Parritt, *Security at Sea: Terrorism, Piracy and Drugs. A Practical Guide*, The Nautical Institute, London, 1991, pp. 13–17; Roger Villar, *Piracy Today: Robbery and Violence at Sea since 1980*, Conway Maritime Press, London, 1985, pp. 57–9.

29 IMO Doc., SUA/CON/15 Rev.1, 10 March 1988, *International Legal Materials*, vol. 27, 1988, pp. 668–90; Glen Plant, 'The Convention for the Suppression of Unlawful Acts Against the Safety of Maritime Navigation', *International and Comparative Law Quarterly*, vol. 39, part 1, January 1990, p. 37; Tullio Treves, 'The Rome Convention for the Suppression of Unlawful Acts Against the Safety of Maritime Navigation', in Ronzitti (ed.), *Maritime Terrorism*, pp. 69–90.

30 Dr Stephen Lushington, cited in O'Connell, p. 978. The United States interprets the law as allowing pursuit 'if contact cannot be established in a timely manner with the coastal nation to obtain its consent . . . [but] pursuit must be broken off immediately upon request of the coastal nation'. US Navy, 'Annotated Supplement to the Commander's Handbook on the Law of Naval Operations', NWP 9 (REV.A)/FMFM 1–10, Department of Defense, Washington DC, 1989, 3.4.3.2, pp. 3/12–13.

31 *Jane's Defence Weekly*, 5 September 1992, p. 34.

32 Straits which fall wholly or partly within territorial jurisdiction but which connect high seas, have customarily been regarded as open to all for continuous and expeditious passage, provided that vessels do not threaten the coastal state or engage in non-transit activity. Chasing pirate vessels is unlikely to be part of direct and expeditious transit. R. R. Churchill and A. V. Lowe, *The Law of the Sea,* rev. edn, Manchester University Press, Manchester, 1988, p. 90.

33 Barry H. Dubner, *The Law of International Sea Piracy*, Martinus Nijhoff, The Hague, 1980, pp. 160–5.
34 Kazuo Takita and Bob Couttie, 'ASEAN Pressured to Act against Pirates', *Lloyd's List*, 29 May 1992, p. 3.
35 *NUMAST Telegraph*, vol. 25, no. 7 (piracy supplement), July 1992, p. i.
36 Teresa Poole, 'Pirates Hoist Jolly Roger in the South China Sea', *The Independent*, 24 February 1992, p. 12; David Sharrock, 'Battle Joined with Pirates Worldwide', *The Guardian*, 2 October 1992, p. 5.
37 'Delincuencia carioca: raptos y pirateria', *Nuevo Herald*, 5 July 1991, p. 3A. See also, Villar, *Piracy Today*, pp. 36–42.
38 P. W. Birnie, 'Piracy Past, Present and Future', in Eric Ellen (ed.), *Piracy at Sea*, ICC Publishing, Paris, 1989, p. 143; Villar, *Piracy Today*, pp. 42–7.
39 International Shipping Federation, *Pirates and Armed Robbers: A Masters' Guide*, 2nd edn, London, 1992, p. 4.
40 *Ibid.*, pp. 8–13. In the UK, the Department of Transport published a Marine Notice in 1993. Department of Transport, *Merchant Shipping Notice No. M1517, Piracy and Armed Robbery*, International Shipping Policy Division, February 1993. Shipping interests and the IMB opened a 24-hour Reporting Centre in Kuala Lumpur on 1 October 1992. *NUMAST Telegraph*, vol. 25, no. 7, July 1992, p. 1; Cal McCrystal, 'Maritime Mafia Rules the Waves', *The Independent*, 14 February 1993, p. 10.
41 In 1992 the Japan Shipowners' Association suggested that the IMO Secretary-General intercede with coastal states. Takita and Couttie, 'ASEAN Pressured to Act', p. 3. The UK's Department of Transport also uses its influence in the IMO to encourage coastal states to act more rigorously. Interview by Michael Pugh with DoT and MoD officials, London, 15 July 1992.
42 'Safety at Sea', submission by NUMAST to Earl of Caithness, Minister for Shipping, London, 9 July 1992.
43 The majority of attacks on British crews are on non-British-registered ships and unionists are hostile to the reflagging of foreign vessels in order to qualify for RN protection. 'No Royal Navy Protection for Non-Brits, Urges RMT', *The Seaman*, June/July 1992, p. 1.
44 'New World Order Full of Curbs on Asean', *The Straits Times*, 28 January 1992, p. 23.
45 NUMAST, 'Observations on Armed Attacks against Merchant Ships', unpublished memorandum, February 1992; John Newman, letter in *Lloyd's List*, 13 April 1992, p. 2.
46 More intensive patrolling by the Thai authorities, compulsory boat registration and paid informers in coastal villages appear to have been effective in the late 1980s, though fewer refugees were leaving Vietnam and more were being rescued by merchant ships under a UN incentive

scheme. Joachim Henkel, 'Refugees on the High Seas: A Dangerous Passage', in Ellen (ed.), *Piracy at Sea*, pp. 108–9; Harry C. Blaney, 'Anti-piracy in South-East Asia: US and International Efforts and Programmes', *ibid.*, pp. 101–6.

47 Takita and Couttie, 'ASEAN Pressured to Act', p. 3; Hyslop, 'Contemporary Piracy', in Ellen (ed.), *Piracy at Sea*, p. 25.

48 See James Cable, 'Naval Humanitarianism', *International Relations*, vol. 12, no. 1, April 1992, pp. 335–45.

49 M. Meyer, 'Principles of Emergency Relief', paper at Congress on International Solidarity and Humanitarian Actions, International Institute of Humanitarian Law, San Remo, 1980, cited in Mohammed El Baradei, M. Bashar, E. Christiansen, J. Connolly, P. de Montalembert, M. Gottleib and T. Pham, *Model Rules for Disaster Relief Operations*, Policy and Efficacy Studies, no. 8, UNITAR, New York, 1982.

50 N. D. White, *The United Nations and the Maintenance of International Peace and Security*, Manchester University Press, Manchester, 1990, pp. 33–5.

51 Article 1b, 'Proposed Draft Convention on Expediting the Delivery of Emergency Relief', Office of the United Nations Disaster Relief Co-ordinator, General Assembly/Economic and Social Council, doc. A/39/267/Add.2; E/1984/96/Add.2, 18 June 1984. A General Assembly resolution, adopted in 1988, refers to: 'Humanitarian Assistance to Victims of Natural Disasters and Similar Emergency Situations', UN Res. A 43/131, 8 December 1988.

52 H. C. Stackpole III, 'Angels From the Sea', *Proceedings*, US Naval Institute, May 1992, pp. 110–16.

53 Mario Bettati, 'Un droit d'ingérence?', *Revue Général de Droit International Public*, vol. 95, 1991, pp. 639–70.

54 Alan James, 'Internal Peace-keeping: A Dead End for the UN?', *Security Dialogue*, vol. 24, no. 4, December 1993, pp. 359–68.

55 Bettati, 'Un droit d'ingérence?', *Revue Général de Droit International Public*, vol. 95, 1991, pp. 658–9.

56 A Disaster Relief Transport Force scheme in the 1980s was rejected by NATO Ministers who quibbled about costs and argued that it was not the job of the military. Hugh Hanning, *NATO and Disaster Relief: An Additional Role for the 1990s*, Report of a Conference, Fontmell Group, London, 13 July 1990. The draft UNDRO Convention made no headway in 1984 at the height of the second Cold War. Interview by Michael Pugh with Jiri Toman (who worked on the draft), Geneva, 24 May 1993.

57 Interview by Michael Pugh with Sergio Piazzi and Rudolph Mueller, Relief Co-ordination Office, DHA–Geneva, 26 May 1993; UN Department of Humanitarian Affairs: Relief Coordination Branch,

'Workshop on Use of Military and Civil Defence Assets in Disaster Relief', Brussels, 14–15 December 1992, Final Report, Project DPR 213/3 (MCDA), DHA–Geneva, April 1993.

58 See, for example, Baradei, *et al.*, *Model Rules for Disaster Relief Operations*, n. 49 above; 'Proposed Draft Convention on Expediting the Delivery of Emergency Relief'; Inter-American Convention for Facilitating Assistance in Cases of Natural Disaster, 12 June 1991; UN General Assembly Resolution 46/182, 19 December 1991.

59 See generally, Peter Macalister-Smith, *International Humanitarian Assistance: Disaster Relief Actions in International Law and Organization*, Martinus Nijhoff, Dordrecht, 1985, pp. 67–9, 164; John Mackinlay, 'The Role of Military Forces in a Humanitarian Crisis', in Leon Gordenker and Thomas G. Weiss (eds), *Soldiers, Peacekeepers and Disasters*, International Peace Academy/Macmillan, Basingstoke, 1991, p. 19.

60 See, Lt-Cdr Kevin M. Mukri, 'Out of the Ash', *Proceedings*, US Naval Institute, Naval Review 1992, pp. 117–19.

61 Interview by Michael Pugh with advisers, Office of UNHCR, Geneva, 24 May 1993.

62 Simon Tisdall, 'Fleet Sails to Head Off Haiti Exodus', *The Guardian*, 16 January 1993, p. 15. The US Supreme Court upheld the presidential blockade order, but the UNHCR refused to monitor or assist the forcible repatriations on the grounds that they were legally suspect. Interview by Michael Pugh with advisers, UNHCR Office, Geneva, 23 May 1993.

63 See T. P. McClement, 'The Environment, Green Issues and the Military', *The Naval Review*, vol. 80, no. 3, July 1992, pp. 201–8.

64 UN Group of Experts on the Scientific Aspects of Marine Pollution in a 1990 report cited in IMO, *IMO's Global Programme*, p. 2.

65 The USSR lied to international regulatory bodies about its dumping programme which continued contrary to the London Dumping Convention. Administration of the President of the Russian Federation, 'Facts and Problems Related to the Dumping of Radioactive Waste in the Seas Surrounding the Territory of the Russian Federation', trans. by Greenpeace Russia, Moscow, 22 April 1993.

66 William M. Arkin and Joshua Handler, *Naval Accidents. 1945–1988*, Neptune Paper, no. 3, Greenpeace/Institute for Policy Studies, Washington DC, June 1989; Michael C. Pugh, *The ANZUS Crisis, Nuclear Visiting and Deterrence*, Cambridge University Press, Cambridge, 1989, pp. 82–99.

67 Russia has nearly 400 marine reactors. Lack of storage space on land means that 140 cores are still being stored in decommissioned vessels. Administration of the President of the Russian Federation, 'Facts and Problems Related to the Dumping of Radioactive Waste in the Seas

Surrounding the Territory of the Russian Federation', trans. by Greenpeace Russia, Moscow, 22 April 1993.

68 'Transport by Sea of Dangerous, Hazardous and Harmful Cargoes . . . ', *Focus on IMO*, August 1992, p. 1.

69 'IMO – The First Thirty Years', *Focus on IMO*, January 1989, p. 20; 'Preventing Marine Pollution', *Focus on IMO*, September 1989, p. 8.

70 Traffic separation schemes in north-west Europe reduced the number of collisions by two-thirds between 1972 and 1989, 'IMO – The First Thirty Years', *Focus on IMO*, January 1989, p. 5. On salvage see, Michael Grey, 'Salvors Worry over Cover They Can No Longer Provide', *Lloyd's List*, 8 January 1993, p. 3.

6 *Jeremy Ginifer*

Multinational naval force structures

In the period since 1945, systemic factors have largely determined that collective action has been occasional and organised in a piece-meal fashion. The ending of the Cold War, however, presents an opportunity for the international community to examine more coherent structures of force organisation. These are likely to become increasingly relevant as the UN's traditional methods of military organisation feel the strain of an unprecedented number of opera-tions. In June 1992 the UN Secretary-General called for the forma-tion of on-call units to bolster the UN's ability to respond effectively and promptly to security threats.[1] However, the international com-munity has been reluctant to move beyond piecemeal mechanisms towards a radical restructuring.[2] Traditional ad hoc approaches con-tinue to be preferred to on-call or standing force structures. Although more structured approaches to collective force organisa-tion would probably yield significant operational benefits, collective force structures are not likely to be arrived at primarily on the basis of military effectiveness, but according to economic and, in particu-lar, political imperatives. This chapter will evaluate the relative utility of ad hoc, on-call and standing naval forces with reference to these variables. It will also sketch a future organisational basis of naval force structures with particular reference to the UN. First, however, it is necessary to explain the meaning of ad hoc, on-call and standing naval force structures.

Definitions and characteristics

Few attempts have been made to rigorously define ad hoc, on-call and standing arrangements. This is unsurprising. Since the late

1940s the notion of collective standing forces drawn from a global constituency was precluded by superpower rivalry, though as discussed later that rivalry led to the formation of regional on-call and standing forces on both sides of the Cold War divide. Furthermore, arriving at conceptually distinct definitions is problematic given the frequently hybrid nature of force organisation. Nevertheless, there are core characteristics which differentiate the three approaches to force organisation (see Table 6.1).

Ad hoc forces
- An ad hoc force is mobilised with the emergence of a threat rather than in anticipation of it. This implies a low level of preparedness.
- Units remain under national command but once the force is constituted operational control is likely to be vested in a state or a group of states.
- The force is likely to be configured for short-term objectives and will usually be temporary in nature.
- Unless the units have a tradition of co-operation there will be a low level of interoperability: state military and political structures will prevail.

A collective ad hoc arrangement can be defined as one in which multinational forces co-operate or co-ordinate for a specific purpose; in which a significant measure of national control is retained; and in which no substantive form of multinational control, or prior organising principle, has been evolved.

On-call forces
- On-call forces are part of a structure that has some prior organising principle. However, they are not normally permanently assigned to this structure and are likely to be utilised for national purposes for much of the time, except for periodic exercises.
- In providing on-call contingents, governments allow themselves scope for determining the desirability, or otherwise, of participating in collective security actions and retain a measure of control over the direction of their forces.

On-call forces can be defined as national units made available to a supranational authority when required, but over which there are still national claims and usually, by implication, national control.

Table 6.1   *Attributes of multinational naval force structures*

	Ad hoc	On-call	Standing
Interoperability:	Variable and unpredictable, dependent on combinations of states involved.	Relatively high; likely to be prepared for collective action.	High, with training and exercising on a constant basis.
Readiness:	Low, except for national contingencies.	Ready for action relatively quickly.	High, but dependent on location.
Integration of command and control:	Highly variable.	Likely to be high once formed and worked up.	Very high.
National versus multinational commitment:	National commitment has overriding priority.	Usually engaged on national priorities; but earmarked for multinational roles.	Permanently dedicated to multinational tasks.
Costs to states of multinational allocations:	Relatively cheap to divert assets temporarily from national functions; but few long-term division-of-labour savings.	Relatively low if dual functioning maximises use of resources.	Initially high to provide new multinational structures; possible long-term savings.
Duration of commitment:	Temporary.	Permanent on a part-time basis.	Permanent.
Flexibility:	High, can readily undertake unilateral, bilateral and multilateral missions.	National roles potentially constrained by multinational role.	Likely to preclude use for national purposes.
National control:	Complete, except when loss volunteered.	Diminished by commitment to multinational duties at short notice.	Minimal or non-existent for fully developed force.

Standing forces
- A standing force consists of a set of integrated national contingents operating in concert, or contingents which have lost their national identity and have assumed a supranational character.
- Standing forces are centrally controlled by an authoritative international or global organisation which takes primary responsibility for their military and political direction.
- Standing forces are likely to have a high degree of integration and interoperability in terms of tactical and strategic direction, military systems, logistics, communications and procedures.
- Standing forces are in place to act immediately in response to a crisis.

In sum, a standing force can be defined as a multinational force formally constituted and operating under a supranational, rather than a national structure, to counter threats to collective interests, and under which there is a substantial devolution of national control.

Although ad hoc, standing and on-call structures have core characteristics, there can be divergences within each type. For the purposes of analysis, rudimentary and advanced types are identified here. A rudimentary ad hoc force, for example, might involve minimal levels of co-operation and co-ordination, while an advanced ad hoc structure of the sort used during the Persian Gulf crisis of 1990–91 involved sophisticated co-operation, much of it deriving from NATO experience. Similar developmental patterns can be projected for standing forces. A rudimentary standing force might be composed of units made available to an international body on a dedicated basis but over which contributing states retain a strong controlling national interest,[3] while an advanced standing force might comprise national contingents under authoritative supranational command and control that would minimise or bypass national inputs. On-call structures might develop in a comparable way.

Political considerations

For radically new force structures to be realised, involving the devolution of significant aspects of state sovereignty, major political changes would have to occur in the international system. It is not the remit of this chapter to be drawn into the theoretical debate over trends in the international system. Nevertheless, it is reasonable to doubt whether the international system, and state authority within it, has developed to the extent that radical approaches to force organisation are feasible.

Even opponents of state-centrism acknowledge the considerable resistance by states to the devolution of decision-making in security matters, either downwards to social groups or upwards to inter-governmental organisations and the UN.[4] In military security, states still constitute authoritative actors, not least within the decision-making apparatus of the UN. Thus there is likely to be weighty resistance to any move towards standing force structures, which in their advanced form call into question the ability of states to control one of their instruments of power – military force. This was evident in the UK's Defence White Paper of July 1993 which dismissed Dr Boutros-Ghali's proposal for the earmarking of forces for the UN with the argument that each case for UK involvement must be judged on its merits and that 'no government will give the UN an unconditional call on their forces'.[5] If states subscribe to radical restructuring, such as a standing force, it will imply a high level of subordination to the collective will. Once engaged in a standing force, the presumption would be that contributors would fulfil their allotted functions, otherwise the organisation's efficiency would be impaired. Within an advanced standing naval force, contingents might increasingly lose their national identity and develop primary loyalty to the UN rather than to national governments.

The dilemmas which states are likely to encounter when divergence between national and collective policies occur will prove more difficult to resolve in standing forces than within looser structures. Standing forces may become engaged in operations contrary to the interests of member states which have close commercial, cultural or ethnic links with the target of sanctions. In rudimentary structures, contributing states might have the freedom to avoid involvement in operations they regard as undesirable. However, in any advanced structure this power of veto might be eroded or states would be, in effect, politically coerced into participating. Commitment to a standing force might also severely limit the scope for withdrawal from an operation which proved domestically unpopular.

The countervailing argument is that collective solidarity, involving the diminution of national interest, can achieve a holistic level of security greater than that possible through a disparate approach where states often pursue competing interests. Furthermore, the benefits of a supranational collective system would lie in its authority and legitimacy as a body theoretically representative of the international community, a legitimacy frequently absent in ad hoc coalitions.

The difficulty in arriving at a common conception of what constitutes an appropriate mode of collective force organisation resides in the diversity of historical experience, capabilities and expectations inherent in the state system. Ultimately, factors such as a state's degree of assimilation within the international system, its experience of international intervention and its disposable power are likely to determine its preference.

A hegemon, such as the United States, is likely to see considerable advantages in ad hoc or on-call forces where it might exercise a controlling influence. By devolving command and control to a supranational organisation, the United States would yield this hegemony. The United States is not averse to 'chopping' operational control to trusted allies and has occasionally seconded units to peacekeeping operations under the operational or tactical control of a foreign commander. But ceding national command of components is another matter.[6] Although US naval forces have been placed under NATO operational control as a matter of routine, both major NATO commanders to whom they have been assigned are American: SACLANT (Supreme Allied Commander Atlantic) and SACEUR (Supreme Allied Commander Europe). Regional hegemons, such as China and India, are likely to resist standing forces in case they pave the way for external intervention in their spheres of influence. Although attitudes vary within the developing world, there are certainly general concerns that standing forces might promote the development of global policing implemented by powerful developed states. However, 'weak' states confronted by military threats might see considerable benefits in joining a standing force structure in anticipation of gaining protection from fellow contributors.

Nevertheless, in the 1990s, more states, including key UN members, Russia, Germany and Japan have proved willing to contribute forces on a 'structured' ad hoc basis for peacekeeping and humanitarian operations in which a measure of control has been conceded to the UN. This may be in the process of being extended, with states contributing forces that increasingly come under the control of the Security Council or the Secretary-General. This might result in some states incrementally surrendering national control over certain forces as their confidence in the UN increased.

Financial considerations

Assessing the financial implications of the alternative force structures is a complex and speculative task. First, many navies do not make available appropriate financial data, either because it is secret or because a relevant cost breakdown is not readily available.[7] Second, the modes of force organisation frequently involve navies in missions that require differing capabilities and, hence, differing levels of expense. The deployment of a 25-year-old frigate may be satisfactory for certain ad hoc operations, whereas standing structures may require more sophisticated and expensive warships. Third, the extra cost involved in contributing units to advanced standing forces, for example, may be only marginally greater than the costs of a normal fleet programme. Any navy which wishes to be considered fully operational deploys vessels at sea for considerable periods as a matter of routine.

Setting up a standing force structure will involve considerable extra costs if new administrative, C[4]I, and operational capabilities are required, adding to or duplicating existing national capabilities. For less sophisticated navies, also, participation in anything other than the most basic of standing force structures would require upgrading of equipment and capabilities in order to operate effectively, unless they are assigned undemanding roles.

In the longer term a standing force may prove more cost effective than ad hoc arrangements. Once start-up costs have been met and navies are configured to operate within a standing structure, there may be savings through economies of scale and division of tasks. A standing force could be said to provide a 'public good', and navies operating within standing forces may drop certain duties and allow them to be undertaken collectively.[8] Start-up costs of standing forces would be further offset by improved training, increased operational readiness and experience.[9]

Short-term cost perspectives, however, seem likely to prevail given the UN's financial predicament and cuts in the national military budgets of major maritime powers. The creation of a UN standing naval force structure would almost certainly be financially pro-hibitive. As the Secretary-General has commented, albeit with land forces in mind: 'A standing United Nations force would be too expensive, wasteful and inappropriate for the organisation while it is in the process of a vital restructuring exercise aimed at minimising inefficiency and duplication.'[10] High costs would be a short-term problem for even a modest UN standing naval force in which some vessels were donated 'free' by national navies.

One approach to estimating the type of expenditure involved is to examine the costs of an existing national surface patrol force. New Zealand operates the kind of patrol mix that might be similar to a basic UN standing force – comprising four 'Leander' class frigates and four unarmed inshore patrol craft (IPCs). The personnel and operating costs for the four frigates amount to approximately £26m per annum and the four IPCs a further £0.37m per annum.[11] For a UN standing force, additional costs would have to be added: auxil-iary and tanker support, transport of the IPCs to operating areas, costs of base facilities, and special costs associated with training and the development of interoperability. The annual costs of such a patrol force would approach the entire costs (£40m) of monitoring the peace agreement and election in Angola (UNAVEM II) in 1992. To put this in perspective, the total UN peacekeeping budget for 1992 was £875m.[12]

The naval peacekeeping element of the UN Transitional Authority in Cambodia (UNTAC) provides another indicator of possible costs. For the period 15 March 1992 to 31 July 1993 the estimates were: $US2.735m in preparation costs (to repair the Cambodian boats, provide safety equipment, radars and navigation equipment); $US11.083m in fuel at 12 hours per vessel per day for 15 months; $US11.935m in maintenance and component replace-ment; and $US1.320m in rental of landing craft. The total running costs for this localised, and small-scale operation were estimated at just over $US27m (£18m), excluding personnel costs.[13]

It is not clear how costs for a UN standing naval force would be apportioned. In the modest UN naval peacekeeping operation con-ducted by the Argentine Navy in the Gulf of Fonseca, the UN met most of the costs including collision insurance, fuel, daily allowances, the transportation of boats and crew between Ushuaia and the Gulf of Fonseca and the repainting of boats. However, as Juan Neves notes:

the small size of the naval vessels, low number of crew members, and simple technology favoured the feasibility of the operation. In actions that involve larger ships, over longer periods of time, funding may be the most crucial issue to be resolved. In some cases a Member State might be able to afford the financial burden of its own fleet operations dedicated to a UN peace-keeping mission. But this financial self-sufficiency that is available only to a few rich countries, may be seen for other U.N. Member States as affecting the indispensable independence of the mission's operation and jeopardize the U.N. image.[14]

Whether or not more substantive operations would require different arrangements, naval forces are clearly expensive and there will be pressure on the UN to minimise its costs. Thus, global standing forces are likely to prove too expensive in the immediate future unless national governments are prepared pay a significant proportion of the cost. Ad hoc or on-call arrangements, where naval contingency costs are largely borne directly by national governments, are more likely to eventuate.

Operational considerations

A detailed examination of the technical and operational requirements in multinational operations is given in Chapter 9 below, but we note here that if naval forces are to regularly act collectively, the cohesion that a standing force structure imposes is likely to be operationally beneficial. A standing force has considerable operational advantages over ad hoc arrangements if its structure is purposefully designed rather than arrived at through a process of evolution or trial and error. Standing forces should address more effectively three key areas of difficulty in multinational force operations – command and control, crisis response, and interoperability – though as the development of NATO standing forces has demonstrated, considerable difficulties need to be overcome before even basic levels of operational efficiency can be attained.

Command and control
Within standing forces clear command-and-control structures can be developed, in contrast to the untidy duplication or lacunae that can bedevil ad hoc arrangements. An advanced standing naval force

might have circumvented many of the difficulties and delays that were faced in creating a multinational naval force in the Persian Gulf, where initially navies operated with varying degrees of international integration. The approach to command and control adopted during the blockade of Iraq in 1990–91 was to allocate zones to individual navies or groups of navies. Within an advanced standing force structure, it would be theoretically possible to improve upon such arrangements.

Rapid response
The ad hoc approach implies reactive rather than pre-emptive action. It does not necessarily foster the political will and organisational expertise to pre-position crisis response units and establish prior organising principles. A form of standing force or on-call arrangement may be a prerequisite for timely or preventive action. The type of ad hoc mechanisms used in the Gulf and the Adriatic, drawing on a core of US and allied naval expertise, are sometimes capable of rapid response, but are highly dependent on the convergence of political interests. Such convergence may only be briefly sustained. However, on-call forces, as favoured by the Secretary-General, could enhance the UN's 'repertoire of options at a time of crisis'.[15]

Interoperability
Multinational interoperability is difficult to achieve in ad hoc structures without considerable experience of joint operations. In the Persian Gulf it took time for ships from the 'Atlantic' and 'Pacific' theatres to develop interoperability. Although the major navies in the Gulf were able to work together reasonably coherently, there were problems in integrating ships from states with less multinational experience. The problems were starkly revealed when Russian ships participated in continued sanctions enforcement after the war. These vessels had to learn even the most basic operational progressions, such as replenishment at sea from non-national auxiliaries. Interoperability is not necessarily a goal within ad hoc structures, and there will be a reluctance to develop integration in sensitive areas, such as intelligence and surveillance, when co-operation may be regarded as only transient. However, when a navy joins a standing force it is obliged to develop interoperability to demonstrate commitment and permit the proper functioning of the structure.

Multinational force structures in operation

The Middle East
Events in the Gulf beween 1987 and 1991 demonstrate both the difficulties and the potential of ad hoc arrangements. During the
Iran–Iraq War states sought to pursue independent policies which
limited the degree of integration of their forces. For this reason ad
hoc force structures were generally preferred. The Soviet Union
favoured an integrated UN force but this was opposed by the
Western powers.[16] Even the latter were far from united. When the
United States requested help from the Europeans in clearing mines,
the UK Government refused to place RN units under US command
due to concerns over American policy in the region.[17] The UK only
sent minehunters to the Gulf in response to Iranian minelaying in
the south, where the RN's Armilla Patrol operated. Italy showed a
similar reluctance to act collectively – until galvanised by an attack
on an Italian merchantman in early September. Even then this was
essentially a national effort, as was that of France (though France
did warn Iran that its warships would fire on Iranian gunboats
which failed to break off attacks on any neutral merchant ships that
French vessels were trying to assist).[18] It was observed that 'the
Italians seem to operate completely on their own, their domestic
political difficulties having prevented any more definite co-operative
arrangement . . . . The French, always anxious to maintain freedom
of action, remain formally uncommitted to any other European
navy's support despite their possession of the most powerful forces
in the area'.[19]
    The Dutch and Belgians operated together but refused to send
vessels without an informal agreement from the UK to supply cover.
This was later extended to a fully integrated UK–Benelux force. The
WEU also eventually arrived at a degree of 'concertation' between
all the European forces involving tactical and political co-operation
(see Chapter 8), and also operated in informal co-operation with the
Americans. However, national contingents remained under national
command and operational control. There was no WEU commander,
and in no sense were the European forces a WEU flotilla.[20]
    Multinational operations in the Gulf during the Iran–Iraq War
were a low-level ad hoc arrangement. Yet they created a foundation
for further co-operation. Remarking on the coalition Maritime
Interception Force (MIF), following the invasion of Kuwait, the US

Department of Defense reported that the co-operative protection of reflagged ships in the Persian Gulf had 'improved working relationships among the participating nations, particularly between the USA and France, and deepened trust and cooperation between the US and GCC (Gulf Cooperation Council) states. This helped pave the way for the successful Coalition effort during Operations *Desert Shield* and *Desert Storm*.'[21]

Following the Iran–Iraq War, WEU members met to discuss future co-operation. Most member states favoured a reactive approach, refusing to set up special structures or pre-defined consultation procedures. As the WEU's Permanent Council put it: 'It is not WEU's responsibility to announce in advance that member states are prepared to co-ordinate such action. Any national decisions to commit forces should be taken with due regard for the overall political context.'[22] Following the invasion of Kuwait, the MIF was co-ordinated overall by the United States, again on an ad hoc basis.[23] As NAVCENT, the American co-ordinating authority noted, 'each naval force received Maritime Interception Force tasking . . . from its own national command authority'.[24] Monthly co-ordination meetings were held by NAVCENT with representatives from each participating nation. Operating sectors were assigned, with the senior naval officer in each appointed as a co-ordinator.[25]

The Europeans adopted their own co-ordination mechanisms within this overall system. The first meeting of WEU staff chiefs to be held adopted guidelines to facilitate admiralty co-ordination and naval points of contact, mainly for dissemination of information. A naval co-ordination authority was established in Paris in January 1991 to deal with transport to the theatre of operations, including escorting through the Mediterranean and Red Sea, and to draw up logistic requirements. At task force level, commanders met on board ships to reach agreement on patrolling.[26] However, the WEU did not create significant new mechanisms for co-operation and did not take full operational control of the naval contingents. Indeed, some WEU members operated outside the 'WEU' task force structure, for each state decided independently on force deployments and missions.[27]

The sanctions operation was governed by political variables, including the level of domestic political support and dependence on Middle East oil supplies, rather than by compelling operational criteria or commonly held goals. States chose where they operated and the level of rules of engagement their ships could use. Yet an effective operation was carried out: 'By mixing and matching, like a puzzle, everyone could have a role and participate up to the limits of their authority.'[28] The peacetime exercising and co-operation among NATO commanders and units greatly facilitated operations, and even without a formal international command and control structure 'the MIF demonstrated superb international cooperation', with monthly conferences leading to 'enhanced mutual protection and reduced redundancy'.[29]

Operational control (OPCON) was retained by national naval commanders in theatre although (tactical control) TACON of one nation's unit by another was sometimes conceded.[30] Once hostilities began, however, co-ordination was not enough. OPCON, or at least TACON, became a necessity for those forces directly engaged. National sensitivities were, however, reflected in the commitment of units. Even the UK, which generally had the least inhibition about placing forces under US OPCON, specifically retained national operational control over minehunters, giving the United States only tactical control.[31] The UK also insisted on separate logistic arrangements from the common underway replenishment area controlled by the Canadian Naval Force Commander. France eventually placed a frigate under US OPCON but only to escort the combat logistics ships and not to engage in 'offensive operations'.[32] Despite these sensitivities a large multinational naval force was assembled (see Figure 6.1). Ships were deployed according to their operational effectiveness, degree of interoperability and level of national commitment. Belgium, for example, specified that its three vessels could not participate in any action involving direct contact with ships trying to break the embargo.[33] A down-threat escort 'box' was also allocated to the Argentine and French ships. The force was thus a notable example of a 'developed' ad hoc arrangement that managed to achieve some of the operational benefits normally associated with on-call and standing arrangements.

NATO *standing and on-call forces*

The most extensive experience of standing and on-call force structures during peacetime has been within NATO. At sea, earmarking was the rule until the 1960s when extended MATCHMAKER exercises were held in an attempt to improve interoperability. In 1962 the US Secretary of Defense, Robert McNamara, and President Kennedy pressed NATO to establish a Multilateral Force (MLF) of

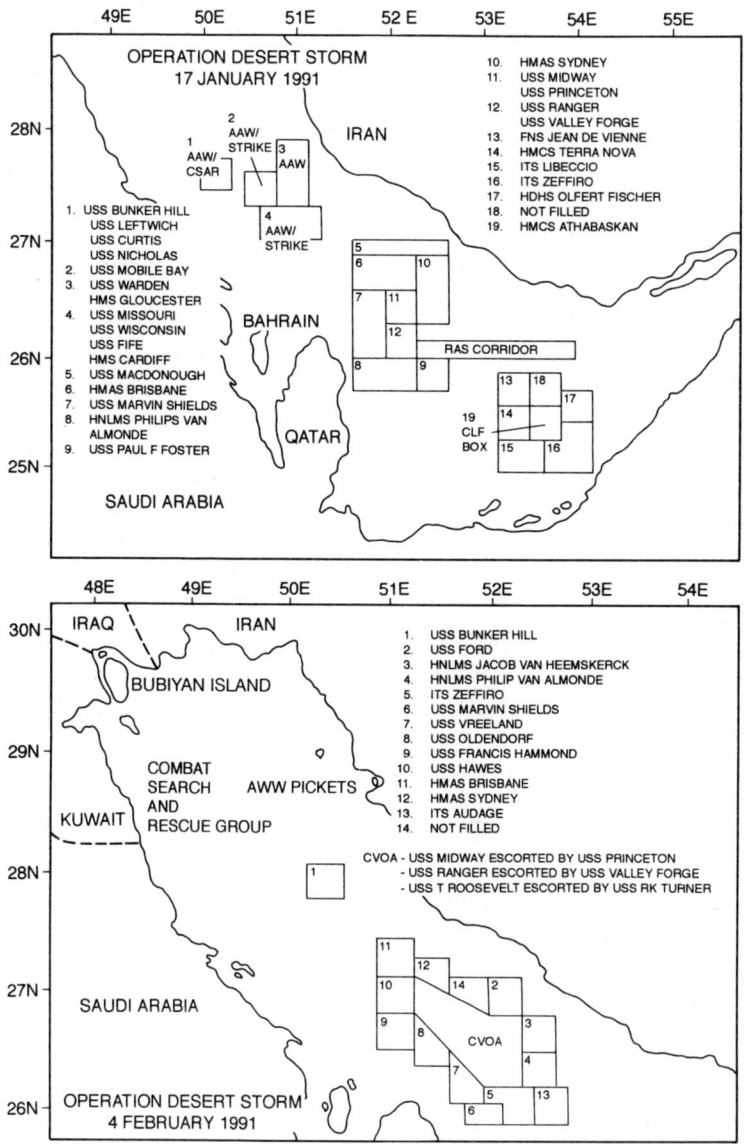

Figure 6.1 *Naval deployments for Operation* Desert Storm

surface ships equipped with Polaris nuclear missiles. In essence the idea reflected US concerns about the development of independent nuclear deterrents and the prospect that Germany would demand nuclear weapons. A special NATO Committee produced a study at the end of 1964, assessing such issues as mission configuration, political control, military operations and finance. The most radical aspect of the MLF was that the ships would have mixed crews. Indeed an experiment in multinational manning was conducted from early 1964 to late 1965 on the USS *Ricketts*. Armed with anti-submarine and anti-missile missiles, but not strategic weapons, the ship was worked up under SACLANT with a crew complement from all NATO states except Belgium. It then visited NATO ports to demonstrate the success of the experiment. The planners concluded that the scheme would be militarily effective and operationally feasible, provided the crews were highly trained. Although the MLF foundered at the political level, and the idea of mixed crews was dropped, the planners carried forward many of the integration principles into the establishment of Standing Naval Force Atlantic (SNFL) in 1967, after Allied vessels had been deployed as combined forces for a number of months.[34]

Typically, SNFL comprised between five and nine frigates and destroyers, providing SACLANT with an initial crisis response force. In order to provide SACEUR with a similar capability (albeit on a less permanent basis) Naval On-call Force in the Mediterranean (NAVOCFORMED) was formed in 1969 and a standing force in the English Channel (STANAVFORCHAN) was formed in 1987.[35] With the increased post-Cold War emphasis on standing multinational forces, NAVOCFORMED was converted in April 1992 into the Standing Naval Force, Mediterranean (SNFM), consisting of eight surface vessels. Both SNFM and SNFL have participated in the embargo operations against former Yugoslav states.[36]

Once formed, the units were intended to fight as an integrated multinational force. Joint exercises were undertaken and doctrine developed, to improve co-operation and readiness. As well as providing NATO commanders with their own rapid response force, the standing forces were able to demonstrate the solidarity of the Alliance in port visits. A high level of integration and cohesion has been achieved within NATO standing forces but the extent to which this can be replicated in new standing global structures is open to question. First, the integration was largely a function of the system of superpower rivalry. Second, NATO is not fully international in the sense envisaged here; it was not designed to act globally or undertake the range of tasks that might be expected of UN forces.

As suggested in Chapters 8 and 9 below, NATO has achieved high levels of interoperability and standardisation in weapon systems, fuel requirements, logistics channels, tactical procedures and communications. Nevertheless, problems remain with navies possessing differing levels of technology, notably in the field of communications. Some NATO navies have been unable to meet their commitments due to budgetary constraints or their inability to function in certain environments, such as rough seas. At times, NATO forces have had to operate according to the lowest common denominator – the capability of the least efficient contributor – and this has been a cause of concern. Training has been undertaken to address this problem and ensure that all units reach a common standard, but in practice it has not always proved possible.[37]

Nevertheless the degree of multinational operational integration demonstrated in the NATO exercises of the late 1980s was of a high level.[38] Indeed, NATO's interoperability proved an asset for naval operations in the Adriatic Sea during 1992–93. According to Rear-Admiral J. J. Blackham, who commanded a Royal Navy task force, co-ordination between national contingents was facilitated because the ships of NATO navies were accustomed to operating in mixed national groups of all shapes and sizes. When one of Blackham's escorts was replaced by a Dutch frigate, it made no difference to his group's effectiveness, and 'all that was needed to convert the disparate national groups into a true multinational force was an appropriate command and control (C²) architecture'.[39]

As NATO is not a supranational authority, the decision-making process places a premium on consensus, sometimes involving protracted discussion.[40] This is hardly conducive to rapid crisis response. To address the problem, NATO developed a flexible range of operational plans, combining national and alliance structures. Grove notes that:

> These contingency plans are very flexible in the scale of forces they generate and how they may be applied. As tension increases and each plan is approved . . . more and more units would be transferred by nations to NATO control so that forces can be positioned to maximise their deterrent effect. SACLANT is helped greatly in

this process by the fact that many of the Allied commanders involved are also national commanders: e.g. Commander Striking Fleet is Commander US Second Fleet, Commander Eastern Atlantic is the Royal Navy's CINCFLEET. These commanders can make anticipatory moves using national authority.[41]

The future relationship between NATO and the UN is uncertain, but it is conceivable that in particular circumstances NATO might undertake subcontracting duties on behalf of the UN. NATO institutions and procedures could provide a model and 'industrial standards' for UN on-call forces or a small standing force which might parallel that of the three NATO standing naval forces. The feasibility of proposals for global standing naval forces and other more radical forms of force organisation are examined next.

The UN and future naval force organisation

Standing forces have been advocated throughout the twentieth century. In the aftermath of the First World War, a proposal for a League of Nations standing naval force was put before the United States Navy,[42] and abortive discussions took place in the UN Military Staff Committee, over the formation of standing forces after the Second World War (see Chapter 7 below). The validity of standing forces has been re-examined after the Cold War and navies are regarded as prime candidates for structural integration.

One of the first modern proposals for a UN Standing Naval Force (UNSNF) was made by a Norwegian organisation. It suggested that national ships be earmarked for a UN squadron on a rotational basis under the control of a UN commander who would be supported by an international staff of experts. Ships would join the UN squadron for three to six months. The annual sailing programme would be approved by the UN Secretary-General.[43]

The idea of an experimental UN naval unit was also aired in the former Soviet Ministry of Foreign Affairs, growing out of a proposal by Eduard Shevardnadze in September 1987 for a UN task force to convoy merchant ships and ensure freedom of navigation in the Persian Gulf. Subsequently, at UN seminars in 1989 and 1990, the Deputy Foreign Minister, Vladimir Petrovsky, argued for an extension of UN activities to maritime operations. In its October 1990 Memorandum to the Security Council on strengthening the UN, the

Soviet Government urged analysis of appropriate contingents provided by the permanent members of the Security Council. The MSC
would be required to plan options and procedures for joint actions
and control the naval forces of any UN members which were put at
the Security Council's disposal. Regional structures might be developed and authorised by the UN to conduct operations. The costs
would be borne by UN members according to their force contributions and ability to pay. Standing Joint Task Forces in each of the
Atlantic and Pacific Oceans, with ships regularly rotated, would
provide the basis for UN responses to regional conflicts. Joint training to co-ordinate fleet operations would be required, and perhaps
a large exercise once every 2–3 years under UN auspices.[44]

Michael Vlahos takes the view that the United States would be a
key component of any UN standing force and has called for the
United States to take the lead in establishing a 'Standing Naval
Force, World'. He proposes that such a navy should move beyond
the alliance concept which defined NATO and should become a
permanent global force divided into Eastern and Western naval divi-
sions. Vlahos stops short of suggesting that the UN should control
this global force in any substantive sense. Instead, he envisages it as
a permanent military coalition, in 'co-operative, voluntary association', with a permanent US naval contingent as its core.[45]

Gwyn Prins has also suggested the creation of a global UN naval
force structure and the development of UN standard operating procedures. This would be augmented by the development of a United
Nations Command Centre which would liaise with the National
Command Centres of those states contributing forces to UNSNF at
times of crisis. UN as well as national pennants would be flown. In
certain high intensity operations Prins envisages the switching of
military command from National Command Authorities to the UN
Command Centre.[46]   If such proposals are to be implemented, two
principal difficulties must be addressed. First, there is the question
of resources – territorial disputes are likely to remain the UN's priority. Second, the rationale for a UN standing force would need to be
elucidated. It can be argued that the political convergence or a perceived monolithic threat that would justify the costs, and the
devolution of sovereignty that a 'purpose-built', developed standing
force structure involves, do not exist. These factors will remain
formidable obstacles to a change in the manner in which UN force
organisation is approached.

More feasible is an incremental approach towards UN naval integration. This might encompass the provision of on-call units to circumvent some of the objections surrounding standing forces. Costs to the UN and contributing states are likely to be minimalised. Existing command structures within the UN can be utilised, albeit with modifications, and national operational control would be only temporarily devolved. Conceivably, a number of developed states might eventually provide on-call naval units for the UN, based on the notion of earmarking which Canada and Scandinavian states have adopted in the peacekeeping context. These states might be prepared to extend the territorial peacekeeping model to naval forces, with the UN exercising tactical control of forces through the Secretariat.

Another approach would be for the UN to authorise NATO to adopt rapid reaction, crisis management roles on a case-by-case basis, perhaps 'attaching' non-NATO naval forces in an attempt to overcome concerns about Western domination. Whether these navies will be capable of integrating is open to question, as is the nature of the relationship between the UN and NATO (see Chapter 8 below). NATO–WEU forces have acted as agents of the UN in enforcing the embargo in the Adriatic Sea. Inevitably, however, the further evolution of such co-operation will depend on wider political developments.

Conclusion

The opportunity exists to create a more structured approach to the organisation of collective forces given the more co-operative relationship among permanent members of the UN Security Council. However, it is not yet clear whether the international community is willing to proceed in this direction. Issues of finance, loss of sovereignty and conflicting political objectives will continue to preclude the integration of national contingents into a global force. The co-operation within the UN Security Council since the late 1980s has encouraged the belief that the interests of key actors are converging and that an effective collective security system can be constituted on this basis. This may be premature. The international community may continue with rudimentary forms of ad hoc collective force action as its primary mechanism to address international security. A developmental approach may lead to the creation of more sophisticated ad hoc arrangements; and perhaps on-call arrangements. But the constitution of mature standing forces, in spite of their theoretical advantages, appears to be a distant prospect. Conflicting priorities and differing historical perspectives are likely to mean that if the international community does move towards integrated collective responses, progress will be incremental and characterised by setbacks.

In the maritime context, the international community is likely to give the development of new naval force structures a low priority because of the low incidence of maritime security threats to international peace and security. As NATO standing naval forces require only a limited financial or organisational input from the UN, there are strong practical arguments in favour of their use, though difficulties of political representation and legitimacy would have to be surmounted.

Notes

1 'An Agenda for Peace: Preventive Diplomacy, Peacemaking and Peace-keeping. Report of the Secretary-General pursuant to the statement adopted by the Summit Meeting of the Security Council on 31 January 1992', doc. A/47/277; S/24111, 17 June 1992.

2 In response to 'An Agenda for Peace', France promised stand-by troops and the United States promised bases and exercise facilities for the UN. But, with the exception of Austria, the Security Council members are believed to have tried to block further discussion. Peter Bardehle, 'Internal Peacekeeping: Concept and Reality in Cambodia and Former Yugoslavia', paper at 34th ISA Convention, Acapulco, 23–27 March 1993; George Bush, address to the United Nations General Assembly, 21 September 1992, USIS official text; Hella Pick, 'UN Peace Force Plan "Ready in Months"', *The Guardian*, 2 October 1992, p. 9.

3 Unit commanders serving under foreign commanders as part of a multinational force are issued with detailed terms of reference which include instructions to communicate immediately with the next higher *national* commander if the unit has been ordered or requested to undertake a task not in keeping with its capabilities or in apparent conflict with national interests. 'Who Commands Whom?', *Peacekeeping & International Relations*, vol. 22, no. 3, March/April 1993, p. 15.

4 See Ken Booth, 'Security in Anarchy: Utopian Realism in Theory and Practice', *International Affairs*, vol. 67, no. 3, July 1991, p. 542.

5 Ministry of Defence, *Statement on Defence Estimates*, HMSO, London, July 1993.

6 The Clinton Administration argued that any US forces sent to Bosnia should be channelled through NATO. James Bone, 'US Rejects Control of Peace Force by Boutros-Ghali', *The Times*, 6 May 1993, p. 12.

7 See Philip Pugh, *The Cost of Seapower: The Influence of Money on Naval Affairs from 1915 to the Present Day*, Conway Maritime Press, London, 1986, for an assessment of financial parameters.

8 See Gavin Kennedy, *Defense Economics*, Duckworth, London, 1983, pp. 23–44.

9 Capt. A. J. Goode, 'Multinational Cooperation in the Atlantic Region', paper at Conference on Multinational Naval Cooperation, Royal Naval College, Greenwich, 12–13 December 1991, p. 3.

10 Boutros Boutros-Ghali, 'UN Peace-keeping in a New Era: A New Chance for Peace', *The World Today*, April 1933, p. 69.

11 Personnel costs comprise pay and allowances. Operational costs are fuel, ammunition and maintenance. Personnel costs make up a high proportion of total costs on the RNZN's elderly 'Leander' class vessels which have crew complements of 230–50. On the other hand, the IPCs have low personnel costs as they are manned by volunteer reserves. Figures for FY 1990–91 and FY 1992–93 were kindly provided by the Naval Staff, Headquarters New Zealand Defence Force, Wellington.

12 Paul A. Volcker *et al.*, *Financing an Effective United Nations: A Report of the Independent Advisory Group on UN Financing*, Ford Foundation, New York, NY, 1993, pp. 2, 15; Simon Duke, 'The UN Finance Crisis: A History and Analysis', *International Relations*, vol. 11, no. 2, August 1992, pp. 127–50.

13 Report of the Secretary-General, 'Financing of the United Nations Advanced Mission in Cambodia, Financing of the United Nations Transitional Authority in Cambodia', UN doc. A/46/903, 7 May 1992. Personnel costs borne by national governments vary per head. In Somalia, New Zealanders in theatre are not classed as being on active service and receive about a fifth of that paid to Australians and far less than that paid to US forces, Jock Vennel, 'Appointment in Somalia', *New Zealand Defence Quarterly*, no. 1, winter 1993, p. 39.

14 Juan Carlos Neves, *United Nations Peace-keeping Operations in the Gulf of Fonseca by Argentine Navy Units*, Report 01–93, Strategy & Campaign Dept., US Naval War College, Newport RI, 12 January 1993, p. 27.

15 Boutros-Ghali, 'UN Peace-keeping in a New Era', p. 69.

16 Eduard Shevardnadze, cited in *The Times*, 24 September 1987, p. 1.

17 Eric Grove, 'From Concertation to Co-ordination: The Western European Union and Naval Operations in the Gulf 1987–91', paper at

Conference on Maritime Interests, Conflict, and the Law of the Sea, Dalhousie University, Halifax, NS, 20–23 June 1991, pp. 1–2.

18 Francis V. Russo, Jr, 'Targeting theory in the law of armed conflict at sea: the merchant vessel as military objective in the tanker war', comments by D. Fleck, in Ige F. Dekker and Harry G. H. Post (eds), *The Gulf War of 1980–1988: The Iran–Iraq War in International Legal Perspective*, T. M. C. Asser Instituut, Martinus Nijhoff, Dordrecht, 1992, p. 197.

19 Grove, 'Birth of a Western European Navy?', *Naval Forces*, vol. 9, no. 1, 1988, p. 13.

20 *Ibid.*

21 Department of Defense, 'Conduct of the Persian Gulf War. Final Report to Congress', Washington DC, April 1992, appendix I, p. 21.

22 Willem van Eekelen, 'Developing the WEU', *International Defense Review – Defense '92*, 1991, p. 36.

23 The WEU reactivated its three-tier co-ordination arrangements used during the 'Tanker war' in the Persian Gulf. However, new guidelines only extended co-operation into areas such as: definition and performance of missions; definition of areas of action; co-ordination of deployments; exchange of information; logistic and operational support. Arnaud Jacomet, 'The Role of the WEU in the Gulf Crisis', in Nicole Gnesotto and John Roper (eds), *Western Europe and the Gulf*, Institute for Security Studies of the WEU, Paris, 1992, pp. 162–7.

24 Department of Defense, 'Conduct of the Persian Gulf War', appendix I, p. 21.

25 *Ibid.*

26 Defence Committee of the Assembly of the Western European Union, *Consequences of the Invasion of Kuwait: Continuing Operations in the Gulf Region*, by De Hoop Scheffer, doc. 1248 addendum, WEU, Paris, 4 December 1990, appendix 1, p. 26.

27 Dov S. Zakheim, 'An Old Alliance Comes to Life', *Proceedings*, US Naval Institute, December 1991, p. 68; Van Eekelen, 'Developing the WEU', p. 36.

28 Eric Schmitt and Michael R. Gordon, 'A Lot of Hurdles on the Way to Winning the War', *The New York Times International*, 26 March 1991.

29 DoD, 'Conduct of the Persian Gulf War', p. 64 and appendix I, p. 15.

30 *Ibid.*, appendix J, p. 16. OPCON is defined as: 'authority delegated to a commander to direct forces assigned so the commander can accomplish specific missions or tasks, usually limited by function, time or location; to deploy units concerned, and to retain or assign tactical control of those units; does not necessarily include administration or logistics'. TACON is defined as: 'detailed and usually local direction and control of movements or maneuvers needed to accomplish missions or tasks assigned'. Glossary, pp. 31–9.

31　This may have reflected concern about the vulnerability of these lightly protected vessels. *Ibid.*, Ch. 7, p. 276.

32　*Ibid.*

33　René Van Beveren, 'Belgium and the Gulf crisis, August 1990–March 1991', in Nicole Gnesotto and John Roper (eds), *Western Europe and the Gulf*, Institute for Security Studies of Western European Union, Paris, 1992, p. 10.

34　The UK and France were hostile to the dilution of their goals for nuclear independence and wary of a German 'finger on the button'. In negotiations on non-nuclear proliferation the USSR vigorously opposed any hint of German involvement in nuclear deployments. J. W. Boulton, 'NATO and the MLF', *Journal of Contemporary History*, vol. 7, nos 3/4, July/October 1972, pp. 275–94.

35　For a history and analysis of NATO standing forces, see: John B. Hattendorf and Stan Weeks, 'NATO's Policeman on the Beat', *Proceedings*, US Naval Institute, September 1988, pp. 66–71; David D. Dunn, 'Naval Collaboration in NATO', *Naval Forces*, vol. 8, no. 5, 1987, pp. 20–3; Robert Stephens Staley II, *The Wave of the Future: The United Nations and Naval Peacekeeping*, International Peace Academy Occasional Paper, Lynne Rienner, Boulder, Col., 1992, pp. 30–2.

36　*Atlantic News*, no. 2414, Brussels, 11 April 1992, p. 1; *Jane's Defence Weekly*, 18 January 1992, p. 90.

37　Interview at the Norwegian Institute for Defence Studies, National Defence College, Oslo, 5 February 1993; Goode, 'Multinational Co-operation in the Atlantic Region'; Hattendorf and Weeks, 'NATO's Policeman on the Beat', p. 71; Geoffrey Till and R. King, 'A Standing Naval Force for Northern Waters', *Naval Forces*, vol. 8, no. 5, 1987, p. 17.

38　See generally Eric Grove with Graham Thompson, *Battle for the Fiords: NATO's Forward Maritime Strategy in Action*, Ian Allan, London, 1991.

39　Rear Admiral J. J. Blackham, 'Maritime Peacekeeping', *RUSI Journal*, August 1993, p. 22.

40　Dunn, 'Naval Collaboration in NATO', pp. 20–33.

41　Grove, *Battle for the Fiords*, p. 20.

42　US Navy, Memorandum for Chief of Naval Operations, 'Proposed Plans for Establishment of League of Nations Army and Navy', 11 November 1919, PD–179–1, Record Group 80, Secretary of the Navy, National Archives, Washington DC, cited in Jeffrey Sands, *Blue Hulls: Multinational Naval Cooperation and the United Nations*, paper for the Center for Naval Analyses, Alexandria, Va., 1992, Appendix, p. A–17.

43　World Association for World Federation, *A Proposal for United Nations Security Forces*, Amsterdam, 1989.

44 See *The Times*, 24 September 1987, p. 1; USSR, 'The United Nations in the Post-confrontation World', UN Doc A/S–15/AC.1/12,16; Vladimir F. Petrovksy, speech at Seminar on Problems of UN Peacekeeping Operations, Salzburg, 4 August 1989, official Austrian text, and address at Seminar on UN Peacekeeping Operations: Experience and Prospects, Moscow, 22 May 1990; Michail E. Kocheev (Soviet Ministry of Foreign Affairs), 'Naval Nuclear Disarmament', in Sverre Lodgaard (ed.), *Naval Arms Control*, PRIO/Sage, Oslo, 1990, pp. 198–205.
45 Michael Vlahos, 'A Global Naval Force? Why Not?', *Proceedings*, US Naval Institute, March 1992, pp. 40–4.
46 Gwyn Prins, 'The United Nations and Peace-keeping in the Post-Cold War World: The Case of Naval Power', *Bulletin of Peace Proposals*, vol. 22, no. 2, June 1991, pp. 135–55.

UN management of naval operations

Although the UN has been increasingly involved in naval operations, there is at present no clear overarching naval management structure for their oversight. This has been evident in the UN naval initiatives in the Persian Gulf, the Adriatic and Cambodia where differing management structures have been the product of expediency rather than a rigorous management logic. This chapter conceptualises the types of naval management arrangements, for strategic and operational military command and control, that are available to the UN and evaluates their effectiveness. It will be argued that the process of creating an effective UN naval management system will be incremental, and that calls for specialised UN naval agencies will not be practical, given political and financial constraints in the UN. Nevertheless, naval operations, rather than being seen as an adjunct form of activity within the UN, should ultimately be conducted within a unified management system linking all three services. In order to achieve this, naval forces will have to be represented in the new UN structures, such as the Situation Centre.

The UN has failed to evolve a coherent organisational structure for naval forces. Two distinct types of naval management structure have emerged: UN-*controlled* operations, such as peacekeeping in Cambodia and UN-*mandated* operations, such as the Persian Gulf enforcement action.[1] We begin by explaining why, historically, this 'dual-track' approach has evolved under which the UN has usually mandated action rather than taking direct control of naval operations.

The history of UN naval management

Following the Dumbarton Oaks Talks in 1944–45, the Military Staff Committee (MSC) was constituted with a remit to undertake the strategic direction of all UN forces. In order to explore this and other issues, a series of discussions took place in the MSC over the period 1946–48. These represented the first detailed attempts to create a viable management structure for UN forces. The discussions also revealed the inherent problems of creating a centrally managed UN force. It is significant that in the text of the UN Charter and in the MSC deliberations navies were to have a central role in maintaining international peace and security.[2]

MSC deliberations, 1946–48

The Permanent Five Members of the Security Council (P5) envisaged that the MSC would be a powerful joint UN military staff, advising and executing Security Council directives. The term 'strategic direction' is not defined in the UN Charter. However the Draft Statute of the Military Staff Committee, approved by the Security Council in February 1946, envisaged the MSC as having roles in:

- advising states on the preparation and training of UN forces;
- formulating the aims and mandate of a mission;
- advising on contributors to UN military missions;
- oversight and advisory functions regarding the conduct of an operation;
- outlining military requirements.

It was expected that forces made available to the Security Council would be part of the contributing nations' normal order of battle and allocated to specific operations as required. The UN would not be creating standing forces. The forces made available would remain under national command, except when operating under the strategic direction of the MSC for Article 42 (enforcement) operations. They would, however, retain their national character as regards discipline and regulations, and their commanders would have direct access to national authorities.[3] The size of contributions would be negotiated as Special Agreements between the Security Council acting on the advice of the Military Staff Committee and the contributing member.

However, even these relatively limited attempts at creating some form of overarching UN management soon ran into difficulties due to diverging national interests. The Soviet Union, for example, was concerned that the Western powers would use the Special Agreements to institutionalise an encircling strategic superiority based on maritime and air power deployed from a network of foreign bases. This was compounded by the inability of the Soviet armed forces to rival the strategic reach available to the Western powers. For their part, the Western powers were unwilling to be denied the use of forces such as aircraft carriers just because they were unavailable to the Soviet Union. Also, they insisted on the right to use bases where they had rights of access.[4] France and China, facing internal problems, were also concerned that they should be allowed to withhold forces for national emergencies, whereas the United Kingdom, the United States and the Soviet Union believed that this would leave too much scope for reneging on promises. The UK and France differed from the other powers in supporting the concept that a Supreme Commander of a UN operation should have functional land, sea and air subordinate commanders, rather than national deputies commanding the whole national contribution. They wanted their officers to play a significant role in the command structure of any UN operation.[5]

Further disagreements broke out in the MSC over the naval force levels that should be made available to the Security Council. The British Chiefs of Staff argued, for example, that the total strength of a UN naval force might comprise: 2 battleships, 4 carriers, 6 cruisers, 24 destroyers, 24 frigates, 24 minesweepers, 12 submarines and assault lift for 2 brigades. This would be intended more for 'demonstration, blockade and bombardment', rather than 'the actual overpowering of aggressor forces'. The United States proposed much bigger forces, giving the impression that it envisaged UN forces fighting a great power war, possibly against a communist aggressor.[6] Although France and China were much closer to the UK view, the Soviet Union firmly opposed any battleships or carriers being assigned because it would not be represented at this level of force, having no carriers and no combat-worthy battleships.[7] By the end of 1947, however, a compromise seemed achievable on a naval force of about 3 battleships, 6 carriers (4 fleet, 2 light), 12 cruisers, 33 destroyers, 64 frigates, 24 minesweepers, 14 submarines and assault lift for 4 brigade groups (16,000 men).[8] As East–West relations deteriorated, however, the MSC became another front in the developing Cold War. There was little prospect of compromise and further MSC meetings became occasions for displays of acrimony. The MSC talks demonstrated that political imperatives precluded the co-operative behaviour required for the activation of the MSC.

The Korean and Persian Gulf Wars

The MSC deliberations, then, represent the only substantive attempt to establish workable parameters for UN-managed naval forces. Subsequently during the Cold War, direct UN management was still not usually politically feasible, though the UN mandated a number of naval operations as we have seen in Chapter 4 above. These rarely engaged a central UN management function. The UN was informed or consulted rather than taking on a directive role itself. In Korea, the United States was invited by the Security Council to designate a commander of the multinational forces. This Commander, General MacArthur, was not responsible to the UN but to the Joint Chiefs of Staff in Washington and through the chain of command to the President. Although the United States considered itself an agent of the UN, it did not consider the UN as an organisation entitled to determine strategic goals or to exert authority over the forces. Indeed, the UN was only sent factual summaries of operations after they had taken place.[9]

Interestingly, the US initially proposed that a UN enforcement committee be set up to control the Korean operations. However, this radical idea was dropped after objections from the UK and the US Joint Chiefs of Staff.[10] In addition, key P5 members, the UK and the United States, also strongly resisted any use of the MSC. Ernest Gross, US Deputy Permanent Representative to the UN, commented:

Quite apart from the fact that the Military Staff Committee was not capable of doing any practical work an impossible situation would arise if the Russians suddenly turned up and demanded to see any plans which the Military Staff Committee had been preparing.[11]

The UK Foreign Office endorsed the views of Gross and also thought the MSC was probably only legally competent when the Security Council conducted its own military operations under Article 42 of the Charter.[12] The command structure eventually adopted for the Korean operation in fact owed much to the concern of the military chiefs in London and Washington to interpose themselves between the UN and the forces fighting under its banner in Korea.[13]

The Persian Gulf operation initiated in 1991 involved greater consultation with the UN, but was still essentially a US-dominated operation. The chain of command passed from field commanders through the force commander, to the US President before involving the UN Secretary-General and the Security Council.

Peacekeeping
Nevertheless, the UN was able to assume direct management of more benign forms of military action, namely peacekeeping. Under the peacekeeping management model the Secretary-General assumed operational command of UN forces, following Security Council Resolutions which laid down the key objectives. This was adopted for naval operations such as the Gulf of Fonseca peacekeeping effort (see Chapter 3). In the Gulf of Fonseca vessels came under the command of an Argentine-appointed Squadron Commander who reported to the UN-appointed chief of the Verification Centre, through the Chief Military Observers of ONUCA, to the Secretary-General and on to the Security Council (Figure 7.1). In essence it was a classic peacekeeping chain of command.

As argued in Chapter 2 above, the nature of peacekeeping has been undergoing a change, and the UN Secretariat has increasingly directed operations that have moved beyond the traditional peace-keeping remit of impartiality, minimal use of force and the consent of conflicting parties. Indeed, in Somalia the Secretary-General found himself heading a Chapter VII operation. Already, from the late 1980s, a re-examination of UN management issues had been undertaken by the Special Committee on Peacekeeping Operations (the Committee of 34).[14] Developments in the 1990s triggered further reappraisals of how the UN might manage its military forces.[15]

Reform of UN-directed operations

It has become increasingly apparent that the old UN management structure is inadequate for the efficient direction of naval operations, other than in relatively benign peacekeeping operations. There is, for example, no central planning or advisory function of any substance attached to either the Secretary-General or the Security Council for the more substantial types of naval operations occurring in the post-Cold War era. Furthermore, responsibility

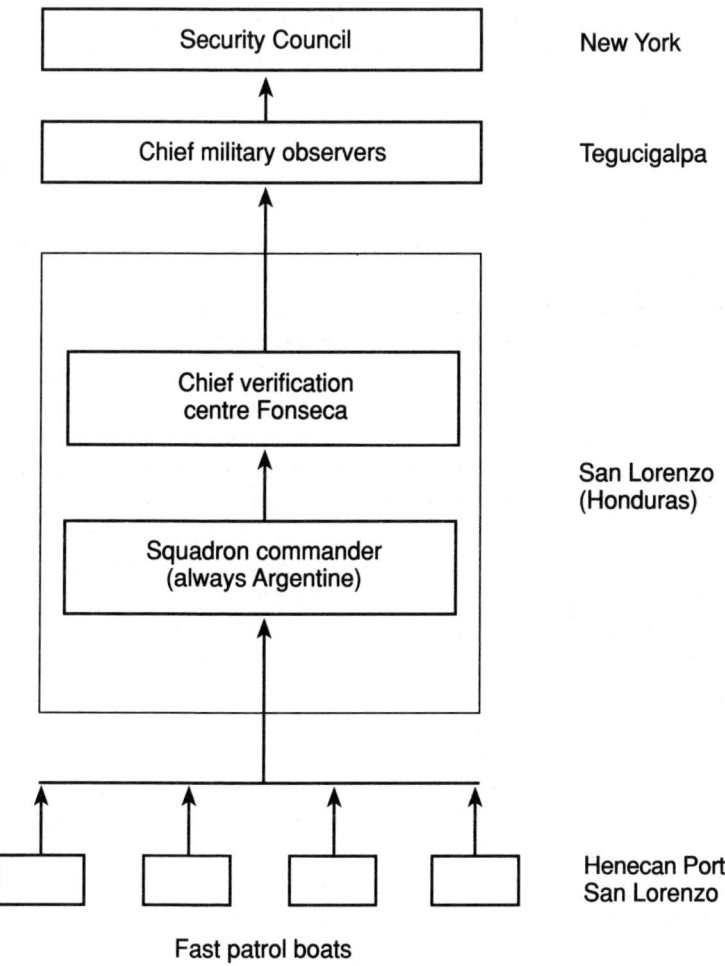

Figure 7.1 *The ONUCA chain of command*

within the Secretariat for the planning of new peacekeeping missions, budget drafting, recruitment and supplies, is fragmented between various groups. Historically, the UN has had only a small operational planning capability, no military chief of staff and no peacekeeping operations centre. The UN's military adviser, responsible to the Secretary-General and also with a link to the Under-Secretary for Peacekeeping Operations, has been assisted by a small military planning staff of five to six personnel. A similar number of officers work in the UN's administrative offices planning transport and logistics.[16] The UN's Field Operations Division, a civilian body, operates with a degree of independence from its military counterparts, a factor which has led to confusion and inefficiencies. Furthermore, the Secretariat management structure makes no specific provision for naval forces because peacekeeping has been primarily land-based.

The Security Council's capacity to manage naval operations is even more limited. There is at present no substantive Security Council organisation to undertake military direction. The Security Council meets to formulate Resolutions and reviews the conduct of UN military operations, but that is the present limit of its involvement. It is clear that reform of UN management is required if the UN is to function effectively and that such reform should include more formal and rigorous arrangements for naval forces.

One of the most apparent shortcomings of the UN management system is the absence of an active body undertaking strategic direction, as defined in the MSC's Draft Statute. Without such a body, UN-directed multinational action is likely to lack purpose. Various suggestions have been made for reactivating the MSC to fulfil this strategic function and a number of some of these have had naval elements. In addition to the Shevardnadze proposal for MSC co-ordination of escorts during the Iran–Iraq War, the Russians suggested in 1990 that the MSC should co-ordinate embargo duties following the invasion of Kuwait. The United States agreed to an MSC review of the military embargo arrangements, which may have been part of the price for securing Russian compliance during the Gulf crisis.[17] Security Council Resolution 665 of 25 August 1990 requested the relevant states concerned to co-ordinate their actions regarding sanctions, using 'as appropriate' mechanisms of the Military Staff Committee.[18] However, the MSC was not involved in the enforcement action which was subsequently authorised by Resolution 678.[19]

France and the Soviet Union also submitted similar proposals to provide the MSC with strategic direction of land forces.[20] In 1987 Soviet President Mikhail Gorbachev urged that the MSC be activated and given the job of co-ordinating UN peacekeeping operations, a proposal reiterated by former Deputy Foreign Minister, Vladimir Petrovsky in October 1989.[21] In January 1992, France

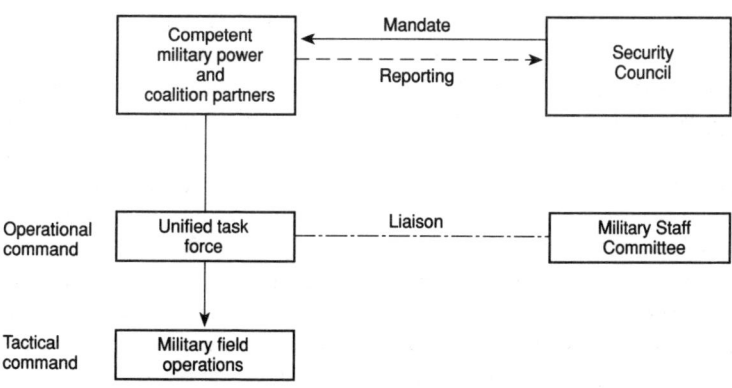

Figure 7.2 *An MSC role in management of coalition operations*

suggested that the MSC be activated – following its offer to make 1,000 troops available to the Security Council at 40 hours' notice for peacekeeping duties.[22] Information in the public domain gives few clues as to the substance of these proposals.

However, a number of theoretical models have been postulated for the MSC adopting a naval role. These have varied from suggestions for relatively minor advisory and planning functions,[23] up to some form of strategic control and command function in consultation with the Security Council. A view of how the MSC might have a limited, partly liaising, function is outlined in Figure 7.2. In a more prominent role it could be supported by a military planning cell (or International Military Support Staff).[24]

In addition, the MSC could play a central directing role within a dedicated UN naval system employing both UN standing and national force contingents. As visualised by Gwyn Prins,

the Military Staff Committee would interpret its responsibilities for strategic direction under Article 47(3) in two ways: First it would inform the Security Council through the Secretary-General of its assessment of the situation; secondly, it would nominate a regional coordinator, most probably a ranking officer from those national flotillas present in the crisis area. The responsibility of the Regional Coordinator would be to ensure that national flotillas were acquainted with and using UNSOPs [United Nations Standard Operating Procedures] for purposes of *liaison and coordination.* This is an important point to stress because the line of command to these national flotillas would remain from their National Command Authorities. The line of political communication from the United Nations to those national authorities would be through requests directed to national authorities by the Security Council, upon information provided to it by the Military Staff Committee and through the agency of the Secretary-General.[25]

Robert Staley goes further than this to suggest that naval forces require a new and powerful United Nations Maritime Agency (UNMA) responsible for overseeing all United Nations maritime concerns. The implications of a UNMA for maritime regime management is discussed in Chapter 11 below. In terms of operation it would supervise education and training, force constitution, rules of engagement, equipment and support, and command, control and communications. It would have a professional maritime leadership under a senior naval or coast guard officer, chosen by the UN Secretary-General and confirmed by the Security Council from among the nominees of member states. The maritime chief would 'leave the service of his or her country for United Nations service . . . the leader's staff could likewise be composed of permanent UNMA personnel'.[26] The UNMA would undertake standing agreements to draw on member states' ships and crews which would report to the UNMA task force or fleet command when necessary. However, Staley argues that 'a United Nations maritime command structure must accompany the institution of a parallel land command structure, and both must come under the control of an overall Peacekeeping Operations office'.[27] Similarly, the World Association for World Federation's proposal for a UN standing force (see Chapter 6 above) visualises the appointment of a UN commander, selected on a rotating basis, who would be assisted by a staff of experts. The sailing programme would be approved by the Secretary-General.[28]

Steps were taken in the early 1990s to improve the responsiveness of UN management. The existing command system for peace-keeping operations within the Secretariat was examined with a view to strengthening it, and the creation of a military structure attached to the Security Council was also considered. However, the prospect of an active Military Staff Committee, controlled by the permanent members (P5) of the Security Council caused alarm in the developing world, even though the idea consistently failed to gain support from P5 members such as the United States and the UK.[29]

Although the adoption of a strategic planning function within the UN remained a theoretical possibility, in April 1993 the UN did establish a 24-hour Situation Centre staffed by seconded national officers to collate information from the field and provide a better link between UN forces and the Security Council and the Secretary-General.[30] There appeared to be no intention for this to acquire any planning, command and control or directive function, or for any naval officers to be seconded to the Centre.[31] Although substantive naval force management restructuring is attractive in theory, there are constraining institutional, political and financial factors, which will make reform problematic in practice. As this book has continually emphasised, regional sensitivities to 'gunboat diplomacy' will be exacerbated by the fact that naval resources are concentrated largely in states with an 'interventionist' past. The principal actor in most UN naval initiatives is likely to be the United States. In the development of any substantive UN management structure there would be fears among some contributing or non-contributing navies that the system would be an instrument of the United States or the Western naval powers and therefore unrepresentative.

Further, some naval forces have a history of institutional autonomy which may not be conducive to the reform process. The US Navy, in particular, has a reputation for independence though this is changing in response to the new strategic context and developments in command and control. This trend is gradually being reflected internationally with navies becoming more integrated into overall force structures. However, naval establishments may remain conservative about reform processes.

At the political level, there is considerable resistance within the Security Council, most notably from the United States, China and the UK, to the MSC taking an active role in the strategic direction of UN forces. The United States in particular appears to fear that giving access to military decision-making to other P5 members would lead to indecision or may even be used to block UN operations. In the developing world there are concerns that the MSC would be a P5-dominated institution reflecting P5 interests rather than those of the UN as a whole. Article 47(2) allows for any non-P5 UN member to be associated with the MSC when 'the efficient discharge of the Committee's responsibilities requires the participation of that Member in its work'. However, according to Section IV of the Draft Statute of the MSC these will not be regarded as MSC members. The MSC was clearly constituted in a manner intended to minimise non-P5 input.[32] There are also conceptual differences over what constitutes 'strategic direction' and whether in fact this is the proper role for the MSC.

The uncertainty surrounding future UN management structures extends to the issue of which UN authority should be vested with the power to direct naval operations. There are growing ambiguities as to the respective roles of the Secretary-General and the Security Council in the new types of UN peace support operations. Under the traditional territorial peacekeeping model, the Secretary-General assumes operational command, including the organisation, conduct and direction of forces. Although in Somalia (UNOSOM II) the Secretary-General has assumed a directive role, despite the fact that it is a Chapter VII operation, it is not yet clear whether this will be the case in future Chapter VII operations. Delineation of roles is further complicated by the reform process noted above. What will be the nature of the relationship between the Secretary-General and the MSC in a more interventionist UN? What access will the Secretary-General have to a strategic planning body if it is set up? How can these and other management tensions be alleviated within the UN-management system? These management issues are further complicated by the involvement of regional organisations, such as NATO and the WEU, in certain UN operations. Already, there has been considerable friction between NATO and the UN over the conduct of operations in Bosnia. In these circumstances, a coherent naval management structure is problematic.

Reform of UN-mandated operations

As well as undertaking internal reform the UN also needs to address its capacity to devolve management to external organisations or international coalitions.[33] The problematic nature of UN and NATO force co-ordination in Bosnia has demonstrated the inherent difficulties of UN regional authorisation, particularly when the UN retains an operational interest.

Bosnia has been a particularly difficult case as NATO forces form a subset within an overall UN force contingent. The UN has yet to determine a coherent basis for 'allied' forces to operate in such circumstances. Although, as argued in Chapter 8 below, there are constraints on regional co-operation at sea, the UN has sometimes mandated regional organisations to proceed with peace and security initiatives and left operational conduct to those organisations. This was the case in the UN-mandated Economic Community of West African States (ECOWAS) operation in Liberia, for example. Similar 'hands off' arrangements have also prevailed in the WEU–NATO naval operations in the Adriatic. In the past, the fact that UN involvement has been circumscribed has not been of great importance.[34] However, regional security, particularly in former Yugoslavia, has assumed a new importance. In the case of the NATO retaliatory strikes in Bosnia, the Secretary-General made it clear that his position of operational authority over peacekeeping efforts in former Yugoslavia, gave him the right to determine whether NATO air strikes could go ahead. There are likely to be continued difficulties where two effectively distinct force and command structures are involved in a common UN operation.

In the Adriatic two regional organisations developed a reasonably effective system for co-ordinating embargo duties, but the UN's input into the process has been limited. The two distinct naval operations initially set up – *Maritime Guard* and *Sharp Fence* – and conducted independently by NATO and the WEU have been merged into operation *Sharp Guard* with a joint command and common rules of engagement.[35] It seems probable that in the future the UN will want to have a greater input into these types of operations.

UN-mandated coalition operations have proved contentious. Management problems have arisen at a national level between the various force contingents, but more significantly they have been apparent between the UN and the coalition leader. In the two coalition enforcement operations in Korea and the Persian Gulf the UN devolved operational responsibility to a US command. In both Korea and the Persian Gulf, there were concerns within the Security Council and the Secretariat over lack of consultation and divergence from mandates. As former Secretary-General Javier Pérez de Cuéllar commented with regard to the Persian Gulf operation:

> What we know about the war, which I prefer to call hostilities, is what we hear from the three members of the Security Council which are involved . . . which every two or three days report to the Council after the actions have taken place. The Council, which has authorised all this . . . [is informed] only after the military activities have taken place.[36]

Similar reservations were expressed about Korea:

> Concern was expressed in both the British Parliament and Cabinet that General MacArthur and possibly the US government, or elements within it, were pursuing objectives not shared by other contributing countries or endorsed by the UN. Existing machinery did not allow the UN to have any say in the instructions issued to General MacArthur.[37]

Even though UN-mandated coalitions have operational advantages, where the contributing states have already developed norms of co-ordination, there are likely to be calls for the UN to adopt a more active or 'directive' role.[38]

A new UN naval management structure

The creation of a dedicated naval agency and similar radical management schemes is unlikely to be realised for reasons that have already been outlined. Naval management reform will take place within the wider context of UN reform which has tended to be incremental and limited in its scope. Rather than pursue radical agendas, the central challenge for navies and proponents of naval power may be to articulate the need for greater representation in the overall UN management structure. At the time of writing, the naval 'point-of-view' has virtually no bearing on UN decision-making and management. The apparent lack of any naval representation in the UN Situation Centre, even though it is only an informational body at present, and the absence of plans to introduce any, is indicative of the sidelining of naval forces. There is a strong case for integrating naval forces into a unified, three-service, UN management system to oversee peace support operations. Such a system would be able to act more cohesively in the increasing number of UN operations that required a mix of naval, land- and air-based capabilities.

There should, then, be naval representation in any new or evolved management structures that are created within the UN, including the UN's new intelligence system – the Joint Deployable Information Support System – and also a possible Peace Operations Department which the United States has advocated. There will be UN operations which will not initially require a naval response, but this should not preclude naval involvement in the management process. It is frequently overlooked that naval or maritime forces often support UN territorial operations through the supply of material and provide a means of evacuation should ground operations prove problematic.

Naval operations should not be regarded as adjunct activities that are contracted out of the UN, to regional organisations, or merely undertaken on an ad hoc basis for the political and operational reasons eluded to above. Naval forces are part of a mix of instruments that are required to regulate international peace and security. Just as it is recognised that aircraft have a distinct function in UN operations, such as patrolling 'no fly' zones in Iraq, so naval forces should receive recognition for the specialised UN tasks they are undertaking, such as embargo duties in the Adriatic.

Reform of the present structure of NATO-type 'subcontraction' is urgently required. In the absence of UN naval expertise it is tempting to devolve operational direction to the 'subcontractor' and restrict UN involvement to the framing of Security Council Resolutions and general oversight. There may sometimes be political advantages in this approach but it is unlikely to prove satisfactory as a general principle. As has been shown on the ground in Bosnia, tactical and operational objectives can diverge with detrimental consequences for the effectiveness of the mission. Further, the exclusive West European and North American representation in NATO forces is unsatisfactory in the UN context. This could be addressed by some form of NATO 'associate' membership being extended to some navies or greater co-ordination between NATO and non-NATO navies, but this process has considerable operational, and for that matter political, difficulties. Establishing a formal institutional relationship between the UN and NATO, giving the UN greater participation in the decision-making process, might be highly desirable. But achieving it may be problematic. Intermeshing UN and NATO management structures would open up problems of hierarchy and organisational competition, and is thus likely to be unproductive. One approach might be to place the strategic direction of NATO forces undertaking UN operations in the hands of the Security Council with operational control vested in NATO. This would consolidate the authority of the UN while allowing NATO to exercise its operational expertise. This relationship could be institutionalised by setting up co-ordinating mechanisms and procedures between the two institutions. Whether it could be implemented effectively given different levels of military competence in the two bodies is open to question. Further, it is uncertain whether Russia and China would be in favour of NATO assuming a formal operational stake in UN operations. The difficult issue of where a strategic function should be situated within the UN would also have to be addressed.

However, nothing in the discussion so far precludes non-UN maritime–naval operations. The UN is not a monolithic organisation capable of controlling all global security activities. Even if UN management is reformed, there will be circumstances where the UN is unable to act cohesively or where it may judge that a state or a coalition of states is in a position to act more effectively. In these circumstances, the UN will provide a mandate and forgo a management input. There will be cases where powerful states choose to undertake independent naval action and there will be little that the UN can do about it. Nevertheless, the UN should seek to establish procedures and norms which ensure that its input into UN-mandated coalition operations is increased. This will not necessarily take the form of strategic or operational direction, but perhaps a greater input at the political level. The UN might be regularly consulted as to how coalition operations are progressing, rather than merely being informed after events have occurred.

Conclusion

This chapter has stressed the lack of consideration that has been given to the question of naval management within the UN. There have been good reasons for this. Territorial operations have historically taken precedence because most conflicts have originated on land. Further, the specialised nature of maritime–naval forces and the concentration of sophisticated capabilities in a limited number of states has encouraged the UN to contract out naval activities. However, the more fluid strategic environment since the Cold War allows an increased prominence for naval forces with their access and support potential, a prospect that has been recognised by the US Navy with its new concept of littoral operations.[39]

If the UN is to authorise maritime deployments more frequently it will no longer be able to ignore the naval management issue. Rather than view naval operations as something that can be 'tacked on' to land operations, it should apportion them equal substance in its emerging management structure. This means that naval officers should serve in the Situation Centre as a matter of policy and if a Peace Operations Centre is set up, there should be naval representation. In the case of the latter, there is a strong argument for a naval cell to co-ordinate naval operations. In addition, the naval institutional arrangements between the UN and regional subcontractors need to be formalised with the UN adopting a strategic management role.

It may be time, then, to dispense with the old dichotomy of UN-mandated and UN-directed operations under which the UN took formal responsibility for naval peacekeeping but effectively devolved all other forms of naval operations to coalitions or regional organisations. The UN should take a firm hand on the tiller and assume an overarching responsibility for naval operations.

Notes

1 Sands suggests four management types: UN authorisation; UN designation; UN direction; and standing naval forces. Jeffrey I. Sands, *Blue Hulls: Multinational Naval Cooperation and the United Nations*, CRM 93–40, Center for Naval Analyses, Arlington, Va., July 1993, pp. 27–9.

2 Indeed naval forces, in conjunction with air forces, were envisaged as the most applicable instruments for this purpose. The British Chiefs of Staff, for example, concluded that 'the main elements of the United Nations force will . . . be the air and naval forces', Cabinet Defence Committee, CAB 131/4, 'Overall Strength and Composition of the United Nations Armed Forces', DO (47) 51, p. 3, paras 15–17, Public Record Office, Kew.

3 *Report of the Military Staff Committee on General Principles Governing the Organization of the Armed Forces Made Available to the Security Council by Member Nations of the United Nations: Report by the Chiefs of Staff*, MS/264, Articles 3, 4, 36–40, in DO (47) 46, CAB 131/4, PRO.

4 The divergent views are set out in MS/264, *ibid.*, Annex A.

5 *Ibid.*

6 United Nations, *Yearbook of the United Nations, 1947–48*, Department of Public Information, New York, 1949, p. 495.

7 'Overall Strength of the United Nations Armed Forces, Report by the Joint Planning (JP) Staff', JP (47) 159, Annex, 23 December 1947, DEF 6/5, PRO.

8 *Ibid.*, p. 6, para. 19.
9 Oscar Schachter, 'Authorized Uses of Force by the United Nations and Regional Organizations', in Lori Fisler Damrosch and David J. Scheffer (eds), *Law and Force in the New International Order*, Westview Press, Boulder, Col., 1991, pp. 72–3. See also David Cox, 'Enforcement, Deterrence, and the Role of the United Nations: Introduction and Summary', in Cox (ed.), *The Use of Force by the Security Council for Enforcement and Deterrent Purposes: A Conference Report*, The Canadian Centre for Arms Control and Disarmament, Ottawa, 1990, p. 3.
10 Richard Bevins, 'Command and Co-ordination of UN Forces in Korea', in, *Korea*, FCO Historical Branch: Occasional Papers, no. 5, Foreign and Commonwealth Office, London, April 1992, p. 37.
11 *Documents on British Foreign Policy*, series II, vol. IV, no. 10, note 7: Gross to Jebb, 28 June 1950, cited in FCO, *ibid.*
12 *Ibid.*, p. 37.
13 *Ibid.*
14 The Special Committee on Peacekeeping Operations was commissioned to produce inventories of requirements and potential contributions, to assess the financing of operations, and to examine the reorganisation of services and operational procedures. However, it resisted the formulation of a coherent body of operational principles and directives on the grounds that each operation was different and would lose flexibility, UN doc. A47/253, 4 June 1992, para. 33. For a discussion of the Special Committee's work, see Serge Lalande, 'L'Assemblée générale et les forces de maintien de la paix: le rôle du Comité des 34', *Le Trimestre du monde*, 4e, 1992, pp. 117–19.
15 Major-General Indar Jit Rikhye (ret.), *Strengthening UN Peacekeeping. New Challenges and Proposals*, United States Institute of Peace, Washington DC, May 1992; Brian Urquhart, 'The United Nations in 1992: Problems and Opportunities', *International Affairs*, vol. 68, no. 2, April 1992, pp. 311–19.
16 William J. Durch, *The United Nations and Collective Security in the 21st Century*, Strategic Studies Institute, US Army War College, Carlisle Barracks, PA, February 1993, pp. 16–17.
17 Paul Lewis, 'France's UN Plan at Odds with US', *The New York Times*, 2 February 1992.
18 Benjamin Rivlin, *The Rediscovery of the UN Military Staff Committee*, Occasional Paper, no. 4, The Ralph Bunche Institute on the United Nations, City University of New York, New York, May 1991, p. 2.
19 *Ibid.*
20 Foreign and Commonwealth Office document on the MSC, RADN 18/92, DD 1992/255, London, September 1992, p. 10.

21 Frank J. Prial, 'Crisis Breathes Life Into a Moribund UN Panel', *The New York Times*, 6 September 1990.

22 Lewis, 'France's UN Plan at Odds with US', n. 17 above.

23 Rivlin, for example, suggests that 'a more limited advisory role than originally envisaged in the Charter may . . . be feasible', in 'Regional Arrangements and the UN System for Collective Security and Conflict Resolution: A New Road Ahead?', *International Relations*, vol. 11, no. 2, August 1992, pp. 103–4.

24 United Nations Association (UK), 'Memorandum on an Agenda for Peace', for the House of Commons Select Committee on Foreign Affairs, Session 1992–93, 12 November 1992, p. 36.

25 Gwyn Prins, 'The United Nations and Peace-Keeping in the Post-Cold War World: The Case of Naval Power', *Bulletin of Peace Proposals*, vol. 22, no. 2, June 1991, p. 146.

26 Robert Stephens Staley II, *The Wave of the Future: The United Nations and Naval Peacekeeping*, International Peace Academy occasional paper, Lynne Rienner, Boulder, Col., 1992, pp. 43–4.

27 *Ibid.*, p. 44.

28 World Association for World Federation, *A Proposal for United Nations Security Forces (UNSF)*, Amsterdam, 1989, p. 8.

29 *The Guardian*, 2 October 1992, p. 9.

30 Larry J. Bockman, Barry L. Coombs and Andrew W. Forsyth, 'The Employment of Maritime Forces in Support of United Nations Resolutions', Research Report 6–93, Naval War College, Strategy and Campaign Department, 11 August 1993, p. 59.

31 Interview by Jeremy Ginifer with Barry Coombs, US Naval War College, 22 August 1993.

32 Jim Whitman and Cdr Ian Bartholomew, *The Chapter VII Committee – A Policy Proposal: Military Means for Political Ends: Effective Control of UN Military Enforcement*, Global Security Programme, University of Cambridge, August 1993, pp. 21–3.

33 For a description of the role of regional organisations in collective security see R. M. Connaughton, *Peacekeeping and Military Intervention*, Occasional Paper, no. 3, Strategic and Combat Studies Institute, Staff College, Camberley, HMSO, London, 1992, pp. 20–2.

34 See Rivlin, 'Regional Arrangements and the UN System', pp. 103–4.

35 Assembly of Western European Union, 39th Ordinary Session (First Part), 'WEU initiatives on the Danube and in the Adriatic – Reply to the Thirty-eighth Annual Report of the Council', report by Mr Marten and Sir Keith Speed, doc. 1367 (revised), 15 June 1993, pp. 23–4.

36 *Ibid.*, p. 19.

37 Bevins, 'Command and Co-ordination of UN Forces in Korea', n. 10 above, p. 38.

38 Sands outlines the advantages of these types of arrangements, see n. 1 above, pp. 39–40.
39 'From the Sea: Preparing the Naval Service for the 21st Century', US Navy and Marine Corps White Paper, Department of the Navy, Washington DC, September 1992.

Regional co-operation at sea

From the discussion of management issues in the previous chapter, it is apparent that one of the options open to the international community is to organise naval peacekeeping and enforcement on a regional basis. Indeed, given an increase in the number of internal and minor conflicts since 1989, it seems reasonable to expect regional organisations to be more active in peacekeeping and related activities.[1] It might also be thought that given the UN's lack of resources, the delegation of naval operations to a competent regional organisation would be a rational enough policy. However, as Benjamin Rivlin has pointed out, there are problems in defining a region and finding agencies which are truly representative of all regional interests.[2] In practice, external involvement may be more acceptable in regional disputes than dominance by one or more regional powers. Nor are most regional groupings sufficiently coherent or institutionally strong enough to deal with military security issues. Nevertheless, the principle of decentralisation should be explored and this chapter examines the possibilities as well as the problems of the regional approach to naval operations. It argues that naval–maritime co-operation in many regions will be at functional levels rather than in the management and resolution of conflicts.

Regionalism and globalism

There has been a long-standing controversy over the respective merits of regionalism or globalism as the more suitable means to promote international peace and security. The lively debate which occurred at Dumbarton Oaks in 1944 over the structure of post-war international organisation even saw Winston Churchill, contrary to Foreign Office advice, arguing for regional structures, including a federated Council of Europe, as a half-way house between nationalism and universalism.[3] Although Churchill lost the argument, and lost interest in European federalism, concessions to the regional idea were incorporated into the UN Charter. Chapter VIII states that nothing precludes regional arrangements from dealing with peace and security, provided that they are consistent with the purposes and principles of the UN. Regional organisations are encouraged to make the initial steps to resolve disputes and the Security Council can use regional institutions, if necessary, for enforcement actions. However, the UN has ultimate responsibility for peace and security, and no enforcement action is permitted without Security Council authorisation except for collective self-defence under Article 51 of the Charter (or, in an anachronistic provision, against the former enemies in the Second World War). In other words, the UN can lend its weight and support to regional initiatives and delegate implementation of mandates, but regional institutions cannot assert jurisdiction which weakens the UN.[4]

The possible harnessing of regional security arrangements for UN peacekeeping was studied on several occasions during the Cold War, but interest increased with the ending of the Cold War. The UN General Assembly proposed studies on UN co-operation with regional agencies, and Dr Boutros Boutros-Ghali, himself a scholarly expert of regionalism, devoted a section of his 1992 report, 'An Agenda for Peace', to the regional concept.[5] Formal arrangements were not essential according to the Secretary-General but the potential for decentralisation, delegation and co-operation should be utilised in order to parcel out tasks and lessen the burden on the UN. In April 1993 he wrote to 52 organisations requesting them to study means of strengthening their regional peace support measures and improving links with the UN. In part a new approach seemed feasible because regional organisations which were geared to the purposes of Cold War confrontation, in Europe particularly, had lost their old roles and were open to suggestions for new ones.

In practice, the UN has regularly consulted regional interests and organisations. The Organisation of African Unity, the League of Arab States and the Organisation of the Islamic Conference, were consulted over Somalia, for example. Furthermore, the European

Community, NATO and WEU have undertaken various diplomatic and military–naval roles, approved by the UN, in response to the conflict in the former Yugoslavia, including plans for a force of 50,000 NATO peacekeepers to underpin an agreement for Bosnia, which, however, was turned down by Bosnian-Muslim leaders in September 1993.[6] Ad hoc arrangements have sometimes proved more serviceable than existing structures. A complex and fluid grouping, rather than the Organisation of American States, was involved in the negotiations which led to the establishment of ONUCA in Nicaragua, and for the dispute in El Salvador an improvised group of 'Friends of the Secretary-General' was assembled.

In both theory and practice, then, regional arrangements for the kinds of naval operations considered in this study seem both a legitimate and appropriate response to disputes affecting international peace and security. Yet the regional concept is difficult to apply, especially, it would appear, in maritime contexts.

Regions and navies

To begin with, the general notions of 'regions' and 'regionalism' lack precision. Particular regions may have imprecise boundaries, shifting memberships and feature any one, or a combination of, indices (such as cultural homogeneity, economic links, common political orientations and geographical properties). Although emphasis is usually placed on clusters of resemblance and the notion of congruent interests,[7] some regions, such as the Middle East, could be defined as much by disharmony as by harmony. Nor is it a simple matter to define regions where the sea is a focus. Although, for example, the Baltic Sea might be relatively easily characterised as the focus of a sub-region of Europe, the Mediterranean basin cannot be so easily defined. It is a European sub-region in the sense that conflicts affecting the Adriatic and Aegean areas are of direct concern to Europe as a whole. But the Mediterranean might also act as a potentially dangerous security frontier between contrasting world views – the Arabic and European, and between South and North. The Pacific Ocean, by contrast, does not so much demarcate a region as permit links between diverse states and regions.

Even where regions are clearly identifiable, structured naval co-operation may be absent and difficult to achieve. One reason is that for many developing states, the priorities are national coastal constabulary work and the protection of EEZs. Another is that regional foci are perhaps less significant for the major naval–maritime powers and authorities than for continental powers and land-oriented defence establishments. This is not to deny that naval cultures have been influenced by concepts of territorial and regional defence, especially in states where a land-based strategic culture has predominated. A zonal philosophy dominated Soviet naval thinking about contingencies for major war and led to an emphasis on maritime 'sanctuaries' and defence perimeters.[8] Nevertheless, for the major maritime powers (the United States, UK, France, Japan and Russia), the use of the sea entails crossing zones, securing sea-lanes or projecting power – as if in defiance of regional theorising. In their ability to roam the high seas and provide a powerful diplomatic presence, ships are ideal instruments for challenging regional claims at a much lower level of risk than would be the case with troops massed on a frontier.

In order to strengthen, rather than weaken, international responses to disputes, regional naval arrangements would have to offer political and operational as well as financial advantages.

In terms of political legitimacy, regional arrangements have the potential to be more representative, and therefore more accountable than can be claimed, say, for the UN Security Council. At regional levels, too, the normative understandings between naval powers may be organic and more durable. But this legitimacy might be challenged by two further considerations.

First, is there a solid political basis for the development of common security interests? In areas where political groups within states seek absolute gains there will be little serious negotiation between them. Where states are relatively weak and competition for influence strong, states may also be fearful of implementing any political accords reached without an impartial extra-regional involvement that would temper any concerns about the ambitions of regional powers.

Second, to what goal is the regional arrangement directed? Is it to regulate the activities of states within the region or to organise states to meet a perceived threat from outside? For Third World regional groups, the domestic and intra-state threats are likely to be more significant than external threats, and regional organisations may not want to address these problems through military co-operation.[9] By contrast, if a regional arrangement has reached the stage of establishing a 'security community', in which armed conflict between the members is remote, then the integration of national military capabilities is facilitated and reinforced. Mechanisms may be needed to contain hostile relations between members, as in the case of Greece and Turkey in NATO. But in general a regional security community will not have to police itself. Therefore it is only likely to prove useful against non-members within the region, as in the case of NATO and WEU naval forces in the Adriatic Sea, or extra-regionally. Indeed a security community such as NATO may only become operationally effective when there are common perceptions of an overwhelming external threat. In this respect, defence alliances against specific threats are more cohesive than collective security systems without a predetermined adversary.[10] If the *raison d'être* of the regional structure is to meet external problems, then the regionalisation of security could foster hostility between regions and undermine international peace and security. However, it is also true that for many states, naval power has not been overwhelmingly dependent for its development on specific, manifest threats. In addition to the protection of coasts against invasion, the major naval powers also protected commerce and sustained colonial development against diffuse threats. The Cold War era may have been an aberration in narrowing the outlooks of some naval establishments.

In terms of operational effectiveness, regional naval arrangements would address several problems which the UN cannot do, given its overstretched condition and the absence of a naval command system. The case for delegation has been forcefully made in the light of the experience of UN-authorised operations by NATO and WEU ships in the Adriatic Sea.[11] The argument is that the key to implementing Security Council, or other international, mandates must be at regional level because that is where a coincidence of security interests and capabilities is to be found. It would have the advantages of coherent, rehearsed command and control, concepts of mutual support, operational procedures and guidelines, compatible training and relatively unrestricted access to base facilities.

In brief, the argument for implementation of global decisions at regional level assumes that regional entities have a unity of political purpose as well as appropriate naval capabilities which could be harnessed for multilateral operations. NATO's achievements in developing standing naval forces have already been recognised in this study, and the operational and technical standards which NATO could propagate internationally are discussed in the next chapter. But it is a moot point whether the North Atlantic–Western Europe experience of naval integration should be considered as a model for developing regional competence or an exception. It is hardly possible to do justice, here, to the maritime concerns and potential for security co-operation in all regions of the world, but a brief survey indicates that Europe has a range of multinational security structures, arguably too many. Elsewhere, however, regional arrangements are institutionally weak and multinational naval co-operation is comparatively rudimentary.

Cross-currents in Europe

Arguments for the regional approach gain strongest support from the co-operative actions by European navies, especially since their protection of shipping in the Persian Gulf in 1987. In political terms, however, Europe's ability to provide a coherent regional response to crises has been affected by the disorderly and competitive evolution of security frameworks, leading at times to an 'acrimony of acronyms'! Naval forces have not been immune from this bruising process, but the flexibility with which naval units can be deployed has meant that co-operation at service level has occurred in spite of the political incoherence which weakens Europe's ability to act on behalf of the UN.

The Western European Union (WEU) emerged as a significant maritime actor in the late 1980s – partly because Article VIII(3) of the modified Brussels Treaty extends the WEU's security interests beyond Europe, whereas NATO has no remit to operate 'out-of-area'. For example, France, Spain (which are not formally integrated in NATO's military structure), Germany and Italy insisted that NATO was not a competent authority to deal with Iraq's invasion of Kuwait. It was also argued that a WEU presence might be more acceptable to states in the developing world than a NATO operation which would have overtones of US hegemony.[12] But the WEU has no permanently assigned forces, has no right to call upon US assets and no more represents the whole of Europe than does NATO.

European naval units were co-ordinated by the WEU in the

'Tanker War' of 1987–88. It was referred to as 'concertation' by WEU officials – mutually planned operations at ministerial, admiralty and task-force levels. But, as indicated in Chapter 6 above, units remained subject to national policies, command and control and ROE, and the operations relied on NATO doctrine, procedures and logistic support. European naval contributions were also successfully integrated for the Coalition War against Iraq, in spite of differing foreign policy and domestic preoccupations. Indeed the untidy Coalition structure suited European states politically. Spain's decision to undertake escort missions was legitimised by the European context; so was Italy's first combat mission since the Second World War. Both states were concerned to distance their participation from US policy in order to safeguard relations with the Maghreb.[13] Germany's involvement outside the immediate war zone and its post-war mineclearing, generated a domestic debate about amending the Basic Law to allow German participation in actions within the framework of the UN Charter. In June 1993 the Supreme Court ruled that the Bundeswehr could participate in peacekeeping with the approval of the Bundestag (which agreed to send personnel to Somalia).[14] The Gulf experience also shook assumptions about France's ability to operate unilaterally and contributed to the subversion of Gaullism.[15]

These states, as well as the WEU Assembly and Secretariat, saw an opportunity to carve out an operational role for the WEU as the future military component of European Union.[16] The WEU's Hague Platform of 1987 had not only called upon members to 'concert their policies on crises outside Europe' but also to 'pursue European integration including security and defence'. There were hopes that the WEU would develop stronger mechanisms for naval integration, co-ordination of logistics, harmonisation of decisions, solutions to rules of engagement problems, and the establishment of an independent satellite intelligence capability.[17] In truth, however, the WEU states had problems in providing capabilities independently of NATO.[18]

The NATO Council summit in Rome in November 1991 accepted the concept of enhanced Europeanisation, and at Maastricht, in December 1991, the WEU states agreed to 'develop a genuine European security and defence identity', both as a defence component of the future EU and to strengthen the alliance.[19] New WEU operational arrangements included the creation of a Planning

Cell and regular Chiefs of Staff meetings. However, the post-Cold War restructuring of West European security also produced tensions. The United States, the UK, Denmark, Portugal and the Netherlands feared that a stronger WEU would undermine Atlanticism and NATO's military strength. The UK argued that rather than becoming the military arm of European Union the WEU's functions should be limited to ad hoc responses and confined to areas where NATO could not operate.[20] Consequently the WEU members decided not to press for pre-determined military tasks or force commitments.[21]

This decision, and the lack of dedicated ground forces, reinforced the tendency of WEU members to rely on ad hoc, but concerted, naval deployments as the preferred means of action in a crisis. In the Yugoslavian débâcle it was also less risky to do something at sea rather than commit large-scale ground forces to Bosnia. Both the WEU and NATO sent task groups to the Adriatic to monitor the trade and arms embargo against Serbia–Montenegro (UN Security Council Resolutions 713 and 757). The WEU group patrolled the Strait of Otranto, using Taranto base in southern Italy and a command HQ in Rome. By August 1992, this force comprised frigates from France, Belgium, Spain, Portugal, Italy (2) and a joint (Italian) supply ship. The WEU also co-ordinated French, German, Italian and Dutch maritime air patrols based at Sigonella in Sicily (see Chapter 3).[22] For its part, NATO deployed seven frigates off the Montenegrin coast, utilising Standing Naval Force Mediterranean which had been created in April 1992. This duplication of effort was clearly wasteful and NATO staffs may have resented the WEU's claims to competence (given its plundering of NATO procedures and assets). But the WEU deployment had the politically symbolic goal of declaring a European defence identity. Once this had been expressed the two naval groups were combined, with French participation, on 15 June 1993 (see Appendix).[23]

A clear definition of roles in Western Europe has thus been problematic because of Cold War legacies, the divergent security perceptions of EU members, and the uncertain future of US and Canadian involvement in European security. However, the future of NATO, as well as the WEU, would be jeopardised by any unravelling of European integration or a re-nationalisation of defence policy.[24] The signs of Europeanisation have been unmistakable, and the tasks projected for the multinational European corps, which France and Germany launched in 1992, included assignment to the UN, NATO or European Union for peacekeeping and humanitarian missions.[25] The WEU also declared its willingness to improve contacts with the UN. However, like NATO, it disavowed claims to be a regional organisation under the legal constraints of Chapter VIII of the UN Charter, but remained a collective defence organisation under Article 51.[26]

Neither the WEU nor NATO represents the whole of Europe though they have sought ways to co-operate with the states of the former Warsaw Treaty Organisation. NATO established the North Atlantic Co-operation Council in 1991 to give the former adversaries consultative status, and in January 1994 offered them eventual membership and security through the 'Partnership for Peace' programme. In June 1992, Germany pressed the WEU Council to accept that intra-state disputes required a European response, perhaps under the Conference on Security and Co-operation in Europe (CSCE), with the possible development of a European Security Council and CSCE peacekeeping forces.[27] Otherwise, instead of providing a regional framework in which the UN could have confidence, Europe would be divided anew. Indeed schisms arose in 1993 when Russia opposed NATO's interest in offering full NATO membership to the states of Eastern Europe. Russia argued strongly for endowing the CSCE with greater competence as a pan-European organisation to help contain crisis situations.

During the Cold War the CSCE had been a political process rather than an organisation. Institutionalisation began with the Paris Charter of 1990 and the subsequent creation of new secretariats. The Helsinki document of June 1992, 'Challenge of Change', empowered the CSCE to undertake peacekeeping in internal as well as inter-state disputes, but it has tougher conditions for involvement than the UN and excludes operations in situations where political violence is occurring.[28] The chain of command would be through the CSCE Secretary-General, the standing Committee of Senior Officials and an ad hoc group of participating states, rather than through structures offered by NATO or the WEU. But the CSCE's regulatory and operational mechanisms remain weak and consensus among the 54 members about democratic and human rights is absent. It has made little impact on the six disputes where it has been engaged in conflict management.

The Mediterranean and the Middle East

Inspired by the CSCE process, Mediterranean states have engaged in multilateral security dialogues from the 1970s. An Italo-Spanish proposal in 1990 for a Conference on Security and Co-operation in the Mediterranean consciously sought to determine norms and rules which might help prevent the Mediterranean becoming a frontier between Islam and the West and perhaps forestall an increase in refugees moving north.[29] Problems arose, however, from linkages with issues in the Middle East. The United States was hostile to any discussion of naval confidence-building measures (CBMs), and was supported by Germany and the UK in opposing the inclusion of Libya. This was followed by a Western Mediterranean dialogue (five European and five Maghreb states) which became a casualty of poor Franco-Libyan relations on the issue of terrorism. In 1992 an Interparliamentary Union initiative for the whole Mediterranean agreed on measures for improving stability but, mindful of US sensibilities, excluded naval CBMs.[30] Anticipation of greater progress followed from the Israeli-Palestinian settlement of 1993, but the Libyan issue and a revival of Islamic fundamentalism in Algeria complicated the search for common ground.

The interim Israeli-Palestinian settlement held out the prospect of greatly improved stability in the Middle East proper. But the region has no overarching security structure and resolution of conflicts on a purely regional basis seems remote. Regional states are notoriously important arms purchasers, and the naval forces of the Persian Gulf states have grown significantly since Iraq took delivery of Soviet torpedo boats in 1960. By the 1970s, Iran had become the dominant regional naval power, though Iraq also disrupted neutral shipping in the Tanker War before its small navy was eliminated by the Coalition in the Gulf War. In 1993 Iran's surface combatants included 6 destroyers/frigates, 13 fast-attack craft and the first of 3 Soviet 'Kilo'-class submarines. Iran's shore-based missiles and air-craft can also cover offshore facilities and trade routes through the Sea of Oman. Saudi Arabia's Navy has a similar configuration (4 major combatants and 13 fast-attack craft). The small Gulf states have bought counter-mine ships and fast-attack offshore patrol craft. However, there is no indigenous naval tradition in the Gulf and naval development has not been a priority. Moreover, as ana-lysts have indicated, the general procurement pattern has been quite normal for developing states seeking to improve their coastal defence.[31] Nevertheless, the build-up has been partly competitive and naval co-operation has been insignificant.

Trials in Africa

The UN frequently interceded in African affairs as a consequence of civil wars and the decolonisation process. UN co-operation with regional parties rather than autonomous regional conflict resolution has been the norm. The most representative institution, the Organisation of African Unity (OAU) has had some successes, including delimitation of the maritime boundary between Gabon and Equatorial Guinea in 1972. It has also co-operated with the UN, but has frequently been divided on particular issues and members have stuck firmly to Article III (2) of the OAU Charter, which upholds the principle of non-intervention in the sovereign affairs of states.

In the 1970s the OAU initiated a diplomatic process to tackle conflict in the Western Sahara, but was bitterly divided in the 1980s over recognition of a Polisario state. The OAU provided observers for the Mission for the Referendum in the Western Sahara (MINURSO), but it was very much a UN operation.[32] In Angola and Namibia the OAU merely endorsed the peace processes (which gathered momentum with the thaw in the Cold War and changes in South African foreign policy). An OAU Neutral Military Observer Group sent to Rwanda revealed inadequacies which prompted the OAU Secretary-General to submit 'Proposals for Resolving Conflicts in Africa' (July 1992).[33] The OAU was represented at a UN Conference on Somalia in March 1993, but the crisis was quite beyond its competence to handle. In the view of a critic: 'The OAU secretary general has not visited Somalia; no delegation of respected African elders has been dispatched to attempt a dialogue between conflicting factions; no concerted campaign has been launched to place or keep Somalia on the U.N. Security Council agenda.'[34]

Most African states have small coastal fleets of limited capability and limited experience of co-operation. However, an important experiment in African conflict management began after the Liberian civil war broke out in December 1989. The US Navy led an evacuation of foreign nationals, but the United States was anxious to avoid further involvement whilst the Persian Gulf crisis was developing, preferring rather to support a regional response through the Economic Community of West African States (ECOWAS). In August 1990, seven ECOWAS members developed the 1981 Mutual Assistance and Defence Protocol to legitimise an intervention with an ad hoc ceasefire Monitoring Group (ECOMOG). As Guinea was the only francophone state to participate (because it was affected by a refugee influx), the United States subsidised Senegal's involvement to increase ECOMOG's credibility. Nigeria appears to have seen its role in the Liberian operations as helping to consolidate its bid to be the regional hegemon in West Africa.[35] Nigeria supplied the vast majority of the 'peacekeepers' and the largest naval task group, comprising 2 corvettes, 2 fast-attack boats, an LSD, 2 MCMVs and 4 merchant ships. Ghana contributed 2 fast-attack craft and 2 merchant ships. Guinea and Sierra-Leone provided small craft. The naval operations were controlled nationally but covered a wide range of tasks: sealift, coastal patrolling to prevent arms importing, a blockade of Buchanan Port, civilian and military evacuation, port control and communications between ECOMOG and the outside world.[36]

By December 1990 ECOMOG was engaged in enforcement which became a full-scale war involving bombardment of the coast from naval vessels. ECOMOG's lack of success in containing the war led the West African states to ask the UN to take more positive action, and a complete arms embargo was adopted by the Security Council at the end of 1992. A peace accord, reached in July 1993, proposed a more representative OAU force, to include contingents from Egypt, Zimbabwe and Botswana, but implementation is likely to be problematic and dependent on US funding.[37]

South America and the Caribbean

The text of the 1947 Treaty of Inter-American Reciprocal Assistance (Rio Treaty) cites the UN Charter at regular intervals and declares that the Security Council has overriding jurisdiction for enforcement action. Generally speaking, however, the Treaty and its associated Organisation of American States (OAS) has been ineffective unless acting in conformity with US interests. The OAS has dispatched several missions, including a force to the Dominican

Republic in 1965, ceasefire monitors to El Salvador–Honduras (1969) and Ecuador–Peru (1981). But the OAS played a marginal role in the Central American peace process in the 1980s because overall relations between the United States and Latin America were fragile. The United States feared it would not be able to exercise control through the OAS. Mexico and Central American States feared it would have too much control, and formed the ad hoc Contadora Group in 1983 to promote peace.[38] However, the OAS has fostered information exchanges, memoranda of understanding on military issues, links between military forces and associated naval exercises.

The primary role of navies in South America, Central America and the Caribbean has been to engage in constabulary work, to protect EEZs and combat crime. In South America, only Brazil and Argentina have regionally significant navies. But one of the interesting developments since the Falklands/Malvinas War in 1982 has been the contribution of the Argentine Navy to operations for international peace and security authorised by the UN. Argentina appears to have grasped opportunities arising from the monitoring in Nicaragua, the Coalition War against Iraq and the blockade of Haiti, to improve its standing in the UN and to provide operational benefits for its navy which is attempting to acquire experience and regain prestige. Whether this policy will trigger other regional states into matching Argentina's internationalism at sea remains to be seen. If it did, then Uruguay, Brazil and Venezuela might be expected to contribute, though political instability within such states will tend to undermine their reliability. Indeed, possible scenarios for multilateral naval operations include embargoes to influence the internal politics of states similar to the blockade of Haiti (see Appendix).[39] Within the region, the possibility of inter-state conflict seems low, in spite of long-standing rivalries, unsettled issues including the future of the Falklands/Malvinas and the potential for disputes over maritime resources. In fact, Argentina, Uruguay, Paraguay and Brazil have co-operated in surveillance and shipping control off the east coast of the continent and in the South Atlantic.[40] In Central America and the Caribbean, political instability, the drug trade and the displacement of people in search of economic or political security are incentives for other states, especially the United States, to intervene. As noted in Chapter 5, US military–naval drug interdiction has had mixed results for confidence-building and made little impact on the drugs trade. But between regional states there have been some co-operative developments, relating to maritime resource conservation and exploitation, research and navigation, reflected in a series of bilateral arrangements between Colombia, Haiti, Costa Rica and Panama.[41]

Asia–Pacific contrasts

The Asia–Pacific region provides a salutary reminder of the problems which confront proponents of decentralisation under the UN's umbrella.

Maritime security is a major preoccupation in the Asia–Pacific region. The sea is an important source of food and other resources, and for many states seaborne trade through strategic straits and waterways has underpinned economic growth. Cross-Pacific trade among the ASEAN states, China, Japan, Taiwan, the United States, Canada, Australia and New Zealand represents about 10bn tonnes or 37.4 per cent of the world's total.[42] There are thus common interests which in theory should provide the basis for naval–maritime co-operation. However, states do not share threat perceptions and there are outstanding disputes over sovereignty and maritime delimitations. Although, as indicated in Chapter 2 above, states in the region have developed quantitative and qualitative surface-combatant capability, the United States and its allies retain a clear naval superiority and few other states have the surveillance and anti-submarine warfare capabilities to protect shipping on the high seas. The major growth in Asian navies is at the level of coastal patrol craft.[43] Moreover, the region is politically fractured and encompasses several security complexes.

Four areas offer contrasting illustrations of the problems and potential for regional maritime co-operation: South Asia (India, Pakistan, Bangladesh, Sri Lanka, and Burma); the North Pacific (China, Japan, Taiwan, Hong Kong and North and South Korea); Indochina and the archipelagos of South-East Asia; and the South-West Pacific (Papua New Guinea, Micronesia, Melanesia, Polynesia, Australia and New Zealand). There is considerable overlap, of course. Australia, for example, looks outwards to the Indian Ocean, the South Pacific and South-East Asia.

There is no security institution in South Asia and the Indian

Ocean, an area marked by continuing potential for conflict especially between India and Pakistan. In the event of war with India,
Pakistan's priority is coastal protection, boosted by US systems and
French-supplied submarines and missiles. India's apparent quest for
regional maritime dominance is based on a blue-water surface fleet
with organic air power (though in poor repair), a long-range submarine force and an indigenous ship-building industry. However,
there are significant gaps in India's capabilities, quality of equipment is questionable, and New Delhi's strategic purposes have been
severely affected by the end of Soviet patronage.[44] China has
extended its influence by supplying military–naval equipment to
nearly all India's neighbours including Pakistan. India has therefore
drawn closer to the United States and the two navies exercised
together in May 1992. The US Navy has long regarded the Indian
Ocean as a sanctuary, dominated by Diego Garcia's facilities, to
allow projection of force into the Middle East. Although there were
opportunities for the United States to co-opt regional states for
support in the Coalition War against Iraq, the absence of common
political interests makes the prospects for even functional multilateralism rather remote. The so-called Indian 'peacekeeping' operations in Sri Lanka had a naval dimension which continued after
ground forces pulled out in 1990 (see Appendix) but is hardly a substantial basis for a regional subcontracting arrangement by the UN.
   In the North Pacific, regional naval and maritime co-operation
continues on a bilateral basis between the United States and Japan,
South Korea and Taiwan. Multinational exercises involving ships
from Canada and US allies from further afield are also held regularly. Diplomatic rapprochements between China and USSR/Russia
from the late 1980s, China and South Korea (1991), Russia and
Japan (1993), and Korea and Japan (1993), the settlement of
Cambodia and disorder in Russia's Far Eastern Fleet have all eased
the risk of conflict. Further, the dispatch of 1,800 Japanese troops
abroad, for peacekeeping in Cambodia, proved less disturbing to
neighbouring states than anticipated – though deep suspicion of
Japan's future regional role remains unallayed. Uneasy Sino-
Japanese relations and North Korea's nuclear policy also impede
substantial progress.
   A particular focus for maritime disputes is the South China Sea
and the Spratly and Paracel Islands. Significant for strategic, navigational and resource reasons, the EEZs in the South China Sea have

not been properly charted but might yield energy resources. The Spratlys have long been contested by China, Taiwan, Vietnam, Malaysia, Brunei and the Philippines (see Figure 8.1). Many of the islands have been fortified by the claimants, and Chinese naval vessels clashed with Vietnamese boats in March 1988.[45] China is developing air-cover capabilities, has strengthened marine and special forces and pledged the protection of its navy for a joint energy venture with a US company, but like other contenders has not yet realised a blue-water capability. None of the claimants has the economic capacity to fully exploit resources in the sea bed and this may explain why Vietnam, Malaysia and the Philippines have indicated a willingness either to participate in joint development, or to examine the issue on a multilateral basis. Whilst maintaining its claim to exclusive sovereignty, China also proposed, in August 1990, the pursuit of common interests in hydrography and exploitation. Likewise, China is apparently anxious not to allow a dispute with Japan over the Senkaku/Diaouyutai Islands in the East China Sea to hinder wider foreign policy objectives. A framework for joint ventures could help to establish confidence-building between the participants, despite the absence of a regional security regime.[46]

Canada successfully launched a common security dialogue for the North Pacific which has semi-official standing.[47] But proposals by Australia and Canada in the early 1990s for institutionalising co-operation, to include incidents-at-sea agreements, military transparency, non-proliferation measures and environmental protection, were originally rejected by the United States and Japan as challenging US hegemony at a time of graduated US force reductions. Other states regarded the proposals as unrealistic and were suspicious of ideas clearly inspired by the CSCE process in Europe.[48] But by June 1993, the ASEAN Ministerial Conference and its dialogue partners (including the United States, Russia, China and Japan) launched a new Asia Regional Forum to examine non-offensive defence, control of arms proliferation and nuclearism and common security.[49]

From its creation, ASEAN had deliberately avoided military-security issues in order to protect the norms of non-interference in South-East Asia. Instead of creating a regional security structure, members maintained separate links with external powers, and the Five Power Defence Arrangements (the UK, Australia, New Zealand, Malaysia and Singapore) continues to form a basis for multinational naval co-operation.[50] The pattern of naval

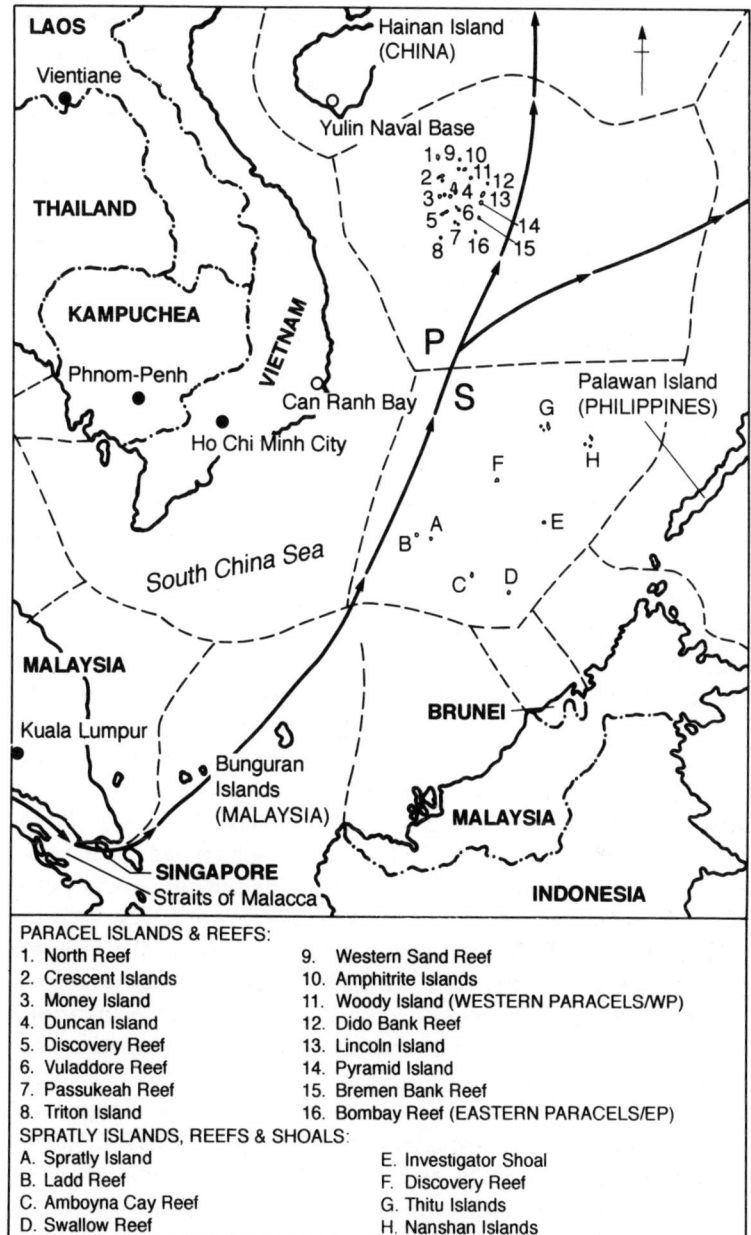

PARACEL ISLANDS & REEFS:
1. North Reef
2. Crescent Islands
3. Money Island
4. Duncan Island
5. Discovery Reef
6. Vuladdore Reef
7. Passukeah Reef
8. Triton Island
9. Western Sand Reef
10. Amphitrite Islands
11. Woody Island (WESTERN PARACELS/WP)
12. Dido Bank Reef
13. Lincoln Island
14. Pyramid Island
15. Bremen Bank Reef
16. Bombay Reef (EASTERN PARACELS/EP)
SPRATLY ISLANDS, REEFS & SHOALS:
A. Spratly Island
B. Ladd Reef
C. Amboyna Cay Reef
D. Swallow Reef
E. Investigator Shoal
F. Discovery Reef
G. Thitu Islands
H. Nanshan Islands

Figure 8.1 *The Spratly and Paracel Islands*

co-operation in exercises between ASEAN states tends to be bilateral. However, the prospect for developing maritime CBMs has increased with the dissolution of the Cambodia–Vietnam problem, the retreat of Soviet/Russian naval power, the drawing down of US naval forces and the absence of any military crisis requiring management. CBMs proposed by the Australian Government and Australian researchers in 1991 emphasised the potential for common procedures to handle safety at sea and co-operate in maritime surveillance. The measures would cover functional constabulary roles outside the context of threats involving the UN:

- surveillance and the sharing of information and intelligence, including the compilation of a shipping plot of all vessels within the designated area;
- monitoring illegal activities such as smuggling, piracy and unlicensed fishing;
- search-and-rescue and maritime safety;
- controlling and monitoring maritime pollution and taking remedial action;
- planning the control and protection of shipping transiting the area.[51]

As explained in Chapter 5, some co-operation has already occurred to suppress piracy. But the density of shipping in the Straits of Malacca and other narrow waters multiplies the general risk of collisions and spillage. CBMs would address these problems which have been of great concern to the International Maritime Bureau and the littoral states. At the ASEAN summit of January 1992, the Malaysian Prime Minister, Dr Mahathir Mohammed, emphasised that regional states were expected to monitor and police such waterways, though wealthier countries were the major users. 'Is it too much', argued Mahathir, 'to ask that those who use the passages, and the maritime nations, contribute towards the cost of keeping them free and safe?'[52] Enhancing use of existing resources might also be achieved by functional confidence-building, leading perhaps to joint task forces to deal with the problems. The process is likely to begin in selected functions and from the bottom up. Naval representatives from states throughout the Pacific region have begun by holding biennial symposia since 1988, to discuss the procurement of compatible systems, identification of hydrographic and oceanographic priorities for joint surveys, maritime training provisions, naval control of shipping, the impact of the law of the sea and EEZ assistance to smaller states.[53] Political agreement on common purposes is, however, jeopardised by divergent views on human rights and Indonesia's policy on East Timor.

By contrast there is already exemplary maritime co-operation in the South-West Pacific where there has been sufficient coincidence of strategic purpose to create the South Pacific Nuclear-Free Zone. Most instability arises from economic, social and environmental problems (notably the threat of rising sea-level). Navies and civilian agencies co-operate in constabulary missions, such as surveillance, disaster relief and providing support to the Pacific Forum Fisheries Agency (FFA) and the 1986 Convention for the Protection of Natural Resources and the Environment.[54] However, further tension derives from the issue of interventionism where there is internal or secessionist unrest as in Fiji and Bougainville. The smaller states rely on sovereignty to survive in the international system and are vulnerable to external interference – including interference by Australia and New Zealand. Indeed the prospect for consensus on norms relating to minority rights seems slight, with Australia and New Zealand taking different stances to other members of the Pacific Forum.[55]

Conclusion

The UN has considerable experience in peacekeeping, unequalled by regional organisations. However, its apparent weakness as an organisation for deploying naval forces, especially in embargo and enforcement operations, may mean that it will have to delegate operational control to competent regional forces. The Charter's lack of precision in defining the concept a region may be an advantage here, allowing flexibility for various levels of informal and improvised co-operation between the UN and regional networks.[56] Regional peacekeeping centres to enhance the capacity of regions to engage in confidence-building, arms control and general peace support measures might be explored.[57] But the UN should continue to be responsible for action that it has authorised and contractors should be answerable to the UN. The relationship, as noted by Adam Roberts, should be a partnership and not a shuffling of responsibilities.[58] Nor should regional channels be devices delaying or avoiding UN commitments.

Regional bodies have played only a limited role in peace settlements. Without a strong global organisation to act coercively, there is little pressure on regions to settle disputes.[59] Moreover, the only well-integrated organisations that can call upon powerful multinational naval capabilities are binding alliances designed to defend one part of the world against another. These are not necessarily conducive to stability. Paradoxically, the most highly integrated naval forces are in NATO which spans two continents and has not become a regional organisation under Chapter VIII of the Charter. As stressed throughout this study, the prospect of sophisticated 'First World' warships sailing into Third World trouble spots could damage the framework of a global structure based on interdependence between states and regions. From a globalist perspective, of course, peace is indivisible and 'world problems simply do not recognize regional boundary lines'.[60] In this respect, ships with reach and sustainability are ideally suited to ignoring such frontiers and acting globally as well as regionally.

There will be occasions when major naval capabilities are required for UN-authorised enforcement. Equally important, the major naval powers should be prepared to export concepts of maritime confidence-building and offer expertise and training for low-level operations. The purpose of most regional co-operation is likely to be concerned with functional welfare rather than dealing with armed conflicts. The naval–maritime capabilities in Third World regions are generally deployed on coastal work or EEZ protection. Joint regional constabulary work, such as surveillance, fishery protection, ensuring safety at sea, and hydrographic surveys could encourage more institutional development and the holding of naval exercises. But the exploration of common interests is first and foremost a political exercise.

Notes

1 Peter Wallensteen and Karin Axell, 'Armed Conflict at the End of the Cold War, 1989–1992', *Journal of Peace Research*, vol. 30, no. 3, August 1993, pp. 331–46.

2 Benjamin Rivlin, 'Regional Arrangements and the UN System for Collective Security and Conflict Resolution: A New Road Ahead?, *International Relations*, vol. 11, no. 2, August 1992, pp. 95–110.

3 E. J. Hughes, 'Winston Churchill and the Formation of the United Nations Organization', *Journal of Contemporary History*, vol. 9, no. 4, October 1974, pp. 187–94.

4 This was the view generally taken by the framers of the UN Charter. Francis O. Wilcox, 'Regionalism and the United Nations', *International Organization*, vol. 19, no. 3, summer 1965, p. 792.

5 The Special Committee on the Charter of the United Nations has been asked to consider regional arrangements, UN Doc. A/Res/46/58, 9 December 1991; 'An Agenda for Peace: Preventive Diplomacy, Peace-making and Peace-keeping. Report of the Secretary-General pursuant to the statement adopted by the Summit Meeting of the Security Council on 31 January 1992', doc. A/47/277; S/24111, sect. VII, 17 June 1992.

6 But too rigid a separation of diplomatic and military functions led to misunderstanding in 1991 when Dr Boutros-Ghali became alarmed that EC negotiators appeared to commit the UN to action which he had not approved. Annika Savill and Leonard Doyle, 'Hurd tries to end row with UN on Yugolsavia', *The Independent*, 23 July 1992, p. 1.

7 Bruce M. Russett, *International Regions and the International System: A Study in Political Ecology*, Rand McNally, Chicago, 1967, pp. 218–26.

8 Michael MccGwire, *Military Objectives in Soviet Foreign Policy*, Brookings Institution, Washington DC, 1987, pp. 90–140.

9 See, Amitav Acharya, 'Regional Military–Security Cooperation in the Third World: A Conceptual Analysis of the Relevance and Limitations of ASEAN', *Journal of Peace Research*, vol. 29, no. 1, February 1992, p. 9.

10 See Josef Joffe, 'Collective Security and the Future of Europe: Failed Dreams and Dead Ends', *Survival*, spring 1992, pp. 36–50.

11 Rear-Admiral J. J. Blackham, 'Maritime Peacekeeping', *RUSI Journal*, August 1993, pp. 18–23.

12 Willem van Eekelen, 'WEU and the Gulf Crisis', *Survival*, vol. 32, no. 6, November/December 1990, p. 523.

13 Carlos Zaldivar and Andrés Ortega, 'The Gulf Crisis and European Cooperation on Security Issues: Spanish Reactions and the European Framework', in Nicole Gnesotto and John Roper (eds), *Western Europe and the Gulf*, Institute for Security Studies of the WEU, Paris, 1992, pp. 129–36.

14 Karl Kaiser and Klaus Becher, 'Germany and the Iraq Conflict', in Gnesotto and Roper (eds), pp. 54, 62–3; Anatol Lieven, 'Bonn Opposition Votes for Role in UN Peacekeeping', *The Times*, 18 November 1992, p. 12.

15 François Heisbourg, 'France and the Gulf Crisis', in Gnesotto and Roper (eds), p. 25.

16 For example, Jacques Delors, 'European Integration and Security', Alastair Buchan Lecture, IISS, 7 March 1991, in *Survival*, vol. 32, no. 2, March–April 1991, pp. 99–109.

17 Van Eekelen, 'Developing the WEU', *International Defense Review – Defense '92*, 1991, p. 38; Assembly of the WEU (Defence Committee), *Consequences of the Invasion of Kuwait: Continuing Operations in the Gulf Region*, doc. 1248, Report by de Hoop Scheffer, WEU, Paris, 7 November 1990, p. 10; *WEU: the Operational Organisation*, Report by Sir Dudley Smith, doc. 1307, WEU, Paris, 13 May 1992, p. 14.

18 The Portuguese Government considered that its Navy's enthusiasm to participate in missions in the Red Sea or Indian Ocean was reckless because its frigates lacked air and missile defence. Alvaro de Vasconcelos, 'Portugal, the Gulf Crisis and WEU', in Gnesotto and Roper (eds), p. 114.

19 Provision was also made to enable EC members to accede to the WEU (or become observers), and for other NATO members to become associate members (giving them participation but no involvement in decisions). In 1992 Greece joined and Turkey became an associate. 'Declaration of the Member States of Western European Union issued on the occasion of the 46th European Council meeting on 9 and 10 December 1991 at Maastricht', Press and Information section, London, WEU. See also Anand Menon, Anthony Forster and William Wallace, 'A Common European Defence?', *Survival*, vol. 34, no. 3, autumn 1992, pp. 98–118.

20 France opposed both a peacekeeping and an out-of-area role for NATO, but in May 1993 participated in voting on peacekeeping issues in NATO's Military Committee (on which it is normally an observer).

21 Van Eekelen, 'WEU and the Gulf Crisis', pp. 522–4; Arnaud Jacomet, 'The Role of the WEU in the Gulf Crisis', in Gnesotto and Roper (eds), *Western Europe and the Gulf*, pp. 161–2.

22 Miguel González, 'La "Extremadura" no podrá acercarse más de 457 metros a los buques que controle', *El País*, 22 July 1992, p. 2; General Assembly of Western European Union, 'WEU Initiatives on the Danube and in the Adriatic – Reply to the Thirty-eighth Annual Report of the Council', report by Mr Marten and Sir Keith Speed, doc. 1367, 15 June 1993.

23 Assembly of Western European Union (Defence Committee), 'An Operational Organisation for WEU: Naval Co-operation – Part One: Adriatic Operations', report by Mr Marten and Sir Keith Speed, doc. 1396, 9 November 1993, pp. 5–8.

24 On this point see, François Heisbourg, 'The European–US Alliance: Valedictory Reflections on Continental Drift in the Post-Cold War Era', *International Affairs*, vol. 68, no. 4, October 1992, pp. 665–78.

25 Assembly of Western European Union (Defence Committee), 'The European Corps', report by Mr Zierer, doc. 1400, 23 November 1993, p. 6.

26 The arguments are addressed in Assembly of Western European Union (Political Committee), 'Political Relations between the United Nations and WEU and Their Consequences for the Development of WEU', report by Mr Soell, doc. 1389, 8 November 1993, pp. 13–18.

27 Petersberg-at-Bonn Declaration, 19 June 1992, WEU text. In June 1993, partly in an attempt to heal the political rifts over Yugoslavia, France proposed a political European Stability Pact comprising EU states, the United States and Canada plus Eastern Europe and European CIS republics to co-operate in peacekeeping. Assembly of Western European Union (Defence Committee), 'Lessons drawn from the Yugoslav conflict', report by Sir Russell Johnston, doc. 1395, 9 November 1993, pp. 13–14.

28 Victor-Yves Ghebali, 'CSCE's velvet clout', *International Defense Review*, April 1993, pp. 285–6.

29 For a full discussion of the abortive efforts see, Victor-Yves Ghebali, 'Toward a Mediterranean Helsinki-Type Process', *Mediterranean Quarterly*, vol. 4, no. 1, winter 1993, pp. 92–101.

30 Inter-Parliamentary Union, *Final Document of the 1st Inter-Parliamentary Conference on Security and Co-operation in the Mediterranean*, Malaga, 15–20 June 1992, para. 25.

31 Michael Lindberg, *The Persian Gulf Naval Arms Race: Myth or Reality?*, Occasional Paper, Centre for Defence and Security Studies, University of Manitoba, Winnipeg, September 1993; Paul George, 'The Persian Gulf and the Northern Indian Ocean', paper at Colloquium on Maritime Security and Conflict Resolution, Centre for Foreign Policy Studies, Dalhousie University, Halifax, NS, 24–27 June 1993.

32 See, William J. Durch (ed.), *The Evolution of UN Peacekeeping: Case Studies and Comparative Analysis*, St Martin's Press, New York, 1993, pp. 408–24.

33 Oluyemi Adeniji, 'Regionalism in Africa', *Security Dialogue*, vol. 24, no. 2, June 1993, pp. 211–20.

34 Jeffrey Clark, 'Debacle in Somalia', *Foreign Affairs*, vol. 72, no. 1, spring 1993, p. 117.

35 Adeniji, 'Regionalism in Africa', pp. 211–20.

36 Capt. Olutunde A. Oladimeji, 'Behold, African Peacekeepers', *Proceedings*, US Naval Institute, March 1993, pp. 64–6.

37 Mark Hubbard, 'Liberia's Hopes Depend on Goodwill of African States', *The Guardian*, 27 July 1993, p. 9.

38 Larman C. Wilson and Raúl González Díaz, 'The Central American Peace Process, 1983–1993', paper at 34th ISA Convention, Acapulco, 23–27 March 1993.

39 Bruce A. Donaldson, 'Regional Security Perspectives: The Caribbean Basin and the Americas', paper at Colloquium on Maritime Security and Conflict Resolution, Centre for Foreign Policy Studies, Dalhousie University, Halifax, NS, 24–27 June 1993.

40 *Ibid.*, n. 15.

41 See, Jonathan I. Charney and Lewis M. Alexander (eds), *International Maritime Boundaries*, Martinus Nijhoff, Dordrecht, vol. 1, 1993, pp. 463–502, 519–49, 615–89.

42 Michael O'Connor, 'The Security Sea Lanes of Communication in the Pacific: Proposals for Enhanced Co-operation', paper at 7th Asia–Pacific Roundtable Conference, Kuala Lumpur, July 1993.

43 Robert Holzer, 'Small Patrol Craft Will Dominate Sales', *Defense News*, 1–7 November 1993, pp. 8, 28.

44 Paul George, 'The Persian Gulf and the Northern Indian Ocean', see n. 31 above.

45 Peter Kien-hong Yu, 'Protecting the Spratlys', *Pacific Review*, vol. 3, no. 1, 1990, pp. 78–83; Marko Milivojevic, 'The Spratly and Paracel Islands Conflict', *Survival*, vol. 31, no. 1, January/February 1989, pp. 70–78.

46 Joint exploitation was discussed at a non-official level in workshops held in Indonesia in 1990–93. Eric Hyer, 'The South China Sea Territorial Dispute: Implications of China's Earlier Settlements', paper at 34th ISA Convention, Acapulco, 23–27 March 1993. B. A. Hamzah, 'Conflicting Maritime Claims in the South China Sea: The Scope for Resolution', in Ross Babbage and Sam Bateman (eds), *Maritime Change: Issues for Asia*, Allen & Unwin, St Leonards, NSW, 1993, pp. 96–109. In early 1990 Japan raised the issue of sovereignty over the Senkaku/Diaouyutai Islands by sending armed vessels and aircraft to warn off Taiwanese fishing boats. Jung-Hoon Lee, 'Asian Reaction to Japan's "Peace Cooperation" Debate', paper at Japan and Peacekeeping Operations Workshop, East Asia Centre, University of Newcastle, 19 March 1991.

47 Gerald Segal, 'North-East Asia: Common Security or à la carte', *International Affairs*, vol. 67, no. 4, 1991, pp. 759–64.

48 See generally, Andrew Mack (ed.), *A Peaceful Ocean? Maritime Security in the Pacific in the Post-Cold War Era*, Allen & Unwin, St Leonards, NSW, 1993.

49 Nicholas Cumming-Bruce, 'Pacific Rim States Launch Security Forum', *The Guardian*, 27 July 1993, p. 9.

50 Amitav Acharya, 'Regional Military–Security Cooperation in the Third World: A Conceptual Analysis of the Relevance and Limitations of ASEAN', *Journal of Peace Research*, vol. 29, no. 1, February 1992, pp. 17–18.

51 Sam Bateman, 'Maritime Confidence and Security-Building Measures in the Asia Pacific Area', in Kevin Clements (ed.), *Peace and Security in the Asia Pacific Region*, United Nations University/John Dunmore, Tokyo and Palmerston North, NZ, 1993, pp. 281–9.

52 Cited in, 'New World Order Full of Curbs on ASEAN', *The Straits Times*, 28 January 1992, p. 23.

53 O'Connor, 'The Security Sea Lanes of Communication in the Pacific', see n. 42.

54 D. J. Doulman, 'An Assessment of Australia's Role in the South Pacific Forum Fisheries Agency', in W. S. G. Bateman and M. W. Ward (eds), *Australia's Maritime Interests – Views From Overseas*, Canberra, Australian Centre for Maritime Studies, 1990, pp. 90–101.

55 Peter King, 'Redefining South Pacific Security', in Ramesh Thakur (ed.), *The South Pacific: Problems, Issues and Prospects*, London, Macmillan, pp. 55–7.

56 'An Agenda for Peace', UN doc. A/47/277; S/24111, pp. 35–7.

57 See, Christian Harleman, 'Regional Conflicts: Peace-Keeping and Disarmament', *UN Disarmament Quarterly Review*, no. 3, 1992, pp. 183–4.

58 Adam Roberts, 'The United Nations and International Security', *Survival*, vol. 35, no. 2, summer 1993, p. 8. Somalia 'has shown how premature abandonment of responsibility by the UN to a regional organization like the OAU can lead to neglect and disaster'. Adeniji, 'Regionalism in Africa', p. 217, see n. 33.

59 Francis O. Wilcox, 'Regionalism and the United Nations', *International Organization*, vol. 19, no. 3, summer 1965, pp. 795–8.

60 *Ibid.*, p. 807.

Operational and technical requirements

Analysis of the key operational and technical problems facing multilateral maritime–naval forces might prevent either unrealistic expectations or excessive pessimism as to the potential of international naval action to help underpin global security. Technological arrangements, however, cannot provide solutions to political problems. The success of operational integrity depends initially on political agreement between participants about what the common policy should be and the approach that needs to be adopted. The political objectives should be clearly understood by naval planners. Operational and technological arrangements are then adapted to serve needs.

We discuss here the probable requirements for different kinds of naval task which might be agreed upon politically, and the technical issues which affect the integration of national naval assets, whether in ad hoc, on-call or standing force structures. The degree of political consensus and assimilation will permit a particular level of operational integration.

Levels of integration

The levels of integration in multinational naval operations can be divided into three types: co-operative, co-ordinated and combined.

Co-operative operations are those in which navies deploy in the same area independently pursuing national objectives. However, they may exchange information, conduct exercises with each other, alert each other to forthcoming events and exchange visits to familiarise each other with their operational procedures (as occurred between West African units during the Liberian civil war and between British and US ships in the Persian Gulf area during the Iran–Iraq War). These activities may be politically 'concerted', that is to say arranged nationally but within the framework of an overall common cause (as WEU operations were during the Iran–Iraq War).[1]

They might then cross the threshold of *co-ordination* whereby forces are formally allocated areas in a co-ordinated plan, for example for blockade or surveillance. During Operation *Desert Shield*, under overall US direction, a large-scale blockade was carried out with ships and aircraft being assigned to a system of 'boxes'.

Combined forces are, however, fully integrated when they are collated into a fighting force under a single agreed command structure – as for most states in the Gulf during Operation *Desert Storm* or in NATO or similar operations once forces are 'chopped' to Allied operational control.

These levels should not be confused with the three types of force structure discussed in Chapter 6 above. It is possible to have co-operative, co-ordinated or combined integration within ad hoc and on-call force structures. However, a standing force is most likely to operate at the combined level.

A major factor affecting the success of a multinational operation will be the extent to which the level of integration and the forces committed match the type of operation, and the constituent tasks which have been authorised.

Types of operation

As discussed in Chapter 4 above, multinational naval operations can be divided into three broad categories: peacekeeping, second generation operations and enforcement.

Peacekeeping
To recapitulate, peacekeeping ideally takes place when there is an effective ceasefire with good prospects of its holding, all parties to the dispute give their consent to the presence of the force and there is a political process in train to resolve the dispute. The kinds of duties include monitoring for any breaches of ceasefire agreements

and supervising the cantonment of vessels, where the environment is likely to be benign with a low level of threat. The platforms required will be surface ships of small and medium size and perhaps at the level of fast coastal protection vessels. Indeed, there is a general trend in the world's navies towards procuring this kind of capability.[2] Danish shipyards, for example, have three new designs for low-intensity operations, 'peacekeeping' and offshore patrol missions. They are: a 500-ton vessel based on the 'Standard Flex 300' class adapted to carry a helicopter; a 1,500-ton vessel based on the Danish missile 'Corvette' class, also lengthened to carry a helicopter; and a 3,000-ton ship based on the 'Thetis' class.[3] The emphasis in these kinds of operation is much more on seaworthiness, endurance and surveillance capability than on high-level combat potential.

Patrols are not necessarily cheap and, as the Beira Patrol indicated (see Appendix), the number of ships required to keep a frigate on station may be as high as nine, depending on the distance from home bases.[4] In certain contexts (as occurred in Cambodia) the leasing of indigenous craft might be better than vessels deployed from distant bases.

'Second generation' operations
Increasingly in the post-Cold War world, however, multinational forces are being sent to areas where ceasefires are not holding, where at least some parties are hostile to the presence of the force and where the political process to obtain a settlement is unstable. These peace support operations fall within the hazy area between peace-keeping and full-scale enforcement action of a conventional warlike character. The tasks include:

- naval diplomacy to effect a presence, show the flag, or demonstrate commitment;
- mine-countermeasures to provide access, prevent incidents and to clear up the effects of the conflict;
- maintaining an amphibious evacuation capability if the situation begins to deteriorate seriously;
- seaborne humanitarian, logistic and medical support (and its protection) where other access is difficult;
- escort and protection of civilian vessels;
- dealing with seaborne refugee problems;
- constabulary tasks as discussed in Chapter 6, such as pollution control and maintaining law and order at sea.

The capabilities required by the forces engaged in such operations are dependent on the potential threat on, over or perhaps even under the sea. Their minimum armament requirements are thus the same as those for normal patrol tasks, no more than light guns, although heavier weapons might be necessary for deterrence and flexibility against unexpected resistance. 'Type-23' frigates in the Royal Navy are suitably multifunctional, though for many interventions they would not need to be fully combatant provided they were equipped with radar and preferably a helicopter for surveillance and for underway boarding. For mine-countermeasure work, minehunters are generally essential although a few nations can deploy diving teams independently from mercantile shipping. An ability to work in seas distant from base means that seaworthiness will be an important asset.

Specialist amphibious and logistic support shipping is likely to be useful, if not vital, both for evacuation and other support roles. Japan, for example, is improving its long-range logistic support with the purchase of an 8,900-ton amphibious landing ship, for which expanding Japan's ability to participate in UN operations was a justification.[5]

Land-based maritime patrol aircraft, both fixed and rotary winged, would also provide useful support for surveillance and for directing ships to investigate suspicious activity. Such patrols have been operated in the Adriatic by members of NATO and the WEU from bases in Italy in support of the UN-authorised embargo of Serbia and Montenegro. There are, however, fundamental problems with land-based air cover, as the provision of effective cover and surveillance requires many aircraft, airfield space, maintenance and support facilities and possibly overflight rights. Consequently, land-based airborne surveillance may not be a cost-effective option.

Whilst peacekeeping and more assertive operations might occur at any of the three levels of integration discussed earlier in the chapter, forces expected to operate together against powerful maritime opposition ought to be at least co-ordinated and at best fully combined.

Enforcement
If the mandate involves enforcement, the situation shifts to one of potential or actual belligerency in support of the land operations. Thus sanctions can be enforced by a naval blockade backed up by

the threat of force and a naval presence. This entails the proximity of heavily armed warships, either forward deployed or in a covering role. Aircraft carriers and frigate/destroyer-type platforms are essential in operations identical to the combatant roles defined in US maritime strategy statements: for power projection with air, missile and amphibious forces; and for battlespace dominance.[6]

For providing logistic support to major land operations, fast sealift is also essential. Approximately 80 per cent of the supplies sent to the UN forces in the Korean War and over 90 per cent used by the Coalition forces in the Gulf War went by sea. Sealift is not generally a naval task. The United States uses state-owned vessels and has eight pre-positioned logistic ships. Other states rely on commercial vessels to sustain land operations. But sealift may well require naval protection by escorts.

In addition to protection and amphibious capability, hospital ships might be necessary if shore-based medical facilities were unavailable or overloaded. No force can match the sophistication of US sea-based medical support and the Military Sealift Command ships, USNS *Mercy* and *Comfort*. But these facilities are expensive to maintain, and a lower level of medical capability would suffice, though its Red Cross status might be compromised by military operations.[7] Given that such vessels are scarce, a hospital ship could be the type of vessel which, in practice, might be deployed jointly by nations in a task force, perhaps supplied and crewed by a state which for political reasons preferred to avoid combat missions.

Combined forces are highly desirable for mutual support against air and subsurface attacks. Developing countries are acquiring modern capabilities which, although unlikely to cut sea lines of communication (SLOCs) or prevent multinational sea control, need to be taken into account. Submarines are, or will soon be, operated by, among others: Albania, Algeria, Argentina, Brazil, Bulgaria, Chile, Colombia, Cuba, Ecuador, Egypt, India, Indonesia, Iran, Israel, both Koreas, Libya, Pakistan, Peru, Romania, Serbia–Montenegro, South Africa and Venezuela.[8] The unsophisticated quality of many of the submarines, and immature domestic support structure, may mean that although such submarine forces are regionally significant, and generate kudos, they may not be very effective. However, submarines have a psychological impact and any hostile submarine threat would inevitably affect the tactics and options of multinational forces.[9] Considerable efforts would have to be expended on precautionary anti-submarine warfare (ASW) operations, and full tactical integration and adequate training of a multinational force would be essential.

Equally problematic would be sophisticated attack aircraft and anti-ship missiles for air or surface launch. These are more widely dispersed than submarines and require less expensive infrastructures. Small, fast ships can launch surface-to-surface missiles, weapons which have been acquired by about 70 states.[10] Missile boats are, however, very vulnerable to air attack, provided they can be identified. Although the air-launched missile threat was successfully contained in the Gulf War by the neutralisation of the Iraqi Air Force, naval operations close to the shore reduced the capabilities of even the most sophisticated radar and fire-control systems, and placed a premium on integration with the anti-air warfare (AAW) vessels of other navies. The cruiser, USS *Leyte Gulf*, was able to track Iraq's 'Scud' missiles efficiently with its 'Aegis' fire control system. But configured for open-ocean 360-degree horizon search to meet the former Soviet threat, the 'Aegis' system was occasionally degraded in the Persian Gulf by proximity to mountainous terrain, by temperature inversion and clutter generated by events on land. Control of defence aircraft was also attenuated, and adequate radar transmission coverage could only be achieved by working in combination with UK, Canadian, Dutch, Italian and French AAW vessels.[11] In these circumstances close international operational integration was vital and seems to have been successfully achieved.

In contrast to the air threat, mines are a weapon of comparative advantage to small powers – being cheap, simply laid by almost any vessel and potentially disruptive, especially in narrow seas. By setting 1,200 ground and moored mines over a large area, including beaches, Iraq caused disruption and deterred Coalition amphibious landings. A moored contact mine crippled the USS *Tripoli* and two influence mines severely damaged the cruiser USS *Princeton*.[12] Ships can be fitted with their own mine-avoidance sonars, but this would not obviate the need for specialist mine-countermeasure vessels.

Dealing with such threats is slow and time-consuming, and the vulnerable assets so engaged require protection from other threats. Thus mine-countermeasures against opposition, potential or actual, require a well-integrated force with modern C⁴I (command, control, communications, computers and intelligence). Nor should it be assumed that the operating conditions for peacekeeping, policing or enforcement would be anything but difficult. UN-authorised operations are likely to be closely related to land-based operations, and the ability of multinational forces to operate in restricted, perhaps shallow, waters where merchant shipping is also conducting business will be the rule rather than the exception.

Availability of naval units

National naval forces have multipurpose capabilities and a flexibility which in theory should allow them to form part of task forces without having to be geographically separated as usually occurs in land-based peacekeeping. Nevertheless, modern surface combatants also have different specialisms: ASW, AAW and anti-surface unit warfare (ASUW) capabilities. Such assets are surprisingly widespread. Specialist amphibious ships, for example, are deployed by South American states as well as by the main West European navies, the United States and Russia. Several states have small- to medium-size aircraft carriers or, like Thailand, will soon deploy them. Only large aircraft carriers are unique to the United States.

However, these widely held assets would not necessarily be available for an international operation, and perhaps only the United States, UK and France possess a sufficient number of 'blue water' ships to allow a response at short notice for operations anywhere on the globe. Japan has a large navy capable of participating in worldwide deployments but under its peacekeeping law would not be permitted to engage in interdiction or enforcement operations. China's potential for global co-operation is limited, especially in ASW and AAW capabilities. Only with the deployment of the first 'Luhu' class ships from 1993–94 will truly modern major surface combatants be available, assuming political willingness to co-operate in multinational operations.

The Russian Navy has modern ocean-going vessels in the 'Udaloy' and 'Sovremenny' classes which ought to be capable of fighting anywhere at high levels of conflict in three dimensions (when Russia can afford to deploy them). The deployment of a 'Udaloy' and an auxiliary in the Persian Gulf in 1992 saw experimental co-operation with UK, French and US vessels. A basic level of interoperability was soon achieved and the *Admiral Vinogradov*, the first Russian ship on station, took part in the exercise, GULFEX

15. The *Admiral Tributs*, the next Russian ship on station, developed co-operation further. However, most Russian warships lack appropriate C⁴I facilities to combine effectively with Western forces.[13]

Therefore, for international deployments at higher levels of enforcement the inescapable conclusion is that the United States, France and the UK would have to provide the core around which a force was organised. A US aircraft carrier, escorted by a multinational group, as during the Coalition War against Iraq, would be the obvious model.

Procedural and technical requirements for integration

The greatest constraint on operational integration will be the degree of political consensus in the multinational force, closely followed by economic considerations. Integration should be governed primarily by political agreement about the level of operations expected and by the threat envisaged. As discussed in Chapter 7, it will also require considerable political agreement to establish appropriate command-and-control structures. If significant opposition is encountered, data communications for maritime fighting platforms working to common rules of engagement (ROE) would be ideal. Furthermore, naval intelligence collection, analysis, classification and distribution levels probably need to be reviewed in the context of multinational operations. This section focuses on five areas: ROE, communications, strategic intelligence, sustainability and training.

Rules of engagement
ROE are among the most problematic issues faced by command authorities. The concept of ROE and procedures for obtaining political authorisation to move from one stage to another during operations may differ considerably from one state to another. It may also be difficult to get agreement even between national commanders on an interpretation of ROE in a crisis, as the Falklands/Malvinas conflict demonstrated.[14] Moreover, the shooting down of the Iranian airliner by the USS *Vincennes* in July 1988 also indicates that it may be even more difficult to implement ROE in low-intensity situations than in enforcement actions. As with land-based interventions where there is civil unrest, it will be difficult to identify threats. Also,

it may be impossible to create stand-off zones around warships or regulate local shipping in coastal waters.[15]

The level of integration of navies has, of course, a fundamental impact on the degree to which rules of engagement need to be harmonised. Co-operative operations are, by definition, run under independent national ROE, though perhaps with some level of formal or informal co-ordination. As the co-ordination threshold is crossed, however, some harmonisation of ROE is essential to prevent the activities of one set of co-ordinated forces leading to attacks on another. For a multinational blockade it would be necessary to establish ad hoc arrangements, with commanders communicating back to national commands, to prevent blockade-runners taking advantage of different ROE to escape from one navy's sector to another. In theory, a combined force requires ROE that are as integrated as possible. However, formal integration proved unnecessary in the circumstances of Operation *Desert Storm* in 1991. It is possible that this situation was only tolerable because of the limited air threat, but it demonstrates that quite a high level of multinationality is possible under co-ordinated national ROE. Commanders can deploy assets in the light of ROE contexts, as well as in accordance with more technical operational factors. Governments will wish to monitor closely the ROE of their own vessels, especially in ill-defined situations. They may also wish to prevent secret national rules being revealed.

Nevertheless, if the political situation allows, agreed international ROE are in theory feasible. In practice, they already exist in the NATO framework. Forces within the NATO command structure use ROE listed in classified publications and can be chosen according to the situation. A closely related ROE system is used by the COMBEXAG system (US–UK–Canadian–Australian–New Zealand Combined Exercise Agreement) used for exercises in the Pacific. Japan, Malaysia, Singapore, South Korea and other participants in RIMPAC, STARFISH, as well as exercises under the Five Power Defence Arrangements for Malaysia and Singapore, also have access to these ROE and plunder them to make their own joint ROE system. There is thus a multinational ROE system that could be the basis for a universal ROE system for use by multinational forces when required, either for co-ordination or for complete integration. It would also be feasible to write *sui generis* menus of ROE, specifically for particular operations. Of course this does not mean that even similarly formulated ROE will always be observed in the same way, given different national naval cultures and perspectives. Neither does it mean that it would be easy to agree on their adoption in the first instance. Nevertheless, a degree of ROE integration, with obvious operational advantages, is in theory possible for multinational naval forces.

Communications

Interoperability in communications requires agreement on many variables: frequencies, modulation (whether AM or FM), mode (morse, voice or data), language, coding (encryption, forward error correction, electronic counter-countermeasures), procedures (for example, for signing on and off) and formats (open or SEASPEAK).

All maritime vessels use the International Maritime Organisation's International Code of Signals for which there are flag, light, morse and voice codes. The standard system of flag signals has provided an adequate means of tactical communication in the initial stages of co-operation between navies. In addition, the VHF International Maritime Mobile (IMM) band is widely used for line-of-sight communications, and is the basic channel for voice communications between warships from different nations. The range is normally not greater than some 18–25 miles, depending on aerial height.[16] The English language and a simple format, known as SEASPEAK, are in general use. All the same, an ability to converse in English is not necessarily a condition for the appointment of officers in the non-English-speaking world. One of the important lessons drawn by the Argentine from its naval participation in ONUCA was the need for its personnel to be able to understand colloquial English.[17]

VHF and the English language were also the agreed means for communications relating to the Incidents at Sea agreements beginning with that of 1972 between the Soviet Union and the United States.[18] This reflected the Soviet Union's preference for VHF for their line-of-sight naval communications. Western navies, however, have moved into the higher UHF band for this purpose. Experience in the Persian Gulf shows that Russian ships can communicate on UHF if required. The question is more one of operator training and quality than hardware. The presence of liaison officers on board has proved to be a major factor in improving radio communications between units.[19]

Satellite communications have also become increasingly vital for the naval systems deployed by the United States, the UK, France and Russia. These systems are not entirely compatible. The American FLTSAT system operates in the UHF band while the others operate in the super high frequency band. Only the later versions of the British system are compatible with US UHF frequencies. The RN, like other allied vessels, carry US antennae both to give them access to the US satellite system and for use in line-of-sight ship-to-ship and ship-to-air communications.[20] The British and NATO satellites, together with the American super high frequency tri-service Defense Satellite Communications System can, however, be said to operate 'on a cooperative basis to the mutual advantage of all parties'.[21]

For co-ordination and combined operations, a close-knit system of common communications and operational doctrine exists for some of the world's navies. In the early days of the Pacific War in 1941–42, great difficulties were experienced by allied navies in tactical co-operation, notably during the Battle of the Java Sea. This led the allied Combined Chiefs of Staff to establish common codes, procedures and communications security arrangements. A Combined Communications Board (CCB) was set up, originally comprising the United States, UK and Canada (Australia and New Zealand joined later, though New Zealand was reduced to observer status after the ANZUS Crisis in 1985). The 'famous five', known as the 'AUS–CAN–NZ–UK–US states', established a Technical Co-operation Programme to promote naval interoperability. Naval subgroups were formed, notably the NAVCOMM's Organisation and, since 1978, a Naval Command and Control Board. Ocean surveillance systems and naval intelligence were shared, using facilities developed by the United States. The CCB co-ordinates frequency requirements so that the 'famous five' present a united front to the International Telecommunications Union workshops. Although the numerous AUS–CAN–NZ–UK–US agreements set the United States and British Commonwealth apart from the rest of the world, there is considerable overlap with NATO's Allied Naval Communications Agency which ensures harmonisation of developments between members. A Latin American communications 'club' also exists as a result of the UNITAS exercises regularly carried out between Latin American navies and the US Navy.[22]

Secure communications are desirable and often an operational necessity. Common cryptographic systems were developed for the

Cold War alliances. As early as 1949, the UK, United States and Canada released cryptographic systems for NATO use.[23] But there are obvious security problems in sharing systems too widely. Possible solutions to this problem might be placing personnel in other ships to look after sensitive cryptographic equipment or the use of commercially available systems.

The advent of computerised data handling allowed the development of digital data links for information sharing in real time, thus combining various platforms into an integrated operational unit. Data links were developed internationally from the start – a Canadian, UK, US Naval Data Transmission Working Group being formed in 1954. Its main product was Link 11, an HF/UHF system widely but not universally used by US and allied navies. Its high cost led the UK to develop a simpler, lower-capacity system (Link X or 10) which was also sold to the Belgian, Dutch, Greek and Turkish navies. A commercial version, Link Y, has been supplied to several states, including Argentina, Brazil, Egypt and Thailand.

Other, cheaper alternatives are a 'receive-only' version and Link 14, described as a: 'computer-generated teleprinter broadcast which enables non-computer-fitted ships to plot manually, or semi-automatically, a summary of the most important information available to better equipped ships'.[24] This has already proved useful in NATO and might well have a wider relevance. The UK also developed a technique whereby ships equipped with both Link 10 and 11 could serve as channels for redistribution, known as 'gateways'. This assists in the integration of ships equipped with different data systems. Buffer systems between different datalinks can also be developed, though at some cost. The United States deployed the Mobile Universal Link Translator System in Italy, Greece and Turkey during the Gulf War to help maintain multinational sea communications.[25] Such systems require a van trailer and a generator and can only be sited at particularly important C^4I nodes.

Paradoxically, technological development creates problems for communications interoperability. It seems that NATO's improved Link 11, although providing better security and jam-resistance, may not be fully interchangeable with the original Link 11. And the highly sophisticated American Link 16 which, unlike other Links can be transmitted by satellite, may well be too expensive for deployment by all but the richest states.[26]

The ability of individual ships to interconnect electronically must always be an important factor in choosing units to participate in any joint military action, but functional interoperability is a viable solution for multinational forces. Naval commanders performing different functions do not require the same communication suites. Thus, a simple voice net communication system, preferably secure, would suffice for blockading vessels tasked with monitoring merchant ships. Simple, 'bolt-on' communication systems, provided by partners if not already available, and perhaps even manned by non-allied personnel, would be quite practical. American equipment has been supplied to both Argentine and Russian vessels in the Gulf to allow co-operative operations, though communication problems were still experienced.[27]

Access to global command and control systems makes blockade-type operations potentially much more effective but this need not be extended to all ships. By contrast, task and group force commanders would require a full panoply of communications systems, including datalink systems, as would commanders of rapid reaction units such as air-defence ships. In effect, not all contingents need high levels of investment for sophisticated communications equipment. By the same token, states which cannot afford expensive equipment must be reconciled to the fact that they are unlikely to be accorded the higher command of a task force.

Strategic intelligence

The issues surrounding C⁴I affect strategic as well as operational integration. The US Navy and its allies now have the benefit of a global intelligence and data distribution system that can transmit detailed intelligence pictures to coloured monitors in the operations rooms of warships anywhere in the world. The allied Joint Operational Tactical System provides a remarkable distributive capability. If the United States is willing to share data this can be quickly fitted to ships of other nations, as happened during the Persian Gulf Crisis of 1990–91.

As with tactical links this raises interesting questions of classification and information sharing. It should be possible, however, for the Force Over The Horizon Track Co-ordinator to create 'sanitised' data that can be transmitted to vessels with limited security clearance within a multinational force. What cannot be altered is reliance on US satellites and other ocean surveillance assets for creating the critical database and communicating it to the forces. It is hard to imagine an alternative system being built, or the UN developing a comparable, independent capability. The parallel but much more limited Russian system may well waste away. Any major international enforcement operation will probably have to rely on US assets in this vital area even if most of the units in the operation fly other flags. The United States might well consider C⁴I to be its appropriate contribution to an international effort when it did not wish to participate more fully in the front line. Such a contribution would be invaluable.

Sustainability, reach and logistic support
To a limited extent, peacekeepers, such as the naval personnel in UNTAC (Cambodia), may have access to available logistic support in the host state. But this may not always be available or practical, and sustainability away from bases is a consideration which force-contributing states need to take into account. Indeed the Argentine naval force in the Gulf of Fonseca as part of ONUCA (see Chapter 3 above) found that to sustain a high level of patrolling required a continual maintenance effort which relied heavily on the competence of the crews and the national logistic system.[28] For all types of operation, navies are likely to rely upon a high degree of logistic autonomy. Most, but not all, navies possess fleet auxiliaries. The established Western navies are all reasonably well equipped, but some major fleets, notably India, Japan and China, are less well off. This could provide opportunities for Western states to contribute significantly to operations in ways that would prevent the appearance of Western hegemony.

Common connections and pooling of spares and stocks are quite feasible. During the Coalition War in the Gulf, some nations integrated their auxiliaries into a common logistical pool organised and escorted by the Canadian Navy. This was based on the progress made by NATO in the provision of common buffer equipment for logistical support. Russian ships in the Gulf have also exercised refuelling operations with Western warships. Although achieving common fuel standards does not pose a great difficulty, more serious problems could arise in providing spares and ammunition stocks for weapons not standardised in the force. However, just as Western equipment in its various forms is widely dispersed so Russian and Chinese equipment has a certain commonality that could be exploited. Where vessels reveal serious shortcomings, airlift might be available from another participant to bring in vital spares or equipment. Good logistic planning can be of considerable assistance. In one case during Operation *Desert Storm*, a US Navy ammunition ship was pre-stocked with Australian ammunition in a southern Gulf port before moving north.

Nevertheless, ships and aircraft of a multinational force may require passage through territorial waters to facilitate access to an area (as is the case with ships transiting Croatian waters to gain the northern Adriatic Sea), and entry into ports for supplies, refuelling and rest and recreation for crews. Inevitably, this entails diplomatic activity involving delicate political issues. Thus whilst Italy granted blanket clearance to ships and aircraft on NATO–WEU embargo patrols in the Adriatic Sea which were under Commander Allied Naval Forces Southern Europe (an Italian), ships on national duties were obliged to seek diplomatic clearance on separate occasions, perhaps to ensure that the embargo operations were not compromised and perhaps to exercise political discretion in an area where Italy's relations with neighbouring states may continue to be problematic for many years.[29]

Training and doctrine
Even national forces need time to work up together before becoming fully combat effective. Multinational forces require longer work-up periods. NATO's Mediterranean on-call force required six weeks to work up and even then it was not perhaps as effective as a national force of similar size.[30] The need for prolonged training and working up is also a leading argument against developing the concept of integrated multinational crews. Although feasible in an alliance context, as demonstrated by the NATO Multilateral Force experiment of the 1960s (see Chapter 6 above), the costs are likely to be high. However, where national units have worked closely together in the past, understandings at service level will be possible, even in the absence of formal inter-government agreements. This was demonstrated when the HMS *Ark Royal* task force was sent to the Adriatic Sea to support British troops in the former Yugoslavia in January 1993. Although there was no formal political accord for operational co-ordination, the UK, US and French carrier forces made their own arrangements to exercise together and co-ordinate with those naval units engaged in blockade enforcement activities under WEU and NATO command.[31]

In situations where multinationality and readiness are to be completely combined, Standing Forces become operationally attractive alternatives. Another, and probably quicker, way of creating a multinational combination would be to attach suitable individual units into a basically national or allied operation. However, the attachment of ships to a force from states which have not been closely allied, or which lack training and equipment, are likely to present practical difficulties to a force commander. An attached ship might be incapable of receiving a complete intelligence picture of the theatre of operations and might add nothing to that picture on its own account. Even if allocated a low-risk task, it will require a prolonged period of working up to reach the required level of preparedness, and may require 'nursing', to the extent that it presents something of an operational burden – however valuable its contribution in a political sense.

Forces that are expected to fight together need to build up habits of co-operation in regular joint exercises. In the light of his experience as a commander in the Adriatic, Rear-Admiral Jeremy Blackham of the Royal Navy emphasises that: 'The continued value of multinational exercises perhaps in groupings which we have not imagined before, and the value of Commanders knowing both each other and their respective units cannot be overstated.'[32] As well as very large set-piece exercises such as the NATO TEAMWORK series, activities such as the multinational Joint Maritime Courses held to the north of the British Isles provide essential experience in multinational operations. These are AAW and ASW orientated, organised by the UK, comprising small teams working largely within NATO guidelines. Such training could be expanded both within the existing courses and other similar frameworks, and cover coastal surveillance, mine-countermeasures, amphibious and evacuation operations and boarding and search techniques. Common shore training of officers and simulation exercises are also vital, with courses sanitised if necessary to maintain national secrecy. Interservice training should give some priority to the possibility that UN-authorised forces may need to be withdrawn from an area by sea, and that a fighting retreat may be necessary. In Bosnia, for example, one could envisage a situation where a faction which was benefiting from UN protection tried to prevent the withdrawal of UN forces.

The end of the Cold War should see more cross-training of personnel in standard operating procedures. The manual, *Allied Tactical Publication, vol. I, Allied Naval Manoeuvring Instructions*, has been so widely disseminated that its classified status has little more than nostalgia value. It has been superseded by a modified version in the leading navies allied to the United States, but the original still provides an indispensable source of tactical principles for disposing an anti-submarine screen and taking up manoeuvring formations. Volume II provides a common signal book. Consideration might be given to ensuring their wider distribution, though this is likely to be resisted in Washington and London. In the meantime a useful half-way house has proved to be the production of an agreed Multinational Force Operations Order with a set of agreed signals taken from the International Code.[33]

Conclusion

Multinational naval operations have been developed to a high degree by NATO since the establishment of the Atlantic Command in 1952. Given this background, NATO procedures have become an 'industrial standard' for multinational operations. This does not necessarily mean that NATO procedures should automatically be adopted. It is conceivable that the states engaged in a multinational operation would have no connection with the Western Alliance or experience of operating with its forces. Nor may there be an equivalent regional structure which the UN could call upon. Whether NATO could be an agent for the UN must also depend on its political acceptability in specific instances. However, as a model, the NATO experience indicates the key elements for *any* successful multinational naval endeavour. These elements are:

• agreed politico-military authorities;
• appropriate command and control structures;
• an agreed menu of ROE;
• secure communications channels and common data links;
• standardised operational procedures.

The NATO framework has considerable potential to be applied more widely. It is already being adopted by the WEU and it is not inconceivable that it might be adopted by the UN. If so, the wheel would have turned full circle. NATO was set up as a collective organisation at a time when the UN was failing to develop its own military authorities and enforcement capability. After some forty years of developing integrated naval forces, NATO's technical and operational experience could facilitate future maritime peace-keeping, peacemaking and internationally legitimised enforcement against aggression. However, political understandings are a pre-condition for multinational maritime operations and, as examined in the next chapter, so are understandings about the role of international law.

Notes

1 Although international ground forces in Bosnia–Herzegovina are under UN command, support ships not engaged in embargo operations in the Adriatic Sea are under national command. The naval and ground opera-tions are 'concerted'. Should the UN commander require offshore assis-tance, the request would have to be addressed through the national command chains or, if naval aircraft, through NATO command.

2 Robert Holzer, 'Coastal Defense Redefines World's Navies', *Defense News*, 1–7 November 1993, pp. 8, 14.

3 'Danes Join on Exports', *Jane's Defence Weekly*, 5 December 1992, p. 13.

4 In addition, two RFA's were continually needed for the Beira patrol. F. E. G. Gregory, 'The Beira Patrol', *RUSI Journal*, December, vol. 124, no. 656, 1969, pp. 75–7. Taking personnel tempo, overhauls and transit time into account, it has been estimated that it takes 4–5 ships to keep 1 US ship forward deployed in the Mediterranean, 5–8 for the Indian Ocean and 4–6 for the Western Pacific. Ronald O'Rourke, 'Naval Force-Structure Planning: New Environment, Old Habits of Thought', paper at Defense and Arms Control Studies Program Seminar, Center for International Studies, Massachusetts Institute of Technology, Cambridge, Mass., 14 April 1993.

5 Barbara Opall and Naoaki Usui, 'Japan Fights Logistics Woes', *Defense News*, 1–7 November 1993, pp. 8, 28.

6 US Department of the Navy, '. . . From the Sea: Preparing the Naval Service for the 21st Century', Navy and Marine Corps White Paper, Washington DC, September 1992.

7 The Royal Navy's general-purpose Fleet Auxiliary, RFA *Argus*, was fitted with primary casualty-receiving facilities for the Gulf War, but did not qualify for Red Cross status because it was used to support military helicopter missions.

8 James Fitzgerald and John Benedict, 'There Is a Sub Threat', *Proceedings*, US Naval Institute, August 1990, pp. 57–63.

9 During the Falklands campaign the Royal Navy knew that the Argentine submarine capability was very limited, but there were several scares. In turn, the RN's own submarine operations kept the bulk of the Argentine Navy in port. See, Admiral Sandy Woodward (with Patrick Robinson), *One Hundred Days: The Memoirs of the Falklands Battle Group Commander*, Harper Collins, London, 1992, pp. 97, 105, 123.

10 US Congress, HASC, Subcommittee on Seapower, Strategic and Critical Materials, *Hearings on Intelligence Issues*, statement by Rear-Admiral Thomas A. Brooks (Director of Naval Intelligence), Washington DC, USGPO, 1990.

11 Joris Janssen Lok, 'Naval Radars and Fire Control', *Jane's Defence Weekly*, 3 December 1992, p. 45.

12 Antony Preston, 'Naval Aspects of the Gulf Conflict', *Military Technology*, vol. 15, no. 4, 1991, pp. 58–61.

13 Tripartite Adderbury Talks on International Naval Co-operation, RN College Greenwich and other locations, 3–6 May 1993. For the unofficial origins of these talks in 1988 between delegations from the UK, United States and the Soviet Union, see Eric Grove, *Maritime Strategy and European Security*, Brassey's, London, 1990. The annual dialogues became official, and the 1993 meeting included a simulation of joint blockade and evacuation operations in a regional context.

14 In the conflict with Argentina, RN commanders had to decide whether to attack Argentine surveillance aircraft and spy ships, how to interpret ROE and whether to obtain permission from London to change ROE. See Woodward, *One Hundred Days*, pp. 102, 106–8, 154–8, 163, 194.

15 Steven G. Smith, 'Naval Operations in the Third World', unclassified paper for the Operations Department, US Naval War College, Newport, RI, 1 July 1991.

16 Information in this section is from Capt. Gordon Wilson (RN ret.) and Capt. David Whitehead (RN ret.). See also Capt. W. T. T. Pakenham, *Naval Command and Control*, Brassey's, London, 1989, pp. 69–77.

17 Ricardo Enrique Schroeder, '"Operacion Gaucho" en CentroAmérica', *Puestos de Maniobra*, yr. 3, no. 4, September 1991, p. 21.

18 See, 'Agreement on the Prevention of Dangerous Military Activities', Moscow, 12 June 1989 and 'Agreement between the Government of the United States of America and the Government of the Union of Soviet Socialist Republics on the Prevention of Incidents on and over the High Seas', Moscow, 1972.

19 Discussions at the Tripartite Adderbury Talks, RN College, Greenwich, 3 May 1993.

20 Norman Friedman, *The Naval Institute Guide to World Naval Weapons Systems, 1991/92*, Naval Institute Press, Annapolis, 1991, pp. 17–23.

21 Pakenham, *Naval Command and Control*, p. 77.

22 Interview by Michael Pugh with David Whitehead, Racal Training Services Ltd, Heckfield Place, 5 February 1993.

23 See Jeffrey T. Richardson and Desmond Ball, *The Ties That Bind*, Allen & Unwin, Boston, 1985, pp. 156–60, 198–227; Michael C. Pugh, *The ANZUS Crisis, Nuclear Visiting and Deterrence*, Cambridge University Press, Cambridge, 1989, pp. 41–53.

24 Pakenham, *Naval Command and Control*, p. 106.

25 Capt. A. J. Goode, 'Multinational Cooperation in the Atlantic Region', paper at Conference on Multinational Naval Cooperation, Royal Naval College, Greenwich, 12–13 December 1991.

26 Friedman, *World Naval Weapons Systems*, pp. 18–19.

27 Interviews by Michael Pugh with Capt. Alberto Secchi, Argentine Naval Attaché, London, 17 December 1992, and by Eric Grove with Russian officials, Moscow, February 1992.

28 Juan Carlos Neves, *United Nations Peace-Keeping Operations in The Gulf of Fonseca by Argentine Navy Units*, Report 01–93, Strategy & Campaign Dept, US Naval War College, Newport RI, 12 January 1993, pp. 21–3.

29 Discussions with a source involved in naval operations in the Adriatic Sea.

30 Eric Grove, 'Birth of a Western European Navy?', *Naval Forces*, vol. 9, no. 1, 1988, pp. 12–13.

31 Rear Admiral J. J. Blackham, 'Maritime Peacekeeping', *RUSI Journal*, August 1993, pp. 18–22.

32 *Ibid.*, p. 23.

33 Tripartite Adderbury Talks, 3–6 May 1993. In mid-1944 an unclassified version of *Allied Tactical Publication* was in fact issued by NATO.

Naval peacekeeping and the law

Changes in the international system since the end of the Cold War have clearly affected the expectations of states. After the second Gulf War it seemed as though the will existed to create an effective international mechanism for the upholding of international law and the enforcement of the will of the Security Council. Following diffi- cult experiences in Somalia and the former Yugoslavia, however, the international community appeared to seek more modest goals, espe- cially in regard to enforcing international law.[1]

These developments and expectations involve different approaches to the UN Charter. The arguments are not primarily legal but they have important legal secondary effects. They also highlight the particular nature of international law. The more politi- cally sensitive the subject area, the more likely it is that the relevant law will be manipulated for political purposes. When it comes to determining the scope of enforcement measures available to the Security Council, whether or not involving the use of armed forces, there is likely to be an argument as to what the law actually is.[2] This reflects the ambivalent role of states which are not only the creators of international law but also its subjects and its arbitrators in decid- ing breaches of the law.

In general there is a contrast between politically sensitive areas, such as the UN Charter, and areas where the law represents a balance between competing interests and has attained a greater degree of stability and objectivity. In the latter areas, there is less room for dispute about the scope of law. States are then likely to argue about the applicability of an accepted rule to the particular facts.

That said, the fields of international law relevant to maritime peacekeeping are, in fact, almost as contested as the provisions of the Charter. This is attributable to different factors in the various fields. So, for example, the rules of the law of the sea are evolving because the UN Convention on the Law of the Sea which provides a fairly comprehensive package, balancing different interests, has barely entered into force.[3] It is difficult to determine whether any particular provision has the status of customary international law, either as formulated in the Convention or as a general principle. In the relationship between the law of the sea and the law of naval warfare, the reason for the confusion is that the relationship has not been the subject of multilateral negotiation and agreement.[4] In the case of the law of naval warfare itself, the law is uncertain because the treaty provisions, for the most part, date back to 1907.[5] This is also true of the law of neutrality.[6] Practice since then has not stood still but it is necessary to distinguish between practice which represents customary international law and that which has not attained such status – an issue likely to attract disagreement.

In other words, it is to be expected that, in a period of uncertainty, the law of the UN Charter should be contentious. That reason alone does not explain the confusion in the law relating to maritime operations. The law at sea is, itself, all at sea. When taken together with the law of the UN Charter, it is extremely difficult to put forward uncontroversial statements of the law applicable to maritime security operations including sanctions enforcement.

With that major caveat well to the fore, this chapter examines the authority for such operations, the legal implications of the purpose behind the deployment of force, the law relating to maritime zones, the legal relationship between the naval force and the state against which action is being taken as well as third states and, finally, the law of naval warfare, with particular emphasis on the rules of engagement in multinational maritime operations.

The mandate of a peacekeeping or peace enforcement maritime operation

The peacetime law enforcement activities of one or more states do not, as such, involve the United Nations. Constabulary functions are not merely within the power of the coastal state but, in some cases, may be its duty. But where the UN is likely to be involved, the state needs to invoke special rules to justify its actions. Their applicability is triggered by a change in the situation. In other words, peaceful co-existence is the norm.

If an armed attack occurs against a UN member, it can invoke its right of self-defence stated in Article 51 of the Charter, though the right is described as 'inherent', implying that it derives its existence from outside the UN Charter.[7] The classic statement of the right of self-defence in customary international law is contained in the formulation sent to the British Government in 1841 by Secretary of State Webster regarding the *Caroline* case. It will be for the

> [British] Government to show a necessity of self-defence, instant, overwhelming, leaving no choice of means, and no moment for deliberation. It will be for it to show, also, that the local author-ities of Canada, even supposing the necessity of the moment authorised them to enter the territories of the United States at all, did nothing unreasonable or excessive; since the act justified by the necessity of self-defence must be limited by that necessity, and kept clearly within it.[8]

This introduces the concepts of necessity and proportionality.

Article 51 of the UN Charter is framed in terms of 'if an armed attack occurs'. There has been disagreement as to whether this authorises pre-emptive strikes.[9] On the face of it, the words could not cover pre-emptive strikes. It is, however, unrealistic to expect a state to wait until the enemy is crossing its borders before invoking the right of self-defence. If there must be some element of anticipa-tory self-defence, efforts are better spent in avoiding abuse of a nec-essary but potentially dangerously loose concept. The formulation in the *Caroline* case may be useful in that context.

Where the state can invoke a right of self-defence, it can ask for the assistance of other states under Article 51.[10] For state X to regard an attack against state Y as somehow against itself, some prior joint or collective identity might be thought to be necessary. But state practice suggests that 'collective self-defence' does not just apply to attacks on states already part of military alliances. In the Gulf conflict of 1990–91, it was enough for a state entitled to invoke the right of self-defence to ask for assistance and for any help offered to come within 'collective self-defence'.[11] In other words, states may collectively defend one state. Those states which did not invoke such an argument themselves do not appear to have objected to its use by others.[12]

Whilst the right of self-defence arises outside the Charter, the exercise of the right is in certain respects subject to the Charter.[13] Most significantly, the state will have to justify its actions before the Security Council. This has both political and legal implications. Legally, the right of self-defence can be exercised 'until the Security Council has taken measures necessary to maintain international peace and security'. During the Cold War, this qualification was of limited significance, given the usual inability of the Security Council to agree on any measures at all. The situation has been very different since then, at least potentially. Where the threat to state X is external, invoking its right to self-defence will be an interim measure, pending the taking of effective Security Council action. That may become the usual pattern. It may make a difference to the organisation and conduct of a peacekeeping or enforcement operation whether or not it happens against the backdrop of a state exercising its right of self-defence.

So far, the situation has been considered from the point of view of the individual state. The United Nations itself has two different bases on which it can take action. Whilst the legal basis of the operation may not be very different in the two cases, its character is likely to be materially affected by the nature of the operation. On the one hand, there is the defence of the victim of aggression. Although action may be taken in the name of the United Nations itself, it may look like a form of collective self-defence. The operation against Iraq in 1990–91 is such an example. In the other type of action, the UN is not only acting in the name of the UN but is serving a UN interest, the maintenance of international peace and security. The balance shifts from a combination of a collective interest and an individual state's interest in opposing aggression to a collective interest in preventing a breakdown in international peace and security. In the second situation, the attitude of the state from which the threat comes may appear to be less significant. In theory, the UN can act without its consent. In practice, as the UN has found to its cost in Angola, Somalia and the former Yugoslavia, it operates without the consent of all the parties at its peril.

From the point of view of the UN, it can become seized of a dispute which is likely to endanger the maintenance of international peace and security. Under Article 35 of the Charter, any member of the UN can bring such a dispute to the attention of the Security Council. Under Chapter VI of the Charter, the Security Council has a variety of pacific dispute settlement mechanisms at its disposal. They all depend on the willingness of the parties to co-operate. Where the situation is internal, as in the case of Somalia and initially the former Yugoslavia, the Security Council may positively seek out something it can recognise as a domestic authority for the purpose of seizing the Security Council with the issue.[14] Where the parties agree, a peacekeeping operation could be established under Chapter VI.[15] The difficulty is that the principal function of Chapter VI is the settlement, not the freezing, of a dispute. A peacekeeping operation might buy time but it is most unlikely to solve the underlying dispute. That requires political negotiation or legal resolution.

This highlights the difference between a Chapter VI and Chapter VII response by the UN. Under Chapter VI, the UN is neutral in the ordinary sense of the word. It seeks to facilitate the resolution of the dispute. Its interest is not materially different from that of the parties. Where, however, the UN deploys forces without the consent of one or more of the parties, its role changes. If the UN is taking action to forestall a threatened breach of the peace, it may be frustrating parties who want to fight. The UN is not taking the side of one party against another, but its interest diverges from that of the parties. That is even more marked where it is assisting a victim of aggression. In that case, the UN appears to have taken sides. It does not matter that it is upholding international law rather than supporting state X. As far as state Y is concerned, they both look the same.

These represent two different types of problems with Chapter VII enforcement operations. Although their common feature is that the interest of the UN is different from that of one or both of the parties, the two situations which can arise are materially different from one another. Where consent is lacking but the UN is trying to enforce peace even-handedly, its overriding desire for peace interferes with the scope for mediation. Nevertheless, there is still some room for negotiation. Where, on the other hand, enforcement action is being taken against a perpetrator of aggression, the violation of international law requires the taking of sides. There is limited scope for mediation since the effects of the aggression must be undone. The fundamental distinction between conciliation, which is based on the idea that neither party will get all its own way, and recourse to law, in which one party can emerge as the winner, is reflected in Chapters VI and VII of the Charter.

Under Chapter VII, the Security Council can order that measures be taken not involving the use of armed force, such as complete or partial interruption of economic relations. If such measures are thought to be or have proved to be inadequate, under Article 42 the Security Council 'may take such action by air, sea, or land forces as may be necessary to maintain or restore international peace and security. Such action may include demonstrations, blockade, and other operations by air, sea, or land forces of members of the United Nations.'

The provision with regard to the interruption of economic relations expressly refers to measures not involving the use of armed force. Maritime forces might monitor the effectiveness of the measures but they would not be empowered, under that provision, to enforce the sanctions. That requires a Security Council resolution under Article 42. Nevertheless, the possibility of stationing ships on the high seas to monitor compliance provides considerable potential benefits.[16] It enables great flexibility in the response. Unlike the deployment of land forces, which requires the consent of the territorial sovereign, the vessels can be outside the territorial jurisdiction of a state whilst at the same time being sufficiently close to the embargoed state to exert pressure. Should authority be given to enforce the sanctions order, the ships are already on station. The monitoring of activities can also include internal waterways, particularly where they form an international border.[17] However, the evidence suggests that sanctions without provision for enforcement are usually ineffective, especially where a state has land borders and neighbours who, for whatever reason, are not too punctilious in the enforcement of sanctions, as in the case of Serbia–Montenegro.[18]

As discussed in Chapters 6 and 7 above, the UN Charter provided for action by UN standing forces where sanctions proved to be inadequate and for national air-force contingents to be held in readiness for combined international enforcement action. A Military Staff Committee (MSC) was to be responsible for the strategic direction of any armed forces placed at the disposal of the Security Council. Following the end of the Cold War and the dramatic increase in the number of UN operations, some of which involve enforcement rather than traditional peacekeeping, various proposals have been made for transforming the MSC into a body capable of meeting the need.[19] There are two fundamental difficulties, of a very different order of magnitude. The reaction during the 1990–91 Gulf conflict suggests that the Security Council has a problem of legitimacy which is exacerbated where the Council is perceived as simply doing the bidding of one member.[20] A system is needed for involving the General Assembly in some way if this difficulty is to be addressed, perhaps through a reporting procedure between the Security Council and/or the MSC and the General Assembly.

The second difficulty is much more serious. Clearly, the MSC as it has evolved cannot meet the demands placed upon it by the plethora of operations of considerable complexity. Less clear is whether the difficulties can be met by changes in military doctrine and practice, since political difficulties are likely to mean that the MSC will never be able to develop into the type of structure necessary to assume the role envisaged. In that case, UN delegation to a competent military organisation such as NATO may be the only effective procedure for enforcement operations, without precluding the participation of other states. NATO C^{3}I was adapted and used successfully in the Gulf and is being used in the former Yugoslavia. Although delegation is not envisaged in the UN Charter it is not inconsistent with it, and current practice represents a *de facto* revision which poses fewer problems than trying to amend the Charter formally.

The precise mandate of an operation will depend upon the terms of the Security Council resolution establishing the force.[21] If, as seems likely, the UN moves back to a traditional peacekeeping role, it has precedents which form a pattern. In the area of second generation operations, however, there is likely to be a greater range of mandates, together with a greater risk of national divergence in their interpretation.

Legal issues arise within the organisation of a peacekeeping operation.[22] These include the selection of the states invited to participate, the calculation of the costs which may be attributable to the operation, the payment of those costs, the state's choice of which forces to send, control over those forces and the circumstances and manner in which the state can withdraw its component. A substantial body of practice has been built up, at least for land forces involved in traditional peacekeeping. Peace enforcement operations may be more likely to involve significant naval support, perhaps requiring the participation of different states from those which have traditionally provided peacekeeping forces. As argued in the previous chapter, the number of ships needed to keep even a small contingent deployed would often exclude all those without a blue-water capacity. Indeed there is no necessary connection between the deployment of naval and land forces. For example, the naval support of land forces is a function different from the enforcement of sanctions, as indicated by the type and function of ships currently on station in the Adriatic (see Chapter 3 above).

It is too soon for norms to have developed with regard to the organisation of peacemaking operations, but they would probably be significantly different from those applicable in traditional peacekeeping operations. This needs to be borne in mind, given the greater likelihood of the deployment of maritime forces in the former type of operation. We can now turn to the legal implications of the functions that might be performed by maritime forces under the UN Charter.

The legal implications of the possible functions of maritime forces

The function that a deployment is supposed to perform is likely to affect its location, the powers it will need and its impact on other states. The four most significant types of function are influencing events on land, constabulary duties, enforcing embargoes and sanctions and simply being there, as a naval presence. An operation may be expected to fulfil more than one function either at the one time or over time.

Military, political and geographical variables will also affect the manner in which the naval force carries out its tasks. The military variables concern principally the degree to which the situation on land has deteriorated, whether the naval force is engaged in deterrent peacekeeping or whether fighting is already going on. In the latter case, one needs to know whether it includes fighting between naval forces and the attitude being taken to the peacekeeping/making force. The other type of military variable is whether the force is designed to facilitate operations on land and whether it is a floating platform for air operations.

Examples of political variables include the deterioration of the situation on the ground, the attitude of the parties in dispute, and the attitude of third parties. The last of these is one of the most significant ways in which maritime operations differ from peacekeeping operations on land. Adjacent coastal states are likely to be affected in some way by a maritime peacekeeping force as are, to a lesser extent, all states with a significant merchant fleet. The interests of the latter will be overwhelmingly commercial but affected adjacent states are likely to have a combination of commercial and political interests which the peacekeeping force will need to take into consideration in the conduct of its operations.

To speak of geographical variables is simply to emphasise the degree to which the configuration of the coast in relation to political boundaries can affect the conduct of (and hence the legal difficulties that can arise in) peacekeeping operations with apparently identical functions.

The function being performed in the light of all the variables will shape issues such as the maritime zones in which the force needs to operate and the powers it needs in relation to both the source of the threat to international peace and third states. Only when those powers have been identified will it be possible to determine whether the force needs to be able to take action not normally permitted. In that case, it may need the authorisation of the Security Council.

Two examples will illustrate the difference. A maritime peacekeeping force based on the high seas whose sole function is the support of land forces from the high seas will not usually need special powers. It does not need authority over other vessels and the components of the force are not subject to the authority of a state other than the flag state. Where, on the other hand, a maritime peacekeeping force needs to be able to venture into the territorial sea of one or more states and is supposed to be enforcing an embargo or sanctions, it needs to know to what extent the mandate given to the force overrides the normal rule that there is only a right of innocent *passage* in the territorial sea and what measures it is entitled to take against shipping of the territorial state or third states. The force will also need to consider whether the parties in conflict have proclaimed any special zones and whether it wishes to declare a special zone around the force itself.[23] Whilst the existence of areas close to land, but outside the jurisdiction of any state, potentially gives maritime peacekeeping operations greater flexibility than operations on land, it also gives rise to uncertainty. In so far as general norms applicable to all maritime peacekeeping operations are thought to create too great inroads into the rules usually applicable in certain maritime zones, special *ad hoc* declarations may be preferable.[24] They provide some rational basis of calculation for shipping, without conceding the general principle. An example would be a declaration as to what will generally be interpreted as 'hostile intent' within what distance of the maritime peacekeeping force.[25]

Reference has been made to two maritime zones, the territorial sea and the high seas. The issue can now be examined in greater detail.

Maritime zones and peacekeeping/enforcement operations

Historically, the most important function which states wanted to regulate was passage. This led to the creation of three maritime zones. In order to protect its land territory, a state could control activities within a belt of appurtenant water, subject to a right of innocent passage. In order to calculate the outer limit of that zone, it was necessary to know the baseline from which the zone was calculated. Ships had to be in a position to know what zone they were in. This pointed to the need for a more or less straight territorial sea/high seas demarcation line. One which reflected the vagaries of a heavily indented coastline but at X miles out to sea would make life impossible for the mariner. This led to the use, in some cases, of straight baselines. It was not uncommon for there to be water on the landward side of the baseline. These waters would be regarded as the internal waters of the state, subject to its complete control.[26] From the baseline to a distance of three miles out to sea was the territorial sea and beyond that was high seas. The most significant feature of the zones was passage. On the high seas a ship could engage in any activity lawful under international law. The ship was subject to the exclusive jurisdiction of the flag state. In the territorial sea a ship only had a right of innocent passage. This contains two requirements. The vessel had to be engaged in passage: it could not take up permanent station. Furthermore, the passage in question needed to be innocent. This posed certain obvious difficulties in relation to warships.[27] Practices developed as to the conduct of a surface fleet when engaged in innocent passage, and submarines passing through the territorial sea must navigate on the surface, though it is not clear whether this applies to passage through international straits.

This relatively straightforward system has given way to one of much greater complexity. Pressure arose from the need to protect states from certain threats in relation to which they needed to be able to exercise a certain control over more than a three-mile belt of sea. Second, as competition over maritime resources led to the need to regulate activities such as fishing, pressure was also exerted to regulate not zones but activities. The first example is still centred on the protection of the state's land territory. The second is not. The ability to exploit the resources of the continental shelf also had an impact on regulation of the superjacent water. Claims to a wider territorial sea would also have the effect of isolating areas of high seas previously connected by straits wide enough to contain a belt of high seas within them, in other words, straits between 6 and 24 miles wide.

These competing pressures led, over a period of years, to the negotiation of the United Nations Convention on the Law of the Sea.[28] The negotiations were significant in three respects. First, the arrangements represent a 'package deal'; states are not free to pick the bits they like and to reject the rest. Second, it was adopted by consensus. Third, and most important for these purposes, there were more conflicts of interest within than between states. The naval interest of both NATO and the Warsaw Pact was for a narrow belt of territorial sea and as much high seas as possible, in order to reduce to a minimum the restrictions on passage. Against this were pitted their constabulary interests such as drug interdiction, the interception of illegal immigrants and the protection of the coast from pollution.

There are currently five significant maritime zones and one of them contains sub-zones. The coastal state still exercises full sovereignty in its internal waters, including water landward of the baseline, subject to the sovereign immunity of warships. A territorial sea of up to 12 miles may now be claimed and there is still a right of innocent passage in the territorial sea. Some effort has been made to spell out what this means for warships but ambiguities and uncertainties still remain.[29] These are only compounded by the uncertain status of individual provisions of the Convention and the general uncertainty about the effect of a Security Council peacekeeping/peacemaking resolution on the rights otherwise exerciseable. The expansion of the width of the territorial sea created a problem for passage rights in straits, such as the English Channel, which no longer contained an area of high seas all the way through them.[30] This led to the establishment of a special transit passage regime for the straits. This was even more of a problem in the case of archipelagic states and led to the creation of an archipelagic sea-lanes passage regime.[31]

The coastal state has legislative competence over certain activities in its territorial sea, notably navigation, the protection of cables and pipelines, fisheries, pollution, scientific research and customs, fiscal, immigration and sanitary regulations.[32] Any legislation adopted must not have the effect of hampering innocent passage. States which insist on exercising legislative jurisdiction may be inclined to turn a blind eye when it comes to the exercise of enforcement jurisdiction against foreign vessels in their territorial waters. States have certain duties with regard to the territorial sea, notably the obligation to warn of known navigational hazards. In the case of transit passage, the coastal state can protect its interests in such matters as pollution, traffic separation schemes and safety standards but only by making internationally agreed standards applicable.[33]

Beyond the territorial sea, the waters are high seas, with the traditional right of passage. The designation of the waters as contiguous zone or exclusive economic zone affects the activities in the zones which the coastal state can regulate. That may have a knock-on effect on the way in which passage rights may be exercised but does not affect the characterisation of the waters as high seas for the purpose of passage. The coastal state may take certain measures in a contiguous zone up to 12 miles from the outer limit of its territorial sea. It has limited powers for the enforcement of customs, fiscal, sanitary and immigration laws. These resemble constabulary functions, as described in Chapter 5 above. It would appear from the wording of Article 33 of the Law of the Sea Convention that the coastal state was only to have enforcement and not legislative jurisdiction in the contiguous zone (that is, action can only be taken in respect of offences committed within the territory or territorial sea of a state) but state practice appears to vary.[34] Co-operative constabulary operations would obviously make good sense, particularly where the configuration of the coast results in overlapping contiguous zones. It might provide an alternative to demarcation.[35]

The designation of an area as an exclusive economic zone may affect the use of the high seas.[36] The zone can extend for up to two hundred nautical miles from the baseline. The coastal state's sovereign rights include exploring, exploiting and managing the living and non-living resources, principally fish. It seems unlikely that the zone will have much impact on the conduct of a maritime peace-keeping operation except possibly for pollution controls to protect fish stocks. Likely to be of more impact are the effects on navigation of the state's exploitation of its continental shelf resources, notably oil and gas. The coastal state has jurisdiction to establish and use artificial islands, installations and structures. It can designate safety zones of up to five hundred metres round installations.[37] The need to protect such installations from two different types of threat may well affect both the movement and deployment of a maritime peace-keeping force. In addition to the normal risks attached to such installations, there is the risk of deliberate sabotage. In view of the effects, both on the economy of the coastal state from the loss of resources and on the maritime environment from possible pollution, the coastal state is likely to be sensitive about the protection of such installations, even from the peacekeeping forces themselves.

Areas of high seas outside the exclusive economic zone are subject primarily to the control of the flag state over its ships. That includes not only rules for the maintenance of good order on board ship but also rules arising out of the international obligations of the state, notably in the field of pollution. In addition, any state may assume jurisdiction over a vessel engaged in piracy and flying no flag.[38]

The extension of the rights of coastal states into areas outside the territorial sea also carries with it certain responsibilities for effective policing, though many coastal states do not have the requisite naval forces to patrol the areas effectively.

Clearly, the captains of ships in a naval peacekeeping force need to know not only through what type of zone they are sailing but also the claims and regulations of the coastal state.[39] This can include traffic separation schemes. The easiest way to avoid difficulties is to take nothing for granted and to seek to proceed only with consent. In some instances this may not be possible. The reaction of the force will then depend on the significance of the obstruction which it encounters.

This raises the general issue of the relationship between the mandate of the peacekeeping force and the usual rules applicable in the zone. Whether a resolution is permissive or mandatory will obvi-ously make a difference but, even in the case of mandatory resolu-tions, it is not clear who determines their impact on the rule normally applicable in a maritime zone.[40] A further potential complication is that the coastal state may modify the peacetime rules by indicating that it intends to follow a policy of strict neutrality. The impact on a peacekeeping force which does not see itself as a belligerent has not been resolved.

Relationship between the naval force and the state in relation to which the force has been deployed

Where the peacekeeping operation has the consent of the parties, there should not be undue difficulties, even if the force is stationed within the territorial sea. Problems are more likely to arise when the force does not have the consent of all the parties. Where the parties are both states, they are bound by mandatory Security Council resolutions. Where, however, they are different fighting groups within a state whose disintegration threatens international peace and security, problems could well arise. It is more difficult for such parties to control the fighting, as in Somalia and Yugoslavia. Much may depend on the location of the naval peacekeeping force, the types of ships in the force, the ships available to the parties and the message being projected by the peacekeeping force. These variables in turn depend on the function of the force. Where it is merely monitoring shipping to determine whether sanctions are being evaded, or an embargo breached, it is not much of a threat. Where, however, the force is mandated to enforce sanctions or an arms embargo, it may need to be stationed closer to the shore and it interferes more with the activities of the parties, particularly if there is no alternative supply route. Whilst this emphasises the desirability of operating with consent whenever possible, it does not mean that operations cannot be contemplated without such consent.[41] It then becomes more important to consider carefully the composition of the force. Moreover, the force should give as much information as possible as to how it will fulfil its mandate and protect itself, so that those who may come into conflict with the force have a clear idea of the different thresholds operating (see Chapter 3 above).

Relationship between the naval force and third states

The peacekeeping force is likely to need the positive co-operation of one or more third states for port facilities, medical evacuation and so on. A decision to afford such positive co-operation will obviously depend on a variety of political factors.

More problematic will be the attitude of third states which are hostile to the deployment of the peacekeeping force, which side with one party to the conflict or which invoke neutrality as the basis for their response. All member states of the UN are bound by mandatory resolutions but that only means that they are bound to give effect to them. It does not follow that they are bound to accept international inspection of areas within their control to ensure that they are giving effect to, for example, mandatory sanctions. This allows for shades of response to the requests of a peacekeeping force which needs the co-operation of third states. Another material distinction lies between a UN force and a UN-sanctioned force. In the Gulf conflict of 1990–91, for example, mandatory sanctions were imposed on Iraq. The force that was assembled was not a UN force but a force sanctioned by the UN. States were invited to participate but it was not mandatory. Jordan and Iran had to apply the sanctions regime, but did not have to participate in the military operation. Iran appears to have notified Iraq that it intended to behave with the strictest neutrality.[42]

Where the Security Council approves the enforcement of mandatory sanctions, it can presumably have an impact on the otherwise applicable regime in the waters of third states. Where a vessel flying the flag of state A is passing through the territorial sea of state B but is intercepted and fired upon for failing to stop, by a sanctions-enforcing vessel flying the flag of state C, it would seem unlikely that state A could claim redress against state B. In practice, it would appear that ships enforcing sanctions or an embargo seek the consent of the coastal state.

Consent is even more necessary in the case of non-mandatory operations but may be more difficult to obtain, since the state does appear to have a choice. In naval operations, unlike land-based ones, it will sometimes be possible to avoid the problem by keeping the force on the high seas. Another way of skirting round the problem is to exercise only the right of innocent passage in the territorial sea of a third state. Whether a vessel on UN peacekeeping duties is exercising a right of *innocent* passage is not altogether clear; it would not appear to be directly hostile to the third state, even if it does complicate the relations of the third state with the state against which sanctions are being enforced or enforcement action taken.

The biggest difficulty, legally speaking, will arise where a third state claims to invoke neutrality. That is a special status in relation to the parties to a conflict, carrying with it specific rights and obligations.[43] At the inception of the UN, doubts were expressed about the compatibility of UN membership with permanent neutrality. Sweden did not appear to experience any particular difficulty and was able to participate in peacekeeping operations, at least those which were clearly of a UN character.[44] Problems are most likely to arise where the operation is authorised by the UN but is not a UN operation as such, where it is taking place without the consent of the parties and where participation is permitted but not mandatory. In such a situation, if an adjacent third state invokes neutrality, it appears to be viewing the UN-authorised force as a belligerent. States which wish to claim the benefits of neutrality, most notably not being the target of attack, assume certain obligations. These include impounding for the duration of the conflict belligerent vessels which enter their jurisdiction.[45] Furthermore, a neutral state is obliged to police areas effectively, within its jurisdiction, in order to prevent violations of its neutrality.[46] Iran's apparent claim to neutrality in the 1990–91 Gulf conflict could have complicated the task of the Coalition. In practice, it does not seem to have inhibited operations unduly.[47]

The other side of the coin is easier to deal with. Where shipping from an allegedly neutral state encounters a UN peacekeeping force, it will probably be subject to whatever rights of inspection and enforcement the force has.[48]

Most of the problems which could arise between a maritime peacekeeping force and third states are more likely to be resolved by seeking consent than by reliance on rules of law which do not adequately address the relationship between the rights of a UN peacekeeping force and the jurisdiction of coastal states.

Rights of the peacekeepers

The peacekeeping force needs to know in what circumstances it can open fire and what rules will apply to the conduct of any naval engagement. As far as the commanding officer is concerned, the legal rules surface in the form of rules of engagement (ROE).[49] Any naval peacekeeping force has the right to defend itself from attack but the practice of different national contingents may vary as to what constitutes an attack and/or presumed hostile intent.[50] This not only points to the need for similar, if not identical, ROE for the different contingents but, perhaps more importantly, the need for elements of the force to have experience in working together. Identical words do not guarantee an identical reaction when the ROE have to be applied to a particular configuration of facts. Only the habit of working together can try to assure close similarity of conduct.[51]

The need for a similarity of response is greatest where the peace-keeping force is fully integrated and not operating as separate national contingents. Even in the latter case, however, from a legal point of view one would expect to find the same response to what is a common legal basis applicable to all contingents.

This, so far, has presupposed that the peacekeeping force has come under attack. What if it needs to resort to the use of armed force in order to carry out its mandate? Again, the ROE should provide for this eventuality.

In traditional peacekeeping, the UN forces are present with consent. If fighting breaks out between the parties, the UN peacekeepers seek a new ceasefire by political means; they do not intervene militarily. They only resort to force to defend themselves if they come under attack.

Once one moves away from the restricted view of peacekeeping and contemplates the use of force to achieve a defined purpose, new ROE problems arise. Sanctions enforcement is clearly perceived as enforcement action. The situation is more ambiguous where the force is given an objective to pursue and empowered to use 'all necessary means' to achieve it. The difficulty is the uncertainty as to when force may be resorted to and the limits on the scope of the force used. The experience with sanctions enforcement at sea suggests that captains of merchant vessels have a clear idea of the graduated response that will follow their refusal to comply with an order to stop.[52] There may be more uncertainty where the objective is more vaguely defined, such as to secure the delivery of humanitarian relief. It is not necessary for the mandate to be clearly defined in order for the peacekeeping forces to indicate what will be the response in defined situations. A naval peacekeeping force gains certain advantages from ambiguity of intentions and flexibility of response. Nevertheless, if mistakes are to be avoided, parties need to know what will trigger a particular response. That is not incompatible with a flexibility of function.

A peacekeeping force needs to know whether, in the event of fighting breaking out, it is bound by obligations in the Geneva Conventions of 1949, particularly the second and third conventions on shipwrecked persons and prisoners of war. This is much less of a problem for a naval peacekeeping force than land forces.[53] The sailor has less scope for individual action than the soldier and is also less likely to come across civilians. That, however, does not resolve the issue of whether the force is bound by the Geneva Conventions. The answer usually given is that since all states supplying national contingents are bound, the force as a whole is bound. The rules on the conduct of hostilities at sea date, for the most part, from 1907, as amended by customary law. Discussions have been under way for some time in an attempt to produce a more up-to-date code or manual.[54] It is not clear whether those discussions include issues specific to maritime peacekeeping and other peace support operations.

A final issue which requires clarification is the jurisdiction over an individual who interferes with lawful sanction enforcement. If a boarding party from a vessel forming part of a maritime peacekeeping force lawfully boards a vessel flying the flag of state A and, during the course of the inspection, a member of the boarding party is injured by a crew member, who can exercise criminal jurisdiction?[55] On normal principles there is exclusive jurisdiction for the flag state of the boarded ship, unless the injury occurs in the territorial sea of another state and the coastal state can show that the events are likely to have a prejudicial effect on land. Much will depend on whether the ship is in territorial waters and, if so, whose. It might be desirable to provide that the state supplying forces has jurisdiction in such circumstances. However, the political ramifications, such as the vulnerability of the whole boarding party, may deter the enforcement of the jurisdiction. An alternative would be to provide for a notification system, reinforced by state responsibility. In other words, the peacekeeping forces would notify state A of the complaint against a member of the crew of a ship flying its flag. If it failed to take effective action, it would be liable in damages to the state whose national the crew-member had injured.

Conclusion

There are areas of legal certainty in matters relevant to naval peace-keeping, but not many. It is clear, for example, that there is a right of innocent passage in the territorial sea and a right of passage on the high seas, subject to contiguous zone or exclusive economic zone jurisdiction. In other areas, the rule is either uncertain or its status unclear. There is generally some confusion as to the impact of a UN-sanctioned peacekeeping operation on the application of the normal rules. This is only exacerbated where there is any ambiguity in the mandate of the peacekeeping operation. The nature of traditional peacekeeping, above all the fact that it is based on consent, is likely to keep the impact of the legal uncertainties at a minimum level. The greater the likelihood of confrontation, however, the greater the impact of these areas of legal uncertainty. It is perhaps impractical to seek the comprehensive legal regulation of these issues, not least because they depend on so many variables. It is probably better to solve them on an *ad hoc* basis and gradually to develop a series of precedents. It is important, however, that those in charge of operations should at least *recognise* the legal problems. It is one thing to sail in uncharted waters; it is quite another not to know that they are uncharted.

Notes

1 Report on President Clinton's speech to the General Assembly of the UN in *The Independent*, 28 September 1993, p. 1, and on the UN Secretary-General's in *The Times*, 29 October 1993, p. 1.

2 Ian Brownlie, for example, argues that the UN Charter does not permit humanitarian intervention, 'The Principle of the Non-Use of Force in Contemporary International Law', in W. E. Butler (ed.), *The Non-Use of Force in International Law*, Martinus Nijhoff/Kluwer, Dordrecht, 1989, pp. 17–28. There was also disagreement as to whether the 1990–91 Gulf operation was the exercise of the right of collective self-defence or enforcement action, see Christopher Greenwood, *Command and the Laws of Armed Conflict*, Occasional Paper no. 4, Strategic and Combat Studies Institute, Camberley, 1993, pp. 9–11.

3 On the Law of the Sea generally, see R. R. Churchill and A. V. Lowe, *The Law of the Sea*, Manchester University Press, Manchester, 2nd edn, 1988. The United Nations Convention on the Law of the Sea entered into force on 16 November 1994 for those states which have ratified it.

This will not resolve the uncertainty as to the status of its provisions for those states which have not (yet) ratified.

4 A. V. Lowe, 'The Impact of the Law of the Sea on Naval Warfare', *Syracuse Journal of International Law & Commerce*, pp. 657–75 (1988). See also B. Vukas, 'Peaceful Uses of the Sea, Denuclearization and Disarmament', and T. Halkiopoulos, 'Interference between the Rules of the New Law of the Sea and the Law of War', in R.-J. Dupuy and D. Vignes (eds), *A Handbook on the New Law of the Sea*, vol. 2, Hague Academy of International Law, Martinus Nijhoff, Dordrecht, 1991, pp. 1233–320, 1321–31.

5 Natalino Ronzitti (ed.), *The Law of Naval Warfare: A Collection of Agreements and Documents with Commentaries*, Martinus Nijhoff, Dordrecht, 1988. The *San Remo Manual on International Law Applicable to Armed Conflicts at Sea*, prepared 1988–94 by legal and naval experts, provides a contemporary restatement of the law.

6 D. Schindler, 'Aspects Contemporains de la Neutralité', *Recueil des Cours de l'Academie de Droit International*, vol. 121 (1967 II), pp. 221–322; M. Bothe, 'Neutrality at Sea', and A. Gioia and N. Ronzitti, 'The Law of Neutrality: third states' commercial rights and duties', in Ige F. Dekker and Harry G. H. Post (eds), *The Gulf War of 1980–88: The Iran–Iraq War in International Legal Perspective*, T. M. C. Asser Instituut, Martinus Nijhoff, Dordrecht, 1992, pp. 205–11 and 221–42 respectively; Schindler, 'Transformations in the Law of Neutrality since 1945', and Bothe, 'Neutrality in Naval Warfare: What is Left of Traditional International Law', in A. J. M. Delissen and G. J. Tanja (eds), *Humanitarian Law of Armed Conflict: Challenges Ahead*, Martinus Nijhoff, Dordrecht, 1991, pp. 367–86 and 387–405 respectively; F. V. Russo, 'Neutrality at Sea in Transition: State Practice in the Gulf War as Emerging International Customary Law', 19 *Ocean Development and International Law*, pp. 381–99 (1988).

7 See generally, D. W. Bowett, *Self-Defence in International Law*, Manchester University Press, Manchester, 1958; Ian Brownlie, *International Law and the Use of Force by States*, Oxford University Press, Oxford, 1963.

8 *British Foreign and State papers*, vol. 29, pp. 1137–8; R. Jennings, 'The *Caroline* and McLeod Cases', 32 *American Journal of International Law*, p. 89 (1938).

9 Bowett, n. 7 above, pp. 187–93; contra Brownlie.

10 But see L. Doswald-Beck, 'The Legal Validity of Military Intervention by Invitation of the Government', 56 *British Yearbook of International Law*, pp. 189–252 (1985).

11 This appears to have been the justification used by the United States from 17 to 25 August 1990, when Resolution 665 gave the Coalition forces the power to sustain the embargo imposed on 6 August 1990

(SC Res. 660), by force if necessary; Capt. S. Lyons, 'Naval operations in the Gulf', in A. V. Rowe (ed.), *The Gulf War 1990–91 in International and English Law*, Routledge/Sweet & Maxwell, London, 1993, pp. 155–70 at pp. 156–7.

12 *Ibid.*, pp. 160–1.

13 C. Greenwood, 'The Relationship between *jus ad bellum* and *jus in bello*', *Review of International Studies*, vol. 9, no. 4, 1983, pp. 221–34.

14 For example, in the case of Somalia, the UN appears to have taken the initiative and persuaded the leader of one of the warring groups to ask for help: *The Times*, 16 December 1991, 6 February 1992; *The Independent*, 28 January 1993. The creation of a 'safe haven' to protect the Iraqi Kurds without the consent of Iraq was unique.

15 On peacekeeping operations generally, see A. J. T. Dörenberg, *General Report on Legal Aspects of Peacekeeping Operations*, 11th Congress of the International Society of Military Law and the Law of War, 1988; D. W. Bowett, *United Nations Peacekeeping: A Legal Study of United Nations Practice*, Stevens & Sons, London, 1964; Rosalyn Higgins, *United Nations Peacekeeping 1946–1967: Documents and Commentary*, Oxford University Press, Oxford, 1969–81.

16 P. Nailor, 'The Contemporary Use of Maritime Power', in R. P. Barston and P. W. Birnie (eds), *The Maritime Dimension*, Allen & Unwin, London, 1980, pp. 142–53.

17 See the Appendix to this book on the riverine patrols of the UN Transition Authority in Cambodia and on monitoring on the Danube to enforce the economic sanctions against Serbia–Montenegro.

18 Capt. R. H. Thomas, 'The Use of Naval Forces in Imposing and Enforcing Sanctions, Embargoes and Blockades', Colloquium on Maritime Security and Conflict Resolution, Dalhousie, Halifax, NS, 1993; A. B. Siegel, 'Enforcing Sanctions: A Growth Industry', *Naval War College Review*, vol. 46, no. 4, autumn 1993, pp. 130–4.

19 See John Mackinlay and Jarat Chopra, 'Second Generation Multinational Operations', *Washington Quarterly*, vol. 15, no. 3, summer 1992, pp. 113–31; Sir Julian Oswald, Admiral of the Fleet, 'UN Maritime Operations: Realities, Problems and Possibilities', *Naval War College Review*, vol. 46, no. 4, autumn, 1993, pp. 124–9.

20 M. Weller, 'The United Nations and the *jus ad bellum*', in Rowe (ed.), n. 11 above, pp. 29–54 at p. 54.

21 Authorities cited at n. 15 above.

22 R. C. R. Siekmann, *National Contingents in United Nations Peace-keeping Forces*, Martinus Nijhoff, Dordrecht, 1991.

23 'There is an imbalance between the technology for seeing and the technology for killing'; this is one of the most pressing reasons for the creation of zones such as the Total Exclusion Zone in the Falklands/Malvinas conflict. See W. J. Fenrick, 'Military Objectives in the Law of

Naval Warfare', in W. Heinstschel v. Heinegg (ed.), *The Military Objective and the Principle of Distinction in the Law of Naval Warfare*, Bochumer Schriften zur Friedenssicherung und zum Humanitären Völkerrecht, no. 7, 1991, pp. 1–44 at p. 37. See also by the same author: 'The Use of Exclusion Zones in the Falklands Naval Conflict', *Canadian Defence Quarterly*, vol. 15, 1986, pp. 22–8. and the 'Exclusion Zone Device in the Law of Naval Warfare', 24 *Canadian Yearbook of International Law*, pp. 91–126 (1986). On the impact of an Iranian zone in the 1990–91 Gulf Conflict, see Lyons, n. 11 above, at p. 162. On 'Yugoslavia', see Appendix and Chapter 3 above.

24 For example, the UK only recognised a limited right on the part of belligerents in the 1980–88 Gulf War to visit and search neutral merchant vessels on the high seas; Lyons, note 11 above, p. 160. See generally, A. de Guttry and N. Ronzitti (eds), *The Iran–Iraq War (1980–1988) and the Law of Naval Warfare*, Grotius, Cambridge, 1993, and Lowe, n. 4 above.

25 Oswald, n. 19 above.

26 Subject to a right of innocent passage where straight baselines are adopted which have the effect of enclosing as internal waters areas not previously regarded as such, Churchill and Lowe, n. 3 above, p. 51.

27 *Ibid.*, pp. 74–6.

28 *Ibid.*, pp. 13–16.

29 On the territorial sea generally, see *ibid.*, pp. 67–83. See also B. H. Oxman, 'The Regime of Warships Under the United Nations Convention on the Law of the Sea', 24 *Virginia Journal of International Law*, pp. 809–63 (1984).

30 The right of 'transit passage' was created for straits as defined in Art. 37 of the Law of the Sea Convention. This allows the coastal state less control than does the innocent passage regime but more control than it would have had, had the waters been treated as high seas; Churchill and Lowe, n. 3 above, pp. 90–96.

31 *Ibid.*, pp. 105–8.

32 *Ibid.*, pp. 77–84.

33 *Ibid.*, pp. 91–3.

34 *Ibid.*, pp. 116–18.

35 There is an overlap between constabulary functions as described in Chapter 5 above and certain aspects of self-defence. How, for example, should reflagging and minesweeping by non-parties to the 1980–88 Gulf Conflict be analysed? See W. J. Fenrick, 'Legal Limits on the Use of Force in Canadian Warships engaged in Law Enforcement', 18 *Canadian Yearbook of International Law*, pp. 113–45 (1988). On reflagging and co-operative minesweeping, see A. V. Lowe, 'Self Defence at Sea', in Butler, n. 2 above, pp. 185–202; B. R. Tuzmukhamedov, 'The Principle of Non-Use of Force and Security at

Sea', *ibid.*, pp. 173–84; H. S. Levie, *Mine Warfare at Sea*, Martinus Nijhoff, Dordrecht, 1992, pp. 166–70.

36 For example, foreign shipping is subject to the coastal state's powers of pollution control. It is not clear whether and to what extent a coastal state, in the exercise of its sovereign right to exploit and manage living resources, can regulate foreign shipping in order to reduce conflicts with fishing in its EEZ. Other texts may be of assistance, such as the 1972 Convention on the International Regulations for Preventing Collisions at Sea. Nor is it clear precisely how extensive are the rights of warships in the EEZ. See generally, Churchill and Lowe, n. 3 above, pp. 136–44. In June 1993, a 'Yugoslav' patrol boat opened fire on a fishing boat in the Adriatic Sea, killing one fisherman and injuring another. It is not clear what zone the boat was in. The boat was escorted to a Montenegrin port. The 'Yugoslav' navy said that it had opened fire because the boat was violating 'Yugoslavia's' territorial waters. Italy claimed that the incident apparently occurred in international waters, and ordered a naval alert in the Adriatic. Press reports made no reference to the ships enforcing sanctions: *The Times*, 4 June 1993; *The Guardian*, 3 June 1993.

37 Churchill and Lowe, n. 3 above, pp. 127–30, 138–9.

38 *Ibid.*, pp. 168–76 and Chapter 5 above.

39 Lyons, n. 11 above, p. 162 (and n. 41).

40 The decision of the ICJ in the 'Case Concerning Questions of Interpretation and Application of the 1971 Montreal Convention Arising from the Aerial Incident at Lockerbie' (*Libya v. USA*) Order of 14 April 1992, para. 42, might suggest that a specific Security Council order takes precedence over the law otherwise applicable. In that case, however, the order was directed to the state in question. The type of mandatory resolution envisaged might impose sanctions but it does not stipulate how the resolution is to be implemented in areas incidental to the sanctions, such as passage rights for sanction-enforcing vessels in a maritime zone under the sovereign authority or jurisdiction of a state not subject to sanctions.

41 Mackinlay and Chopra, n. 19 above. This would mean that a state was able to dictate the activities of other states and/or frustrate the will of the international community.

42 Lyons, n. 11 above, p. 161 (and n. 38).

43 See n. 6 above.

44 B. H. Blix, *Sovereignty, Aggression and Neutrality*, Almqvist & Wiksell, Stockholm, 1970.

45 Lyons, n. 11 above, p. 161 (and n. 38). Certain Latin-American states took similar action with regard to aircraft in the Falklands/Malvinas conflict.

46 See n. 6 above.

47 Lyons, n. 11 above, pp. 161–2; see also US Department of Defense, 'Conduct of the Persian Gulf War: Final Report to Congress', Washington DC, 1992, Appendix O.

48 Lyons, n. 11 above, p. 160.

49 Admiral Sandy Woodward, *One Hundred Days: The Memoirs of the Falklands Battle Group Commander*, Harper Collins, London, 1992, illustrates clearly how, in the case of fighting at sea, legal requirements as to the circumstances in which a captain can open fire, against which objectives and using which type of weapons, all become translated into ROE.

50 Oswald, n. 19 above.

51 Lyons, n. 11 above, p. 166. Even that is not sufficient to avoid problems if the ethos or culture of the two forces is even slightly different; F. J. Hampson, 'Means and methods of warfare in the conflict in the Gulf', in Rowe (ed.), n. 11 above, pp. 89–110 at pp. 108–9.

52 Siegel, n. 18 above.

53 On the issue generally, see U. Palwankar, 'Applicability of International Humanitarian Law to United Nations Peace-keeping Forces', *International Review of the Red Cross*, no. 294 (May–June 1993), pp. 227–40; Y. Sandoz, 'The Application of Humanitarian Law by the Armed Forces of the United Nations Organization', *International Review of the Red Cross*, no. 206 (September–October 1978), pp. 274–84; D. Schindler, 'United Nations Forces and International Humanitarian Law', in C. Swinarski (ed.), *Studies and Essays on International Humanitarian Law and Red Cross Principles, in Honour of Jean Pictet*, ICRC/Nijhoff, Dordrecht, 1984, pp. 521–30.

· 54 For example, Heintschel v. Heinegg (ed.), note 23 above; see also by the same editor, *Methods and Means of Combat in Naval Warfare*, Bochumer Schriften zur Friedenssicherung und zum Humanitären Völkerrecht, no. 8, 1992. See *San Remo Manual*, n. 5 above.

55 Lyons, n. 11 above, pp. 163–4.

Towards a maritime regime?

Although focusing on peacekeeping at sea as an aspect of military operations, this study has also taken a broad view of the compass of security. Maritime security can incorporate unhindered oceanic trade, safe navigation, the safeguarding of coastal communities and their livelihoods, protecting the food chain and preserving the oceanic contribution to the health of the planet. Obviously, many problems affecting the maritime domain derive directly from the land. It was noted in Chapter 5 that most pollution affecting the seas is land-based run-off. Also, global climate change caused by industrial pollution will cause rises in sea-level which, even if small, will have devastating consequences for low-lying islands and coasts.[1] This implies that it is artificial to distinguish between maritime and other sorts of regimes and that a holistic approach to global security is necessary. However, this chapter considers whether the wealth of existing functional provisions in the maritime sector might be strengthened as a contribution to a wider regime. An integrated sectoral approach might thus be an intermediate level of operation – between fragmented governance and a global system.

The maritime environment is the arena for a host of interrelated human activities. Some are plainly co-operative, others competitive, and whilst some protect the environment, more exploit it. The impact of increasingly intensive use of the seas and pressures on the ecological balance has led to measures to codify, regulate and govern the maritime domain. As shown in the previous chapter, international law already reflects the concerns of states about control over maritime zones. To some commentators this implies that the territorial security problems of the land may be replicated at sea in the future, requiring a new Law of the Sea Convention[2] – and perhaps an extension of peacekeeping and peace support activities to maritime areas.

Our contention is that although fears of territorialisation are probably exaggerated, maritime forces may be expected to play a part in sustaining a maritime regime as instruments of a future global organisation. This is not to say that maritime forces would often be the most appropriate instruments to deal with the economic, social and environmental sources of conflict. The militarisation of non-military security could have a negative effect on regime-building processes. We have also already argued that it is difficult to translate peacekeeping concepts to the sea except in support of land operations. Nevertheless, looking ahead to the middle of the twenty-first century, states may wish to move beyond constabulary functions at a local and regional level to deploy forces to monitor the effectiveness of a global maritime regime and take preventive action to safeguard it.

The chapter considers the characteristics of the emerging maritime regime. Second, it assesses insecurity at sea and the impact of jurisdiction. Third it examines the weaknesses of the primary UN organisation which exists to deal specifically with maritime governance: the International Maritime Organisation (IMO). Finally, it considers the prospect of using maritime forces as part of a new maritime organisation.

Regime characteristics of the maritime domain

Some 70 per cent of the planet is covered by sea, and the international community could hardly avoid addressing issues affecting the maritime domain and the marine environment. The sinews of governance extend to a complex of legal codifications, programmes of action, and formal structures. Even a cursory glance would take in significant achievements including: the 1982 Law of the Sea Convention (UNLOSC), with its implications for maritime delimitation and resource exploitation; the UN Environmental Programme (UNEP), with 10 per cent of its budget directed towards the oceans; the 1972 London Dumping Convention; the International Maritime Satellite (INMARSAT) Organisation; and the 1987 Convention on the Physical Protection of Nuclear Materials, applicable to the carriage of nuclear waste by ships. In addition, most coastal states are parties to regional arrangements, examples of which range from the 1936 Montreux Convention regulating use of the Turkish Straits to the 1979 South Pacific Forum Fisheries Agency. The peacetime use of the oceans has become so highly regulated that we might speak of an emerging maritime regime.

Critics can point to limitations which weaken this thesis. The UNLOSC can be said to threaten the global commons by extending the areas of national jurisdiction. The UNEP's annual budget for safeguarding the oceans is only $3.5m. Many regulatory measures are unratified or inadequately enforced. Further, the UN's maritime policies have been weakly co-ordinated. As discussed below, the fragmented approach to safeguarding the global commons has prompted calls for new structures to develop a more integrated approach, for example through the creation of a new UN Maritime Agency with sweeping powers of regulation and enforcement.

Such criticisms beg questions about the qualities of regimes. These are meant to strengthen international order by establishing principles, norms, rights and rules which lead to predictability of behaviour and better management. Regime analysis mirrors debate about the nature of sovereignty and the locus of power in the international system. A state-centric view regards regimes as merely arenas for sparring between competing national interests. Agendas are determined by hegemonic powers.[3] By contrast, a functionalist view stresses the extent to which states allow their interests to be negotiated in the interests of external harmony or through a sense of obligation. A third view is that clear definitions of national interests are no longer possible, and hegemony difficult to exert because state sovereignty is collapsing, assailed by global processes and the impacts of non-state actors.[4] Indeed, as discussed below with regard to safety at sea and oceanic pollution, states are not necessarily the most powerful actors in maritime regulation.[5] Moreover, as indicated at the outset of this study, the maritime domain has always had peculiarities as an arena of contending sovereignties and interests. Over the high seas, the principle of *mare liberum* pertains. Jurisdiction develops as territory is approached, but even within territorial seas, foreign states claim explicit rights of transit and have risked conflict to assert those rights, notably the Royal Navy's celebrated claim to transit the Corfu Channel as an international strait in 1946.

Existing governance of the oceans can be said to conform to a 'soft' regime. As defined by Stephen Krasner, it features 'governing arrangements constructed by states to coordinate their expectations and organize aspects of international behaviour in various issue-areas'.[6] Other theorists argue that regimes should be limited to agreements which regulate permissible action by establishing explicit and enforceable injunctions.[7] However, this underestimates the degree to which international management relies on implicit as well as explicit aspects of normative regulation. In 'soft' regimes, compliance may be maintained through such devices as rewards of status for good behaviour and threats of low esteem for bad, and appeals to precedent in making decisions. Moreover, although functional criteria provide the basis for a regime, it may operate not because it can be shown to work (when in fact it may be honoured in the breach), but because participants have confidence in its efficacy.[8] This, in effect, is how the maritime regime has been emerging through such instruments as the UNLOSC and the IMO. Virtually by definition, political interactions within soft regimes are difficult to trace because of the informal political processes and implicit norms which affect decisions. Thus, although the UNLOSC, which came into force on 16 November 1994 after ratification by 60 states, had not been ratified by the major maritime powers and global ocean users, state practice may increasingly give it the status of 'a comprehensive constitution for the oceans'.[9] The main issue, however, is whether the maritime regime should or can be strengthened. Much depends on the ability of existing regulatory networks to cope with sources of instability affecting the sea.

Insecurities and the delimitation approach

In addition to oceanic effects of climate change, several insecurities of coastal communities were identified in a 1990 study by the United Kingdom's Ministry of Defence including the illicit drug trade and its potential to corrupt coastal communities, the protection of fish stocks (with the people of 40 states, mainly in the developing world, relying heavily on fish protein in their diet), and the protection/exploitation of offshore resources including sea-bed mining.[10] Whilst the process of establishing a global regime should be expected to address such issues, sensitivities about jurisdiction, as we have already seen, can inhibit multinational maritime co-operation. The process of extending jurisdiction has been regarded as the answer to the problem of competing claims and a means of regulating behaviour. But it is also possible that jurisdictional claims, particularly those involving states with traditions of hostility such as Greece and Turkey, carry risks of conflict.[11]

Jurisdiction at sea has been increasingly extended and rationalised, along with the technical ability of states to intensify their exploitation of maritime resources. The Law of the Sea Convention legitimises the shrinkage of the common oceanic domain to about 64 per cent of the world's ocean area. States have been encouraged to develop proprietary attitudes, and the 200-mile EEZ doctrine has increased the stakes, giving absolute jurisdiction over minerals to 200 miles and regulation of all economic activity. It has been argued that the seas have become 'territorialised', thereby increasing the area in which, in theory, the activities of foreign vessels might be controlled.[12] Indeed an obstacle to US ratification of UNLOSC is the mining lobby's opposition to potential restrictions affecting exploitation of strategic minerals on the sea-bed such as copper, nickel, cobalt and manganese. As argued in the previous chapter, the impact of the UNLOSC on the 'innocent passage' of warships and the potential impact on peacekeepers is contentious. Coastal states have declared restrictions, claiming for example that warships and warplanes and nuclear-powered craft must obtain prior agreement before passing through territorial waters. In James Cable's view, it is 'a safe bet' that attempts by coastal states to police straits will 'lead to disputes, perhaps even conflicts'.[13]

Nevertheless the risk of conflict should not be exaggerated. Jurisdictional zones and boundaries will not necessarily have the same political significance in the future as on land. As noted in Chapter 10, state practice may be flexible about the presence of foreign ships in territorial seas and contiguous zones, and perhaps this is reflected in law. The Law of the Sea Convention holds that, although 'government ships on non-commercial service', such as warships, are not immune from the 'legislative' jurisdiction of coastal states, only the flag state can 'enforce' the regulations of a coastal state. The only legal recourse to a coastal state if a warship failed to comply with its regulations would be to 'require it to leave the territorial sea immediately', and then to make diplomatic representations.[14] As Douglas Johnston demonstrates, there is rarely any urgency to resolve maritime issues, and policy differences do not become crises overnight. Ocean boundary issues are amenable to rational–functional treatment because they lack symbolic and emotive content, and technical matters intervene to prevent politically significant emotions becoming aroused.[15] In fishery disputes, for example, only exceptionally do fishing interests have sufficient political clout to generate emotions, as in Iceland and in the Maritime Provinces of Canada. Emotive responses are also aroused where island territories are contested, as in the eastern Gulf of Thailand and the South China Sea. Generally, however, functional concepts of delimitation can have a stabilising effect.

In many cases where economic resources have been a major issue, the International Court of Justice (ICJ) and independent, ad hoc tribunals, have successfully delimited boundaries. Although relying primarily on natural, geographical features and sovereign rights derived from land territory, tribunals have also accepted flexibility in the degree to which equitable principles can apply to delimitation, as codified in Article 15 of the UNLOSC. Political matters, such as security, welfare and historic fishing practices have influenced many agreements including India–Sri Lanka (1976), Australia–Papua New Guinea (1978), Iceland–Norway fisheries (1980), Tunisia–Libya (1982), Argentina–Chile (1984), Finland–USSR (1986) and several settlements in the Caribbean.[16] Further, preserving the unity of mineral and energy deposits, or promoting their joint development, is often preferred to dividing them by delimitation, as in cases involving Venezuela and neighbouring states.[17] In practice the threat of competing claims may even encourage states to make arrangements for joint exploitation of resources.[18] In regard to fishery disputes and straddling (transmigrating) fish stocks there has also been a fair amount of co-operative behaviour.[19]

It is probable, however, that the 300 maritime delimitation cases outstanding in 1993 are the most complex ones. And, as Charlotte Ku points out, if each case receives *sui generis* treatment, principles of equitability in the body of case law will not be sufficiently developed to strengthen the normative process.[20] In this respect, one of the most difficult areas for determining jurisdiction is the South China Sea (see Figure 8.1 in Chapter 8 above). The area is significant for strategic, navigational and resource reasons, but has not been properly charted. The prospect for an ICJ boundary delimitation seems remote, partly because the dispute is multinational. Except for the *Rockall* and *North Sea Continental Shelf* cases, there have usually been only two litigants, whereas there could be six in the South China Sea. Moreover, there would have to be a ruling on the sovereignty of the Spratly and Paracel islands before the ocean boundaries could be agreed. As indicated in Chapter 8, the most promising approach may be to set aside the sovereignty issue and encourage joint ventures for exploitation.

Such non-jurisdictional solutions should enhance maritime sectoral co-operation, but would not necessarily deal with other issues of international concern and may conflict with desirable management policies for protecting the global environment. Many environmental and conservation problems are beyond the jurisdiction, competence or perceived legitimacy of single maritime powers. And, whilst regional co-operation may offer frameworks for action, the maritime domain also requires a global approach.

Yet multinational responses to broader security issues such as the monitoring of CO_2 levels in the oceans, protecting endangered species and combating widespread marine pollution have been uncoordinated. Measures of global environmental management did emerge in the 1970s. The UN Environmental Programme sponsors anti-pollution measures in various seas, and Chapter 17 of 'Agenda 21', adopted by the UN Conference on the Environment and Development in Rio de Janeiro in 1992, is concerned with ocean issues. But there is no central, integrated approach to the uses and protection of the maritime domain. Whether the delimitation/jurisdictional approach is adequate to meet the diffuse insecurities affecting the oceans, and whether the regime can be hardened by developing a comprehensive enforcement structure is discussed later in this chapter. It is useful first, however, to examine the powers and limits of the UN's existing maritime organisation.

The International Maritime Organisation

The IMO is an autonomous body in the UN network, a relative of the UN Economic and Social Council, with its own membership, structure and financial arrangements. Its purpose is to regulate commercial shipping and tackle marine pollution.[21] Its activities thus impinge on maritime security, broadly conceived, and indicate how far maritime regulation has been developed.

Regulation began during a period of increasing international commerce and intercontinental migration in the nineteenth century, marked in 1863 by Britain and France agreeing to 'Regulations for the Preventing of Collisions at Sea', the forerunner of many such regulations (COLREG). But, in the words of a maritime historian: 'On many issues it has been only major tragedy which has led to expanded government control over domestic industries and which has compelled governments to forgo some degree of national control in exchange for greater reliance upon international solutions.'[22] The Convention for the Safety of Life at Sea (1914) was not adopted until after the *Titanic* disaster in 1912 and then, on account of the First World War, did not come into force. There were considerable difficulties in creating an international maritime organisation because governments faced 'persistent and formidable resistance' by the powerful shipping interests; it was usual for profits to come before safety.[23] However, the two World Wars brought about control of shipping movements and the allies established the United Maritime Authority in 1944 to regulate shipping for wartime needs.

When, in 1948, the UN's Economic and Social Council pressed for a permanent maritime organisation to improve safety at sea and remove the discriminatory tariff practices operated by the secretive shipping cartels, economic interests had to be balanced, and the 1948 Convention establishing the Intergovernmental Maritime Consultative Organisation took another ten years to ratify.[24] The Organisation's main functions were to 'provide machinery for co-operation among Governments in the field of governmental regulations and practices relating to technical matters of all kinds affecting shipping engaged in international trade' and to 'encourage the general adoption of the highest practicable standards in matters concerning maritime safety and efficiency of navigation'. Independently, governments also moved to curb pollution, an issue of increasing concern in the 1950s. The International Convention for the Prevention of Pollution of the Sea by Oil was adopted in 1954, limiting the discharge of oil waste in the vicinity of coasts, a measure for which the intergovernmental body became responsible when it first met in 1959.

The name was changed to International Maritime Organisation in 1982, but it remained a consultative organ. As of June 1992 the IMO's Assembly had 137 full members (including land-locked states, such as Luxembourg and Switzerland, which hold shipping registers) and 2 associate members. The Assembly elects a governing Council of 32 members, 8 of whom represent states with the greatest interests in shipping services, 8 of whom represent other states with major interests in seaborne trade, and 16 others. Financial contributions are based on a formula which combines a state's gross registered tonnage and its assessed levy to the UN. The main contributors in 1991 are given in Table 11.1.

Table 11.1   *Largest contributors to the IMO in 1991*

	% of total contribution
Liberia	12.00
Panama	8.60
Japan	6.68
USSR	6.26
USA	5.41
Norway	5.25
Greece	4.61
Cyprus	4.06
UK	3.18
China	3.15

Source: 'Basic Facts about IMO', *Focus on IMO*, January 1992, p. 3.

For 1992–93 the budget appropriations amounted to £30.25m, which is very small when set alongside the costs of a single oil tanker accident. Even so, the collapse of governments in Liberia, Panama and the USSR disrupted about 25 per cent of the IMO's income in the late 1980s and early 1990s because it was difficult to apply pressure on or through state authorities, even when offshore registers were used for flags of convenience states (such as the Bahamas, Cyprus, Panama and Liberia).

The internal politics of the IMO are difficult to disentangle because of informal processes and government–commercial linkages which affect the organisation. Some observers wonder quite whose interests the IMO represents and note that it defends a flags of convenience system which has been heavily criticised.[25] The IMO has been concerned with non-political, technical aspects of safety and pollution, as reflected in its committee structure.[26] Most developing states have little incentive to accept, or implement, legislation since they usually lack the infrastructures necessary to support regulation. Indeed, flags of convenience states in 'unholy alliances' with private companies which operate registers offshore can act as brakes, resisting regulation which would adversely affect profitability.

This is not, however, to deny the importance of the IMO's work in the two areas of safety and the environment. The IMO updated and extended the International Convention on the Safety of Life at Sea (SOLAS), which had its origins in the unratified agreement of 1914. The current SOLAS Convention was adopted in 1974, and has been frequently amended, notably after the passenger ferry *Herald of Free Enterprise* sank in 1987.[27] Other significant safety conventions include those on: Load Lines (1966), Tonnage Measurement (1969), mandatory traffic separation schemes inserted in COLREGs (1972), Containers (1972) and Fishing Vessels (1977). Technical advances have facilitated safety improvements. The Global Maritime Distress and Safety System which comes into operation during the 1990s will provide information to safety and rescue authorities, promote the use of position-indicating beacons and radar transponders, phase out Morse Code and exploit the satellites of the INMARSAT. The IMO has also promoted higher training standards through the Convention on Standards of Training, Certification and Watchkeeping for Seafarers (1978), the World Maritime University in Malmö (opened in 1983), a Maritime Academy for short courses in Italy, and a Maritime Law Institute in Malta.

Issues of maritime safety and environmental security are closely related. Many of the measures required to safeguard a ship, its crew and cargo also contribute to reducing risks to the environment from the release of cargoes into the sea. Since the 1954 Convention on oil discharges, the IMO has adopted over 30 instruments to tackle pollution. The first comprehensive measure was the International Convention for the Prevention of Pollution from Ships in 1973 (MARPOL). It covered chemicals as well as oil, specified reductions in operational oil discharges and banned oil discharge completely in the Baltic Sea, Mediterranean, Black Sea, Red Sea and certain other waters. New developments led to the Convention, known as MARPOL 73/78, which came into force in 1983 as advances in cleaning technology reduced the need for operational discharges. The IMO also developed a Dangerous Goods Code (1965) and codes affecting the construction of tankers.[28] The Secretariat also shoulders functions in connection with the London Convention on the Prevention of Marine Pollution by Dumping of Wastes and Other Matter (1972) which regulates the incineration and dumping of land waste at sea, banning altogether such highly toxic substances as mercury. Finally, the IMO co-operates with UNEP in sponsoring Regional Marine Pollution Emergency Centres for the Mediterranean Sea, Red Sea, Persian Gulf, Caribbean, West-Central Africa, South-West Pacific and South Asia.

In 1990 the IMO decided to reflect the maritime concerns expressed in the 1987 Brundtland Report, *Our Common Future*, and established a Global Programme for the Protection of the Marine Environment.[29] Its strategy was to assist developing countries which lack the facilities and expertise to implement anti-pollution measures (see Figure 11.1). At a practical level, for example, the IMO has provided waste facilities for fishermen using the badly polluted harbour at Visakhapatnam on India's East Coast.[30]

The IMO has therefore contributed to the creation of an international regime for maritime security. In particular, its codes and regulations affect the health of the oceans, of the societies which rely on the sea for their everyday existence and of the long-term sustainability of the marine food chain. It recognises that spillage and dumping at sea, marine safety, and the provision of accident compensation and maritime technical assistance are international problems. Moreover, it has developed regime constraints during a period of radical change in world shipping. Global tonnage quadrupled between 1960 and 1980, increasing mainly in the developing world whilst shrinking in traditional maritime nations. The size of tankers has increased dramatically, and specialised vessels are now the rule rather than the exception that they were in the 1970s.

The IMO's conventions and codes have been developed by, and are acceptable to, the maritime community. An 'acceptability factor' should increasingly come into play. Leading conventions in force in 1990 are given in Table 11.2. By setting minimum standards for new ship design and operational procedures, the IMO can increase the risk to companies of having substandard vessels rejected by insurers and turned away from ports. The IMO's goal is to encourage the development of a world-wide port control system, based on the 1990 Paris Memorandum of Understanding on Port State Control which agreed to deter rogue vessels from entering ports in Europe. A similar port control system was introduced in Latin America in 1993 and the Asia–Pacific region scheduled to introduce one in 1994.[31] However, to prevent substandard ships operating internationally there is a need to ensure implementation through a co-ordinated programme of intrusive inspections, the targeting of flag

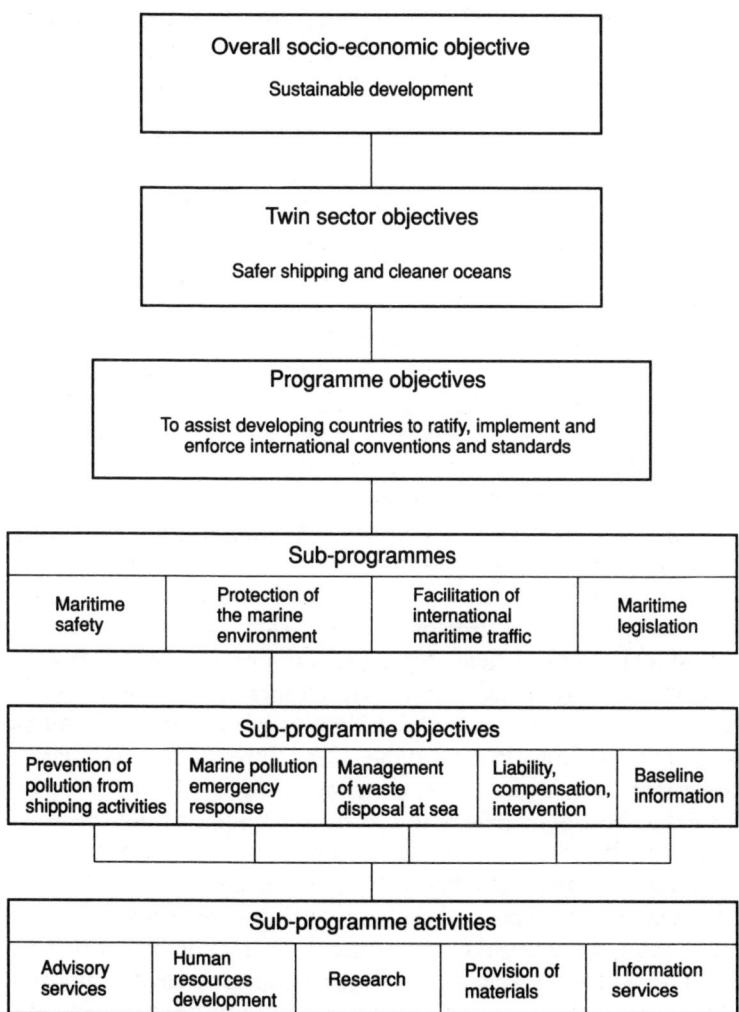

Figure 11.1 *The IMO's global programme*

states with poor records and the computerised distribution of information. In addition, considering that human factors account for most accidents, inspections are needed to ensure that ships are crewed efficiently and that members of the crew can communicate with one another and with any passengers. In several disasters, including the fire on the ferry *Scandinavian Star* in which 159 people died in April 1990, crew competence has been a prominent issue.[32]

Table 11.2   *Leading IMO conventions in force*

	Date in force	Signatories	% of world fleet
SOLAS 1974	25.5.80	108	96.72
MARPOL 73/78	2.10.83	60	85.36
Load Lines	21.7.68	118	98.22
Standards of Training	28.4.84	77	74.53
London Dumping Convention	30.8.75	64	65.12

Source: 'Cleaner Oceans: The Role of IMO in the 1990s', *Focus on IMO*, January 1990, p. 10.

Indeed, critics can point to considerable limitations on the IMO's powers.

• Although the IMO deals with issues which states are unable or unwilling to tackle individually, it seeks co-operation between states rather than developing world society functions. Its decisions are reached by consensus and it has no power to force states to comply with its legislation. The adoption of measures largely depends on consistent lobbying by a state or group of states. Many of its codes have the status of guidelines which are not binding on governments.

• In so far as the IMO reflects transnational concerns, the interests of international commerce have outweighed those of environmental lobby groups or coastal communities. This does not mean that the IMO represents a simple case of 'agency capture'. The composition of national delegations varies, and it should not be assumed that government officials promote their own state's shipping industry. However, some shipping interests are politically influential and contribute to domestic political funds. In the case of flags of convenience states, which are represented in the IMO Council, commercial interests are paramount because government control may be negligible. The Liberian registry is one of several convenience registers run by private companies operating from New York. Given the absence of a functioning government in Monrovia as a consequence of civil war, this might be considered politically 'convenient', but not necessarily conducive to maritime security. The IMO's work borders on industrial self-regulation in which commercial pressures seek the minimum necessary to avoid coercion.[33]

• Many Conventions are limited in scope. For example, the level of the IMO's Oil Pollution Compensation Fund and limited liability for tanker accidents means that the maximum automatic payout may not cover damaged caused.[34] Conventions affecting the design of ships apply to future construction, and much of MARPOL 73/78 applies to ships built after mid-1979. Yet the world's fleet is getting older, and this clearly has an impact on accident rates.[35]

• Conventions generally take many years to come into force, partly reflecting technical complexities of implementation, and partly the resistance of commercial interests and states. Standard tonnage measurement was adopted in 1969 but did not come into effect until 1982. The 1977 Convention on the Safety of Fishing Vessels was still not in force in 1992 because the signatories only represented a combined tonnage of 15.4 per cent of the world's total, the triggering requirement being 50 per cent. Some twenty years will have elapsed between the adoption of the Global Maritime Distress and Safety System and its implementation. Indeed in 1981, the IMO Assembly adopted a policy of slowing down new legislation to enable states to implement existing measures.

• Although conventions are increasingly being strengthened by inspection and certification requirements,[36] there are no explicit sanctions for non-compliance. Conventions which have entered into force have to be incorporated into national law, and enforcement is the responsibility of individual governments. The IMO relies largely on publicity, drawing attention to states which fail to live up to their obligations. But disadvantaged states face vexing legal, technical and administrative problems due to lack of resources.[37] Nor do the flags of convenience states seem willing to enforce safety standards. There is a problem in detecting violations, collecting evidence and proving it in court. In 1989, independent surveys showed that of 300 reported discharge violations in the North Sea, only 18 led to successful prosecutions, and these resulted in derisory fines.[38] After a series of bulk carrier losses around Australia, an official report discovered widespread abuse of the private system for certifying ships and crews.[39]

• The IMO has no independent research capacity. It holds only the information which states, shipping interests and external bodies choose to provide. Its inputs are therefore partly dependent on the level of information technology and research in member states.[40]

• The organisation has a Technical Co-operation Committee but no regular technical co-operation funds. For technical co-operation and the Protection of the Maritime Environment programme there is a heavy reliance on donations from UN agencies, private organisations and individual states, notably Sweden and Norway.[41]

A UN Maritime Agency

Obviously, it is important to retain the expertise which the IMO offers to the UN, and to avoid jeopardising its work. It has begun to recognise, through its programme for protection of the marine environment, that policy and regulation are not easily kept apart. But the IMO has limited power and its financial capacity to assist disadvantaged states is weak and virtually dependent on charitable donations.

Maritime security issues are too serious a business to be left to those with economic interests in maritime trade. Bodies such as UNEP and the Sustainable Development Commission also claim an interest in ocean and maritime management. Any future Conference on the Law of the Sea, mark IV, would likewise have a bearing on maritime security issues. Yet co-ordination between UN agencies, policies and processes is likely to remain problematic, if the difficulties of environmental policy co-ordination through UNEP are anything to go by.[42]

An alternative would be to consider a more radical restructuring to ensure a more rigorous regime for ocean governance. A new multi-functional organisation might be created to take over all the UN's maritime programmes in recognition of the special problems which affect the maritime domain and its users. The IMO's remit might be broadened accordingly and its structure reformed. Or the IMO might be subsumed into a UN Maritime Agency which would have a range of security functions stretching into military spheres and not confined to technical and economic issues.

As noted in Chapter 7 above, a UN Maritime Agency has been proposed by Robert Staley for a wide variety of objectives, many of which would require the tasking of naval forces. The role of the Agency would be to oversee all maritime security issues and devise agreements with states for the constitution of 'on-call' naval forces to carry out UN Security Council resolutions. The Agency would supervise force training and exercising on a multinational basis. Operational missions would cover a broad range, including: the deterrence or defeat of seaborne aggression; crisis prevention, observation and peacekeeping; constabulary work to implement international agreements including those produced by the IMO, and to counter piracy, terrorism and drug smuggling; ecological monitoring and the protection of marine resources.[43]

Such an Agency might offer certain benefits. It could:

- give teeth to the UNLOSC and IMO conventions;
- draw together maritime expertise over a whole range of maritime concerns;
- reflect the fact that the maritime domain has special characteristics and a range of special security problems.

On the other hand, the concept of a UN Maritime Agency, combining several maritime security functions, would have to overcome the various difficulties:

- Linkage between functionalist activities and the diplomatic and political use of naval forces may not be easily sustained. It is frequently argued that the UN's functional agencies work because they are relatively non-political and detached from extraneous political–strategic disputes. To put management of maritime security under one organisation could jeopardise work on technical solutions to problems.
- Linkage between the Maritime Agency and the Security Council would not be at all straightforward, though the proposal envisages the former being a servant of the latter. As currently mandated under the UN Charter, the Security Council is unlikely to direct such an Agency to conduct operations merely to implement regulations affecting, say, infringements of merchant shipping regulations or to reduce the piracy problem.
- Naval presence, suasion and deterrence, crisis prevention, sealift and humanitarian protection is directed at influencing events on

land. In this respect it would be equally important to integrate UN naval deployments with diplomatic initiatives and any land and air operations, and with aid agencies, as to establish a separate maritime–naval institution.

- A new Agency would make new demands on UN finances and, as UK and US opposition to the Sustainable Development Commission revealed, there is a reluctance on the part of some states to fund new organisations.

Conclusion

Nevertheless, there is room for reform of the existing maritime regime, as within the UN security network in general. Whether the regime can be hardened, however, will depend on the willingness of international actors to support world society goals and the means to manage, monitor and, where necessary, to enforce their implementation.

A distinction can be made between ensuring that the civilian use of the oceans is properly regulated and managed, and the implementation of Security Council resolutions to maintain or build peace through the deployment of naval force. The former emphasises legislation, administration, monitoring and constabulary skills, involving close relations with the civilian users of the sea. The latter is essentially concerned with threats to peace on land. This is not to deny the significant degree of overlap which occurs between purely maritime issues and maintaining territorial peace. Nor is it the intention to support a narrow, military based, definition of security. Rather, the concern should be to avoid the unnecessary militarisation of security problems. Although organisations such as Greenpeace have significantly changed world opinion about the maritime domain, through peaceful scientific and political voyages organised on a transnational basis, the only actors with navies are states which have traditionally seen their roles primarily in terms of national military security.

A 'hard' regime would explicitly politicise technical issues in a way that the IMO has so far avoided. But by mid-twenty-first century, a UN Maritime Agency might replace or absorb the IMO for managing the maritime domain more effectively. When maritime constabulary duties are involved, the Agency could certainly facilitate co-operation between states in the deployment of naval, coastguard and fishery protection units. In the foreseeable future, however, the development of higher intensity peacekeeping and peace support functions, related to UN-authorised land operations, is more likely to find expression in a Security Council advisory committee representing all armed services.

Notes

1 See generally, J. Lewis, *The Implications of Sea Level Rise for Island and Low-Lying Countries*, Report for the Commonwealth Secretariat, London, 1988; United Nations Environmental Programme, *Criteria for Assessing Vulnerability to Sea-level Rise: A Global Inventory for High Risk Areas*, Delft, 1989; J. Ince, *The Rising Seas*, Earthscan, London, 1990.

2 Gwyn Prins, 'The United Nations and Naval Power in the Post-Cold War World', in United Nations Department for Disarmament Affairs, *Naval Confidence-building Measures*, Topical Papers 4, UN, New York, 1990, pp. 236–40.

3 Oran R. Young, *International Cooperation: Building Regimes for Natural Resources and the Environment*, Cornell University Press, Ithaca, NY, 1989.

4 Robert O. Keohane, *After Hegemony: Cooperation and Discord in the World Political Economy*, Princeton University Press, Princeton, NJ, 1984, p. 37.

5 Oran Young contends that non-state actors are required to live by rules invented by states. 'Regime Dynamics: The Rise and Fall of International Regimes', in Stephen Krasner (ed.), *International Regimes*, Cornell University Press, Ithaca, NY, 1983, p. 93.

6 Stephen Krasner, 'Structural Causes and Regime Consequences: Regimes as Intervening Variables', *International Organization*, vol. 36, no. 2, spring 1982, p. 186.

7 Stephan Haggard and Beth A. Simmons, 'Theories of International Regimes', *International Organization*, vol. 41, no. 3, summer 1987, p. 495; Volker Rittberger, Manfred Efinger and Martin Mendler, 'Toward an East–West Security Regime: The Case of Confidence- and Security-building Measures', *Journal of Peace Research*, vol, 27, spring 1990, pp. 55–74.

8 Keohane, *International Institutions and State Power*, Westview Press, Boulder, Col., p. 14.

9 T. B. Koh, Introduction to *The Law of the Sea: Official Text of the United Nations Convention on the Law of the Sea with Annexes, Index*

and Final Act of the Third United Nations Conference on the Law of the Sea, St Martin's, New York, 1983, xxxiii. The Preparatory Committee was dismantled in 1993, its work judged to have been completed. Supervisory functions were continued by the UN's office of Ocean Affairs and the Law of the Sea.

10 At present, there are economic, but few technical, obstacles to the exploitation of sea-bed resources in any depth of ocean. Study by the Defence Export Services Organisation cited by Steven Haines, 'The maritime domain – jurisdictional profiles and operational requirements in a developing market', paper at Naval Forecast Conference, Advanced Technology International, London and Brussels, 20–24 May 1991.

11 Douglas M. Johnston, 'Ocean Boundary Disputes and the Risk of Conflict', paper at Colloquium on Maritime Security and Conflict Resolution, Centre for Foreign Policy Studies, Dalhousie University, Halifax, NS, 24–27 June 1993.

12 Ken Booth, *Law, Force and Diplomacy at Sea*, Allen & Unwin, London, 1985, pp. 38–45.

13 See, James Cable, *Navies in Violent Peace*, Macmillan, London, 1989, p. 88; R. R. Churchill and A. V. Lowe, *The Law of the Sea*, Manchester University Press, Manchester, rev. ed., 1988, pp. 307–14; Lowe, 'Some Legal Problems Arising from the Use of the Sea for Military Purposes', *Marine Policy*, vol. 10, no. 3, 1986, pp. 171–84; B. Kwiatkowska, 'Military Uses in the EEZ: a Reply', *ibid.*, vol. 11, 1987, pp. 249–50, and Lowe, 'Rejoinder', *ibid.*, pp. 250–52.

14 Articles 30–32, *The Law of the Sea: Official Text*. See also, Christopher Pinto, 'Maritime Security and the 1982 United Nations Convention on the Law of the Sea', in Jozef Goldblat (ed.), *Maritime Security: The Building of Confidence*, UNIDIR, Geneva, 1992, pp. 13–15.

15 Johnston, *The Theory and History of Ocean Boundary-making*, McGill–Queen's University Press, Kingston, Ont., 1988, p. 226.

16 See reports in Jonathan I. Charney and Lewis M. Alexander (eds), *International Maritime Boundaries*, Martinus Nijhoff, Dordrecht, 2 vols, 1993.

17 Malcolm D. Evans, *Relevant Circumstances and Maritime Delimitation*, Clarendon, Oxford, 1989, pp. 192–4.

18 Stephen Langford, 'Maritime delimitation in the Mediterranean', paper at Naval Peacekeeping Workshop, Mountbatten Centre, University of Southampton, 14 February 1992; Churchill and Lowe, *The Law of the Sea*, p. 161.

19 Robin Churchill, 'Boundaries and Fishing Rights', paper at Conference on International Boundaries: Political, Legal and Strategic Implications', RIIA, 9–10 January 1992.

20 Charlotte Ku, 'Ocean Boundaries: Does the 1982 Law of the Sea Convention Matter?', paper at 34th ISA Convention, Acapulco, 23–27 March 1993.

21 See, Samir Mankabady, *The International Maritime Organization*, 2 vols, Croom Helm, Beckenham, 1986 and 1987.

22 Harvey B. Silverstein, *Superships and Nation-States: The Transnational Politics of the Intergovernmental Maritime Consultative Organization*, Westview Press, Boulder, Col., 1978, p. 13.

23 By taking their own initiatives, creating the International Law Association (1873) and the International Maritime Committee (1897), private interests hoped to forestall government interference. *Ibid.*, p. 10.

24 States accounting for a large tonnage of goods shipped and states with a large tonnage of ships registered were not necessarily one and the same, and their interests in regulation diverged. The Soviet Union objected to potential international control over its growing merchant fleet, and shipping interests in Greece and Scandinavia, influential with their governments, were also prominent opponents of intervention. The market-fixing issue was shunted on to the UN Conference on Trade and Development (UNCTAD) where progress in regulating the shipping 'conferences' was painfully slow. *Ibid.*, p. 27.

25 Gary Slapper, 'Sea Changes', *The Guardian*, 9 June 1993, p. 17.

26 The Maritime Safety Committee is the most senior committee and has sub-committees dealing with navigation, radio communications, carriage of dangerous goods, fire protection and ship design. The Marine Environment Protection Committee deals with pollution of the marine environment from ships. In addition, there is a Legal Committee, a Technical Co-operation Committee and a Facilitation Committee which aims to reduce red-tape in ports.

27 'SOLAS: The International Convention on the Safety of Life at Sea, 1974', *Focus on IMO*, November 1989, *passim*.

28 Some chemicals, such as polychlorinated biphenyls, are so harmful to the environment that the IMO recommends that they should not be carried in bulk by ship at all. 'Preventing Marine Pollution', *Focus on IMO*, September 1989, p. 2.

29 See, The World Commission on Environment and Development, *Our Common Future* [the Brundtland Report], Oxford, Oxford University Press, 1987, pp. 261–89.

30 The programme requires: assessments of pollution and a state's capabilities to meet its obligations; consultation between vested interests on a national level; information and advice; and the installation of equipment. IMO, *IMO's Global Programme for the Protection of the Marine Environment*, London, 1990, p. 6.

31 'Asia–Pacific Boost for Global Port Checks', *NUMAST Telegraph*, December 1992, p. 2.

32 'Three Facing Prison in Ferry Fire Trial', *NUMAST Telegraph*, December 1992, p. 9.

33 Of the largest oil spills in the period 1967–84, 66 per cent involved flags of convenience or Greek-registered vessels. Information from Martin Garside, NUMAST, London. In the 1980s fierce shipping competition encouraged companies to cut costs and keep so-called 'coffin' ships afloat. And there is an obvious contradiction in the way shipping companies accept or even promote safety legislation, and yet register vessels in countries where labour is cheap and standards are low in order to avoid the pay and conditions which well-trained, safety-conscious unionised crews regard as their due. By 1992, about 80 per cent of UK-owned tonnage was registered abroad or offshore. The UK register of ships over 500 g.t. fell from 1,614 ships in 1975 to 303 in 1992, and in this period the number of British nationals working on British-owned ships fell from 90,000 to 25,000. NUMAST, *The Safety Case for British Shipping*, London, July 1992.

34 Compensation for the 1993 *Braer* accident will be in the region of £55 million. Jim Mulrennan, 'Compensation Limits Could be Inadequate', *Lloyd's List*, 7 January 1993, p. 2. However, the US Oil Pollution Act, introduced after the 1988 *Exxon Valdez* disaster in Alaska, confronted tanker companies with unlimited liability in the event of misconduct. Jeremy Leggett, 'Black to the Future', *The Guardian*, 8 January 1993, section 2, p. 6.

35 In the 1980s, the proportion of ships under ten years old fell from 62 per cent to 36 per cent. Of the ships checked by UK surveyors in UK ports in 1991, 60 per cent had defects, and many were prevented from sailing. John Vidal, 'Falling marine standards add to risk of oil disasters', *The Guardian*, 9 January 1993, p. 5.

36 'Preventing Marine Pollution', *Focus on IMO*, September 1989, p. 11.

37 IMO, *IMO's Global Programme*, p. 5.

38 The IMO recognises that there are disincentives for collecting waste. Reception facilities for waste are costly to install and maintain, and the question of payment is an issue between shipping and shore authorities. If the ship owner is levied for disposing a ship's waste on shore, then the temptation is to discharge illegally at sea. 'Cleaner Oceans: the Role of the IMO in the 1990s', *Focus on IMO*, January 1990, pp. 12–13, 14.

39 Australian Commonwealth Parliament, *Ships of Shame: Inquiry into Ship Safety*, Report from the House of Representatives Standing Committee on Transport, Communications and Infrastructure, Australian Government Publishing Service, Canberra, December 1992. Private classification societies, such as Lloyd's of London, choose their own rules to issue seaworthiness certificates for insurance purposes, though huge insurance losses led to tighter requirements in the early 1990s. Declassed ships are not publicly named, however, and their

owners 'shop around' for societies which have lax classification procedures. See House of Lords Select Committee on Science and Technology, *Safety Aspects of Ship Design and Technology*, Session 1991–92, 2nd Report, HL Paper 30–1, HMSO, London, 14 February 1992, recommendations (iv) and (v).

40 Silverstein, *Superships and Nation-States*, pp. 35–6.

41 'Basic Facts about IMO', *Focus on IMO*, January 1992, p. 3.

42 Mark Imber, 'Too Many Cooks? The Post-Rio Reform of the United Nations', *International Affairs*, vol. 69, no. 1, 1993, pp. 55–70.

43 Robert Stephens Staley II, *The Wave of the Future: The United Nations and Naval Peacekeeping*, International Peace Academy occasional paper, Lynne Rienner, Boulder, Col., 1992, pp. 18–20, 43–5.

Conclusion

This study has posed two basic questions: whether traditional peacekeeping is relevant in the maritime environment, and whether, given proposals for broadening UN-authorised involvement in security problems, there are new multinational roles for maritime forces.

In answer to the first question, it has been argued that there have been occasional instances of maritime forces engaging in activity which can either be regarded as analogous to land-based peacekeeping or as having been undertaken in support of operations ashore. But the mainly land-based sources of international disputes, the nature of the maritime environment and the political, jurisdictional and military characteristics of naval vessels have militated against the regular use of maritime forces for peacekeeping.

On the occasions when the international community has legitimised maritime activities, the operational concepts have been derived from the established territorial context of UN peacekeeping activities. This study suggests that the limitation is open to criticism. Territorial and maritime environments are distinct and, hence, give rise to differing peace and security conceptions. Moreover, the traditional basis of territorial collective security actions is itself being challenged by the emergence of concepts of 'second generation' operations. These new concepts may be particularly appropriate to the maritime context.

Thus, in answer to the second question, whether there are new multinational roles tangentially related to peacekeeping, the study indicates that a variety of naval activities have considerable relevance to the emerging international security environment. The kinds of operations which stretch beyond the traditional horizons of peacekeeping, and which are familiar to maritime forces in national or alliance contexts, could certainly be considered appropriate for legitimation by the UN. They include: naval diplomacy, presence and deterrence, interdiction and blockading, mineclearing, disaster relief and humanitarian assistance, maritime housekeeping (environmental monitoring, salvage and hydrographic work) and constabulary work in support of civil and commercial communities.

The study provides a rigorous conceptual framework for UN naval operations. It has also considered the absence of appropriate UN structures for managing naval forces and the institutional bias within the UN towards territorial forces, structures and strategies. This does not mean that policies of exceptionalism are the best way to redress the balance or to harness the unique qualities of sea power. Indeed, integrated naval support for land-based activities may become an increasingly crucial part of multinational operations. Naval operations should be regarded as a mainstream activity with appropriate structures and resources, integrated with land and air operations when relevant, rather than as an adjunct form of activity.

This study envisages a greater role for multinational naval forces in international security. Although some roles, such as disaster relief, will not necessarily be controversial, the authors are mindful of the political sensitivities and constraints which would apply to any concept of 'naval interventionism'. It is also essential that the use of naval forces should not be viewed merely as a technical or operational issue, but as part of broad political processes. Deployment policies should not be driven by the availability of resources but by the requirements of peace and security as legitimised by a competent international authority such as the UN. Moreover, co-operative deployment should be closely concerted with diplomatic activity.

Contexts

At the outset of this study it was considered important to theorise about sea power in the post-Cold War international context. Historically, maritime forces have tended to be associated with state power, competitive security concepts and the pursuit of national interests. Certainly security co-operation at sea during the Cold War tended to occur within well-defined limits. Yet in principle the particular attributes of the maritime environment and of naval–maritime power could foster much wider multinational security co-operation.

Developments in global security were also examined in Chapter 2. The international context in which the UN operates for dealing with world order problems has changed since the end of the 1980s. But the notion that the functioning of the UN network is guided by its continuing reliance on self-interested co-operation between states remains a powerful one. The UN's intercession in crises might be seen as unduly dependent on the interests of a group of powerful states in the Security Council, rather than on a developing international consensus. Indeed, the weight being accorded to state sovereignty and the conditions under which it can be legitimately breached may prove to be increasingly divisive issues between the developed and developing world. The UN-authorised initiatives in Northern Iraq in 1991 and in Somalia in 1992–93 were both justified on humanitarian grounds but have not really resolved fundamental questions about the principles of UN interventionist activity.

The selective or *sui generis* approach to crises is a particular problem in that it condemns the UN to reactive action and expediency, and may jeopardise the UN's legitimacy. Yet selectivity suits state interests and is thus likely to be a continuing feature of the UN network. Nevertheless, the approach may be mitigated by a process of institutionalisation. Unilateral action will be constrained by multinational processes and norms, within which even powerful states seek legitimacy for their actions.

Although 'ideal' peacekeeping has fostered considerable flexibility and innovation, a high priority has generally been given to the principles of consent and impartiality. However, in the context of increased co-operation in the Security Council after the Cold War, further operational experiment has occurred, notably in attempts to offer humanitarian protection. To the extent that these operations have involved the UN in a wide variety of roles and in contested as well as consented intercession, new peacekeeping concepts are useful, allowing for a range of maritime security and peace support roles.

True, the concept of multilateralism has been largely absent from theories of sea power. It is, however, becoming increasingly difficult for the world's major navies to legitimise their roles in terms of traditional sea-control or sea-denial operations, and there are incentives in naval establishments to revise strategies and participate in multinational peacekeeping and peace support operations. The pattern of naval growth also suggests that the global maritime powers will shift away from forces prepared for battle on the high seas, towards protection of economic zones, regional constabulary roles and force projection to facilitate operations ashore.

Naval peacekeeping and force thresholds

From the historical record of UN naval peacekeeping it appears that there have been very few instances of autonomous operations. Maritime activities have tended to be conducted concurrently with land-based deployments. Naval operations, such as those in West New Guinea/Irian in 1962–63, the Straits of Tiran since 1982 and in the Gulf of Fonseca in the early 1990s, were closely circumscribed in terms of their use of force and mandates. However, the deployment of naval forces for peacekeeping has raised distinctive issues, such as the difficulties of providing suitable platforms and sustaining intensive patrolling.

Issues, such as the technical and operational difficulties of multinational force integration, will become more acute if the classical peacekeeping model is overlain by a model which includes overt displays of force and the use of force. One of the chief lessons to be drawn from the historical experiences, is that if maritime units are to be both relevant to the tasks set and perceived to be legitimate, it is vital to appreciate the importance of force 'thresholds'. The notion that peacekeeping and enforcement are becoming blurred should not obscure the critical implications of moving from one role and status of force to another. The fact that naval forces can transit territorial waters, can move freely in international waters, and can evade some of the sovereignty issues that constrain land operations, should not tempt the international community to use naval forces indiscriminately. A UN naval peacekeeping mandate such as the Gulf of Fonseca operation, for example, is a quite different proposition to enforcing sanctions in the Adriatic. In this regard, it is essential to link appropriate levels of force to political and diplomatic initiatives in the management of disputes.

Concepts of maritime operations

The UN has yet to establish an adequate conceptual basis for the type of maritime operations that might be undertaken and has tended to derive concepts of maritime strategy from its territorial experiences. Although this is unsurprising, given the past predominance of territorial initiatives and the low priority accorded to maritime operations, it is no longer intellectually credible to rely on such an approach. If the international community increasingly takes a wider view of security, and if peacekeeping and second generation operations become larger and more complex, maritime forces may play a more prominent role in underpinning security. There is a need for the UN to elaborate coherent concepts to underpin maritime operations. These may diverge significantly from those that have been formulated for land operations.

The maritime environment and the characteristics of ships means that maritime forces can be used in a variety of dispositions without infringing territory. However, they are generally unsuited to the interpositional roles that have characterised traditional peacekeeping. Furthermore, the heavy firepower of many classes of warship appears to undermine the requirements for impartial, non-threatening peacekeeping forces. The fact that they have the capability to circumvent many of the traditional constraints associated with the use of ground forces, such as borders and other physical manifestations of sovereignty, means that they have powerful intervention capabilities. Naval units can thus send ambiguous signals which may be used in an attempt to de-escalate crises, but which also risk creating misperception and heightening tensions.

The freedom of movement associated with naval vessels and the powerful diplomatic signals they can transmit opens up new possibilities for the UN. Naval diplomacy has been traditionally associated with 'gunboat diplomacy' and 'showing the flag' and has unfortunate historical resonances. However, the utility of naval diplomacy should be re-evaluated in the light of the more prominent global role widely advocated for the UN. Naval forces have the capacity to exert deterrent effects, frequently with greater immediacy and credibility than territorial modes of deterrence. Their unique attributes can also be called upon to enforce embargoes or blockades, to provide humanitarian relief and give offshore support

to land forces. In sum, it is essential to incorporate maritime security concepts into theories of international force deployment.

Constabulary functions

Outside traditional peacekeeping concepts there are constabulary
functions which might be organised and performed multilaterally.
Chapter 5 examined four roles regarding naval assistance to civilian
authorities: drug interdiction, piracy suppression, disaster relief and
maritime housekeeping.

For drug interdiction the European and US experiences offer two
models. Although the United States has been involved in multilateral
initiatives and diplomatic activity, the thrust of its policy has been
unilateralist and heavily dependent on military force. In contrast, the
West European approach has been to emphasise co-operation
between law enforcement agencies, and to place less reliance on military forces. The latter approach may prove to be a more appropriate
model for multinational initiatives. However, a UN role is likely to be
limited given the wide-ranging operations already undertaken by
European and US agencies. Asian maritime interdiction might benefit
from a UN input and, more generally, the UN could press for full
international support for the 1988 Vienna Convention.

In deploying maritime forces to suppress piracy, problems arise
from the fact that the definition of piracy in international law is tied
to absence of geographical jurisdiction at sea. The international
community is disadvantaged when a state either lacks the capability to control the problem, or turns a blind eye to miscreants within
its territorial jurisdiction. The use of extra-regional naval forces is
unlikely to be the most appropriate international response. The
answer lies more at the regional level where coastal states should be
assisted with intelligence, funds, training and equipment and other
services. However, a foreign naval presence in international waters
where piracy is a major problem could signal international concern
and stimulate coastal states into taking action.

Navies have traditionally played a valuable role in disaster relief,
a prominent form of military aid to civilian agencies. Disaster relief
guidelines have generally emphasised the importance of relying on
the affected state to issue invitations for assistance, and offshore
naval units have certainly been careful to avoid upsetting local

sensibilities. Ships may be particularly valuable in providing an escape route and a sanctuary for displaced persons and refugees. Although the UN's Department of Humanitarian Affairs, NATO and NGOs have prepared guidelines and standard operating procedures for disaster relief generally, there is a requirement for a new international code on the treatment of persons displaced as a consequence of disasters, who become seaborne.

The concept of co-operative maritime housekeeping recognises that pollution does not respect international frontiers. As public consciousness of the environment has grown, so protection of the world's oceans has become a legitimate goal of international life, and this is likely to require maritime co-operation on a large scale in the future. On specific problems, such as the hazards of naval nuclear reactors, particularly in Russian waters, international naval expertise would be invaluable. But general coastal protection against oil and toxic spills at sea may also require international maritime co-operation.

Maritime forces undertaking international constabulary duties will normally operate according to traditional peacekeeping parameters – firepower, for example, will be of secondary importance to monitoring and boarding duties, medical and evacuation facilities in the case of disaster relief and technical expertise in the case of pollution control.

Force structures

Post-Cold War expectations that the UN can move beyond ad hoc approaches to more cohesive and permanent forms of force organisation are likely to be dashed by political, financial and operational problems. Chapter 6 noted that the gradual development of UN transitional arrangements, such as earmarked or on-call forces or the formalisation of ad hoc arrangements of the type utilised in the Persian Gulf, would be more likely to eventuate.

The main impediment to any development of standing forces is a political one. To forgo or diminish national control of military forces – as implied in advanced forms of standing force structure – raises fundamental issues regarding the authority of the state. The formation of UN standing forces, for example, would be widely perceived as paving the way towards a UN global policing role and erosion of state sovereignty. Given the low priority accorded by the UN to naval forces, it is also unlikely that resources would be made available for advanced naval force structures. Although operationally there are benefits to be realised through the use of standing forces, in practice, as has been shown by the NATO experience, considerable operational difficulties need to be overcome and a strong motivational incentive is necessary before operating efficiency can be achieved. Perhaps the most feasible method of improving maritime operations would be for the UN to draw upon NATO earmarked or standing contingents. However, for the rest of the decade the UN is likely to rely on ad hoc arrangements, whilst perhaps also developing agreements with states for earmarking navies.

Management

The international community needs management structures for regulating maritime security operations. Historically, there has been no special UN management provision for naval forces: naval operations have not been regarded as mainstream UN activities. Naval management has either been part of a territorial peacekeeping management system, or contracted out by the UN to multinational coalitions. But with naval power assuming greater relevance in maintaining international peace and security these approaches may no longer be sustainable. Chapter 7 argued that the UN needs to reconsider naval planning. Management bodies within the UN ought to have naval representation and a maritime perspective in the decision-making process. The UN management system is in a state of flux and future developments are difficult to predict, but a tri-service, unified command is the most appropriate way forward for the UN. In this structure, naval operations, rather than being regarded as an adjunct form of activity, would come under a rigorous management system for co-ordinating air, land and naval initiatives.

Although there is potential for regional structures to develop maritime security functions, most regional institutions lack requisite military competence. As suggested in Chapter 8, naval capability in NATO and the WEU is exceptional. In much of the developing world, naval forces are mainly coastal and used for protecting territorial seas and EEZs. There are opportunities, however, for multinational constabulary work. The South Pacific area provides a model in this respect. But in most regions political will and unity of purpose are absent and the lead will have to come from the UN.

Operational and technical factors

Establishing operational and technical compatibility between navies is a particularly taxing issue in multinational maritime security co-operation. Special difficulties have been experienced with regard to: rules of engagement; communications; strategic intelligence; sustainability, reach and logistic support; and training doctrine. However, it was argued in Chapter 9 that different levels of integration are appropriate for different types of operation, and that not even common rules of engagement are necessarily a prerequisite for the successful conduct of multinational naval operations. In Operation *Desert Storm*, for example, navies operated under differing ROE which were not always disclosed even when co-ordinated. National co-ordination, or the type of arrangements that have evolved within NATO, may form the basis for future multinational integration or co-ordination.

In regard to communications, not all states require sophisticated systems to participate in multinational operations. There are a number of relatively simple, cheap means by which vessels can communicate. Even relatively secure computerised data-handling links are available to many navies. Furthermore, certain operations, such as the monitoring of blockades, might only require a simple voice-net communication system. However, for more complex operations, or for navies hoping to command or co-ordinate naval operations, it will be essential to possess more advanced systems.

Sustainability and reach can be achieved in multinational naval operations through standardised connecting links for refuelling and the pooling of stocks and spares. During the Persian Gulf War some states integrated their auxiliaries into a common logistical pool escorted and organised by the Canadian Navy. Russian vessels also exercised refuelling operations with Western warships.

There are a number of significant problems to be overcome in training and doctrine for multinational naval forces. Joint exercises are required of the sort conducted within the NATO TEAMWORK series. The means already exist for navies to co-operate on standing operating procedures using widely disseminated editions of NATO's manoeuvring instructions and signal book.

If the UN is to consider naval contingencies it will have to establish the basis for interoperability. In this respect, the NATO model may provide key elements worth adopting, notably an agreed menu of ROE, secure communications channels, common data links and standardised operational procedures.

Legal issues and the maritime security regime

Except in regard to well-established rules for the high seas and innocent passage in the territorial sea, international law relevant to naval peacekeeping and peace support operations is generally uncertain. The applicable law of the UN Charter, the law of the sea and the law of naval warfare is a matter of contention. Under the Charter, a state exercising the right of self-defence, or states exercising collective self-defence, are taking interim measures pending the Security Council's involvement. Under Chapter VI the UN maintains neutrality in a dispute, but under Chapter VII the UN's interest, in upholding international peace and security, renders its mediation role more problematic and this may be ruled out altogether by enforcement action. Indeed, legal norms for sanctions and enforcement have not yet been developed as they have for traditional peacekeeping.

It was argued in Chapter 10 that not only is there ambiguity about individual provisions of the Law of the Sea Convention, but also general uncertainty about the impact of UN operations on rights otherwise normally exerciseable. A naval peacekeeping or enforcement force needs to bear in mind the impact of law on an operation in respect of the types of maritime zones it is entering and the claims and regulations of coastal states, including third states which may be attempting to maintain a position of neutrality. Its own powers, as expressed in rules of engagement, will need to reflect the issues which arise from operating in various types of zones – such as the extent to which peacekeepers are entitled to override normal rules regarding innocent passage in territorial seas. The absence of firm customary law in this regard does not absolve commanders from recognising that there are legal problems.

In general, traditional peacekeeping by consent is less likely to trigger problems arising from legal uncertainty than operations where confrontation is likely. With so many variables affecting operations, there seems little prospect of achieving a comprehensive legal regulation and it is probably more feasible to develop precedents in an ad hoc way.

The maritime regime has been characterised as a 'soft' regime in that it relies on consensus rather than enforcement. Chapter 11 considered the type of UN institution that might regulate non-military maritime security in the developing international system. The International Maritime Organisation already has a substantial regulatory function in this area through its conventions on maritime safety and pollution. However, there may be a case for creating a more muscular multifunctional UN body which would regulate non-military (and possibly military) maritime security issues. This could be generated either through broadening the IMO's remit or creating a new body, a UN Maritime Agency. Such an agency, if adequately resourced, could take a firmer line in addressing the burgeoning problems of maritime pollution and depredation. But there are problems associated with this approach mainly related to the willingness of states to set up and empower such an organisation. The present powers of the IMO are severely restricted, both in a legal and operational sense, in part because states are generally unwilling to empower an international organisation to control their commercial activities at sea.

Policy for the future

Our analysis has avoided the strong advocacy of radical steps to maintain and improve maritime security and peacekeeping operations. In part this reflects our recognition of the tension between what may be desirable for global security and what may be feasible in an international system dominated by states whose autonomy is increasingly constrained by multilateralism. In part it also reflects the difficulty of making firm proposals at a time of uncertain international change. All the same, several issues can be identified for the future development of policy.

First, the international community might seek to develop a concept of operations that articulates maritime functions. Clear force thresholds need to be established for naval forces and related to political goals and diplomatic initiatives. Although naval forces have a certain independence of action and a capability to circumvent sovereignty, they should not be used indiscriminately. In regard to force structures, political, operational and financial considerations rule out the formation of standing multinational naval forces, despite their theoretical advantages. The way forward is an evolutionary approach involving greater co-ordination in ad hoc force structures, and perhaps the creation of earmarked forces.

The international community might seek to secure wider political representation within its decision-making and implementation process to bolster legitimacy when peace support activities are undertaken. In practical terms, this involves wide representation in the command and control and constitution of naval forces. Greater naval multilateralism should be encouraged, and efforts made to recruit diverse navies for maritime security operations. In some cases, their operational value may be quite low, but their participation may have political significance.

Steps might be taken to clarify and strengthen international naval management structures. There should certainly be maritime representation within the UN's new Situation Centre and any subsequent body undertaking a strategic management function. Operational integration should extend to amphibious operations, including emergency evacuation and offshore basing for supplies and facilities. The UN should seek to unify naval, land and air operations under a common command system and naval forces should no longer be regarded as an adjunct form of activity.

Although there is a case for restructuring within the UN network, to regulate non-military maritime security issues and to underpin the UNLOSC and IMO regimes, the militarisation of non-military security issues should be avoided. Nevertheless, the UN could promote regional constabulary initiatives and closer co-operation between law enforcement agencies.

The UN should seek to clarify its operational arrangements with regional organisations or multinational coalitions to clearly delineate political and operational responsibilities. There have been many references throughout the study to the experience of NATO's naval forces. This does *not* imply that NATO is the most suitable body to carry out UN functions in a *political* sense. Rather, the point is that NATO has considerable experience in maritime integration which may have both positive and negative lessons for international maritime operations on a wider basis.

Although it is possible to conduct operations with a low level of compatibility between navies, it is imperative in risky operations that a degree of co-ordination takes place. The NATO model has key elements worth adopting in regard to an agreed menu of ROE, secure communication channels and common data links and standardised operational procedures. Common training, exercising and instruction will have a marked effect on multinational efficiency. For operations in support of land-based peacekeeping, planning and training should be tri-service as well as multinational.

Peacekeeping forces, and more especially forces in operations where confrontation is a risk, need to be aware of the legal issues which can have an impact on the varying circumstances of particular operations, even where international law is unclear. More specifically, naval commanders need to know legal issues relating to the types of maritime zone they sail through, the regulations and claims of coastal states, the rights and claims of third states, and the rights of peacekeepers. Comprehensive legal regulation for naval peacekeeping forces may not be possible and it is appropriate for the international community to sustain, and rely upon, the gradual, ad hoc emergence of legal precedents.

The maritime environment and the forces which operate in it have distinctive security attributes which have traditionally been associated with state power. Yet states are increasingly subject to transnational processes and multinational normative pressures. In theory there is considerable scope for building co-operative behaviour at sea through peacekeeping and other peace support roles. Future developments in international relations will determine whether state practice will continue to build upon past and current experiences of co-operative maritime security.

Appendix

Chronology of relevant circumstances

The following is a list of circumstances since the First World War in which naval forces were either actually deployed or might usefully have been deployed to maintain or restore peace, undertake humanitarian measures and secure freedom of navigation, usually as part of a multinational effort authorised by a competent international authority and not simply as a national or alliance operation. The definition of 'competent authority' and issues of political legitimacy are open to interpretation. Instances of gunboat diplomacy and dubious legitimacy, such as China in the 1920s and the Multinational Force in Beirut in the 1980s, have been included to show that although certain naval tasks are commonplace, political circumstances are *sui generis*.

1914 North Atlantic The Convention on Safety of Life at Sea (1914), adopted as a consequence of the *Titanic* disaster in 1912, provided for an international ice patrol in the North Atlantic, but was undertaken in the 1920s by the United States alone.[1]

1920 Schleswig One of the earliest cases of peacekeeping involving navies occurred in Schleswig, occupied by Prussia/Germany from 1864 until after the First World War. It became a test case of the principle of self-determination. Disturbances in central Schleswig in 1919 led the Danish Government to appeal to the Allies to send warships. France sent the cruiser FNS *Marseillaise* which anchored off Sønderborg and later off Aabenraa. An International Plebiscite Commission, comprising UK, French, Norwegian and Swedish representatives supervised plebiscites and the evacuation of German forces in the area. The cruiser HMS *Carisbrooke* and three RN destroyers arrived off Flensburg and 3,000 UK and French troops were deployed in the area from 20 January until 15 June 1920. Overall command fell to Admiral T. Sheppard of the Royal Navy. The force rarely had to intervene and the territory was peacefully divided between Germany and Denmark. For similar plebiscites in Allenstein, Marienwerder and Upper Silesia in 1920, the foreign peacekeepers were supplied by sea and used the port of Danzig as a base.[2]

1922 Smyrna An ad hoc naval force provided by the UK, the United States, France and Italy protected foreign nationals and property. Naval units were ordered to protect only their own nationals, but in effect they offered general protection ashore and protection of merchant ships which had been chartered to evacuate civilians. Over 200,000 Greeks and Armenians were also evacuated, mainly in merchant ships. However, refugees guarded by foreign marines and sailors in Smyrna and on lighters in the harbour were handed over to the Turks who were committing atrocities in the Greek enclaves.[3]

1923 China Protection of Canton Customs House in 1923 by the UK, the United States, Japan, France, Italy and Portugal was followed in 1927 by protection of the International Concession at Shanghai, with the addition of Dutch and Spanish ships. These were ad hoc coalitions exercising rights under the concessions – two of many examples of gunboat diplomacy employed against China to protect or evacuate nationals.[4]

1925 Greco–Bulgar Incident The League of Nations Council considered a naval demonstration to coerce Greece into accepting the Council's resolution requiring Greek and Bulgarian forces to withdraw behind their own frontiers. The UK, France and Italy accepted in principle a demonstration off Piraeus and Phalerum, either under Article 11 (which authorised voluntary action 'to safeguard the peace of nations') or Article 16 (which authorised obligatory sanctions). The UK Government considered it essential that the RN should not undertake the action alone, so avoiding the UK being unduly exposed in dealing with such problems as US merchant ships entering Greek ports. Greece capitulated before action was organised, but the League Council Secretariat subsequently investigated the legal position. One authority argued that a naval demonstration implied the threat of 'something more' such as a bombardment, a precipitate step given that economic pressure had not been tried first. An alternative view was that the 'something more' should be a close blockade of the Athens ports for which the League would have to formulate a legal position to overcome respect for Greece's territorial waters.[5]

1936–39 Spain The Spanish Civil War illustrates problems associated with non-intervention, humanitarian assistance and blockades.

Monitoring and patrolling. To avoid assisting the legitimate Spanish Government, the UK pressured France into proposing an international Non-Intervention Agreement at the beginning of August 1936. Twenty-seven states backed an embargo and an International Board of Control was set up on 8 March 1937 under a Dutch Admiral. International observers were to embark on ships bound for Spain which flew the flag of a participating state. They were to supervise unloading of cargoes and arrival of passengers at Spanish ports. Where contravention of the Non-Intervention Agreement was suspected, observers could report to the state where the ship was registered. An International Naval Patrol was conducted by the UK, France, Germany and Italy, though the last two soon withdrew. Indeed, Italian submarines attacked neutral shipping. Under the Nyon Agreement of 14 September 1937 the UK and France agreed to attack submarines in areas where merchant ships were attacked. The UK tolerated air attacks on her shipping in Spanish ports, but announced the unlimited sinking of submarines in the Western Mediterranean after a UK ship was torpedoed off Cartegena. From mid-April to mid-June 1938, 22 attacks were made on UK-registered ships (many deliberately by Italian aircraft) and 11 vessels were sunk or badly damaged. Prime Minister Neville Chamberlain concluded that protection could only be extended if the UK was prepared to go to war against Franco, and by implication Italy and Germany.[6] The USSR, Italy and Germany ignored the non-intervention policy, and the UK used it to curb French involvement and prevent the Republican Government exercising rights under international law.

Humanitarian assistance. Intervention to evacuate nationals by sea got under way early in the war, involving the UK, France, the United States, Italy and Germany. The RN evacuated all-comers and by the end of January 1937 had rescued 17,000 Spaniards.[7] In April

1937 the UK Consul in Bilbao proposed an evacuation of war refugees from the Basque enclave. The Foreign Office and Admiralty argued that it would constitute intervention on the Republican side, but after the bombing of Guernica public opinion obliged the UK Government to convoy Spanish ships from Bilbao to France and the UK. In September 1937 the Soviet Union chartered a UK ship and was granted Royal Navy protection for the evacuation of children from Gijón. Although such assistance was generally regarded as non-political, there was controversy as to whether it aided the besieged Basques by reducing the mouths they had to feed, whether the refugees would become the agents of communism abroad and whether the children might have been better off staying with their families.[8]

Blockade. Franco proclaimed a blockade of Spanish ports on 17 November 1936. On 6 April 1937 a UK-registered merchant vessel and RN warships were confronted by Nationalist warships off the Biscayan coast. This gave the local RN Commander and the Admiralty reason to argue that the blockade was effective, even though the Nationalist ships had yielded. The UK Government considered it was unsafe to enter Bilbao. Sir Samuel Hoare, First Lord of the Admiralty, wanted to prohibit food supplies to the Basques and withdraw naval protection.[9] However, food ships defied the 'blockade', mines were not a serious problem, Nationalist warships avoided sailing within range of Republican shore batteries, and the RN had no difficulty offering protection beyond the 3-mile limit. Some RN officers were hostile to the communists, who had killed Spanish naval officers. Others were anxious about mines. But the RN had to reverse its assessment of the blockade and resume protection. The concept of an effective blockade had been defined in the Declaration of Paris (1856) as the maintenance of sufficient force to prevent any actual access to the coast. It was incorporated into the 1909 Declaration of London (art. 2) without consensus about what this meant: a chain of anchored warships, intermittent patrols or the establishment of an exclusion zone. As a consequence of the increased range of weapon systems, the traditional rules of law of blockade have become increasingly tenuous.[10] In the Spanish Civil War, the British Admiralty interpreted an 'effective blockade' as the presence of a force which rendered access to the coast hazardous. In fact Nationalist activities in the Bay of Biscay were intermittently hazardous.[11]

Three views are possible. First, assisting merchant ships as far as the 3-mile limit contravened the blockade and represented intervention on the Republican side. Second, the Nationalists had not declared a state of belligerency, therefore they had no legitimate right to operate a blockade. Moreover, failure to protect relief vessels outside the 3-mile limit would represent connivance in the Nationalist cause. Vice-Admiral Geoffrey Blake, the independently minded commander who argued this was relieved of his command. Third, the argument of *force majeure*, is offered by James Cable – that the blockade was only ineffective because of the Royal Navy's presence, and that any British activity could be construed as interventionist.[12]

However, the unenforcible blockade and the Royal Navy's responses had less influence on the outcome of the Civil War than the economic and financial blockade imposed by the UK on the Republican Government. The Admiralty and the Foreign Office were chastened by the UK's relative weakness in the Mediterranean during the Abyssinian crisis and were determined not to antagonise the Axis powers and Japan simultaneously. The Government was also exercised by the prospect, real or imagined, of communist-inspired political turmoil and economic reform which might draw strength from abroad. The Government was anxious to avoid antagonising the enemies of Bolshevism, but was unable to resist the public clamour for humanitarian intervention.[13]

1948 Palestine During the Palestine War the UN Mediator, Count Folke Bernadotte, and the UN Truce Supervision Organisation, could call upon naval units flying UN flags below national ensigns. They included, a French minesweeper, the amphibious cargo ship USS *Marquette*, the aircraft carrier, USS *Palau* (minus its air group) and three US destroyers. The United States also supplied five commercial aircraft for patrols and transport, a Naval medical unit, observers and communications equipment. In July 1948, the vessels patrolled the coast and transported material and personnel. UN officials were evacuated from Haifa, returned and evacuated again by sea. The United States stipulated that its ships were not to use force to board or stop other vessels and were only to be used for transport and observation.[14]

1950–53 Korea This Cold War collective defence operation was legitimised in circumstances which were fortuitous for the United

States. The UN Security Council recommended in the Soviet Union's absence that states assisting the UN should place their forces under an overall Commander to be designated by the United States who was requested to report to the Security Council. Fifteen states contributed forces, but operations were dominated by the United States and US military procedures. General Douglas MacArthur was responsible to the United States and the UN's military authority was nominal. The UK and American Chiefs of Staff objected to an initial US proposal to establish a UN enforcement committee. The option of using the MSC was also turned down by the United States on the grounds that it would not be capable of fulfilling practical tasks. Further, 'an impossible situation would arise if the Russians suddenly turned up and demanded to see any plans which the Military Staff Committee had been preparing.'[15] The Foreign Office in London was also anxious to keep the Security Council at arms length from operations, and the UK Chiefs of Staff reacted negatively to a US proposal to establish a military organisaton within the UN.[16] The participating forces in Korea were, however, authorised to fly the UN flag.

Naval units played vital roles and the vast bulk of personnel and supplies went to Korea by sea. Naval forces destroyed North Korean gunboats in 1950, carried out minesweeping, escorted merchant ships, controlled coastal fishing and conducted air strikes (from US and RN aircraft carriers). They also evacuated forces at Hungnam, and undertook amphibious landings at Pohang, Wonsan and Inchon in September 1950. Naval shore bombardment, notably by four US battleships, supported the land forces. Minesweeping was conducted at Chinnampo, from whence a Canadian-led UN-flagged force also evacuated troops fleeing from the Chinese.

From September 1950, the United Nations Blockading and Escort Force, also known as 'Task Force 95', maintained a blockade, defined as 24-hour surveillance of every section of the coast. Vessels from Australia, Canada, Colombia, France, the Netherlands, New Zealand, South Korea, Thailand, the United Kingdom and the United States participated. For a brief period it was under a Royal Navy Commander, the only occasion that US Navy units have served under non-US, UN-flagged Command. From 3 April 1951, the Commander of the US 7th Fleet took overall responsibility. The Force comprised a US patrol on the east coast and vessels under a British Rear-Admiral on the west coast with a US carrier under command. Both had island protection units. From February 1951, north-eastern ports were subjected to naval siege, and this tied down a large proportion of North Korean forces. Similar operations were launched off the west coast.[17]

1956–67 Egypt Proposals to deter violent incidents in 1956 between Israel and neighbouring Arab states included the suggestion of a UN boat on Lake Tiberius. The idea was acceptable to Syria but not to Israel. After the Suez War, Israel demanded guarantees of freedom of navigation for its shipping in the Gulf of Aqaba before pulling its troops out of Sharm-el-Sheikh. Egypt had blockaded the Gulf, and Israel asked Secretary-General Dag Hammarskjöld, whether the UN would provide a naval unit to ensure freedom of passage. In the event, Israel was satisfied with the presence of UNEF–I at Sharm-el-Sheikh, UN land and air patrols along the Egyptian coast, and guarantees by the United States and other maritime powers that innocent passage in the Gulf would be maintained. UNEF–I had the use of a landing ship, but this was out of commission by 1967 when the force had to evacuate Gaza in haste (see below). The UN also had the task of restoring transit of the Suez Canal which had been blocked. UK and French vessels, made over to the UN, were used at Port Said for the first month, but the main clearing operations were carried out by private salvage companies under the overall direction of a US General.[18]

1959 Panama Members of the Organisation of American States were asked to supply warships and aircraft when 100 Cubans under a Panamanian dissident arrived in Panama to spread Castro's revolution (though disowned by the Cuban Government). The United States, Colombia and Ecuador sent ships to look for further raids and stop vessels approaching the Panamanian coast. The rebels surrendered.[19]

1962 Cuba The United States proposed, and the Soviet Union accepted, the use of UN observers to monitor missile withdrawals. Cuba was prepared to endorse ship inspections by the International Committee of the Red Cross. The ICRC was concerned that its humanitarian functions would be compromised, but eventually agreed to supply Swiss Army personnel. Meanwhile, it was mutually agreed that the United States could conduct helicopter surveillance and inspections from ships alongside.[20]

*1962–63 **West New Guinea*** The UN Temporary Executive Authority (UNTEA), monitored a ceasefire and deployed security forces for the administration of West New Guinea/Irian until the territory was transferred to Indonesia. Thirty-two countries were represented. Pakistan supplied 110 personnel to operate 9 vessels transferred to the UN by the Netherlands. Costs were shared equally by the Netherlands and Indonesia.[21]

*1964 **Cyprus*** The Cyprus Government sent a force to surround villages after reports of arms smuggling and guerrilla infiltrations by sea from Turkey to the fishing ports of Kokkina and Mansoura. A patrol boat was fired upon from the shore at Mansoura. UNFICYP had no mandate to intervene and no coastal patrol to prevent arms smuggling by sea.[22]

*1965–75 **Beira*** A Royal Navy patrol began in December 1965 to help enforce sanctions against Rhodesia. The Royal Navy had no international authority to establish a blockade in the absence of a declared war, and a legal case was brought by Greek shippers. But on 19 April 1966, the UN Security Council authorised the UK to prevent oil tankers supplying the pipeline terminal at Beira in Mozambique. The patrol originally comprised an aircraft carrier group, but was subsequently maintained by two frigates/destroyers and RAF Shackleton patrol aircraft based in Madagascar. The deployment of force against Rhodesian interests and without Rhodesian consent excludes the Beira Patrol from the traditional concept of impartial peacekeeping. The Royal Navy presence was also serving the ulterior motive of keeping an eye on the Soviet Navy in the Indian Ocean. Although nine ships were needed to keep each frigate on station, the environment was benign, fewer than 30 vessels were deemed worthy of interception, and co-ordination with other navies was not required. However, the patrol was circumvented by overland oil deliveries to Rhodesia.[23]

*1967 **Gaza*** The withdrawal of UNEF–I under threat of attack in May and June 1967 was a complex operation which might have been eased considerably by a UN naval presence in the eastern Mediterranean. A landing ship which had been deployed in 1956 had fallen into disrepair and was not replaced. General Indar Jit Rikhye had to ensure the safe evacuation of 3,500 UN troops from the beaches at Gaza. Israel eventually allowed the UN Force to embark at Ashoda whence three charter ships sailed for Cyprus.[24]

1972 Bangladesh The UN made preparations for clearing the ports of Chalna and Chittagong after the Bangladesh war with Pakistan, during which neutral merchant ships had been attacked and sunk. Eventually the UN employed a consortium to deal with the wrecks at Chalna.[25]

1975 Sinai General Siilasvuo, the UNEF–II Force Commander, proposed a naval unit of four coastal patrol vessels to help support the second Sinai Disengagement Agreement. This was not followed up, and violations of the maritime extension of the buffer zone occurred.[26]

1982–84 Beirut The Multinational Force was created at the request of the Lebanese Government and comprised marines from France, Italy and the United States. It provided assistance to the Lebanese Army and facilitated the withdrawal of Palestinian leaders and combatants from Beirut. In August 1982 the evacuation of more than 10,000 Palestinians was completed on Greek-registered, UN-flagged vessels. The MNF was withdrawn but, after worsening violence, forces from the same states plus the UK were reintroduced to provide a 'presence' in support of the Lebanese Army. Israel consistently objected to UN involvement. In September 1983, a US aircraft carrier and French and British vessels patrolled the coast, and naval helicopters and aircraft attacked guerrilla positions. President Reagan granted ground commanders authority to call upon naval gunfire, and on 14 December the battleship USS *New Jersey* shelled Syrian positions. The failure of the intervention led to the gound forces being withdrawn to ships in February 1984. Navy and marine forces were essential to MNF operations. But the second MNF intervention was badly conceived, vague in purpose, without cohesive command, partial and lacking international legitimation.[27]

1982– Strait of Tiran The Multinational Force and Observers, a non-UN force, uses three converted Italian minesweepers, crewed by about a hundred Italians. The Coastal Patrol Unit monitors freedom of navigation through the hazardous Strait of Tiran and the southern part of the Gulf of Aqaba sea-lane to Eilat, much used by freighters and pleasure craft. The Strait is continuously observed from land, and a ship is on patrol for 12 out of every 24 hours. The patrolling is also a confidence-building measure in support of the Israel–Egyptian peace treaty.[28]

1983 *Grenada* After the US invasion a US-dominated, multinational Caribbean Defence Force was established to prevent arms-smuggling and related activities.

1984 *Gulf of Suez* An example of policing to secure safe navigation. The Libyan freighter *Ghat* offloaded mines in the Red Sea in mid-1984 on behalf of the Islamic Jihad. About 18 ships were damaged, and US, UK, French and Egyptian naval forces co-operated in mine clearing.[29]

1984–88 *Persian Gulf* Naval forces were engaged in deterrence, convoying and counter-mine measures outside the orthodox definition of peacekeeping. Iran blockaded the Iraqi ports at the head of the Gulf in 1980, and 23 merchant vessels were attacked in the period to April 1984. Between April 1984 and September 1985 Iraq launched a campaign against tankers carrying Iranian oil and attacked over a hundred. From mid-1986 Iran also increased its attacks and by January 1987 some two hundred ships, many trading with Kuwait, had been attacked. Thirty were sunk, and over a hundred seamen killed, mostly by aircraft.

External powers were reluctant to intervene, largely through fear of widening the Iran–Iraq War into a Cold War confrontation. Intervention was dependent on invitation by Gulf states, and in 1987 Kuwait asked for American and Soviet protection. The Soviet Union offered three tankers under charter, one of which, the *Marshal Chuikov*, hit a mine in May 1987, leading to the deployment of Soviet minesweepers. In March 1987, the US placed 11 Kuwait tankers under the US flag, largely to counter Soviet involvement. US warships escorted tankers for part of their journey through the Gulf, but convoying was only belatedly organised and the *Bridgeton* and the *Texaco Caribbean* struck mines in July and August 1987. Warships usually protected national flags, a pattern broken by the RN.[30] In January 1987 the International Chamber of Shipping raised the possibility of a UN co-ordinated naval force with the UN Secretary-General. In September 1987 the Soviet Foreign Minister, Eduard Shevardnadze, proposed a UN naval task force (and later called for such a force to establish any UN embargo). But Kuwait and the United States opposed any UN reflagging.[31]

However, the mine threat provoked West European states to take action, and a contingent co-ordinated by the WEU cleared mines and escorted merchant ships. The European warships were subject to national command and national ROE, though British, Belgian and Dutch minehunters operated in conjunction. WEU co-ordination, organised from Paris, occurred at ministerial level, admiralty level and task-force level.[32] There were concerns that the foreign naval presence would lead to increased attacks on merchant ships and precipitate a wider conflict, a fear heightened by Iraq's accidental firing on the USS *Stark* on 17 May 1987.[33] Naval forces in the Persian Gulf were reduced after 1988, but US warships and the UK's Armilla Patrol remained on station.

1986 Aden In January 1986 the evacuation of some 6,000 foreign nationals from the civil war in the Yemen was carried out by ships including the Royal Yacht *Britannia* which was en route to New Zealand and diverted to the scene. It was assisted by a British merchant ship and the survey vessel *Hydra*. Soviet and East European merchant ships were also involved, and a Soviet merchant officer was present on the Royal Yacht *Britannia* to provide liaison. The destroyer HMS *Newcastle* and the frigate HMS *Jupiter*, and naval vessels from France and the Soviet Union, provided cover off shore. An ad hoc communications system was established between French ships, the French Embassy and between the French and Soviet Embassies. Information was shared between the ships of all three states.[34]

1987– Sri Lanka In July 1987 the Indian Navy stationed two 'gunboats' off Colombo, with para-commandos aboard, during the signing of the Accord which allowed an Indian Peace-Keeping Force (IPKF) to deploy in Northern Sri Lanka. The Sri Lankan Government was not informed. The Indian Navy's 'peacekeeping' role was to interdict Tamil rebels and arms moving by sea from Malaysia and between Tamil Nadu and Sri Lanka. Patrol boats had a mandate to shoot and sink suspect vessels.[35] Discredited and ineffective, the IPKF pulled out in March 1990. But sea patrols continued and became more important after the assassination of Rajiv Gandhi in May 1991. Maritime surveillance, interception and intelligence increasingly had Sri Lanka's support and co-operation. In effect, the small Sri Lankan Navy came to depend on Indian policing of Sri Lankan territorial waters, as well as international waters. The naval interdictions became more effective than the IPKF's land operations in reducing the effectiveness of the Tamil Tigers. In January 1993 two Indian frigates intercepted the MV *Ahat* and its cargo of weapons. Guerrillas on board blew it up, killing a senior Tiger leader and nine others.[36]

1988– Shatt al-Arab The disputed frontier between Iran and Iraq includes the course of the Shatt al-Arab waterway. After the ceasefire of 20 August 1988, the original plan for UNIIMOG included two patrol boats, but the UN concentrated on observing the land frontier.[37]

1990 Bougainville Ships have often provided neutral and convenient venues for high-level meetings (e.g. the USS *Renville* hosted the Netherlands–Indonesian talks on Indonesia's independence, leading to the *Renville* Agreement of 17 January 1948). In its conflict with secessionists on the island of Bougainville, Papua New Guinea invited New Zealand to help in the negotiation of a ceasefire. HMNZS *Endeavour*, a tanker/logistic support vessel, accompanied by a frigate for protection, was anchored in territorial waters and provided a venue. The two vessels offered status and a neutral meeting ground which led to the '*Endeavour Accords*' of September 1990. The ships also provided medical assistance to people ashore.

1990–92 Gulf of Fonseca As a consequence of initiatives made by the Contadora Group for ending insurgencies in Nicaragua and El Salvador, the UN and the Organisation of American States intervened to hasten progress. In November 1989 the UN Security Council authorised an observer group (ONUCA) to supervise the demobilisation of irregulars and monitor any cross-border military interventions. ONUCA was to be equipped with helicopters and patrol boats. Eventually, and with an eye to largely budget-free operational experience and enhancing its international respectability, Argentina offered four 35-ton Israeli-built Dabur patrol craft from the Ushuaia base and 29 naval personnel.

The boats patrolled the Gulf of Fonseca, bordered by Nicaragua, Honduras and El Salvador and the coastline north and south of the Gulf. The squadron was under an Argentine commander who answered to his government for the deployment and recall of ships and personnel. He reported to the local UN Verification Centre, whose commander, for convenience, was also appointed from the Argentine Navy in 1991. The head of the Fonseca Verification Centre reported to ONUCA HQ in Tegucigalpa.

The boats flew the UN flag from the mainmast and the Argentine flag from the stern. They were painted white with UN lettering, and subsequently re-painted in original colours at UN expense. Argentine uniforms were adorned with UN patches and berets. The UN insisted that all weapons were removed and the crews unarmed. The crews could assist the UN International Military Observers on board in observational tasks, but did not have the right to stop and inspect shipping and the ROE permitted only evasive action if threatened. The naval contingent kept in contact with parties to the disputes to reduce the risk of accidental confrontations, and the squadron's base was moved from El Salvador to the relatively safer port of San Lorenzo in Honduras. Night patrols and combined boat and helicopter patrols became standard. Close liaison with the coastal states and with UN observers on land was essential to monitor Nicaraguan gun-runners to El Salvador using a combination of sea, river and land crossings.

The squadron had a high degree of logistic and maintenance autonomy. But the UN provided all fuel and ground transport, chartered cargo ships to transport the boats between Argentina and the Gulf of Fonseca, and refunded Argentina's support and depreciation costs. Argentina made up the difference between national pay rates and UN allowances. Operation *Gaucho* began on 29 June 1990 and ended on 17 January 1992, after nearly 6,500 patrol hours in which a deterrent presence was established.[38]

1990– Persian Gulf Blockade and enforcement actions against Iraq were authorised by the UN under Articles 39 and 40 of the Charter. From 17 August 1991 a Maritime Interception Force enforced the UN embargo in the Red Sea and Persian Gulf, with US Coast Guard Law Enforcement Detachments. For the most part, NATO procedures were used to facilitate co-ordination between navies. The WEU co-ordinated the naval operations of its members on a zonal basis to conduct interceptions and hunt for mines.[39] The Royal Navy and WEU vessels carried the main burden of minehunting, the former clearing 200 mines during hostilities.

Military action in support of SC Resolution 678 was undertaken by an ad hoc coalition, effectively under US Command and tactical control. The small Iraqi Navy was confronted by the largest armada assembled since the Second World War. The United States was able to sustain six carrier battle groups in the Gulf region and about one-third of the air sorties against Iraq were flown by the naval air component. US ships and submarines in the Gulf and Red Sea also launched over 400 cruise missiles against land targets.

NATO's Naval On-Call Force, Mediterranean, freed naval units from other duties in the Mediterranean and guarded against a perceived potential threat from Libya. About 80 per cent of the supplies and forces for the Coalition were carried by sea via the Mediterranean.

After the war, a selective embargo was continued in order to coerce Iraq into fulfilling ceasefire conditions. Humanitarian air drops to Kurdish-held areas included the participation of US Navy and RN helicopters in April 1991. Marines provided protection for the Kurdish sanctuary in Iraq in Operation *Provide Comfort*.[40]

A multinational ordnance disposal operation to clear Kuwait's harbours and coast of mines and obstacles was undertaken in March–April 1991. It involved 140 personnel from the United States, UK, Australia and France, with the support of a multinational military medical team and a Marine unit for protection. Navy personnel were also involved in humanitarian assistance to refugees in southern Iraq in March–April 1991.[41] In October 1992 Russia joined the Maritime Interception Force with an 'Udaloy' destroyer, *Admiral Vinogradov*, and a tanker, later joined by the *Admiral Tributs*. Basic levels of interoperability were achieved with US Navy ships, and cross-decking of helicopters occurred, but the Russian Navy Commander, Felix Gromov, emphasised that Russian ships would remain under Russian command.

1990– Liberia Marine units of the US Mediterranean Sixth Fleet amphibious group, including an amphibious ship and destroyer, arrived in Liberian territorial waters off Monrovia in early June 1990 to protect US installations and evacuate non-combatants. A Royal Navy frigate and tanker were placed under US tactical command. The Nigerian Navy also sent a naval task group. About 1,600 persons were evacuated.[42]

However, the United States was reluctant to intervene in the fighting and supported a regional response through the Economic Community of West African States (ECOWAS). Seven of the member states activated the 1981 Mutual Assistance and Defence Protocol and set up an ad hoc ceasefire Monitoring Group (ECOMOG) which landed by sea in Liberia in August 1990. No authority existed in Liberia to give or withhold consent. Nigeria supplied the vast majority of the original force of 7,000 which, by December 1992, had reached a total of 15,000. Nigeria also contributed two corvettes, two fast-attack boats, a landing ship, two mine-countermeasure vessels and four merchant ships. Ghana contributed two fast-attack craft and two merchant ships. Guinea and Sierra Leone provided small craft. The naval operations were co-ordinated under national commands and included: sealift, coastal patrolling to prevent arms importing, a blockade of Buchanan Port, civilian and military evacuation, port control and communications between ECOMOG and the outside world.[43]

By October 1992, the foreign troops in Monrovia were engaged in a full-scale war, including naval bombardment, against a guerrilla army of the National Patriotic Front. ECOMOG's lack of success in containing the war led the West African states to ask the UN to take more positive action, and a complete arms embargo was adopted by the Security Council at the end of 1992.

1991 Bangladesh Disaster relief and the distribution of food and medical aid was co-ordinated by government, military and humanitarian agencies after Cyclone Marian ravaged the coastal area of Bangladesh on 29–30 April 1991. An ad hoc coalition of rescue teams from China, the UK, France and Japan, and a US amphibious force of 7,500 was created. The United States had a political interest in supporting the Bangladeshi Government, but legal and sovereignty issues meant that the US military had to operate according to Bangladeshi instructions. Because they could return to ships at night, the troops could be used without intruding on sovereignty, culture and local politics. Working with aid agencies which were trusted locally was an essential part of the operation, but the military could supervise the aid and circumvent local corruption.[44]

1991– Somalia The US Marine Corps rescued 281 people of 30 nations from the Somali capital on 5–6 January, using helicopters from the USS *Guam* under a Special Operations Command. The US Ambassador had argued that Mogadishu civil airport was unsafe for the evacuees to use.[45] Italian and French warships also evacuated foreign nationals, and in November 1992 three French warships answered a distress call by a freighter in the Gulf of Aden crammed with 3,000 Somali refugees. These were independent initiatives. But 3,000 UN troops were then engaged in distributing aid.

The UN Security Council agreed on 3 December 1992 to a US-led force, after a UN-chartered relief ship approaching Mogadishu was shelled and a report by the Secretary-General on the looting of aid. The initial operations were conducted from the amphibious assault ship, USS *Tripoli*, carrying US Marine Corps, with supply ships from their pre-positioning station at Diego Garcia. The Bush Administration made it clear that the force would be under US command and that operations would be limited to about 120 days.[46] However, the UN forces became embroiled in fighting and abortive attempts to capture the warlord held responsible for killing UN troops.

1991– Adriatic International maritime responses to conflict in the former Yugoslavia included: monitoring the crisis on the Dubrovnik coast; monitoring of UN embargoes; enforcement of sanctions and support to UN ground troops.

The Yugoslav Federal Navy imposed a blockade of the Slovenian and Croatian coasts using the islands of Vis and Lastovo as bases, whilst Croatian vessels laid mines in the Bay of Castelli to prevent federal ships leaving the base at Lora.[47] The Federal Navy shelled the coast, including Split and Dubrovnik from early September to the ceasefire of 7 December 1991. EC monitors attempted to land in Dubrovnik with a flotilla carrying emergency supplies organised by UNICEF, comprising a ferry and 29 small vessels. This had to run a gauntlet of mines and gunfire, and was stopped by Federal patrol boats before arriving on 31 October 1991.[48] The flotilla was permitted to evacuate civilians from the Dalmatian coast. The relief of Dubrovnik and evacuation of refugees might have been facilitated by an international escort. But political constraints on British, French and Italian vessels in the Adriatic prevented intervention until an Italian naval vessel and a French hospital ship were permitted to collect wounded civilians by agreement of the warring parties and under ceasefire conditions.

An arms embargo against Yugoslavia (UN SC Res. 713), extended to Croatia and Bosnia, and a trade embargo against Serbia and Montenegro on 30 May 1992 (Res. 757), involved monitoring by two ad hoc naval groups. NATO units in *Maritime Monitor* were stationed off Montenegro and the port of Kotor, using the Augusta base in Sicily and commanded from Naples HQ. The seven NATO ships of SNFM (the standing Mediterranean force created in April 1992) are: frigates or destroyers from Italy, the UK, Netherlands, Germany, Turkey, Greece and the United States. In January 1993 HMS *Ark Royal*, USS *J.F. Kennedy* and FNS *Clemenceau* were deployed with logistics experts, helicopters, escort vessels and auxiliaries. These ships assist in operation *Deny Flight*, the multinational enforcement of a no-fly zone over Bosnia–Herzegovina. Additionally, the RN and FN ships offer support, protection and a withdrawal facility for their UN troops in Bosnia and Croatia. A group co-ordinated by the WEU, *Sharp Vigilance*, patrolled the Strait of Otranto using the base at Taranto and led by an Italian flagship and frigate. France, Belgium, Spain and Portugal each had a frigate, and a joint supply ship. The WEU also co-ordinated French, German, Italian and Dutch maritime air patrols based at Sigonella in Sicily.[49]

Initially the warships had no mandate to stop and search suspect vessels, but could interrogate masters and track merchant ships. This failed to prevent gun-running by speedboats, the occasional arrival of oil tankers in Montenegrin ports, and breaches of the embargoes by overland routes and via the River Danube. The CSCE provided monitors in Bulgaria, and Romania was offered the assistance of US inspectors and patrol vessels to monitor shipping along the Danube, but trans-shipment of oil continued.[50]

From 22 November 1992, in accord with UN Security Council Resolution 787, the Adriatic naval patrols and monitors on the Danube were entitled to enforce a blockade of Serbia and Montenegro. The Adriatic patrols were re-named *Maritime Guard* and *Sharp Fence*. ROE then allowed for firing across the bows of suspected vessels refusing to stop. However, German and Spanish warships remain limited to monitoring rather than enforcement activities.[51] From 31 December 1992 Albania granted NATO unrestricted access to its territorial waters for purposes of embargo enforcement. In a new departure, on 17 April 1993 the UN Security Council's Resolution 820 extended the embargo mandate. All merchant ships were prohibited from entering the territorial waters of Serbia–Montenegro except on a case-by-case basis or in case of *force majeure* and states acting under SC Res. 787 were authorised to use necessary measures *including in the territorial sea* of Serbia–Montenegro. As of 16 May 1993, 10,696 merchant vessels had been contacted by NATO and WEU patrols. Of these, 881 had been inspected or diverted to a port for inspection. Nine ships were found to be in violation of UN sanctions. From 15 June 1993 the two task forces were combined as operation *Sharp Guard*, with single command and control under the authority of the Councils of both organisations. The command is through NATO's Commander-in-Chief Allied Forces Southern Europe and the Commander-in-Chief Allied Naval Forces Southern Europe (an Italian Admiral) whose HQ was reinforced by a WEU element.[52]

Navies also support the Security Council's authorisation of 4 August 1992 for 'all measures necessary' to facilitate the delivery of humanitarian aid to Bosnia. The aid protection forces of UNPRO-FOR can call upon sealift and evacuation capabilities, naval medical facilities and naval air support.[53]

1992–94 Cambodia The mandate of the UN force in support of the UN Transitional Authority in Cambodia (UNTAC) included provision for 376 naval personnel (compared to infantry of 10,200). Coastal, riverine and lake patrols were deployed to: transport UNTAC personnel and equipment; supervise the ceasefire; investigate any allegations of foreign military presence; monitor regroupment, cantonment and demobilisation of the naval forces of parties to the Paris Agreements of October 1991; and to deter and intercept arms smuggling. Check-points were established at the ports of Sihanoukville and Phnom Penh, and at river crossings into Vietnam. Patrol craft provided by Cambodia as part of the 'retained units', comprised: 4 sea patrol and 27 river patrol boats (10 Kano class; 6 landing craft and 11 special boats). An additional 8 landing craft were to be rented. Navy–marine personnel comprised 42 Canadians, 84 Filipinos and 42 Uruguayans. Some 220 UN naval observers on board were provided by the UK, Uruguay, Russia, the Philippines, New Zealand, Chile and Canada.[54] The marines were armed and the ROE provided for self-defence. The Cambodian People's Armed Force also operates river craft.

UNTAC operations were jeopardised by the failure of the Khmer Rouge to comply with the Paris Agreements. Khmer Rouge units attacked opponents and kidnapped UN personnel, including naval observers. In March 1993 ethnic Vietnamese fishing communities living on the Tonle Sap Lake were targeted. After massacres attributed to the Khmer Rouge, hundreds of boats and over 13,000 people migrated south to Phnom Penh and across the border into Vietnam. The exodus was monitored by UNTAC craft and marines whose presence offered an element of protection by deterring attacks.[55] However, after successfully organised elections, the Khmer Rouge were increasingly isolated and UN forces began withdrawing in late 1993.

1992– Haiti From May 1992 the US Coast Guard and the US Navy intercepted Haitians seeking asylum in the United States after the Haitian military coup in November 1991. The UN brokered an accord in July 1993 to restore the exiled Haitian President and allow UN peacekeepers to retrain the Haitian police and military. But the Haitian regime failed to honour this and a US amphibious ship carrying UN specialists was turned back from Port-au-Prince by demonstrators. The UN imposed sanctions and a new blockade was implemented from 19 October 1993 by warships from the United States, Canada and the UK. The heavily armed warships of the US Navy were also poised to facilitate any evacuation of nationals and to intercept seaborne refugees and asylum-seekers.

Notes

1 World Peace Foundation (Denys P. Myers), *Nine Years of the League of Nations, 1920–28, (Ninth Yearbook)*, Boston, 1929, p. 80.
2 Alan James, *Peacekeeping in International Politics*, Macmillan/IISS, London, 1990, p. 29; Sarah Wambaugh, *Plebiscites Since the World War*, 2 vols, Carnegie Endowment for International Peace, Washington DC, 1933, vol. 1, pp. 65–8, 73–4, 113.
3 David Walder, *The Chanak Affair*, Hutchinson, London, 1969, pp. 172–7; James Cable, *Gunboat Diplomacy: Political Applications of Limited Naval Force*, Chatto & Windus/IISS, London, 1971, p. 180.
4 Cable, *Gunboat Diplomacy*, pp. 181, 185.

5 James Barros, *The League of Nations and the Great Powers: The Greek–Bulgarian Incident, 1925*, Clarendon Press, Oxford, 1970, pp. 69, 79–81, appendices A and B.

6 Cable, *Gunboat Diplomacy: Political Applications of Limited Naval Force*, Chatto & Windus/IISS, London, pp. 196–9; Hugh Thomas, *The Spanish Civil War*, Penguin rev. edn, London, 1965, pp. 679–80; Alan James, *Peacekeeping in International Politics*, IISS, London, 1990, pp. 80–83.

7 James Cable, *The Royal Navy and the Siege of Bilbao*, Cambridge University Press, Cambridge, 1979, pp. 27–8.

8 *Ibid.*, pp. 39, 84–6, 148–9.

9 *Ibid.*, p. 65.

10 See, N. Ronzitti (ed.), *The Law of Naval Warfare: A Collection of Agreements and Documents with Commentaries*, Martinus Nijhoff, Dordrecht, 1988, pp. 72–3.

11 Cable, *Bilbao*, p. 92.

12 *Ibid.*, pp. 93–4.

13 K. W. Watkins, *Britain Divided: The Effect of the Spanish Civil War on British Political Opinion*, Nelson, Edinburgh, 1963, pp. 207–11, 234–6; Sandra Gregory (prod.), *Beside Franco in Spain*, BBC TV Timewatch, 1991.

14 James, *Peacekeeping in International Politics*, p. 175; Frank Uhlig, Jr, 'The First United Nations Force', *Proceedings*, US Naval Institute, February 1951, p. 201.

15 Gross to Jebb, 28 June 1950, cited in *Documents on British Policy Overseas*, series II, vol. IV, no. 10, n. 7.

16 Richard Bevins, 'Command and Co-ordination of UN Forces in Korea', *Occasional Papers, no. 5, Korea*, FCO Historial Branch London, 1992, pp. 37–40.

17 Malcolm W. Cagle and Frank A. Manson, *The Sea War in Korea*, US Naval Institute, Annapolis, Md, 1957, *passim*; David Rees, *Korea: The Limited War*, Macmillan, London, 1964, pp. 364–72.

18 Evan Luard, *A History of the United Nations*, vol. 2, Macmillan, London, 1989, pp. 23, 48–54.

19 James, *Peacekeeping in International Politics*, p. 53; Jerome Slater, *The OAS and United States Foreign Policy*, Ohio State University Press, Ohio, Ill., 1967, pp. 84–6.

20 James, *Peacekeeping in International Politics*, pp. 300–301.

21 *Ibid.*, p. 193; William Henderson, *West New Guinea: The Dispute and its Settlement*, Seton Hall University Press, South Orange, NJ, 1973.

22 Bertil Stjernfelt, 'FN 25 år. Fredsbevarande operationer – Cypern', *Kungla Kirgsvetenskapsakademiens Handlingar och Tidskrift*, no. 8, 1970; Michael Harbottle, *Blue Berets*, Leo Cooper, London, pp. 73–4.

23 F. E. G. Gregory, 'The Beira Patrol', *RUSI Journal*, December 1969, pp. 75–7; Adam B. Siegel, 'Naval Forces in Support of International Sanctions: the Beira Patrol', *Naval War College Review*, vol. 45, no. 4, autumn, 1992, pp. 102–4; Cable, *Gunboat Diplomacy*, pp. 105–8; James, *Peacekeeping in International Politics*, p. 178; James Barber, 'Economic Sanctions as a Policy Instrument', *International Affairs*, vol. 55, no. 3, July 1979, pp. 367–84.

24 Discussions with Maj.-Gen. Indar Jit Rikhye, Mountbatten Centre for International Studies, University of Southampton, 6 October 1992.

25 Charles C. Petersen, 'Soviet Port-clearing Operations in Bangladesh', in B. W. and S. M. Watson (eds), *The Soviet Navy: Strength and Liabilities*, Westview Press, Boulder, Col., 1986, pp. 319–40.

26 Stjernfelt, *The Sinai Peace Front*, Hurst, London, 1992, pp. 108, 149.

27 Anthony McDermott and Kjell Skjelsbaek (eds), *The Multinational Force in Beirut, 1982–1984*, Florida International University Press, Miami, Fla, 1991, *passim*.

28 James, 'Symbol in Sinai: The Multinational Force and Observers', *Millennium: Journal of International Studies*, vol. 14, no. 3, winter 1985, pp. 261–3.

29 Eric Grove, *The Future of Sea Power*, Routledge, London, 1990, p. 192.

30 Cable, *Navies in Violent Peace*, pp. 23, 66; Cable, 'NATO Naval Operations Out-of-Area', *Naval Forces*, vol. 8, no. 1, pp. 30–9; James, 'The United Nations and the Gulf War', *Naval Forces*, vol. 9, no. 6, December 1988, pp. 44–51.

31 Sir Adrian Swire, 'Merchant Shipping and the Gulf War', *Naval Forces*, vol. 8, no. 3, 1987, pp. 14–15; *Washington Post*, 16 December 1987.

32 Grove, 'Birth of a Western European Navy?, *Naval Forces*, vol. 9, no. 1, 1988, pp. 12–13; Willem van Eekelen, 'WEU and the Gulf Crisis', *Survival*, vol. 32, no. 6, November/December 1990, pp. 522–4.

33 Cable, 'NATO Naval Operations', p. 35.

34 Anon., 'Multinational Humanitarian Cooperation in Action: HMY *Britannia* and the Evacuation of Aden, January 1986', Tripartite Adderbury Talks on International Maritime Co-operation, Royal Naval College, Greenwich, 3 May 1993; Cable, 'Naval Humanitarianism', *International Relations*, vol. 12, no. 1, April 1992, p. 344.

35 'Indian Navy Blockades "Tigers"', *Navint*, 16 August 1991, p. 7.

36 'India Targets LTTE Arms Shipments', *Tamil Times* (London), 15 February 1993, pp. 13–14, and information kindly supplied by Alan Bullion.

37 James, 'The United Nations and the Gulf War', *Naval Forces*, vol. 9, no. 6, 1988, pp. 44–51.

38 Capitán Ricardo Enrique Schroeder, '"Operacion Gaucho" en CentroAmérica', *Puestos de Maniobra*, yr. 3, no. 4, September 1991, pp. 18–21; Juan Carlos Neves, *United Nations Peace-Keeping*

Operations in the Gulf of Fonseca by Argentine Navy Units, Report 01–93, Strategy & Campaign Dept., US Naval War College, Newport RI, 12 January 1993, pp. 15ff.

39 Willem van Eekelen, 'WEU and the Gulf Crisis', *Survival*, vol. 32, no. 6, November/December 1990, pp. 519–32; Anthony Preston, 'Naval Aspects of the Gulf Conflict', *Military Technology*, vol. 15, no. 4, 1991, pp. 58–61; Nicole Gnesotto and John Roper (eds), *Western Europe and the Gulf*, Institute for Security Studies of WEU, Paris, 1992, *passim*.

40 John H. Cushman, 'Joint, Jointer, Jointest', *Proceedings*, US Naval Institute, May 1992, pp. 78–85.

41 Dana C. Covey, 'Offering a Helping Hand in Iraq', *Proceedings*, US Naval Institute, May 1992, pp. 106–9.

42 Lt-Col. T. W. Parker, 'Operation Sharp Edge', *Proceedings*, US Naval Institute, June 1991, pp. 102–6.

43 Capt. Olutunde A. Oladimeji, 'Behold, African Peacekeepers', *Proceedings*, US Naval Institute, March 1993, pp. 64–6.

44 H. C. Stackpole III, 'Angels From the Sea', *Proceedings*, US Naval Institute, May 1992, pp. 110–16. A mixture of disaster relief, evacuation and asset salvage was also to involve the US Navy after Mt Pinatubo erupted in the Philippines on 4 June 1991, threatening the Subic Bay Naval Base.

45 Adam B. Siegel, 'An American Entebbe', *Proceedings*, US Naval Institute, May 1992, pp. 96–100; Robert A. Doss, 'Out of Africa: Rescue from Mogadishu', *Proceedings*, US Naval Institute, May 1992, pp. 103–5.

46 Some charities opposed the force as jeopardising relief operations which relied on good relations with Somali guards; others were concerned that the US was not prepared for the long stay necessary to restore political stability. Mark Husband, 'Relief Workers in Somalia Reject More UN Troops', *The Guardian*, 10 September 1992, p. 10; Mark Husband, 'Uneasy Landfall for US Marines', *The Guardian*, 5 December 1992, p. 10.

47 Milan Vego, 'War on the Yugoslav Coast', *Proceedings*, US Naval Institute, March 1992, pp. 92–8. During the war for Croatia, the Yugoslav Federal Navy lost vessels to Croatia, which established a navy in September, but the bulk of the Federal force relocated to the Montenegrin port of Kotor. Before the war it comprised: 4 frigates, 5 submarines, 29 missile/torpedo boats and 14 mine-warfare vessels.

48 Ed Vulliamy and Davor Huic, 'Food Flotilla Relieves Dubrovnik', *The Guardian*, 1 November 1991, p. 26. Foreign merchant vessels were also fired upon, and the Maltese-registered *Euroviveri* was sunk near Split.

49 Miguel González, 'La "Extremadura" no podrá acercarse más de 457 metros a los buques que controle', *El País*, 22 July 1992, p. 2.

50 Ian Traynor and Hella Pick, 'US Unveils Quarantine Plan to Squeeze Serbia', *The Guardian*, 27 August 1992, p. 1; David Fairhall and David Gow, 'Bosnian Serbs Fear Croat Troop Influx', *The Guardian*, 14 November 1992, p. 10.

51 M. Simmons and I. Traynor, 'UN Enforces Its Oil Embargo on Serbia', *The Guardian*, 18 November 1992, p. 9; 'New Moves on Blockade', *Jane's Defence Weekly*, 5 December 1992, p. 9.

52 NATO Allied Forces Southern Command Fact Sheet, 18 May 1993; Assembly of Western European Union (Defence Committee), 'An Operational Organisation for WEU: Naval Co-operation – Part One: Adriatic Operations', report by Mr Marten and Sir Keith Speed, doc. 1396, 9 November 1993, pp. 5–8.

53 David Fairhall, 'Nato Role in New British Force for Bosnia', *The Guardian*, 8 October 1992, p. 8.

54 'Report of the Secretary General on Cambodia', UN doc., S/23613, 19 February 1992. Personnel strengths are as of 1 March 1993, UNTAC 'Daily Press Briefing', UN Information Centre, New York, 4 March 1993.

55 UNTAC 'Daily Press Briefings', March–April 1993.

Select bibliography

Documents (published and unpublished)

Administration of the President of the Russian Federation, 'Facts and Problems Related to the Dumping of Radioactive Waste in the Seas Surrounding the Territory of the Russian Federation', trans. by Greenpeace Russia, Moscow, 22 April 1993.

Australian Commonwealth Parliament, *Ships of Shame: Inquiry into Ship Safety*, Report from the House of Representatives Standing Committee on Transport, Communications and Infrastructure, Australian Government Publishing Service, Canberra, December 1992.

International Maritime Bureau, *A Report into the Incidence of Piracy and Armed Robbery from Merchant Ships*, submitted to the IMO, London, 6 June 1983.

International Shipping Federation, *Pirates and Armed Robbers: A Masters' Guide*, 2nd rev. edn, London, 1992.

Inter-Parliamentary Union, *Final Document of the 1st Inter-Parliamentary Conference on Security and Co-operation in the Mediterranean*, Malaga, 15–20 June 1992.

NUMAST:

'Maritime Piracy: Observations on Armed Attacks against Merchant Ships', policy statement, February 1992.

'Safety at Sea: Submission by NUMAST to the Earl of Caithness, Minister for Shipping', Department of Transport, London, 9 July 1992.

The Safety Case for British Shipping, London, July 1992.

United Kingdom

Official Papers, Cabinet Defence Committee Papers, DO (47–51), CAB 131/4, 1947; Joint Planning Staff Papers, JP (47–48), DEFE, 6/4–5, 1947–8; Foreign Office MSC Papers, FO 371/–, 1948, Public Record Office, Kew.

Department of Transport, *Merchant Shipping Notice No. M1517, Piracy and Armed Robbery*, International Shipping Policy Division, February 1993.

Directorate of Defence Policy, *Statement on the Defence Estimates 1992*, HMSO, London, July 1992.

Directorate of Naval Staff Duties, *A Navy for the 1990s: A Rationale for Maritime Forces in the New Strategic Environment*, MoD, London, July 1992.

HM Customs and Excise, *Annual Report*, Cm 1223, 1990 and Cm 1626, 1991, HMSO, London.

HM Customs and Excise, *Drugs Brief*, annual report, 1988–1992.

House of Commons Foreign Affairs Committee, *The Expanding Role of the United Nations and its Implications for United Kingdom Policy*, Session 1992–93, 3rd Report, HC Paper 235, HMSO, London, 23 June 1993.

House of Commons Select Committee on Home Affairs, Session 1988–89, 7th Report, *Drug Trafficking and Related Serious Crime*, 2 vols, HC–370 I & II, HMSO, London, 1989.

House of Lords Select Committee on Science and Technology, *Safety Aspects of Ship Design and Technology*, Session 1991–92, 2nd Report, HL Paper 30–1, HMSO, London, 14 February 1992.

United Nations

'An Agenda for Peace: Preventive Diplomacy, Peacemaking and Peace-keeping. Report of the Secretary-General Pursuant to the Statement Adopted by the Summit Meeting of the Security Council on 31 January 1992', doc. A/47/277; S/24111, 17 June 1992.

The Blue Helmets: A Review of United Nations Peace-keeping, New York, 1985.

The Law of the Sea: Official Text of the United Nations Convention on the Law of the Sea with Annexes, Index and Final Act of the Third United Nations Conference on the Law of the Sea, St Martin's, New York, 1983.

The Naval Arms Race, Report of the Dept for Disarmament Affairs, A/40/535, New York, 1986.

'Proposed Draft Convention on Expediting the Delivery of Emergency Relief', Office of the United Nations Disaster Relief Co-ordinator, General Assembly/Economic and Social Council, doc. A/39/267/Add.2; E/1984/96/Add.2, 18 June 1984.

Report of the Military Staff Committee on General Principles Governing the Organisation of the Armed Forces Made Available to the Security Council by Member Nations of the United Nations, MS/24, 30 April 1947, New York, 1947.

'Situation in Cambodia: Letter dated 30 October 1991 from the Permanent Representatives of France and Indonesia to the United Nations addressed to the Secretary-General', doc. A/46/608; S/23177, 30 October 1991.

The United Nations and the Situation in Somalia, Reference Paper,

Department of Public Information, 15 December 1992.

The UN and Drugs Control, New York, 1982.

UNTAC 'Daily Press Briefings', Cambodia, March–July 1993.

Yearbook of the United Nations, Office of Public Information, New York, annually.

Union of Soviet Socialist Republics, 'The United Nations in the Post-Confrontation World', UN Doc., A/45/626, S/21869, 12 October 1990.

United Nations Department of Humanitarian Affairs (Relief Coordination Branch), 'Workshop on Use of Military and Civil Defence Assets in Disaster Relief', Brussels, 14–15 December 1992, Final Report, Project DPR 213/3 (MCDA), DHA–Geneva, April 1993.

United Nations Institute for Training and Research (Mohammed El Baradei, M. Bashar, E. Christiansen, J. Connolly, P. de Montalembert, M. Gottleib and T. Pham), *Model Rules for Disaster Relief Operations*, Policy and Efficacy Studies, no. 8, UNITAR, New York, 1982.

United Nations Institute for Training and Research (Christopher C. Coleman), 'Report on New York Training Seminar on Peace-keeping 23–27 March 1992', UNITAR, New York, 1992.

United Nations International Maritime Organisation

'Convention for the Suppression of Unlawful Acts Against the Safety of Maritime Navigation', doc., SUA/CON/15 Rev.1, 10 March 1988.

Focus on IMO, background documentary series, IMO, London, 1989–93.

IMO: What It Is, What It Does, How It Works, IMO, London, 1992.

IMO's Global Programme for the Protection of the Marine Environment, IMO, London, n.d. [1991].

'Protocol for the Suppression of Unlawful Acts against the Safety of Fixed Platforms Located on the Continental Shelf', IMO, London, 1988.

United Nations (Security Council)

'Implementation of Security Council Res. 340 (1973)', Secretary-General's Report, doc. S/11052/Rev.1, 27 October 1973.

'Report of the Secretary-General on Cambodia', doc. S/23613, 19 February 1992, and 'Addendum', doc. S/2361/Add.1, 26 February 1992.

'First Progress Report of the Secretary-General on the United Nations Transitional Authority in Cambodia', doc. S/23870, 1 May 1992.

United States

Browne, Marjorie Ann, *United Nations Peacekeeping: Historical Overview and Current Issues*, Foreign Affairs and National Defense Division, Congressional Research Service, Library of Congress, 31 January 1990.

Browne, Marjorie Ann, *United Nations Peacekeeping: Issues for Congress*, Foreign Affairs and National Defense Division, Congressional Research Service, Library of Congress, 7 April 1992.

Center for Naval Analyses, George S. Dragnich, 'The Lebanon Operation of 1958: A Study of the Crisis Role of the Sixth Fleet (U)', research contribution 153, Institute of Naval Studies, Washington DC, September 1970.

Department of the Army, 'FM 100–5: Operations', Washington DC, June 1993.

Department of Defense, 'Annotated Supplement to the Commander's Handbook on the Law of Naval Operations', NWP9 (Rev.A)/FMFM 1–10, Washington DC, 1989.

Department of Defense, 'Report on Naval Arms Control', submitted to the Senate and House Committees on Armed Services, Washington DC, April 1991.

Department of Defense, 'Conduct of the Persian Gulf War. Final Report to Congress', Washington DC, April 1992.

Department of the Navy, 'From the Sea: Preparing the Naval Service for the 21st Century', Navy and Marine Corps White Paper, Washington DC, September 1992.

US Coast Guard, *Annual Report*, 1986–92.

The White House, *National Drug Control Strategy*, Annual Report, Washington DC, 1989–91.

The White House, *National Security Strategy of the United States*, USGPO, Washington DC, August 1991.

Western European Union

Western European Union Assembly (Defence Committee)
'Naval Aviation', report by Mr Wilkinson, doc. 1139, 9 May 1988.

'State of European Security – Intervention Forces and Reinforcement for the Centre and the North', report by Mr Speed, doc. 1183, 26 April 1989.

'Consequences of the Invasion of Kuwait: Operations in the Gulf', report by Mr De Hoop Scheffer, doc. 1243, 20 September 1990.

'Consequences of the Invasion of Kuwait: Continuing Operations in the Gulf Region', report by Mr De Hoop Scheffer, doc. 1248, 7 November 1990, and 'Addendum', 4 December 1990.

'Operational Arrangements for WEU – the Yugoslav Crisis', report by Mr De Hoop Scheffer, doc. 1294, 27 November 1991.

'WEU: the Operational Organisation', report by Sir Dudley Smith, doc. 1307, 13 May 1992.

'United Nations Operations – Interaction with WEU', report by Mrs Baarveld-Schlaman, doc. 1366, 19 May 1993.

'WEU Initiatives on the Danube and in the Adriatic – Reply to the Thirty-eighth Annual Report of the Council', report by Mr Marten and Sir Keith Speed, doc. 1367, 15 June 1993.

'Lessons Drawn from the Yugoslav Conflict', report by Sir Russell Johnston, doc. 1395, 9 November 1993.

'An Operational Organisation for WEU: Naval Co-operation – Part One: Adriatic Operations', report by Mr Marten and Sir Keith Speed, doc. 1396, 9 November 1993.

Western European Union Assembly (Political Committee)
'European Security Policy – Reply to the Thirty-eighth Annual Report of the Council', report by Mr Marshall, doc. 1370, 24 May 1993.
'Security in the Mediterranean', report by Mr Roseta, doc. 1371, 24 May 1993.
'Political Relations between the United Nations and WEU and Their Consequences for the Development of WEU', report by Mr Soell, doc. 1389, 8 November 1993.

Western European Union (Council of Ministers)
'WEU Related Texts Adopted at EC Summit, Maastricht – 10 December 1991', Press & Information Service, WEU, London.
'Declaration of the Extraordinary Meeting of the WEU Council of Ministers with States of Central Europe', Petersberg–Bonn, 19 June 1992, Press & Information Service, WEU, London.

World Association for World Federation, *A Proposal for United Nations Security Forces (UNSF)*, Amsterdam, 1989.
Yomiuri Constitution Study Council, *The First Proposal (Process of Establishing the Constitution)*, Yomiuri Shimbun, Tokyo, 9 December 1992.

Press and periodicals

Atlantic News (NATO, Brussels)
Daily Telegraph
Defense Monitor
Defense News
The Economist
Far Eastern Economic Review
Financial Times
The Guardian
IMO News
The Independent
International Defense Review
International Herald Tribune
Jane's Defence Weekly
Jane's Intelligence Review
Keesing's Record of World Events
Lloyd's List
Military News Bulletin

Le Monde
Moscow News
Naval Forces
Naval Review
NAVINT
Navy News and Undersea Technology (US)
New York Times
NUMAST Telegraph (UK)
Peacekeeping & International Relations (Canada)
El País
Proceedings (US Naval Institute)
Rossijskaya Gazeta
RUSI Newsbrief
The Seaman (UK)
South China Morning Post (Hong Kong)
The Straits Times (Singapore)
The Times
Washington Post
Die Welt

Books

Anthony, Ian, *The Naval Arms Trade*, Oxford University Press/SIPRI, Oxford, 1990.

Babbage, Ross and Bateman, Sam (eds), *Maritime Change: Issues for Asia*, Allen & Unwin, St Leonards, NSW, 1993.

Barros, James, *The League of Nations and the Great Powers: The Greek–Bulgarian Incident, 1925*, Clarendon Press, Oxford, 1970.

Bartlett, C. J., *Great Britain and Sea Power, 1815–1853*, Clarendon Press, Oxford, 1963.

Blix, B. H. *Sovereignty, Aggression and Neutrality*, Almqvist & Wiksell, Stockholm, 1970.

Bloomfield, Lincoln P., *International Military Forces: The Question of Peacekeeping in an Armed and Disarming World*, Little, Brown & Company, New York, 1964.

Booth, Ken, *Navies and Foreign Policy*, Croom Helm, London, 1977.

Booth, Ken, *Law, Force, and Diplomacy at Sea*, Allen & Unwin, London, 1985.

Bowett, D. W., *Self-Defence in International Law*, Manchester University Press, Manchester, 1958.

Bowett, D. W., *United Nations Peacekeeping Operations: A Legal Study of United Nations Practice*, Stevens & Sons, London, 1964.

Boyd, James M., *United Nations Peace-Keeping: A Military and Political Appraisal*, Praeger, New York, 1971.

Brown, B., *Disaster Preparedness and the United Nations: Advance Planning for Disaster Relief*, Pergamon, New York, 1979.

Brown, E. D. and Churchill, R. R. (eds), *The UN Convention on the Law of the Sea: Impact and Implementation*, Law of the Sea Institute, University of Hawaii, Honolulu, 1987.

Brownlie, Ian, *International Law and the Use of Force by States*, Oxford University Press, Oxford, 1963.

Bull, Hedley (ed.), *Intervention in World Politics*, Clarendon Press, Oxford, 1984.

Burns, Arthur Lee and Heathcote, Nina (eds), *Peace-Keeping by UN Forces*, Pall Mall Press, London, 1963.

Cable, James, *Gunboat Diplomacy: Political Applications of Limited Naval Force*, Chatto & Windus/IISS, London, 1971.

Cable, James, *The Royal Navy and the Siege of Bilbao*, Cambridge University Press, Cambridge, 1979.

Cable, James, *Navies in Violent Peace*, Macmillan, London, 1989.

Cagle, Malcolm W. and Manson, Frank A., *The Sea War in Korea*, US Naval Institute, Annapolis, MD, 1957.

Cassese, A. (ed.), *United Nations Peace-Keeping: Legal Essays*, Sijthoff & Noordhoff, Alphen aan den Rijn, Netherlands, 1978.

Charney, Jonathan I. and Alexander, Lewis M. (eds), *International Maritime Boundaries*, Martinus Nijhoff, Dordrecht, 2 vols, 1993.

Chatterjee, S. K., *Legal Aspects of International Drugs Control*, Martinus Nijhoff, Dordrecht, 1980.

Churchill, R. R. and Lowe, A. V., *The Law of the Sea* (rev. edn), Manchester University Press, Manchester, 1988.

Damrosch, Lori Fisler and Scheffer, David J. (eds), *Law and Force in the New International Order*, Westview Press, Boulder, Col., 1991.

Davies, David, *The Problem of the Twentieth Century*, Ernest Benn, London, 1930.

Dekker, Ige F. and Post, Harry G. H. (eds), *The Gulf War of 1980–1988: The Iran–Iraq War in International Legal Perspective*, T. M. C. Asser Instituut, Martinus Nijhoff, Dordrecht, 1992.

Dubner, B. H., *The Law of International Sea Piracy*, Martinus Nijhoff, The Hague, 1980.

Dupuy, R.-J., and Vignes, D. (eds), *A Handbook on the New Law of the Sea*, 2 vols, Hague Academy of International Law, Martinus Nijhoff, Dordrecht, 1991.

Durch, William, J. (ed.), *The Evolution of UN Peacekeeping: Case Studies and Comparative Analysis*, St Martin's Press, New York, 1993.

Ellen, Eric (ed.), *Violence at Sea*, ICC Publishing, Paris, 1986.

Ellen, Eric (ed.), *Piracy at Sea*, ICC Publishing, Paris, 1989.

Eriksson, Gudmundur, *The Law of the Sea, Ocean Management and Confidence-Building*, UN Department of Disarmament Affairs, New York, December 1990.

Evans, Malcolm, D., *Relevant Circumstances and Maritime Delimitation*, Clarendon Press, Oxford, 1989.

Falk, Richard A., Kim, Samuel S. and Mendlovitz, Saul H., *The United Nations and a Just World Order*, Westview Press, Boulder, Col., 1991.

Fieldhouse, Richard (ed.), *Security at Sea: Naval Forces and Arms Control*, Oxford University Press/SIPRI, Oxford, 1990.

Fieldhouse, Richard and Taoka, Shunji (eds), *Superpowers at Sea: An Assessment of the Naval Arms Race*, Oxford University Press/SIPRI, Oxford, 1989.

Finkelstein, Lawrence (ed.), *Politics in the United Nations System*, Duke University Press, Durham, NC, 1988.

Ford Foundation, *The United Nations and the Iran–Iraq War*, Ford Foundation, New York, 1987.

Freedman, Lawrence and Karsh, Efraim, *The Gulf Conflict: 1990–1991, Diplomacy and War in the New World Order*, Faber & Faber, London, 1993.

Friedman, Norman, *The Naval Institute Guide to World Naval Weapons Systems 1991/92*, US Naval Institute Press, Annapolis, Md., 1989.

Friedman, Norman, *Desert Victory: The War for Kuwait*, US Naval Institute Press, Annapolis, Md, 1992.

Fromuth, Peter J., *A Successor Vision. The United Nations of Tomorrow*, UN Association (US)/University Press of America, Lanham, Md, 1988.

Gilchrist, Peter, *Sea Power: The Coalition and Iraqi Navies*, Osprey, London, 1991.

Gilpin, Robert, *War and Change in World Politics*, Cambridge University Press, Cambridge, 1983.

Glassner, Martin, Ira, *Neptune's Domain: A Political Geography of the Sea*, Unwin Hyman, London, 1990.

Gnesotto, Nicole and Roper, John (eds), *Western Europe and the Gulf*, Institute for Security Studies of Western European Union, Paris, 1992.

Gold, Edgar (ed.), *Maritime Affairs: A World Handbook* (2nd edn), Longmans, London, 1992.

Goldblat, Jozef (ed.), *Maritime Security: The Building of Confidence*, UNIDIR, Geneva, 1992.

Gordenker, Leon and Weiss, Thomas G. (eds), *Soldiers, Peacekeepers and Disasters*, Macmillan/International Peace Academy, Basingstoke, 1991.

Green, S., *International Disaster Relief: Towards a Responsive System*, McGraw-Hill, New York, 1977.

Grove, Eric, *From Vanguard to Trident: British Naval Policy Since 1945*, Bodley Head, London, 1989.

Grove, Eric, *The Future of Sea Power*, Routledge, London, 1990.

Grove, Eric, *Maritime Strategy and European Security*, Brassey's, London, 1990.

Grove, Eric with Thompson, Graham, *Battle for the Fiørds: NATO's Forward Maritime Strategy in Action*, Ian Allan, London, 1991.

Guttry A. de, and N. Ronzitti (eds), *The Iran–Iraq War (1980–1988) and the Law of Naval Warfare*, Grotius, Cambridge, 1993.

Hanning, Hugh, *Peace: The Plain Man's Guide to War-Prevention*, Cecil Woolf, London, 1988.

Heiberg, Marianne (ed.), *Subduing Sovereignty: Sovereignty and the Right to Intervene*, forthcoming, 1994.

Heinegg, W. Heinstschel v. (ed.), *The Military Objective and the Principle of Distinction in the Law of Naval Warfare*, Bochumer Schriften zur Friedenssicherung und zum Humanitären Völkerrecht, no. 7, 1991.

Heinegg, Heintschel v. (ed.), *Methods and Means of Combat in Naval Warfare*, Bochumer Schriften zur Friedenssicherung und zum Humanitären Völkerrecht, no. 8, 1992.

Henderson, William, *West New Guinea: The Dispute and its Settlement*, Seton Hall University Press, South Orange, NJ, 1973.

Higgins, Rosalyn, *United Nations Peacekeeping, 1947–1967: Documents and Commentary*, 4 vols, Oxford University Press, Oxford, 1969–81.

Hollick, Anne L., *US Foreign Policy and the Law of the Sea*, Princeton University Press, Princeton, 1987.

Hollis, Martin and Smith, Steve, *Explaining and Understanding International Relations*, Clarendon Press, Oxford, 1990.

Howell, Raymond, C., *The Royal Navy and the Slave Trade*, Croom Helm, London, 1987.

Independent Commission on Disarmament and Security Issues [Palme], *Common Security: a Blueprint for Survival*, Simon & Schuster, New York, 1982.

Independent Commission on International Development Issues [Brandt], *North–South: A Programme for Survival*, Pan Books, London, 1980.

Independent Commission on International Development Issues [Brandt], *Common Crisis, North–South Cooperation for World Recovery*, Pan Books, London, 1983.

International Peace Academy, *Peacekeeper's Handbook*, Pergamon Press, New York, 1984.

James, Alan, *The Politics of Peace-Keeping*, Chatto & Windus, London, 1969.

James, Alan, *Peacekeeping in International Politics*, Macmillan and IISS, Basingstoke and London, 1990.

Johnston, Douglas M., *The Theory and History of Ocean Boundary-making*, McGill–Queen's University Press, Kingston, Ont., 1988

Kearsley, Harold J., *Maritime Power and the Twenty-first Century*, Dartmouth Publishing, Aldershot, 1992.

Kelsen, Hans, *The Law of the United Nations: A Critical Analysis of Its Fundamental Problems*, Stevens & Sons, London, 1950.

Kennedy, Paul M., *The Rise and Fall of British Naval Mastery*, Allen Lane, London, 1976.

Langdon, F. and Ross, D. (eds), *Superpower Maritime Strategy in the Pacific*, Routledge, London, 1990.

Lee, John, M., von Pagenhardt, Robert and Stanley, Timothy, W., *Strengthening United Nations Peacekeeping and Peacemaking: a summary*, International Economic Studies Institute, Washington DC, April 1992.

Levie, H. S., *Mine Warfare at Sea*, Martinus Nijhoff, Dordrecht, 1992.

Lillich, Richard B. (ed.), *Humanitarian Intervention and the United Nations*, University Press of Virginia, Charlottesville, Va, 1973.

Little, Richard, *Intervention: External Involvement in Civil Wars*, Martin Robertson, London, 1975.

Luard, Evan, *A History of the United Nations*, Macmillan, London, 1989.

Luard, Evan, *The Globalization of World Politics: The Changed Focus of Political Action in the Modern World*, Macmillan, London, 1990.

Luttwak, E. N., *The Political Use of Sea Power*, Johns Hopkins University Press, Baltimore, 1974.

Macalister-Smith, Peter, *International Humanitarian Assistance: Disaster Relief Actions in International Law and Organization*, Martinus Nijhoff, Dordrecht, 1985.

MaccGwire, Michael, *Military Objectives in Soviet Foreign Policy*, Brookings Institution, Washington DC, 1987.

McDermott, Anthony and Skjelsbaek, Kjell (eds), *The Multinational Force in Beirut, 1982–1984*, Florida International University Press, Miami, Fla, 1991.

Mack, Andrew (ed.) *A Peaceful Ocean? Maritime Security in the Pacific in the Post-Cold War Era*, Allen & Unwin, St Leonards, NSW, 1993.

Mackinlay, John, *The Peacekeepers: An Assessment of Peacekeeping Operations at the Arab–Israel Interface*, Unwin Hyman, London, 1989.

Mahan, Alfred Thayer, *The Influence of Sea Power upon History 1660–1783*, Little, Brown & Co., Boston, 1890.

Mankabady, Samir, *The International Maritime Organization*, 2 vols, Croom Helm, Beckenham, 1986 and 1987.

Modelski, George and Thompson, William R., *Seapower in Global Politics, 1494–1993*, Macmillan, Basingstoke, 1988.

Morris, Michael A., *Expansion of Third-World Navies*, Macmillan, Basingstoke, 1987.

Moskos, Charles C., Jr, *Peace Soldiers: The Sociology of a United Nations Military Force*, University of Chicago Press, Chicago, Ill., 1976.

Norton, Augustus Richard and Weiss, Thomas G., *UN Peacekeepers: Soldiers with a Difference*, Foreign Policy Association, New York, 1990.

O'Connell, D. P., *The International Law of the Sea*, 2 vols, Oxford University Press, Oxford, 1982, 1984.

Pakenham, W. T. T., *Naval Command and Control*, Brassey's, London, 1989.

Parritt, B. A. H., *Security at Sea*, Nautical Institute, London, 1991.

Pay, John and Till, Geoffrey (eds), *East–West Relations in the 1990s: The Naval Dimension*, Pinter, London, 1990.

Plano, Jack C. and Riggs, Robert E., *The United Nations: International Organization and World Politics*, Dorsey, Chicago, Ill., 1988.

Pugh, Michael C., *The ANZUS Crisis, Nuclear Visiting and Deterrence*, Cambridge University Press, Cambridge, 1989.

Pugh, Philip, *The Cost of Seapower: The Influence of Money on Naval Affairs from 1915 to the Present Day*, Conway Maritime Press, London, 1986.

Rees, David, *Korea: The Limited War*, Macmillan, London, 1964.

Reynolds, Clark G., *History and the Sea: Essays on Maritime Strategies*, University of South Carolina Press, Columbia, NY, 1989.

Richardson, Jeffrey T. and Ball, Desmond, *The Ties That Bind*, Allen & Unwin, Boston, Mass., 1985.

Rikhye, Indar Jit, *The Sinai Blunder: Withdrawal of the United Nations Emergency Force Leading to the Six-Day War of June 1967*, Cass, London, 1980.

Rikhye, Indar Jit, *The Theory and Practice of Peacekeeping*, Hurst/International Peace Academy, London, 1984.

Rikhye, Indar Jit, Harbottle, Michael and Egge, Bjorn, *The Thin Blue Line*, Yale University Press, New Haven, Conn., 1974.

Rikhye, Indar Jit and Skjelsbaek, Kjell (eds), *The United Nations and Peacekeeping*, Macmillan, London, 1990.

Roberts, Adam and Kingsbury, Benedict (eds), *United Nations, Divided World: The UN's Roles in International Relations*, Clarendon Press, Oxford, 1988.

Rodley, Nigel S., *To Loose the Bands of Wickedness: International Intervention in Defence of Human Rights*, Brassey's/David Davies Memorial Institute, London, 1992.

Rogers, Paul and Dando, Malcolm, *A Violent Peace: Global Security After the Cold War*, Brassey's, London, 1992.

Ronzitti, Natalino (ed.), *The Law of Naval Warfare: A Collection of Agreements and Documents with Commentaries*, Martinus Nijhoff, Dordrecht, 1988.

Ronzitti, Natalino (ed.), *Maritime Terrorism and International Law*, Martinus Nijhoff, Dordrecht, 1990.

Rubin, Alfred P., *The Law of Piracy*, Naval War College Press, Newport, RI, 1988.

Rupesinghe, Kumar (ed.), *Internal Conflict*, Macmillan, Basingstoke, 1992.

Saksena, K. P., *Reforming the United Nations: The Challenge of Relevance*, Sage Publications, New Delhi, 1993.

Silverstein, Harvey B., *Superships and Nation-States: The Transnational Politics of the Intergovernmental Maritime Consultative Organization*, Westview Press, Boulder, Col., 1978.

Sokolsky, Joel L., *The Fraternity of the Blue Uniform: Admiral Richard G. Colbert, the US Navy and Allied Naval Cooperation*, Naval War College Press, Newport, RI, 1991.

Stjernfelt, B., *The Sinai Peace Front*, Hurst, London, 1992.

Tarling, Nicholas, *Piracy and Politics in the Malayan World: A Study of British Imperialism in Nineteenth-century South-east Asia*, F. W. Cheshire, Melbourne, 1963.

Taylor, Paul, *International Organization in the Modern World: the Regional and Global Process*, Pinter, London, 1993.

Taylor, Paul and Groom, A. J. R., *Global Issues in the United Nations' Framework*, St Martin's Press, New York, 1989.

Thant, U, *View from the UN*, David & Charles, Newton Abbot, 1978.

Thomas, Hugh, *The Spanish Civil War* (rev. edn), Penguin, Harmondsworth, 1965.

Till, Geoffrey (ed.), *Maritime Strategy and the Nuclear Age* (2nd edn), Macmillan, London, 1984.

Till, Geoffrey, *Modern Sea Power: An Introduction*, Brassey's, London, 1987.

Urquhart, Brian, *A Life in Peace and War*, Weidenfeld & Nicolson, London, 1987.

Verrier, Anthony, *International Peacekeeping: United Nations Forces in a Troubled World*, Penguin, Harmondsworth, 1981.

Villar, Roger, *Piracy Today: Robbery and Violence at Sea since 1980*, Conway Maritime Press, London, 1985.

Wainhouse, David W., *International Peace Observation*, Johns Hopkins University Press, Baltimore, Md, 1966.

Wainhouse, David W., *International Peacekeeping at the Crossroads*, Johns Hopkins University Press, Baltimore, Md, 1973.

Walder, David, *The Chanak Affair*, Hutchinson, London, 1969.

Walters, F. P., *A History of the League of Nations*, 2 vols, Oxford University Press/RIIA, London, 1952.

Wambaugh, Sarah, *Plebiscites Since the World War: With a Collection of Official Documents*, 2 vols, Carnegie Endowment for International Peace, Washington DC, 1933.

Weil, Prosper, *The Law of Maritime Delimitations – Reflections*, Grotius Publications, Cambridge, 1989.

Weiss, Thomas G. and Kessler, Meryl A. (eds), *Third World Security in the Post-Cold War Era*, Lynne Rienner, Boulder, Col., 1991.

White, N. D., *The United Nations and the Maintenance of International Peace and Security*, Manchester University Press, Manchester, 1990.

Wiseman, Henry (ed.), *Peacekeeping: Appraisals and Proposals*, Pergamon Press, New York, 1983.

Woodward, Admiral Sandy (with Patrick Robinson), *One Hundred Days: The Memoirs of the Falklands Battle Group Commander*, Harper Collins, London, 1992.

World Commission on Environment and Development [Brundtland], *Our Common Future*, Oxford University Press, Oxford, 1987.

World Peace Foundation (Denys P. Myers), *Nine Years of the League of Nations, 1920–28, (Ninth Yearbook)*, Boston, 1929.

Articles, chapters and published reports

Abi-Saab, Georges, 'La deuxième génération des opérations de maintien de la paix: quelques réflexions préliminaires', *Le Trimestre du monde*, 4e, 1992, pp. 87–97.

Adeniji, Oluyemi, 'Regionalism in Africa', *Security Dialogue*, vol. 24, no. 2, 1993, pp. 211–20.

Bateman, Sam, 'Maritime Confidence and Security-Building Measures in the Asia Pacific Area', in Kevin Clements (ed.), *Peace and Security in the Asia Pacific Region*, United Nations University/John Dunmore, Tokyo and Palmerston North, NZ, 1993.

Berdal, Mats R., *Whither UN Peacekeeping?*, Adelphi Paper no. 281, IISS, London, October 1993.

Beschorner, Natasha, Gould, St John B. and McLachlan, Keith (eds), *Sovereignty, Territoriality and International Boundaries in South Asia, South West Asia and the Mediterranean Basin*, Geopolitics and International Boundaries Research Centre, School of Oriental and African Studies, University of London, London, 1990.

Bettati, Mario, 'Un droit d'ingérence?', *Revue Général de Droit International Public*, vol. 95, 1991, pp. 639–70.

Bjørgo, Tore, *Maritime Terrorism. A Threat to Shipping and the Oil Industry*, Special Report, Norwegian Institute of International Affairs, Oslo, August 1991.

Blackham, Rear Adm. J. J., 'Maritime Peacekeeping', *RUSI Journal*, August 1993, pp. 18–23.

Blechman, Barry M., Durch, William J., Ellis, W. Philip, Fisher, Cathleen S. and Fitzgerald, Mary C., *The US Stake in Naval Arms Control*, Henry L. Stimson Center, Washington DC, October 1990.

Bockman, Lt-Col. Larry J., Coombs, Cdr Barry and Forsyth, Cdr Andrew W., *The Employment of Maritime Forces in Support of United Nations*

Resolutions, Research Report 6–93, Strategy and Campaign Department, US Naval War College, Newport RI, 11 August 1993.

Booth, Ken, 'Security and Emancipation', *Review of International Studies*, vol. 17, no. 4, October 1991, pp. 313–26.

Boothby, Derek, 'Sailing Under New Colors', *Proceedings*, US Naval Institute, July 1992, pp. 48–50.

Bothe, M., 'Neutrality in Naval Warfare: What is Left of Traditional International Law', in A. J. M. Delissen and G. J. Tanja (eds), *Humanitarian Law of Armed Conflict: Challenges Ahead*, Martinus Nijhoff, Dordrecht, 1991, pp. 387–405.

Boulton, J. W., 'NATO and the MLF', *Journal of Contemporary History*, vol. 7, nos 3/4, July/October 1972, pp. 275–94.

Boutros-Ghali, Boutros, 'Empowering the United Nations', *Foreign Affairs*, vol. 72, no. 1, spring 1993, pp. 90–102.

Boutros-Ghali, Boutros, 'Towards a New Generation of Peace-Keeping Operations', *Bulletin of Arms Control*, no. 10, May 1993, pp. 2–7.

Boutros-Ghali, Boutros, 'UN Peace-keeping in a New Era: A New Chance for Peace', *The World Today*, April 1993, pp. 66–9.

Brownlie, Ian, 'The Principle of the Non-Use of Force in Contemporary International Law', in William E. Butler (ed.), *The Non-Use of Force in International Law*, Martinus Nijhoff, Dordrecht, 1989, pp. 17–28.

Buzan, Barry, *Sea of Troubles? Sources of Dispute in the New Ocean Regime*, Adelphi Paper, no. 143, IISS, London, 1978.

Cable, James, 'NATO Naval Operations Out-of-Area', *Naval Forces*, vol. 8, no. 1, 1987, pp. 30–39.

Cable, James, 'Naval Humanitarianism', *International Relations*, vol. 12, no. 1, April 1992, pp. 335–45.

Canfield, Jeffrey L., 'The Independent Baltic States: Maritime Security Implications', *Naval War College Review*, vol. 45, no. 4, seq. 340, autumn, 1992, pp. 55–81.

Center for Defense Information, 'The US as the World's Policeman? Ten Reasons to Find a Different Role', *Defense Monitor*, vol. 20, no. 1, 1991.

Center for Defense Information, 'The Pentagon's War on Drugs: The Ultimate Bad Trip', *Defense Monitor*, vol. 21, no. 1, 1992.

Chopra, Jarat, Mackinlay, John and Minear, Larry, *Report on the Cambodian Peace Process*, Norwegian Institute of International Affairs, Oslo, January 1993.

Chopra, Jarat and Weiss, Thomas G., 'Sovereignty Is No Longer Sacrosanct: Codifying Humanitarian Intervention', *Ethics and International Affairs*, vol. 6, 1992, pp. 95–117.

Clark, Jeffrey, 'Debacle in Somalia', *Foreign Affairs*, vol. 72, no. 1, spring 1993, pp. 109–23.

Connaughton, R. M., *Peacekeeping and Military Intervention*, Occasional Paper, no. 3, Strategic and Combat Studies Institute, Staff College, Camberley, HMSO, London, 1992.

Cordesman, Anthony H., 'Western Sea Power Enters the Gulf', 2 parts, *Naval Forces*, vol. 9, 1988, no. 2, pp. 26–34 and no. 3, pp. 34–40.

Cox, David (ed.), *The Use of Force by the Security Council for Enforcement and Deterrent Purposes: A Conference Report*, The Canadian Centre for Arms Control and Disarmament, Ottawa, 1990.

Cushman, Lt-Gen. John H., 'Joint, Jointer, Jointest', *Proceedings*, US Naval Institute, May 1992, pp. 78–85.

Daley, Tad, 'Can the UN Stretch to Fit Its Future?', *Bulletin of the Atomic Scientists*, April 1992, p. 40.

Diehl, Paul, F., 'When Peacekeeping Does Not Lead to Peace. Some Notes on Conflict Resolution', *Bulletin of Peace Proposals*, vol. 18, no. 1, 1987, pp. 47–53.

Diehl, Paul F., 'The Conditions for Success in Peacekeeping Operations', in Paul F. Diehl (ed.), *The Politics of International Organizations: Patterns and Insights*, Dorsey, Chicago, Ill., 1989.

Dörenberg, A. J. T., *General Report on Legal Aspects of Peacekeeping Operations*, 11th Congress of the International Society of Military Law and the Law of War, 1988.

Doss, Capt. Robert A., 'Out of Africa: Rescue from Mogadishu', *Proceedings*, US Naval Institute, May 1992, pp. 103–5.

Doswald-Beck, L., 'The Legal Validity of Military Intervention by Invitation of the Government', *56 British Yearbook of International Law*, pp. 189–252 (1985).

Doulman, D. J., 'An Assessment of Australia's Role in the South Pacific Forum Fisheries Agency', in W. S. G. Bateman and M. W. Ward (eds), *Australia's Maritime Interests – Views from Overseas*, Canberra, Australia Centre for Maritime Studies, 1990.

Duke, Simon, 'The UN Finance Crisis: A History and Analysis', *International Relations*, vol. 11, no. 2, August 1992, pp. 127–50.

Dunn, David J., 'Naval Collaboration in NATO', *Naval Forces*, vol. 8, no. 5, 1987, pp. 20–33.

Durch, William J., *The United Nations and Collective Security in the 21st Century*, Strategic Studies Institute, US Army War College, Carlisle Barracks, PA, February 1993.

Eberle, Sir James, 'Naval Cooperation in the Indian Ocean', *Naval Forces*, vol. 14, no. 1, January 1993, pp. 8–11.

Eekelen, Willem van, 'WEU and the Gulf Crisis', *Survival*, vol. 32, no. 6, November/December 1990, pp. 519–32.

Eekelen, Willem van, 'Developing the WEU', *International Defense Review – Defense '92*, 1991, pp. 35–8.

Ellen, Eric, 'Contemporary Piracy', *Commercial Crime International*, vol. 7, no. 12, May 1990, pp. 9–10.

Fenrick, W. J., 'Legal Aspects of the Falklands Naval Conflict', *Revue de Droit Renal Militaire et Droit de la Guerre*, vol. 24, pt 3/4, 1985, pp. 243–64.

Fenrick, W. J., 'Exclusion Zone Device in the Law of Naval Warfare', 24 *Canadian Yearbook of International Law*, pp. 91–126 (1986).

Fenrick, W. J., 'The use of Exclusion Zones in the Falklands Naval Conflict', *Canadian Defence Quarterly*, vol. 15, 1986, pp. 22–8.

Fenrick, W. J., 'Legal Limits on the Use of Force in Canadian Warships engaged in Law Enforcement', 18 *Canadian Yearbook of International Law*, pp. 113–45 (1988).

Fetherston, A. B., 'Putting the Peace Back into Peacekeeping: Theory Must Inform Practice', *International Peacekeeping*, vol. 1, no. 1, spring 1994, pp. 3–29.

Findlay, Trevor, 'Stockholm on the Mekong? CBMs for Asia/Pacific', *Pacific Review*, vol. 3, no. 1, 1990, pp. 55–64.

Franck, Thomas M. and Patel, Faiza, 'UN Police Action in Lieu of War: "The Old Order Changeth"', *American Journal of International Law*, vol. 85, no. 1, January 1991, pp. 63–74.

Freedman, Lawrence, 'Escalators and Quagmires: Expectations and the Use of Force', *International Affairs*, vol. 67, no. 1, January 1991, pp. 15–31.

Friedman, Norman, 'The Seaward Flank', *Proceedings*, US Naval Institute, July 1991, pp. 81–3.

Genet, Raoul, 'The Charge of Piracy in the Spanish Civil War', *American Journal of International Law*, vol. 32, no. 2, April 1938, pp. 253–63.

Ghebali, Victor-Yves, 'Le développement des opérations de maintien de la paix de l'ONU depuis la fin de la guerre froide', *Le Trimestre du monde*, 4e, 1992, pp. 67–85.

Ghebali, Victor-Yves, 'Toward a Mediterranean Helsinki-Type Process', *Mediterranean Quarterly*, vol. 4, no. 1, winter 1993, pp. 92–101.

Ginifer, Jeremy, 'Towards a Concept of UN Maritime Operations', *Arms Control*, vol. 13, no. 3, December 1992, pp. 333–51.

Goodby, James, E., 'Peacekeeping in the New Europe', *The Washington Quarterly*, vol. 15, no. 2, spring 1992, pp. 153–71.

Grazebrook, A. W., 'Regional Navies Still Growing: The Year at Sea', *Asia–Pacific Defence Reporter*, vol. 17, nos 6–7, December/January 1990/1991, pp. 69–71.

Greenwood, Christopher, 'The Relationship between *jus ad bellum* and *jus in bello*', *Review of International Studies*, vol. 9, no. 4, 1983, pp. 221–34.

Greenwood, Christopher, 'New World Order or Old? The Invasion of Kuwait and the Rule of Law', *The Modern Law Review*, vol. 55, no. 2, March 1992, pp. 153–78.

Greenwood, Christopher, *Command and the Laws of Armed Conflict*, Strategic and Combat Studies Institute, Occasional Paper no. 4, Camberley, 1993.

Gregory, F. E. G., 'The Beira Patrol', *RUSI Journal*, vol. 124, no. 656, December 1969, pp. 75–7.

Gregory, F. E. G., *The Multinational Force – Aid or Obstacle to Conflict Resolution?*, Institute for the Study of Conflict, London, 1984.

Gregory, F. E. G., 'Can Military Force Defeat Drugs Trafficking?', *Small Wars and Insurgencies*, vol. 2, no. 1, April 1991, pp. 1–7.

Grove, Eric, 'Birth of a Western European Navy?', *Naval Forces*, vol. 9, no. 1, 1988, pp. 12–13.

Grove, Eric, 'UN Armed Forces and the Military Staff Committee: A Look Back, *International Security*, vol. 17, no. 4, spring 1993, pp. 172–82.

Guillot, Philippe, 'France, Peacekeeping and Humanitarian Intervention', *International Peacekeeping*, vol. 1, no. 1, spring 1994, pp. 30–43.

Haas, E. B., 'Types of Collective Security: An Examination of Operational Concepts', *American Political Science Review*, vol. 49, no. 1, March 1955, pp. 40–62.

Haines, S. W., 'The Maritime Domain: Security, Law Enforcement and Control Requirements in Offshore Zones', *Naval Forces*, vol. 10, no. 4, 1989, pp. 16–18.

Halderman, John W., 'Legal Basis for United Nations Armed Forces', *American Journal of International Law*, vol. 56, no. 4, October 1962, pp. 971–96.

Hammond, Paul Y., *Taking Peacekeeping Seriously*, Ridgway Viewpoints, No. 93–2, Ridgway Center, University of Pittsburgh, Pittsburgh, Pa, 1992.

Hampson, Françoise J., 'Means and Methods of Warfare in the Conflict in the Gulf', in A. V. Rowe (ed.), *The Gulf War 1990–91 in International and English Law*, Routledge/Sweet & Maxwell, London, 1993, pp. 89–110.

Hanning, Hugh, *NATO and Disaster Relief: An Additional Role for the 1990s*, Report of a Conference, Fontmell Group, London, 13 July 1990.

Harbottle, Michael, *What is Proper Soldiering? A Study on New Perspectives for the Future Uses of the Armed Forces in the 1990s*, Centre for International Peacebuilding, Chipping Norton, 2nd edn, 1992.

Harleman, Christian, 'Regional Conflicts: Peace-Keeping and Disarmament', *UN Disarmament Quarterly Review*, no. 3, 1992, pp. 3–4.

Hattendorf, John B. and Weeks, Stan, 'NATO's Policeman on the Beat', *Proceedings*, US Naval Institute, September 1988, pp. 66–71.

Haydon, Peter, 'Naval Peacekeeping?', *Strategic Datalink*, Canadian Institute of Strategic Studies, Toronto, December 1992, pp. 1–4.

Heiberg, Marianne, *Ethnic Conflict, Peacekeeping and Peacemaking Towards 2000: Second Generation Peacekeeping*, Notat Paper no. 442, NUPI, Oslo, April 1991.

Henn, F. R., 'Guidelines for Peacekeeping', *British Army Review*, no. 67, April 1981, pp. 31–9.

Hill, Richard, 'Control of the Exclusive Economic Zone', *Naval Forces*, vol. 6, no. 2, 1985, pp. 84–9.

Holst, Johan, J., 'Enhancing Peace-keeping Operations', *Survival*, vol. 33, no. 3, May/June 1990, pp. 264–75.

Howe, Jonathan T., 'NATO and the Gulf Crisis', *Survival*, vol. 33, no. 3, May/June 1991, pp. 246–59.

Imber, Mark, 'Too Many Cooks? The Post-Rio Reform of the United Nations', *International Affairs*, vol. 69, no. 1, 1993, pp. 55–70.

International Alert, *Preventive Diplomacy: A UN/NGO Partnership in the 1990s*, Round Table Report, 28–30 January 1993, UN University, Tokyo.

James, Alan, 'Options for Peace-Keeping', in Josephine O'Connor Howe (ed.), *Armed Peace: The Search for World Security*, Macmillan, London, 1984, pp. 145–67.

James, Alan, 'Symbol in Sinai: The Multinational Force and Observers', *Millennium: Journal of International Studies*, vol. 14, no. 3, winter 1985, pp. 255–71.

James, Alan, 'The United Nations and the Gulf War', vol. 9, no. *Naval Forces*, 6, 1988, pp. 44–51.

James, Alan, 'Internal Peace-keeping: A Dead End for the UN?', *Security Dialogue*, vol. 24, no. 4, December 1993, pp. 359–68.

Jamieson, Alison, *Global Drug Trafficking*, Conflict Study no. 234, Research Institute for the Study of Conflict and Terrorism, London, 1990.

Johansen, Robert C., 'UN Peacekeeping: The Changing Utility of Military Force', *Third World Quarterly*, vol. 12, no. 2, April 1990, pp. 53–70.

Johnson, Edward, 'A Permanent UN Force: British Thinking After Suez', *Review of International Studies*, vol. 17, no. 3, July 1991, pp. 251–66.

Kocheev, Michail E., 'Naval Nuclear Disarmament', in Sverre Lodgaard (ed.), *Naval Arms Control*, Peace Research Institute, Oslo/Sage Publications, Oslo, 1990, pp. 198–205.

Kosiak, Stephen, 'A New Navy for a New World', *Defense Monitor*, vol. 19, no. 3, 1990.

Kwiatkowska, B., 'Military Uses in the EEZ: A Reply', *Marine Policy*, vol. 11, no. 3, July 1987, pp. 249–50.

Lahneman, William J., 'Interdicting Drugs in the Big Pond', *Proceedings*, US Naval Institute, July 1990, pp. 56–63.

Lalande, Serge, 'L'Assemblée générale et les forces de maintien de la paix: le rôle du Comité des 34', *Le Trimestre du monde*, 4e, 1992, pp. 107–19.

Laurenti, Jeffrey, *Directions and Dilemmas in Collective Security: Reflections from a Global Roundtable*, Fletcher School of Law and Diplomacy, Mass., and UNA–USA, New York, 1992.

Leckow, Ross, 'The Iran–Iraq Conflict in the Gulf: The Law of War Zones', *International and Comparative Law Quarterly*, vol. 37, no. 3, July 1988, pp. 629–44.

Lewis, William H. (ed.), *The Security Roles of the United Nations*, Conference Proceedings, Institute for National Strategic Studies, National Defense University, 9–10 October 1991, Washington DC.

Lewis, William H. and Julian, Thomas, A. (eds), *Military Implications of United Nations Peacekeeping Operations*, Workshop Proceedings, Institute for National Strategic Studies, National Defense University, 17 November 1992, Washington DC.

Lindberg, Michael, *The Persian Gulf Naval Arms Race: Myth or Reality?*, Occasional Paper, Centre for Defence and Security Studies, University of Manitoba, Winnipeg, September 1993.

Liu, F. T. and Wiseman, Henry, *The United Nations Peace-keeping Operation: Recent Experiences and Future Prospects*, Report of the Tokyo Symposium co-organised by the UN University and International Peace Academy, 2–4 September 1991, Tokyo.

Lowe, A. V., 'Some Legal Problems Arising from the Use of the Sea for Military Purposes', *Marine Policy*, vol. 10, no. 3, July 1986, pp. 171–84.

Lowe, A. V., 'The Impact of the Law of the Sea on Naval Warfare', *Syracuse Journal of International Law & Commerce*, 1988, pp. 657–75.

Lowe, A. V., 'Self-Defence at Sea', in William E. Butler (ed.), *The Non-Use of Force in International Law*, Martinus Nijhoff, Dordrecht, 1989, pp. 185–202.

Lyons, Capt. S., 'Naval Operations in the Gulf', in A. V. Rowe (ed.), *The Gulf War 1990–91 in International and English Law*, Routledge/Sweet & Maxwell, London, 1993, pp. 155–70.

McCarthy, James P., 'Commanding Joint and Coalition Operations', *Naval War College Review*, vol. 46, no. 1, winter 1993, pp. 9–21.

McClement, T. P., 'The Environment, Green Issues and the Military', *The Naval Review*, vol. 80, no. 3, July 1992, pp. 201–8.

Macfarlane, Neil, *Intervention and Regional Security*, Adelphi Paper, no. 196, IISS, London, spring 1985.

MacKenzie, Maj.-Gen. Lewis, 'Military Realities of UN Peacekeeping Operations', *RUSI Journal*, vol. 138, no. 1, February 1993, pp. 21–4.

Mackinlay, John, and Chopra, Jarat, 'Second Generation Multinational Operations', *Washington Quarterly*, vol. 15, no. 3, summer 1992, pp. 113–31.

McNamara, Robert S. and Urquhart, Brian, *Toward Collective Security: Two Views*, Occasional Paper no. 6, Watson Institute, Providence, RI, 1991.

Mayall, James, 'Non-intervention, Self-determination and the "New World Order"', *International Affairs*, vol. 67, no. 3, July 1991, pp. 421–9.

Meconis, Charles A. and Wallace, Michael D., 'A Modest Proposal for a UN Naval Peacekeeping Force', in Charles A. Meconis and Michael D. Wallace (eds), *Halting the Arms Race at Sea: Naval Arms Control and Maritime Strategy in the 21st Century*, Lynne Rienner, Boulder, Col., 1991, Ch. 6.

Menon, Anand, Forster, Anthony and Wallace, William, 'A Common European Defence?', *Survival*, vol. 34, no. 3, autumn 1992, pp. 98–118.

Milivojevic, Marko, 'The Spratly and Paracel Islands Conflict', *Survival*, vol. 31, no. 1, January/February 1989, pp. 70–8.

Miller, David, 'The Maritime Importance of the South China Sea', *Naval Forces*, vol. 14, no. 2, March 1993, pp. 32–8.

Nailor, Peter, 'The Contemporary Use of Maritime Power', in R. P. Barston and P. W. Birnie (eds), *The Maritime Dimension*, Allen & Unwin, London, 1980, pp. 142–53.

Neves, Juan Carlos, *United Nations Peace-Keeping Operations in The Gulf of Fonseca by Argentine Navy Units*, Report 01–93, Strategy & Campaign Dept., US Naval War College, Newport RI, 12 January 1993.

Oladimeji, Capt. Olutunde A., 'Behold, African Peacekeepers', *Proceedings*, US Naval Institute, March 1993, pp. 64–6.

Oswald, Sir Julian, 'UN Maritime Operations: Realities, Problems and Possibilities', *Naval War College Review*, vol. 46, no. 4, autumn 1993, pp. 124–9.

Oxman, B. H., 'The Regime of Warships under the United Nations Convention on the Law of the Sea', 24 *Virginia Journal of International Law*, pp. 809–63 (1984).

Padelford, Norman J., 'The International Non-Intervention Agreement and the Spanish Civil War', *American Journal of International Law*, vol. 31, no. 4, October 1937, pp. 578–603.

Padelford, Norman J., 'Foreign Shipping during the Spanish Civil War', *American Journal of International Law*, vol. 32, no. 2, April 1938, pp. 264–79.

Palwankar, U., 'Applicability of International Humanitarian Law to United Nations Peace-keeping Forces', *International Review of the Red Cross*, no. 294, May–June 1993, pp. 227–40.

Parker, Col. T. W., 'Operation Sharp Edge', *Proceedings*, US Naval Institute, June 1991, pp. 102–6.

Parks, Col. W. Hays, 'Rules of Engagement: No More Vietnams', *Proceedings*, US Naval Institute, March 1991, pp. 27–8.

Parliamentarians For Global Action, *From National To UN-Based Security: A Report on Strengthening Collective Security – The Role of Parliamentarians, Mechanisms, and Financing*, New York, May 1992.

Plant, Glen, 'The Convention for the Suppression of Unlawful Acts Against the Safety of Maritime Navigation', *International and Comparative Law Quarterly*, vol. 39, pt. 1, January 1990, pp. 27–56.

Preston, Anthony, 'Naval Aspects of the Gulf Conflict', *Military Technology*, vol. 15, no. 4, 1991, pp. 58–61.

Prins, Gwyn, 'The UN and Peace-Keeping in the Post-Cold War World: The Case of Naval Power', *Bulletin of Peace Proposals*, vol. 22, no. 2, June 1991, pp. 135–55.

Pugh, Michael C., 'An International Police Force; Lord Davies and the British Debate in the 1930s', *International Relations*, vol. 9, no. 4, November 1988, pp. 335–51.

Pugh, Michael C., 'Peacekeeping – a Role for Navies?', *Naval Forces*, vol. 13, no. 4, 1992, pp. 8–10.

Pugh, Michael C., *Multinational Maritime Forces: A Breakout from Traditional Peacekeeping?*, Southampton Papers in International Policy, no. 1, Mountbatten Centre for International Studies, University of Southampton, July 1992.

Pugh, Michael C., 'Multinational Maritime Peace-keeping – Should the UN Put to Sea?', in Kevin Clements (ed.), *Peace and Security in the Asia Pacific Region*, United Nations University/John Dunmore, Tokyo and Palmerston North, NZ, 1993, pp. 255–72.

Pugh, Michael C., 'Piracy and Armed Robbery at Sea: Problems and Remedies', *Low Intensity Conflict and Law Enforcement*, vol. 2, no. 1, summer 1993, pp. 1–18.

Ranken, Michael, 'Desert Shield/Desert Storm – Command Priorities/Principles', *The Naval Review*, vol. 80, no. 3, July 1992, pp. 243–5.

Rikhye, Indar Jit, *The United Nations of the 1990s and International Peacekeeping Operations*, Southampton Papers in International Policy, no. 3, Mountbatten Centre for International Studies, University of Southampton, November 1992.

Rivlin, Benjamin, *The Rediscovery of the UN Military Staff Committee*, Occasional Paper no. 4, Ralph Bunche Institute on the United Nations, City University of New York, New York, May 1991.

Rivlin, Benjamin, 'Regional Arrangements and the UN System for Collective Security and Conflict Resolution: A New Road Ahead?', *International Relations*, vol. 11, no. 2, August 1992, pp. 95–110.

Roach, J. Ashley, 'Rules of Engagement', *Naval War College Review*, vol. 36, 1983, pp. 46–55.

Roberts, Adam, 'The United Nations and International Security', *Survival*, vol. 35, no. 2, summer 1993, pp. 3–30.

Rostow, Eugene V., 'Until What? Enforcement Action or Collective Self-Defense?', *American Journal of International Law*, vol. 85, no. 3, July 1991, pp. 506–16.

Rubin, Alfred P., 'Terrorism and Piracy: A Legal View', *Terrorism: An International Journal*, vol. 3, nos. 1–2, pp. 117–30.

Russet, Bruce and Sutterlin, James S., 'The UN in a New World Order', *Foreign Affairs*, vol. 70, no. 2, spring 1991, pp. 69–83.

Russo, F. V., 'Neutrality at Sea in Transition: State Practice in the Gulf War as Emerging International Customary Law', *Ocean Development and International Law*, vol. 19, 1988, pp. 381–99.

Sabrosky, Alan Ned, 'A War Unwon: The US Fight Against Drugs', *Small Wars and Insurgencies*, vol. 2, no. 1, April 1991, pp. 8–17.

Saferworld Foundation (Andrew Cottey), *The Gulf Crisis: Test Case for the New World Order*, Saferworld Foundation, Bristol, September 1990.

Salmon, Trevor, C., 'Testing Times for European Political Cooperation: the Gulf and Yugoslavia 1990–1992', *International Affairs*, vol. 68, no. 2, April 1992, pp. 233–53.

Sandoz, Y., 'The Application of Humanitarian Law by the Armed Forces of the United Nations Organization', *International Review of the Red Cross*, no. 206, September–October 1978, pp. 274–84.

Sands, Jeffrey I., *Multinational Naval Cooperation in a Changing World: A Report on the Greenwich Conference*, 12–13 December 1991, Center for Naval Analyses, Alexandria, Va., October 1992.

Sands, Jeffrey I., *Blue Hulls: Multinational Naval Cooperation and the United Nations*, CRM 93–40, Center for Naval Analyses, Alexandria, Va., July 1993.

Schachter, Oscar, 'United Nations Law in the Gulf Conflict', *American Journal of International Law*, vol. 85, no. 3, July 1991, pp. 452–73.

Schindler, D., 'United Nations Forces and International Humanitarian Law', in C. Swinarski (ed.), *Studies and Essays on International Humanitarian Law and Red Cross Principles, in Honour of Jean Pictet*, ICRC/Nijhoff, Dordrecht, 1984, pp. 521–30.

Schindler, D., 'Transformations in the Law of Neutrality since 1945', in A. J. M. Delissen and G. J. Tanja (eds), *Humanitarian Law of Armed Conflict: Challenges Ahead*, Martinus Nijhoff, Dordrecht, 1991, pp. 367–86.

Schroeder, Ricardo Enrique, '"Operacion Gaucho" en CentroAmérica', *Puestos de Maniobra*, yr. 3, no. 4, September 1991, pp. 18–21.

Shaw, S., 'Naval Peacekeeping as a UN Option for the Gulf', *Naval Forces*, vol. 9, no. 1, 1988, pp. 8–9.

Siegel, Adam B., 'An American Entebbe', *Proceedings*, US Naval Institute, May 1992, pp. 96–100.

Siegel, Adam B., 'Naval Forces in Support of International Sanctions: The Beira Patrol', *Naval War College Review*, vol. 45, no. 4, seq. 340, autumn 1992, pp. 102–4.

Siegel, Adam B., 'Enforcing Sanctions: A Growth Industry', *Naval War College Review*, vol. 46, no. 4, autumn 1993, pp. 130–34.

Siekmann, R. C. R., *National Contingents in United Nations Peace-keeping Forces*, Martinus Nijhoff, Dordrecht, 1991.

Stackpole, Lt.-Gen. H. C., 'Angels From the Sea', *Proceedings*, US Naval Institute, May 1992, pp. 110–16.

Staley II, Robert Stephens, *The Wave of the Future: The United Nations and Naval Peacekeeping*, International Peace Academy Occasional Paper, Lynne Rienner, Boulder, Col., 1992.

Stedman, Stephen John, 'The New Interventionists', *Foreign Affairs*, vol. 72, no. 1, spring 1993, pp. 1–16.

Stjernfelt, Bertil, 'FN 25 år. Fredsbevarande operationer – Cypern', *Kungla Kirgsvetenskapsakademiens Handlingar och Tidskrift*, no. 8, 1970.

Sur, Serge, 'La sécurité internationale et l'évolution de la sécurité collective', *Le Trimestre du monde*, 4e, 1992, pp. 121–34.

Swire, Adrian, 'Merchant Shipping and the Gulf War', *Naval Forces*, vol. 8, no. 3, 1987, pp. 14–15.

Taylor, Paul, 'The United Nations System under Stress: Financial Pressures and their Consequences', *Review of International Studies*, vol. 17, no. 4, October 1991, pp. 365–82.

Thakur, Ramesh, 'Non-intervention in International Relations: a Case Study', *Political Science*, vol. 42, no. 1, July 1990, pp. 27–61.

Till, Geoffrey, 'A Post-Cold War Maritime Strategy for NATO', *Naval Forces*, vol. 12, no. 3, 1992, pp. 8–15.

Till, Geoffrey and King, Richard, 'A Standing Naval Force for Northern Waters?', *Naval Forces*, vol. 8, no. 5, 1987, pp. 16–18.

Toremans, Guy, 'NATO's New Standing Naval Force Mediterranean', *Naval Forces*, vol. 14, no. 3, May 1993, pp. 6–10.

Trainor, J. C., 'United States Maritime Drug Law Enforcement', *Naval Forces*, vol. 9, no. 3, 1988, pp. 78–9.

Tuzmukhamedov, B. R., 'The Principle of Non-Use of Force and Security at Sea', in William E. Butler (ed.), *The Non-Use of Force in International Law*, Martinus Nijhoff, Dordrecht, 1989, pp. 173–84.

Uhlig, Frank, Jr, 'The First United Nations Force', *Proceedings*, US Naval Institute, February 1951, p. 201.

United Nations Department for Disarmament Affairs, *Naval Confidence-building Measures*, Topical Papers 4, UN, New York, 1990.

Urquhart, Brian, 'The Role of the UN in Maintaining and Improving International Security', *Survival*, vol. 28, no. 5, September/October 1986, pp. 225–31.

Urquhart, Brian, 'Beyond the "Sheriff's Posse"', *Survival*, vol. 32, no. 3, May/June 1990, pp. 196–205.

Urquhart, Brian, 'After the Cold War: Learning from the Gulf', in *Toward Collective Security: Two Views*, Occasional Paper no. 5, Thomas J. Watson Jr Institute for International Studies, Providence, RI, 1991.

Urquhart, Brian, 'The United Nations in 1992: problems and opportunities', *International Affairs*, vol. 68, no. 2, April 1992, pp. 311–19.

Vego, Milan, 'War on the Yugoslav Coast', *Proceedings*, US Naval Institute, March 1992, pp. 91–8.

Vlahos, Michael, 'A Global Naval Force: Why Not?', *Proceedings*, US Naval Institute, March 1992, pp. 40–4.

Volcker, Paul A., and Ogata, Shijuro, *Financing an Effective United Nations: A Report of the Independent Advisory Group on UN Financing*, Ford Foundation, New York, NY, April 1993.

Wallace, William, 'European Defence Co-operation: The Reopening Debate', *Survival*, November–December 1984, vol. 26, no. 6, pp. 251–6.

Weber, Cynthia, 'Reconsidering Statehood: Examining the Sovereignty/Intervention Boundary', *Review of International Studies*, vol. 18, no. 3, July 1990, pp. 199–216.

Weeks, Stan, 'Crafting a New Maritime Strategy', *Proceedings*, US Naval Institute, January 1992, pp. 30–7.

Weiss, Thomas G. and Campbell, Kurt M., 'Military Humanitarianism', *Survival*, vol. 33, no. 5, September/October 1991, pp. 451–65.

Weller, M., 'The United Nations and the *jus ad bellum*', in A. V. Rowe (ed.), *The Gulf War 1990–91 in International and English Law*, Routledge/Sweet & Maxwell, London, 1993, pp. 29–54.

Weston, Burns H., 'Security Council Resolution 678 and Persian Gulf Decision Making: Precarious Legitimacy', *American Journal of International Law*, vol. 85, no. 3, July 1991, pp. 516–35.

Whitman, Jim and Bartholomew, Ian, *The Chapter VII Committee – A Policy Proposal: Military Means for Political Ends: Effective Control of UN Military Enforcement*, Global Security Programme, University of Cambridge, August 1993.

Wilson, Heather A., 'Humanitarian Protection in Wars of National Liberation, *Arms Control*, vol. 8, no. 1, May 1987, pp. 36–48.

Wilcox, Francis O., 'Regionalism and the United Nations', *International Organization*, vol. 19, no. 3, summer 1965, pp. 789–811.

Winnefeld, James A. and Shlapak, David A., *The Challenge of Future Nonstandard Contingencies: Implication for Strategy, Planning, Crisis Management, and Forces*, N–3098/1–DAG, RAND Corporation, Santa Monica, CA, October 1990.

Young, Thomas-Durell, 'Preparing the Western Alliance for the Next Out-of-Area Campaign', *Naval War College Review*, vol. 45, no. 3, summer 1992, pp. 28–44.

Yu, Peter, Kien-hong, 'Protecting the Spratlys', *Pacific Review*, vol. 3, no. 1, 1990, pp. 78–83.

Index